THE TRAITOR OF ARNHEM

The Untold Story of WWII's Greatest Betrayal
and the Moment that Changed History Forever

ROBERT VERKAIK

PEGASUS BOOKS
NEW YORK LONDON

THE TRAITOR OF ARNHEM

Pegasus Books, Ltd.
148 West 37th Street, 13th Floor
New York, NY 10018

Copyright © 2025 by Robert Verkaik

First Pegasus Books cloth edition February 2025

All rights reserved. No part of this book may be reproduced in whole or in part without written permission from the publisher, except by reviewers who may quote brief excerpts in connection with a review in a newspaper, magazine, or electronic publication; nor may any part of this book be reproduced, stored in a retrieval system, or transmitted in any form or by any means electronic, mechanical, photocopying, recording, or other, or used to train generative artificial intelligence (AI) technologies, without written permission from the publisher.

ISBN: 978-1-63936-827-3

10 9 8 7 6 5 4 3 2 1

Printed in the United States of America
Distributed by Simon & Schuster
www.pegasusbooks.com

Eduard Pieter Wilhelm Verkaik
18 July 1909–29 February 1982

And to all those who resist tyranny

Contents

	Foreword	xi
	Prologue	1

Part One: The Dutch

	Dramatis Personae	9
1.	Open Frontiers	11
2.	Rotterdam Playboy	19
3.	Englandspiel	25
4.	Legend of King Kong	30
5.	The End of the Game	41
6.	Cornered Traitor	56
7.	Invasion	65
8.	Crossing the Line	73
9.	A Spy Too Far	82

Part Two: The British

	Dramatis Personae	105
10.	The Second Arnhem Warning	107
11.	Bombed Out	111
12.	Red Orchestra	125
13.	Red Alert	130
14.	Agent Josephine	141

15.	Secrets of D-Day	149
16.	War of Spies	165
17.	Bridge of Spies	172
18.	Arnhem Betrayed	179

Part Three: The Russians

	Dramatis Personae	197
19.	Operation Tolstoy	199
20.	To Catch a Traitor	208
21.	A Traitor Betrayed	217
22.	Caging the Gorilla	223
23.	Betrayal of the Bulge	233
24.	Confessions of King Kong	240
25.	Josephine in Chains	249
26.	Death Throes	268
27.	Bridge of Lies	285
28.	Orders of the Kremlin	290
29.	Drawing Up the Bridge	301
30.	After the Battle	310
31.	Epilogue: Exploding Chocolates	325

Appendix 1	329
Appendix 2	340
Acknowledgements	347
Bibliography	350
Notes	354
Index	384

When Stalin returned to Russia after the Yalta conference in February 1945, he told the following joke.

Churchill, Roosevelt and Stalin went on a hunting trip and finally killed their bear. Churchill said, 'I'll take the bearskin. Let Roosevelt and Stalin divide the meat.' Roosevelt said, 'No, I'll take the skin. Let Churchill and Stalin divide the meat.' Stalin remained silent so Churchill and Roosevelt asked him: 'Mister Stalin, what do you say?' Stalin simply replied, 'The bear belongs to me – after all, I killed it.'

Foreword

For me this book began because I wanted to find out more about my relative Eddy Verkaik, a Dutch regional chess champion who bravely took up arms against the Germans during Operation Market Garden. When the Allies arrived in Eindhoven on 18 September 1944, Eddy led a group of fighters against a German SS unit that was preparing to ambush a column of British tanks that had entered the city. After a bitter firefight the Germans agreed to surrender to the resistance men. But as Eddy walked towards the Nazi officer, who was waving a white flag, the German shot him down in cold blood.

Before Eddy was shot he had informed the British soldiers of a dangerous Dutch traitor, a giant fighter known as King Kong who had betrayed their plans to the Nazis. The fantastical legend of Christiaan Lindemans piqued my interest. I wanted to contrast Eddy's bravery against Lindemans' dark treachery. But as I followed the trail of the betrayal of Operation Market Garden, questions began to stack up until one day my research took me down a completely different, unexpected avenue. There had been a second betrayal. One that had been all but forgotten and that led me to London and the heart of the British establishment. There I found myself in the company of perhaps the most famous traitors of all and a much more chilling story that has never been told.

The secrets of Arnhem, where thousands of British, American, Polish and Commonwealth soldiers sacrificed their lives, are to be found in hidden files held at the National Archives in Kew; the US

National Archives in College Park, Maryland; the Dutch National Archives in The Hague, military history archives in Amsterdam; the German Bundesarchiv; and the Central Archives of the Ministry of Defence of the Russian Federation and the Archive of Foreign Intelligence in Moscow.

This book is not a military history, there are much better-qualified historians for that job.

The Traitor of Arnhem is a spy story, an 80-year-old cold case review of thousands of primary source documents, many of them written and signed by the traitors.

Prologue

'This is a story you will tell your grandchildren.'[1] Lt General Brian Horrocks cannot have known how prophetic his words were as he briefed his tank commanders on the eve of what remains to this day the biggest combined ground and airborne operation ever undertaken. If successful, it promised to end the war by Christmas and allow victorious British and American troops to enter Berlin while the rapidly advancing Red Army was still hundreds of miles to the East.[2]

On 17 September 1944, the British armoured divisions of XXX (30) Corps, commanded by Horrocks, would punch a hole through the German defences on the Belgian–Dutch border and 'drive like hell' along highway 69 all the way to Arnhem, the last bridge across the Rhine and the final major obstacle to Berlin and the heart of Nazi Germany.

The British tanks had just 48 hours to cover the 64 miles and link up with the 10,000 men of the British 1st Airborne Division who were to be landed by glider and parachute around the town of Arnhem. Along the way, another 25,000 American paratroopers would capture nine bridges between Eindhoven and Nijmegen, smoothing 30 Corps' path to their final objective.

At 2pm, 350 British guns unleashed a mighty artillery bombardment on enemy positions. Half an hour later, Horrocks gave the order for the tanks of the Irish Guards to start the charge up the main road towards their first main objective, Eindhoven. The Shermans rolled forward. Field Marshal Bernard Montgomery's daring plan to outflank the Siegfried Line, capture the Ruhr and win the race to Berlin appeared to have started well. Operation Market Garden was under way.

Then without warning, after just half an hour's advance, the well dug in and carefully camouflaged anti-tank weapons of Kampfgruppe Walther, a unit cobbled together from Wehrmacht, SS and Luftwaffe units commanded by Oberst Erich Walther, ripped into Horrocks' column from their position in the trees and halted its advance almost as soon as it had begun.

Horrocks called in the Typhoons of the RAF to clear the Germans from the trees but by then nine British tanks were burning wrecks blocking the road. The supposedly lightning British advance was in trouble before it had even started.

21st Army Group's official report[3] on Operation Market Garden read: 'Anti-tank guns and Spandaus let the leading squadrons through and "brewed" up eight tanks of the second squadron. The enemy positions had been much stronger than expected and the Guards armoured division had to fight savagely to effect their breakout from the bridgehead established over the Meuse-Escaut Canal.'

Tellingly, the report also noted that among the defenders were 'two battalions of the 9 SS Panzer division' – a battle-hardened enemy force that was not supposed to be anywhere near Eindhoven.[4]

An hour earlier, four rifle regiments of the American 101st Airborne Division had landed safely on their drop zone north of Eindhoven. The 101st were responsible for protecting the 15-mile stretch of road and strategic crossings between Eindhoven and Grave, the first section of Horrocks' route to Arnhem. Crucial to the operation's success was the quick capture of the town of Best and the nearby bridges that crossed the Wilhelmina Canal.

When the American commanders were finalising their plans in England, Best was considered to be lightly defended and one of the more straightforward assignments.[5] The paratroopers landed easily

PROLOGUE

and using the church steeple of Best as a guide, advanced through the fields towards the village in good spirits, expecting light resistance.

But as soon as they approached the first houses they came under heavy fire.[6] The Germans, under the command of General Kurt Student, the godfather of airborne warfare, had reinforced the town with 1,800 troops[7] and had set up defensive positions on the intersection of the main street and the Boxtel–Eindhoven highway. Incoming fire from this position was so intense that H Company fell back in disarray. More German troops were dug in along the highway and brought in 88mm and 20mm artillery in support. During the American assault on the road intersection, H Company lost almost half of its 250 men.

As the Americans fell back, more German reinforcements were sent to Best, including units from the 59th and 245th Division and two SS police battalions. These units continued to hold up the capture of the bridges and further slowed XXX Corps' progress out of Eindhoven. The fighting around Best was to be some of the most bitter of the entire operation.

Later that day, Horrocks learned that German demolition squads had blown up the Son bridge before it could be captured by the 101st paratroopers. Major Dick Winters, of Easy Company 506 Parachute Infantry Regiment and *Band of Brothers* fame, was close to the blast and as lumps of concrete crashed down on the road around him, he remembered thinking: 'God damn, what an awful way to die in the war, being hit by a rock.'[8]

A prefabricated Bailey bridge had to be erected over the canal by British sappers, again wasting valuable time, before Horrocks' tanks could roll forward on what would become known as Hell's Highway.

It wasn't until 1900 hours on 18 September that advanced elements of the Guards Armoured Division met up with the American paratroopers on the outskirts of Eindhoven. They were already more than 10 hours behind schedule.

Fifty miles away, the first lift of 20,000 British and American paratroopers had by now flooded on to their drop zones around Arnhem and Nijmegen. They landed virtually unopposed and the battalions were able to form up in good order, ready to march on their objectives.

But stationed nearby were the main force of the 9th SS Panzer Division and its sister unit the 10th SS, refitting after their mauling in Normandy. The 9th SS, the Hohenstaufen, had a Panzergrenadier brigade, a reconnaissance battalion, an artillery battalion, two batteries of self-propelled guns and a company of tanks. The 10th SS, the Frundsberg, was less well equipped. Nevertheless, between them they mustered a formidable fighting unit of some 7,000 soldiers, and significantly, both divisions had also recently undergone training in defending against an airborne landing.

The 10th was immediately sent to head off American airborne troops of the American 82nd Airborne Division at Nijmegen while the 9th was tasked with stopping the British at Arnhem.

One unit in particular reacted very sharply to the landings.[9] Two companies of SS Panzergrenadier Battalion 16, known as Battalion Krafft, after their commander Sturmbannführer (Major) Sepp Krafft, had been training[10] in the woods to the east of Wolfheze, on the edge of Landing Zone-Z (LZ-Z). Krafft knew that the enemy's objective must be Arnhem bridge and, realising that it was his men who were closest to the enemy, he set out immediately to oppose the threat, gathering up every man he had. Although his total force amounted to just 435 soldiers, he managed to establish a defensive line covering the obvious paths from the landing areas to Arnhem.[11] Centred around the Hotel Wolfheze, a mile east of LZ-Z, his front extended from the railway line down to the Utrechtseweg; the routes down which the Reconnaissance Squadron and the 1st and 3rd Parachute Battalions were due to advance. Krafft hoped to convince the British that his force was much larger than it was and, in so doing, delay the enemy long enough for more substantial German forces to relieve him.

British hopes were now pinned on the second lift of paratroopers, the 10th, 11th and 156th Battalions of 4th Parachute Brigade. But this was delayed by bad weather and by the time these reinforcements arrived later that afternoon, the Germans were waiting. The 156th suffered particularly shocking losses, and of the 603 men who jumped that day, just 27 would withdraw back across the river a week later.

Even so, on 18 September the Germans were still confronting a fighting force of 3,000 British paratroopers. 1st, 2nd and 3rd battalions (1st Parachute Brigade) were fighting furiously, trying to push on towards Arnhem. One battalion, Col John Frost's 2 Para, managed to reach and secure the north end of the main Arnhem bridge.[12] Frost had orders to hold the bridge until the arrival of XXX Corps. Neither he nor Horrocks knew how long that would be.

With every hour that passed, the odds were fatally tilting in favour of the Wehrmacht as reinforcements from Germany flooded in. By the evening of 18 September, the Germans had an advantage of more than two to one in men and an overwhelming advantage in heavy weaponry. The delays in constructing a Bailey bridge at Son and capturing the bridge at Nijmegen gave time for the German panzers to mount a successful counter-attack. By now, the remainder of 1st Airborne Division was too weak to attempt to relieve Frost at Arnhem. Eight of the nine infantry battalions (three battalions had landed with the 1st Air Landing Brigade to secure and protect the landing zones and three more had been landed in the second wave) were so badly depleted or scattered that only one battalion still existed as a unit.[13]

Frost and his men, low on water and almost out of ammunition, heroically held on until the early hours of 21 September, when his soldiers at last succumbed to the inevitable and surrendered.

Just as the British were surrendering their hard-held bridge at Arnhem, tanks of XXX Corps' at last crossed the Nijmegen bridge, a few agonising hours too late to link up with the isolated British paratroopers.

Market Garden had failed and the remnants of the British 1st

Airborne Division found themselves trapped in a small pocket west of Arnhem and had to be evacuated on 25 September after sustaining further heavy casualties.

The official Air Operation diary recorded: 'Market has failed and the agony is ended – and what was, perhaps, the finest division this country has ever produced has been almost wiped out.'[14]

Horrocks lamented after the battle: 'As the exhausted paratroopers swam or were ferried across the river in torrential rain, it seemed even the Gods were weeping at this grievous end to a gallant enterprise.'[15]

It was Montgomery's first and only major defeat, although he tried to claim it had been 90 per cent successful. Allied dreams of ending the war before Christmas had come to nothing and the British and Americans were left wondering how was it possible that the largest airborne force ever assembled, supported by overwhelming air power and armour, could have been defeated by an enemy that was supposed to have been on its last legs. Why had German resistance proved so effective and so resolute?

… PART ONE

THE DUTCH

Dramatis Personae

Christiaan Lindemans (aka King Kong & Le Tueur): Dutch resistance fighter and Abwehr informant. A double or treble agent.

Henk Lindemans: Christiaan Lindemans' younger, favourite brother and a member of the Dutch resistance.

Gilberte Letuppe (aka Gilou): Christiaan Lindemans' long-suffering wife. Resistance fighter and nightclub singer.

Mia Meersman: Lindemans' double agent mistress who worked for the SD and the British.

Hermann Giskes: Head of the Abwehr in Holland (and at the end of the war in Belgium). Instigator of Englandspiel and a non-Nazi.

Willy Kup: Giskes' loyal, trusted right-hand man.

Joseph Schreieder: Head of the SD – rivals of the Abwehr and a fervent Nazi.

Cornelis Verloop (aka Satan Face): Dutch ex-French Foreign Legion, Abwehr V-man and thoroughgoing rat.

Matthijs Ridderhof: Dutchman known as 'Georges'. Giskes' chief infiltrator who helped to break down SOE operations in Holland and set up Englandspiel.

Prince Bernhard: Head of the Dutch military and former Nazi who befriended Christiaan Lindemans.

Kas de Graaf: Security chief of communist-run CS-6 resistance group. Lindemans saved his life. He escaped to England and went on to play a prominent role in Dutch security.

Chapter 1

Open Frontiers

August 1941: the portly guard's slumber in the stifling border post outside Swalmen was disturbed by the roar of a high-performance German sports car coming to a halt in front of the red-and-white barrier.

At the wheel of the open-top two-seater was a dapper and impatient Wehrmacht Major.[1]

The barrier rose. 'Pleasant journey, Herr Major,' shouted the man as the car sped off down the asphalt road, crossed the River Meuse and disappeared into the dark frontier forests.

Behind the wheel was Hermann Giskes, an intelligence officer on his way to his new posting at The Hague, headquarters of the IIIF section, Ast-Netherlands of the Abwehr, the military intelligence wing of the German Army.

Giskes had just spent a week's leave with his wife in their Rhineland home town before setting off to take up his promotion as head of German counter-espionage in Holland.

He must have reflected on his good fortune. Only weeks earlier he had been asked to consider a transfer to Ukraine. But his poor Russian and the success of his counter-intelligence operations in Paris had caused Berlin to have a change of heart.

Giskes was five foot ten, with slicked-back blond hair, narrow blue grey eyes and an aquiline nose. His athletic build and distinguished features meant he carried himself with some authority.[2] In the summer of 1941 he was approaching his 41st birthday.

A patriotic German, he had done his duty in the First World War, bravely serving as a teenage soldier at Verdun, the most murderous of all the campaigns on the Western Front. He ended the war a prisoner of the French and was only released in 1920 when he rejoined the family tobacco business.[3]

He had resisted joining the Nazi Party for years, until in 1938, local party officials made it clear to him that his bad example was no longer to be tolerated. So, after meeting an old skiing friend who had already rejoined the Army, Giskes enrolled in the Abwehr, where he was assured he would not be bothered by Nazis.[4]

During his time in the French capital, Giskes built up a reliable network of diplomats, refugees and collaborators who kept him informed about the loyalties of a number of senior French dignitaries suspected of maintaining contact with London.[5] But his real skill lay in recruiting paid agents to ferret out members of the resistance working against the German occupation. These were the so-called V-men (Vertrauensmann, trusted man), whom Giskes placed across northern France to keep watch on the conquered populations. His network delivered results and Berlin had taken notice of the subtle skill of the middle-aged intelligence officer.

Giskes' brilliance lay in his willingness to let enemy agents run. He calculated that they were likely to deliver much more intelligence under surveillance than under torture.[6] He was also wise enough to resist the temptation to claim every intelligence triumph for himself, making sure he shared some of the credit with his rivals in the Gestapo and the SD, the SS security agency. This had won him the respect and confidence of both Admiral Wilhelm Canaris, head of the Abwehr, and Walter Schellenberg, Heinrich Himmler's SS intelligence chief.

Giskes had visited Holland two years earlier and, like most Germans, had felt a kinship with the Dutch. He held a particular fondness for Holland's political centre:

'I had formed the picture of The Hague,' Giskes wrote, 'as an elderly well-connected maiden who likes her creature comforts but still delights in dressing attractively for her many friends and admirers.'[7]

The Dutch had a long and strict policy of neutrality despite the tests of recent years. When the Kaizer ordered his army into Belgium in 1914, Holland's neutrality held firm, sparing its people from the slaughter of the Great War. At the close of the conflict, the defeated Kaizer had bolted by train to neutral Holland. The Western allies wanted him tried as a war criminal but the Dutch refused to compromise their neutrality by surrendering him to the victorious powers. While this made the Dutch unpopular with the Allies, it was a price they were more than willing to pay if it preserved their own national and political integrity.

It had been over 100 years since a Dutchman had fired a shot in anger in Europe, unless in a private quarrel on a duelling ground.[8] These years of peace and a national culture of tolerance had made Holland an ideal location for conducting international business and politics. The grand, cosmopolitan hotels of Rotterdam, Amsterdam and The Hague became oases of luxurious anonymity, offering meeting places for representatives of the world's biggest corporations and the smallest tinpot dictatorships, making Holland a magnet for spies.

As a result, the Dutch population's initial response to the arrival of the Germans in May 1940 had been one of lukewarm acquiescence.

Abwehr Headquarters was a well-furnished house in a quiet street in the Hogeweg district of Scheveningen. A heavy wrought-iron gate and a wide expanse of garden made the house difficult to approach unannounced. Across the road, meadows stretched away to the Scheveningen woods. Hermann Giskes was impressed by the suitability of the building.

His impression of what was happening inside the Abwehr HQ was not so positive.[9]

At 9am on the morning after he arrived, eight men lowered themselves into the red leather office upholstery or basket chairs brought in from the sun room next door ready to meet their new commanding officer and to brief him on their work.

Oberleutnant Walter Wurr, the most senior officer after Giskes, began by declaring there were 'no active individuals or organisations at present known with any certainty to be engaged in secret service espionage or sabotage in Holland'.[10]

Wurr was forced to concede that recent events showed the British knew quite a lot about German activities. These included a recent operation which ended in disaster when the German security unit who had been lying in wait for a British seaplane was shot up by fighter aircraft who had been warned of their presence.

Among his staff, Giskes came to the conclusion that only Wurr and a veteran NCO called Willy Kup had the experience and guile to be of any use to him.

But it was the number of useless V-men which caused him the greatest concern. Too many of them were well known fascists, paid large sums of money to act as agents provocateurs. Others were part of the criminal underworld who only served up intelligence when it suited them.

It was too easy to entrap a Dutchman into saying or doing something against the German occupation, Giskes told his men. Above all, it served no intelligence purpose.

'From now on,' said Giskes, 'we will use only first-class agents who may be highly paid but must be really suited to the work.'[11]

Giskes laid out his new orders: 'Our one main purpose is to discover the secret plans and communications of the London intelligence service in such a way that we can mislead and thwart their sinister projects. By this means we can acquire important information for our High Command, and in order to accomplish it we may have to allow enemy agents and organisations to operate for a while undisturbed, provided that we have identified them properly and can adequately control them.'[12]

Then he added the caveat: 'In cases of armed resistance, make good and timely use of your weapons, but remember again that a defenceless opponent is no longer an enemy but a man whose only crime is to love his country the same as you or I do.'

Giskes then returned to Paris to poach two of his most resourceful V-men: Richard Christmann, a German-born former French Legionnaire, and Matthijs Ridderhof,[13] a Dutchman who had proved himself well suited to the betrayal of his countrymen. His code name was Oswald[14] but most people knew him as 'George'.

Before Giskes returned he reported to his boss, Admiral Canaris, who was on his own stopover in the French capital.

Canaris warned Giskes that whatever problems he had to overcome with the IIIF station in The Hague, the biggest obstacle he faced would not be the British secret service or the poor quality of his staff and V-men. His greatest threat, said the spy chief, came from the Sicherheitsdienst (SD), the intelligence agency of the SS that had been deliberately set up in direct competition with Abwehr IIIF. The two agencies were now battling each other to be the premier counter-intelligence service of the Reich. It was an unfair contest, since IIIF officers had no powers of arrest and had to rely on the SD to apprehend suspects.

Nevertheless, Canaris made it plain that he expected Giskes not to rock the boat: 'Mind you see I'm not bothered in Berlin with your jealousies.'[15]

Joseph Schreieder, the head of the SD in Holland, had a reputation for underhandedness even with his own men.

On his return, Giskes decided to invite his rival to his office in Hogeweg for a friendly chat. It was to prove an instructive encounter.

Schreieder, a small bald man with a heavy round head, entered and sat back in a black leather chair and half extended a flabby, manicured hand, forcing Giskes to stand up and reach across his own desk. Schreieder was dressed in the imposing black and grey uniform of an SS Sturmbannführer. Giskes was in a plain brown suit.

The Abwehr man suggested they retire to the sun room, where he hoped for a less formal exchange.[16]

Once he had exhausted his supply of pleasantries, Giskes tested the water, asking to see a progress report on the recent arrest of a Dutch radio operator and his assistant whom Giskes wanted to question.

Schreieder was all smiles: 'Lieber Kamerad Giskes ... Please rest assured that I should do everything for you which can be reconciled with police requirements. The operator is a tough fellow in spite of his youth and is not to be broken down at the first onslaught. All that we have got out of him so far is that he is a Dutch naval cadet working for an espionage network operated by the Dutch Admiral Furstner in London.'[17]

Schreieder opened his briefcase and handed over a rather slim-looking file: 'I have extracted the interrogation reports so far which may be useful to you.'

Giskes thanked Schreieder for his cooperation before rounding off the conversation with platitudes about his high hopes of their future working relationship.

After Schreieder had left, Giskes read the report: 'They were a series of excerpts from the interrogation that told me virtually nothing except that the agent's real name was apparently Zomer.'[18]

The next Giskes knew was that Zomer had been executed after a summary trial before a German military court. Giskes now understood Canaris' warning about the SD.

'I learnt the lesson that, cost what it may, I must try, given another opportunity, to get the radio operator into my own hands.'[19]

The Germans' initial assessment of the situation in Holland proved to be hopelessly over-optimistic. The Nazis had assumed the support and collaboration of their Dutch cousins but the early muted welcome had soon turned into a widespread, sullen resistance and even open protest.

Most of the first resistance groups had ties either to the Netherlands Communist Party (CPN) or were ex-military. The communists mounted industrial strikes across the country. The most effective of these was CS-6, which had many members of the Amsterdam intelligentsia.

The Ordedienst (OD) was organised along military lines and its leaders swore loyalty to the Dutch Queen. Although they had access to weapons, they sought clearance from the Dutch government in exile in England before mounting any violent act of resistance.[20]

A few weeks after his arrival in Scheveningen, Giskes was visited by one of IIIF's V-men, 67-year-old Jos Hoosemans.[21] He was in charge of a group of half a dozen agents who had infiltrated a resistance group that was running an escape line from Brussels to Paris and into Spain. He reported that the group now trusted them enough that they had asked them to act as couriers carrying important documents along the route to England.

Giskes asked who had initiated the contact but Hoosemans couldn't remember. What he did know was that the following afternoon, he and his group were going to be meeting the resistance leaders in a coffee bar in Haarlem.

It could be the breakthrough Giskes had been waiting for.

Three days later however, Giskes had all but given up hope when there was a commotion outside his office. The V-man had returned. He was unshaven and had been roughed up. Giskes ushered him into the sun room, where the man collapsed on to a chair and spluttered: 'Murder, prison, all dead, Sicherheitsdienst.' It was several minutes before Giskes was able to ascertain what had happened.[22]

The German agents had arrived at the bar on time and were settling down in their seats when without warning the leader of the resistance group had drawn his pistol and fired it into the body of the V-man sitting opposite, killing him outright. At the same time another, a giant of a man, sitting unnoticed at the bar and nursing a concealed Sten gun, swivelled round and emptied his magazine into the group. One of the V-men managed to get off a shot but it went wide. The attack had all the hallmarks of a CS-6 operation.

Giskes considered the terrified V-man: 'had he just realised that war means shooting and death and that no mercy is shown in the shooting affrays of the underground struggle? Had he only just found out that when it comes to the point, the secret struggle between espionage and counter-espionage does not shrink from murder and assassination? And what had led him to take sides against his own people but his own urge to earn dirty money through informing and betrayal? As I looked at him I could only feel angry and disgust at the very figure before me – at the war, at the service in which I worked, and at myself.'[23]

Something else puzzled Giskes, 'Why did it take you three days to report all this?'

Hoosemans replied: 'When the shooting stopped, the SD arrived and although I told them I was working for you they took me away, locked me up and interrogated me for three days.'[24]

Giskes now vowed to accelerate his shake-up of IIIF. From now on, he would use only trusted V-men, each working closely with an individual Abwehr officer.

What he did not know then was that one of the three gunmen who had ambushed Hermann Giskes' V-men in the Haarlem bar, the giant of a man with the Sten gun, was a Dutch fighter who was to attain mythical status among resistance fighters from Holland to Spain. His name was Christiaan Lindemans, but everyone knew him as King Kong.[25]

Chapter 2

Rotterdam Playboy

The Lindemans were well known in Rotterdam. Joseph and his wife Christina had started out with a single garage selling petrol to the passing trade and became the first garage in Holland to stock Shell petrol.[1] Now they were servicing high-end luxury sports cars from a chain of garages throughout southern Holland. Pride of place was their garage in the centre of Rotterdam, where the Lindemans' workshops attracted custom from the city's wealthy car-owning elites. Joseph Lindemans had five sons to whom he hoped to pass on the family business. But not all the Lindemans brothers wanted to spend their lives with their heads buried under the bonnets of motor vehicles – even expensive ones. Brothers Cornelius, Jan, Joseph and Hendrik had no intention of being chained to the family garage. The Lindemans' second youngest son, Christiaan, was different.

Christiaan's formal education had ended after he was expelled aged 15 for taking a gun to class and using another boy's satchel[2] for target practice. His father thrashed him soundly but was secretly proud of his son's marksmanship. His expulsion meant he left school with nothing except a diploma in car maintenance. Outside school, Christiaan's enormous strength and size made him a first choice for the local rowing team, where his coach nicknamed him King Kong after the famous film which had been a recent hit in Holland.

Most of all though, Chris Lindemans loved speed, and that meant he loved cars, motorcycles and even gliders. Anything that came with an adrenaline rush.

In 1936, at the age of 24, his thrill-seeking lifestyle had cost him dearly when he lost control of his high-powered Brooks motorbike in a terrible accident that left him hospitalised for a year.[3] After the accident, Lindemans' rolling, limping gait lent the coach's nickname an altogether more cruel characterisation.[4]

Lindemans was determined that his injuries and disfigurement would not dictate how he was going to lead the rest of his life. The family's Lindo Garage at Baan 18, in central Rotterdam, gave him everything he needed.[5] He spent the weekdays in the workshop mending and polishing cars and the weekends driving them flat out on the same roads where he had come a cropper on his Brooks motorbike.

Christiaan returned to his life as a daredevil Rotterdam playboy, enjoying gambling, drinking, dancing, girls and lots of noise. When not behind the wheel of a fast car he was at his most content sitting at a table in a nightclub. His huge size and strength combined with his daredevil nature made him a centre of attention. But there was a darker side. Friends said his accident had affected the balance of his mind. People had to be careful not to fall victim to his volcanic temper, which could erupt without warning. He began to gain a reputation for enjoying fighting almost as much as he loved drinking and womanising.

He could also become detached from events when he took on a softer, vacant expression that his adversaries mistakenly mistook for simple-mindedness. In these moods he felt removed from the company he kept. Withdrawn, unable to fit in, nothing could coax him from his introspection.

Yet Chris Lindemans always remained very close to his family, especially to his youngest brother Henk, who hero-worshipped his playboy brother.

The fast-living, fearless Christiaan Lindemans soon attracted interest from other quarters outside the world of cars and casinos. In 1938 the Rotterdam police department[6] paid him a few hundred guilders a month to pass on information about the local communists while a British company rewarded him for informing on the owners and crews of foreign ships.

* * *

In the early hours of 10 May 1940, the skies above Holland filled with black waves of Luftwaffe bombers on their way to attack the airfields at Valkenburg and Ockenburg. At the same time, thousands of German paratroopers landed near the parliament and the Royal Palace in The Hague, where fierce fighting broke out in what was later called the Battle for The Hague and the Five-Day War.

In Rotterdam, a Dutch garrison force under Colonel P W Scharroo held the north bank of the Nieuwe Maas, preventing a German crossing. The Dutch faced daunting odds, including the crack paratroopers of General Kurt Student and the newly arrived 9th Panzer Division and the Leibstandarte Adolf Hitler under General Schmidt. A Dutch counter-attack led by brave soldiers from a marine company had failed to recapture the key bridge at Willemsbrug, but the Germans were unable to cross because of heavy fire being levelled at the structure from Dutch defensive positions.

The battle had fought its way to a stalemate. On 14 May, General Schmidt set in train plans for a combined bridge and air assault using tanks of the 9th Panzer supported by flame throwers. The paratroopers under Student were to make an amphibious crossing of the river upstream and then a flank back through the outskirts of the city.

Before Schmidt ordered the attack, he issued the Dutch leaders with an ultimatum of surrender which the Dutch, outnumbered and outgunned, knew they had to consider.

Two hours after the negotiations for the surrender of the city had begun, 54 Heinkel 111 bombers could be heard approaching from the east. A smaller group of 36 Heinkels began their run from the south. Then the whirring turned to whistling as, without warning, the bombs started falling.

A total of 1,150 50-kilogram (110 lb) and 158 250-kilogram

(550 lb) bombs were dropped on the defenceless city, mainly in the residential areas of Kralingen and the medieval centre and unleashing a firestorm that raged through Rotterdam for several days. The thriving cosmopolitan district of Coolsingel was reduced to rubble. And one bomb had scored a direct hit on the Lindemans' garage.

Nearly 1,000 Rotterdam residents perished before their leaders had a chance to answer the terms of surrender.

Not since the Nazi attack on Guernica during the Spanish Civil War had the world witnessed such indiscriminate targeting of a civilian population.

When the Germans threatened to repeat the air bombardment against Utrecht, the Dutch supreme command agreed to sign what amounted to an unconditional surrender. The rest of Holland followed suit.

The terrible events of 14 May instilled in Lindemans a burning hatred for the Germans. He blamed[7] the weak liberal elite for his country's spineless capitulation, especially Queen Wilhelmina, her government and the general staff who had run away to London.

His initial instinct was to lash out at the invaders, to find some way of avenging the destruction of his city and the loss of the family business.

The British had followed the Dutch leaders into the night and disembarked for England in a mini Dunkirk, but in the first few months of the occupation, the country actually enjoyed an economic boom, driven by orders from Germany for foodstuffs and building materials to support the rampaging Third Reich and its newly conquered territories. In Rotterdam, the order books of the shipyards were bulging as Hitler focused on the next phase of his grand plan – the invasion of Britain.

The Reichskommissar of the occupied Netherlands, Austrian Nazi Arthur Seyss-Inquart, hoped to exploit a shared heritage with the German peoples and rule by velvet glove. Greater enrolment in the Dutch Nazi Party assisted in the smooth transfer of power from the civilian administration to the German overlords.

Lindemans decided his own long-term interests might be best served working for the Nazis.

In July 1940, his garage contacts led him to a job with the Luftwaffe transport division as a petrol tanker driver on the route between Paris and Lille, in northern France.[8] It meant an overnight stay in Lille where Lindemans found accommodation with the Vermeulen family, who had a large house in the town.[9] Vermeulen was living with his second wife and her 19-year-old daughter, Gilberte, from her first marriage.

Gilberte and her stepfather were working for the French resistance, passing Allied soldiers, agents and Jews along an escape line through France and on to the Channel ports. Gilberte drove a French Red Cross ambulance, which she used to transport escapees safely through the German checkpoints. In the evenings, under her stage name Gilou, she sang and danced at a local nightclub. Lindemans was smitten. For Gilou the feelings were mutual, and soon the hulking Dutch lorry driver and the petite songstress were a couple, and by late 1941 Lindemans had taken a job as a caretaker at a German fighter base near Lille so he could spend more time with his new girlfriend. He had even started to become more closely involved with the resistance, working with Gilou and her stepfather.[10]

Vermeulen senior's activities had not escaped the attention of the local Abwehr. Lille was crawling with V-men and radio detection vans.

One of these V-men was another Dutchman from Rotterdam called Cornelis Verloop, an ex-French Foreign Legionnaire[11], who had fought the Germans in Norway, losing three of his fingers on his left hand.[12] Verloop, who had come to Lille looking for work, had tangled with the SD over identity papers and had been imprisoned for a few weeks.[13] When he emerged from custody, Verloop had a new calling and a ruthless determination to get the job done. It earned him the nickname 'Satan Face'.

One of the first men he betrayed was British soldier Paul 'Harry' Cole, who had gone into hiding after Dunkirk and was helping Allied servicemen along the Pat O'Leary escape line.[14]

Cole's arrest was a devastating blow to the French resistance and the British escape lines. Before the war, the British soldier had been a petty criminal and a confidence trickster.[15] He needed little encouragement to betray his comrades to the Germans in return for promises of cash.

Monsieur Letuppe had let the resistance use his home for a cache of machine guns and other weapons.[16] In December 1941, he was warned that a squad of SS soldiers accompanied by two SD officers was on its way. The family had just enough time to heave a large wooden trunk, packed with Sten guns and ammunition, into a deep well at the back of the garden.[17]

Despite this, when the SD men searched the house they found some Allied flags and a dagger belonging to a Pole, Stanislas Sobovv, whom they arrested. Everything pointed to Satan Face as the V-man who had masterminded the raid.

Lindemans was away working at a Luftwaffe air base at Montescourt near Saint-Quentin, but his absence didn't save him and he was arrested several days later.

He was questioned every day for a fortnight but the Germans were unable to prove he was working for the resistance and so he was released.[18] It was not the last close call he was to have and must have underlined in his mind just how risky the life he was leading was. In late 1942 he was to be imprisoned again and would serve five months in solitary confinement before he was eventually released. He was to emerge a changed man.

Chapter 3

Englandspiel

RAF Tempsford, between Bedford and Cambridge, was arguably Bomber Command's foggiest and boggiest airfield. As the home to 138 and 161 Squadrons responsible for Special Operation Executive (SOE) missions all across Europe, it was undoubtedly the most secret.

The appropriately named Operation Catarrh was to be the new service's first attempt to gain a foothold in Holland and establish a link with the Dutch resistance. On the evening of 6 November 1941, Huub Lauwers, a rubber plantation worker, and Thijs Taconis, a mathematician and keen chess player, boarded an RAF Whitley bomber. They had been issued with identity papers, a good supply of Dutch florins and Webley pistols. In addition they carried three sets of pills – 'knockout' drops to spike an enemy's drink; Benzedrine to combat fatigue and a single cyanide capsule which brought death in five seconds in case of capture.[1] Strapped to their backs were their parachutes and in the case of Lauwers, the mission's radio operator, a WT set. Last of all they were handed their secret orders. The two agents landed safely near Ommen, east of the city of Zwolle in the heart of Holland.

It was now that their troubles began.

As they set out to make contact with a resistance network in Amsterdam, they realised they were wearing exactly the same British-made suits – a sartorial oddity that was bound to draw comment. Then, when they attempted to spend their money, they discovered the coins they had were no longer in circulation. And a close examination of their identity cards revealed that the pair of royal Dutch lions in the watermark were facing the wrong way. The worst of their setbacks concerned the radio – it had faulty wiring and left Catarrh with no means of contacting London.[2] It wasn't until several weeks later when Taconis paid a visit to an electrical engineer at Leiden University that the wireless problem was solved.

On 4 January 1942, two months after their arrival, Catarrh sent its first message to London. SOE in Holland was up and running. Taconis had even managed to make contact with a friend who he believed was working for the Ordedienst (OD), the resistance group loyal to the Queen. His friend put him in contact with an affable Dutchman who ran a transport business. Taconis needed a lorry to collect an aeroplane drop in Assen and carry the explosives and weapons to a nearby safe house. This man gave his name as 'George' and assured Taconis and Lauwers he could help them in their clandestine endeavours. George was Matthijs Ridderhof, the V-man recruited by Hermann Giskes in Paris.

Giskes, when he was first told about it, was sceptical. It was surely too good to be true, and he told his trusted NCO Willy Kup: 'Gehen Sie zum Nordpol mit solcher Geschichten,' ('take stories like that to the North Pole') – and from that day on, the Abwehr name for the counter-intelligence operation against SOE in Holland was Operation Nordpol, although Schellenberg, with an instinct for a title better calculated to please Hitler, was to rebrand it as *Englandspiel*, the England Game).

When his agents confirmed that the RAF aircraft had indeed made the drop and Ridderhof had the guns and explosives in the back of his lorry, the German intelligence chief realised he had a unique opportunity to turn the intelligence tables on the British. The successful drop meant that he knew the British agents had access to a radio operator in direct touch with London. Giskes briefed Schreieder of the SD, who agreed to deploy his own radio detection vans to help track down the British wireless operator.

With 'George' Ridderhof's help it didn't take long for the Fu-B-Stelle-ORPO radio intercept unit to home in on Lauwers' location in The Hague.

On the evening of 6 March, Lauwers was sitting behind his transmitter wrapped in an overcoat with a blanket over his knees to keep out the cold as he tapped out a message to London giving the new location for the German cruiser *Prinz Eugen*, a prize naval target. As he finished Lauwers' lookout burst into the room, warning him there were three police cars in the street.[3] Lauwers dropped the radio set out of the window and left the building. He was immediately stopped and searched. Two scraps of paper sealed his fate – one had the address of the flat from where he had sent his message and the other contained the cipher text of the message he had just sent.

He was taken to Giskes for questioning and to begin with the Dutch radio man gave only his false name. But Giskes had a trick up his sleeve. An hour into the questioning, one of Giskes' men handed Lauwers' coded message to the German interrogator: 'Ah, I see the *Prinz Eugen* is now in Schiedam,' exclaimed Giskes.

It would have been impossible for the Germans to break the British code in such a short period of time. But Lauwers could not know that and the apparent speed of the revelation shattered his confidence and he started to talk.

What Lauwers did not know was that the source of the intelligence about the *Prinz Eugen* was Giskes himself, passed on to Lauwers by Ridderhof. Three days later the Germans captured Taconis near Arnhem.

Giskes now told Lauwers that the only way he could save himself and Taconis from torture and death at the hands of the SD was by cooperating fully with him.

So, on 12 March 1942, Lauwers sent another message to London about the location of a new drop zone.[4]

Even then, the Dutch agent followed his SOE training, omitting security checks designed to flag that the operation had been compromised.

Lauwers had been fastidious in the use of checks in all his previous messages so this was noted by a junior officer in the SOE cipher team and passed on to Charles Cecil Blizard, the officer in charge of SOE operations in Holland. Unfortunately, Blizard had a lot on his mind. He had recently split up from his wife because he was having an affair with a much younger female intelligence officer, his future wife, whom he was also trying to have assigned to his section. Already under something of a cloud because of his messy private life, he was reluctant to admit to his superiors that the only wireless operator SOE had infiltrated in the whole of Holland may now be working for the Germans. He was to ignore this and many future red flags. It would result in the worst British intelligence disaster of the war.[5]

Two weeks later, SOE parachuted Lieutenant Arnoldus Baatsen to a moonlit drop zone north of Steenwijk, where he was warmly greeted by Ridderhof and two police officers dressed as resistance fighters. As they helped gather up Baatsen's parachute, the group was arrested by German soldiers. All four of them, including Ridderhof, were handcuffed and marched off to a waiting truck. Baatsen was extremely angry at his arrest, which Giskes cheerfully assured him was the result of intelligence provided by a German agent in London. Baatsen immediately turned on his British controllers, revealing names and operating procedures, information that Giskes added to his growing bank of knowledge about British intelligence.

In the coming weeks, 50 more agents and more vital supplies and weapons intended for the resistance fell into Giskes' hands. The RAF even lost a third of the aircraft used for these missions, picked off by night fighters who knew the British flight paths.

There was great glee in Berlin and Walter Schellenberg was able to personally brief Hitler on the astounding counter-intelligence success in Holland.

By early summer 1943, Giskes had control of an astonishing 14 SOE radio transmitters communicating with London. Nearly every resistance group and the escape line out of Holland had been compromised. Those who survived did so because they shunned contact with SOE. These were the communist groups, the so-called Rote Kapelle or Red Orchestra. They took their orders from Moscow, not London.[6]

Chapter 4

Legend of King Kong

In May 1943, Christiaan Lindemans walked out of Abbeville prison[1] after five months of solitary confinement. The experience had toughened him, and it is now that the legend of King Kong begins to be born. He made his way to Cherbourg to take a new job with a Dutch company working for the giant Todt construction agency responsible for building Nazi infrastructure across Europe, including the massive Atlantic Wall to defend against an Allied invasion.

The pay was good and it would have allowed Lindemans to turn his back on the war. But that was far from his intention.

Instead, Lindemans persuaded a young female secretary called 'Johnny' to provide him with blank Todt identity cards that he passed on to a forger he had met in Saint-Quentin, where they were reissued to escapees who joined construction parties heading to Cherbourg and Abbeville.[2]

However well paid his job was, it was nothing compared to what he could earn ferrying his high-paying human cargo across Europe and the Todt construction sites and labour camps were perfect cover.

The identity and travel documents produced by the master forger 'Monsieur Lacoche', who ran the Saint-Quentin 'shoe shop' (the name Moscow gave to false ID card factories)[3] allowed him to pass Allied airmen, Jews and Onderduikers (Dutch men and women in hiding to avoid deportation to Germany) through the demarcation zones policed by the Nazi security forces.

Lindemans had discovered he was born for this kind of resistance work. The excitement he had once found driving fast cars was no match for the thrill of running escape lines through northern France.

Back in Holland, his brothers, Jan and Hendrik, were working in a communist group, passing refugees between Amsterdam and Rotterdam. So far they had restricted themselves to hiding refugees in safe houses, barely venturing outside Holland.

But the year before, in 1942, Jan and Henk Lindemans had received a letter with a Lille postmark. It contained a single request asking the two brothers to find people who wanted to leave Holland. The letter was signed 'King Kong'.[4]

Lindemans travelled back to Rotterdam so he could personally accompany by train the first batches of escapees to within 20 kilometres of the Belgian border.

Lindemans, the 'passeur', arranged for bicycles to carry his 'customers' the last part of the journey to Esschen, bypassing the main railway checkpoints, where they crossed the border into Belgium, and then on to Paris, where they made their way via Bordeaux to the Spanish frontier. The travellers then crossed the border on foot or by taxi – depending on how much they could afford. Lindemans' reputation was growing, not just with downed airmen but also wealthy Dutch families who longed to get to England and were prepared to pay a fortune to do so. Lindemans accepted jewellery and fine art, anything with value that he could trade on the black market. He recruited other members including 'Wim' van der Meer[5] and 'Harry', two Dutch resistance workers he knew from the old days in Rotterdam.

By the autumn of 1943, Lindemans was becoming a rich man and in September he moved into the Hotel Berne, Boulevard de la Saussaie, Paris,[6] with the now pregnant Gilou Letuppe. For

Lindemans it was a return to his carousing before the war, although of course the nightlife of Paris was far superior to that of Rotterdam.

Lindemans' growing reputation brought him into contact with other resistance networks. One of these was led by a Dutch university student called Victor Swane, who received funds and help from Baron van Boetzelaer, and Baron van Heemstra, the mayor of Arnhem and the aristocratic grandfather of the film actress Audrey Hepburn. Van Heemstra, one of the richest landowners in Holland, had maintained a position of neutrality on the war until the Nazis arrested his son, Audrey Hepburn's uncle, who was executed in August 1942 as a Nazi reprisal for attacks carried out by the Dutch resistance.[7]

Lindemans discovered he also had a special talent for persuading wealthy women to bail him out whenever he needed funds for his resistance ventures. One such benefactor was Freule von Vredenburgh, who lent him money and let him hide out in a grand house in Paris. Three years of living under Nazi occupation had hardened Christiaan Lindemans' political outlook. He noticed how the poor were getting poorer while the wealthy were making fortunes by supporting the German war effort.[8]

The Lindemans brothers were working closely with CS-6 and Lindemans himself became a leading figure in the newly established Raad van Verzet (RVV), the resistance council of Holland that brought together many of the anti-Nazi groups.[9]

CS-6 was a broad socialist church whose 1,000 members comprised Stalinists, Trotskyists and national communists.[10] CS-6's willingness to engage in sabotage and assassinations led to Whitehall wags dubbing it Centrum Sabotage 6.[11] Two of its bravest fighters were Kas de Graaf and Nicolaas Celosse and the group had scores of successful actions under their belt. It was led by Dr Gerrit Kastein, a neurologist who had served as a medical officer in the Spanish Civil War.[12] By the start of the war he had established himself as an outspoken anti-racist and critic of fascism.

In September 1941, his activities had attracted the attention of the Nazis and after a tip-off that he was about to be arrested by the SD, he went into hiding.

On the morning of Friday 5 February 1943, Lieutenant General Hendrik Seyffardt answered a knock on the door of his grand seaside home in Scheveningen, not far from Abwehr headquarters.[13]

The 70-year-old veteran soldier, Dutch nationalist and fierce anti-communist had been brought out of retirement to recruit and lead a Dutch legion of fascists destined for the Russian Front.

Seyffardt had taken to his new role with gusto, travelling the length and breadth of the country enrolling suitable young men for his Vrijwilligerslegioen. His enthusiasm had earned him the title 'the most hated man in Holland', and when he opened his front door, two shots were fired into him from point-blank range. As the assassin fled the scene, the general fell back into his hallway, managing to stumble to the telephone to summon assistance even though he succumbed to his wounds the next day.

The gunman was Jan Verleun, a young communist assassin trained by Kas de Graaf. Two days later, Verleun shot down another collaborator, Hermanus Reydon, a key figure in the fascist National Socialist Movement of the Netherlands (NSB).

The German response was swift and brutal.

The SD executed 50 Dutch students as well as a number of well-known Dutch patriots.

German intelligence soon picked up the trail of Kastein and Verleun. By now the success of Englandspiel had forged a close working relationship between Giskes and Schreieder. Aided by SOE's inept leadership from London, they had become formidable opponents of the resistance.

Van der Waals and 'George' Ridderhof had had some success in penetrating CS-6 and identified Kastein as its leader. Schreieder told his own V-man to arrange a meeting with Kastein in a cafe in Utrecht, where the SD pounced and bundled him into a waiting car. The Dutch communist resistance chief drew a concealed pistol and shot the SD driver before making his escape on foot, but he was quickly recaptured and taken to a prison outside Utrecht. There, Kastein was tied to a chair in an interrogation cell on the second floor of the building.

Kastein held out under the initial brutal questioning, but he knew it was only a matter of time before torture would force him to betray the other members of CS-6. During a break from interrogation, Kastein, who was still tied to his chair, managed to manoeuvre himself to the open windows and throw himself out on to the concrete below, sustaining cranial injuries from which he died a few hours later.

Kastein's heroic sacrifice gave the other members of CS-6 valuable time to go into hiding. Kas de Graaf, now head of CS-6 security,[14] had been tipped off that his name and activities were known to the Germans. His friend Nicolaas Celosse received the same warning. They knew they had to leave Holland immediately.

However, word had also reached de Graaf that several CS-6 members had been taken to Utrecht police station, where they were being held by the Gestapo before being transferred to Amsterdam. De Graaf delayed his departure to mount a rescue operation. On 22 October 1943, de Graaf, Celosse and Jan Verleun led a group of 11 heavily armed fighters into the police station. Aiming his British Sten gun at the astonished German and Dutch officers, he ordered them to put their hands up 'in the name of the Queen', a phrase designed to encourage the Germans to think they were members of the patriotic OD group.[15] As soon as de Graaf had neutralised the Germans, he released his imprisoned comrades and locked the Dutch policemen in their own cells.[16]

Kas de Graaf, who had been a waiter before the war, now began making urgent plans to slip the Nazi dragnet and escape to England.[17] He knew there was one man who had the resources and contacts to carry out the perilous exfiltration.

The passeur he turned to had a fearsome reputation among the Dutch underground. Some knew him as 'Le Tueur', 'the killer', but most called him 'King Kong' on account of his huge build and extraordinary strength. Nobody was quite sure how many Germans he had killed or how many escape lines he and his brothers were running. Nor indeed how many rich and beautiful women he had seduced. Only a few trusted members of CS-6 were allowed to know his real identity, but everyone knew that his exploits in resisting the German occupation were legendary.

Lindemans' flawlessly forged travel documents allowed the group to join a train full of German soldiers on leave travelling from Maastricht to Paris. Lindemans escorted them to the Dutch railway station and then melted away into the crowds of travellers, refugees and soldiers.

In Paris, de Graaf was met by a French woman called 'Madame Clichy',[18] who took the Dutch security chief and his group to an apartment on the Boulevard Victor Hugo.

Lindemans reappeared a few days later with some bad news. He told de Graaf that the SD had made several arrests in Paris and it was no longer safe for them to stay with Madame Clichy. In particular he was worried about another Dutchman who had just made contact with him in the city. The man called himself 'George' and claimed to be a British agent sent by London.[19]

Lindemans, however, told de Graaf that he suspected George of working for the Germans. De Graaf now believed this was the Dutch traitor who had also infiltrated CS-6, leading to the arrests and executions of many of their members that year. Lindemans said they had no choice but to kill 'George'[20] and he would lead the mission to eliminate the dangerous double agent.

He and de Graaf and a small number of trusted fighters combed the city. Their first port of call was a house in the northern banlieues, but George was not there. Next they visited a bar in the Rue Faubourg just behind the Gestapo headquarters where

Lindemans had been told George was a regular customer. There was no sign of 'George' there either. After hours more fruitless searching, Lindemans called off the hunt, telling de Graaf he now believed 'George' had left the city and had returned to Amsterdam.

It was Christmas Eve when Lindemans escorted the group by train to Bordeaux, where they were joined by Henrietta Luret, a local passeur who would help them cross the Pyrenees.[21]

As they neared the Spanish border, Lindemans split them into two parties – one group would accompany some other Dutch refugees while Lindemans and de Graaf would cross the border alone through a little-known mountain pass.[22] In the summer this mountain crossing presented few obstacles, but this was the middle of winter and there were swollen rivers, cavernous drops and deep snow in which they would leave tracks.

Lindemans led the ascent. They climbed silently for several hours before he signalled for de Graaf to stop. They were no longer alone.

'We're being followed,' he quietly told his companion. 'I knew it was too good to last.'[23]

De Graaf asked his friend what he meant.

'In the last village, I didn't want to say anything to you, but I noticed that a man was very interested in us; in that cafe he must have given the alert.'[24]

De Graaf scoured the downward slope for any sign of their pursuer. 'It may be a shepherd … or a mountain smuggler,' he suggested.

Lindemans just shook his head and waved de Graaf forward, while he hung back in the cover of the trees. Soon their pursuer appeared, striding up the pass. He had already seen de Graaf and had drawn his revolver. Lindemans made his move. The man turned to meet the rushing giant ploughing through the snow towards him. But he was unable to get off his shot before he had been smothered by Lindemans, who knocked him to the ground.

Lindemans held the man's throat in his giant hand and used his knees to pin him to the snow. With his free hand he repeatedly punched his face. De Graaf, too far away to help, could only stand and watch the savagery of the attack, which was over in just a few seconds.

The victim's bloody body lay still in the white carpet of snow.

'You should have fired,' said de Graaf; 'he was going to.'

'Noise travels too far in the mountains.'[25]

From inside one of the man's pockets, Lindemans produced a Gestapo identity card.

The Germans were closing in on the France/Spain escape routes and Lindemans was pleased to get de Graaf safely to Orbaiceta, where they bade farewell to each other.[26] De Graaf eventually reached Pamplona where he was joined by the rest of the group. A few days later, the CS-6 resistance man had safely arrived in Gibraltar and boarded a twin-engined Vickers Warwick that flew him to an airfield in Devon.

Lindemans and his brave fighters continued to risk their lives running their escape lines and no sooner had they helped de Graaf and Celosse get back to London than they were to find themselves caught up in the aftermath of one of the most iconic raids of the Second World War.

On 15 September 1943, crews from 617 Squadron, the famous Dambusters, prepared for another mission deep inside enemy territory. Canadian air gunner Fred Sutherland and British navigator Sydney Hobday were among eight Lancaster crews that took part in the ill-fated Operation Garlic to destroy the Dortmund–Ems canal in Germany. The Lancasters ran into trouble as soon as they reached Holland. Flying low over the small town of Nordhorn, the lead Lancaster was hit by flak and the aircraft exploded, killing all the crew.

Fred Sutherland in the front gunner turret of his Lancaster saw everything: 'It was so close I could almost reach out and touch it. … All you can do is think, "Thank God it wasn't us."'[27] Two hours later, Sutherland's low-flying Lancaster had hit the top of a clump of trees, sustaining damage to the radiators of its port engines. Flight Lieutenant Les Knight, who was piloting the plane, shut down the damaged engine and jettisoned his bomb. He managed to climb to 1,400 ft before ordering his crew to bail out. Once everybody had successfully left the aircraft, Knight attempted to crash-land the plane in open fields rather than bail out himself and risk it hitting houses, but he was unable to slow the speed of the descent and his plane blew up on impact with the ground, killing him.

Sutherland and Hobday landed safely in a field near the city of Zwolle. They were helped by a Dutch boy whose parents ran a hotel near Baarn. The two RAF flyers were led to a hut in the middle of a wood in the grounds of a Catholic convent. Here they were held by a group of seven teenagers, brandishing pistols and rifles, who locked them in a shed until they could make sure they weren't Nazi agents masquerading as downed Allied pilots – a ruse often tried by Giskes and Schreieder to infiltrate escape lines.[28] Once their story had been checked out and the boys had located the crashed Lancaster, they were released and invited to mix with the group.[29]

After a month they were told arrangements had been made for their escape from Holland.

Their escort was Nijs van den Dool, a Dutch policeman working at the Scheveningen prison in The Hague.[30]

Hobday recalled during the car and train journey to Rotterdam that the country was crawling with Germans. Both airmen had switched to civilian clothes and shaved off their moustaches because they were told Dutchmen didn't have facial hair. If challenged, the policeman would explain that they were foreign workers from an airfield in northern France who didn't speak Dutch.

Van den Dool took them to an address in Rotterdam, Noordsingel 182 Rotterdam.[31] The airmen were warned to lie low for two days until they were collected by a man who would take them on to Paris. Sure enough, two days later they heard someone using a key to open the door. Standing in the doorway was the giant figure of Christiaan Lindemans. He told the two Dambuster heroes to collect their belongings and prepare to leave. Then he handed them two flawless Todt identity cards made out in the names of two French workers.

The Paris-bound train was so overcrowded that they had to stand next to the toilets for the whole journey, although it also meant that they weren't bothered by inquisitive guards.[32] But when they reached the French border both men were called forward to have their documents examined. Hobday and Sutherland didn't know it, but after their names had appeared in the British press[33] celebrating their part in the Dambusters mission, the Germans had placed the flyers on a blacklist of Allied crew who were to be shot if they ever fell into Nazi hands.

'There were two Gestapo guards on either side of the door,' recalled Hobday after the war. 'I didn't speak German or Dutch and I was supposed to act out the part of a deaf and dumb worker. It was a bit far-fetched really. They were about to ask me a question when they just waved us through.'[34] Lindemans had somehow worked his magic.

Once in Paris, Lindemans handed them over to an elegant old lady named Madame Theresa Viellot. 'Every night,' said Hobday, 'the three of us sat around and drank a bottle of wine.'[35] They stayed in Paris for another month.

The next part of their journey followed that of Celosse and de Graaf, through southern France and across the Spanish Pyrenees. After a train ride to Toulouse, they reached a house at the foot of the mountains, where they were joined by some American flyers and an assortment of other refugees led by two Basque guides, who safely delivered them to Allied contacts in Spain and from Gibraltar they were flown back to England in an American Liberator.

The two RAF airmen would be the last to be helped by the Lindemans brothers. The war in the West had reached a critical point and in Berlin all eyes were on the build-up of Allied troops in southern England.

Chapter 5

The End of the Game

The arrival in England of Kas de Graaf and Nicolaas Celosse finally alerted the British to the idea that something may have gone wrong with the Dutch operation.[1] SOE decided to pause flights while they investigated. At IIIF Abwehr headquarters in The Hague, Hermann Giskes knew that Englandspiel was delivering diminishing returns. The supply of British-sent agents had dried up and radio requests to London were being ignored. It seemed obvious to Giskes that SOE had finally cottoned on to the deception. Furthermore, the working relationship between himself and Schreieder had broken down. Schreieder had tried to cut Giskes out by running his own Funkspiel (sending fake encrypted radio messages to London). This had been handled so badly that it only served to increase British suspicions about their SOE operators in Holland.

Englandspiel had begun to unravel.

To add to Giskes' woes, two captured SOE agents had managed to escape. Code-named Chive and Sprout, Johan Ubbink and Pieter Dourlein had parachuted into Holland separately. Both had been captured immediately and sent to Haaren prison. On the night of 29 August 1943, they escaped through a bathroom window. It would take them five months to get back to Britain.[2]

A few weeks later, three more SOE agents escaped from Haaren. Jan van Rietschoten had managed to hide an SOE-issued miniature hacksaw in his shoe. Working night and day with two other Dutch prisoners, Aart van der Giessen and Antonius Wegner, they cut a small hole in the ceiling and climbed up through the attic and then used tight knotted bed sheets to drop down the prison wall.

The rope was several metres too short and Wegner injured his foot on landing, leaving him unable to run. A team of guards with dogs was sent after them. Van Rietschoten and van der Giessen had no choice but to leave Wegner to fend for himself.[3] Both men successfully evaded the German hunting party.

Because of the escapes, Hermann Giskes now believed the fumbling SOE would know for certain their Dutch operations had been blown. The German spy chief decided to deliver his own *coup de grâce*.

He sat down with his loyal Willy Kup and composed a short message, which they transmitted to London in unciphered plain text:

> To Messrs. Blunt [here, Giskes was referring to Blizard, who had adopted the cover name Blunt], Bingham & Co., Successors Ltd., London. We understand that you have been endeavouring for some time to do business in Holland without our assistance. We regret this the more since we have acted for so long as your sole representatives in this country, to our mutual satisfaction. Nevertheless we can assure you that, should you be thinking of paying us a visit on the Continent on any extensive scale, we shall give your emissaries the same attention as we have hitherto, and a similarly warm welcome. Hoping to see you.[4]

It was a message which must have turned the blood cold in Baker Street as the vast scale of the disaster began to dawn on the SOE chiefs.

SOE sent a feeble response to Giskes' message a few days later:

> With reference to your message of April 1st we have tried your agency once more but consider it to be so terribly

inefficient as to warrant our changing for good. Please do not worry about entertainment as that matter will be in our hands and now have a detailed list of you all, may rest assured that it will hardly be pinpoints [sic pin pricks].[5]

The reaction among some members of the Dutch government in London was much more damning, prompting the accusation that Englandspiel must have been part of a deliberate British deception to feed misleading intelligence to the Germans about D-Day.

By now, the Netherlands had endured more than three years of occupation and the privations and struggles were taking their toll. Everything was scarce – meat, milk, butter, chocolate, tea, coffee and sugar. Even fruit and vegetables, the once bountiful staples of the Dutch farming economy, were difficult to find in the cities. Queues snaked around every corner. Queues for bread; queues for the labour camps; queues of Jews waiting for transportation to the concentration camps. Young children wandered the streets scavenging for morsels of food or something to trade on the black market. Some of them little more than bags of bones while others had bloated stomachs from being fed on a diet of watered-down gruel. Even the wealthy suffered. Audrey Hepburn, granddaughter of Baron van Heemstra, was hospitalised with malnutrition at the end of the war.

Christiaan Lindemans was largely unaffected by the privations, cushioned by the hefty booty he had claimed from the rich refugees he had given a safe passage to freedom.[6]

But the war did take its toll on his family.

Lindemans could see that his mother, a proud woman, was finding it hard to cope with the daily assaults on the family's much-reduced circumstances. Her once-colourful wardrobe of stylish skirts and dresses had been bartered away so that Mrs Lindemans had to make do with a sackcloth skirt and a pre-war threadbare sweater.[7] She too wandered the streets from queue to queue with a basket on her arm, mostly returning at night with little to show for her patience and perseverance. Lindemans helped where he could – but his resources were stretched by the exorbitant prices of the black market and the ever-present bribery payments needed to sustain his escape lines. Plus, there was always another nightclub to go to.

Every day brought news of another arrest of someone he knew – a friend caught up in a razzia or a resistance fighter betrayed for a handful of guilders. Giskes' V-men seemed to be everywhere and if not them, the Gestapo were constantly on the prowl. He had tried to keep them at arm's length with bribes and threats, but with the success of Englandspiel he could see an arrogant triumphalism among the rats and spies who reported everything they saw and heard to their Nazi masters. The glaring shortcomings of British intelligence were not merely staring Lindemans in the face, they were threatening his very life.

Recent Allied air raids only compounded Dutch anger towards their Western Allies. In one attack on the Rotterdam docks on 31 March 1943, 102 USAAF bombers missed their dockyard targets, causing 400 civilian deaths and making 10,000 people homeless. The Allies had now killed more Dutch than the Luftwaffe had during its infamous attack on the city at the beginning of the war.

Lindemans began to worry that the British and Americans could not defeat the Germans and that the best the Allies would settle for was a peace that would leave the Nazis in occupation of Holland.[8] That was not something Lindemans could ever accept.

His anxieties were heightened by the fact that his personal circumstances had also changed. He was now the father of a young girl and Gilou Letuppe, who despite his inveterate philandering was still in love with him, was expecting their second child.

Lindemans realised the Dutch needed to do more to turn the tide. He decided to reach out to Belgian resistance groups and travel to Brussels. where he hoped to use his seniority in the

THE END OF THE GAME

communist-dominated Raad van Verzet or Council of Resistance (RVV)[9] to unite the Belgian and Dutch underground forces under one properly resourced organisation.

But while Lindemans was away in Belgium, events in Rotterdam were about to change his world forever and indirectly affect the closing chapters of the Second World War.

Towards the end of 1943, Henk Lindemans received a phone call from Nijs van den Dool, a policeman working at the Scheveningen Prison, who had helped the Dambuster airmen. He said he had more escaped Allied airmen who needed to be met and hidden in Rotterdam. Van den Dool gave Henk the names of the flyers and a house in The Hague where he could pick them up.[10] Henk wasted no time and rushed to the address.

It was a trap. A squad of SD officers grabbed him and bundled him into a police car and took him to Scheveningen Prison, where he joined his frightened one-time friend van den Dool, who had already been picked up by the Germans.

Ridderhof's penetration of the Lindemans escape line had borne its first fruit.

Not only had he discovered van den Dool was a key member of the Dutch-Paris escape line, he was able to tell Giskes that the two British airmen helped by van den Dool were 'Dambusters'. This was important because their names had been published on Gestapo death lists. The moment had come to reel in the rest of the group.

In a coordinated action, the Germans worked their way back along the line. The Rotterdam network was systematically broken up. Giskes was even able to track back to the boys of Baarn who had hidden Sutherland and Hobday. Six of them were imprisoned and one of them was summarily executed.[11]

Lindemans was staying at the Montholon Hotel in Paris when word reached him of the arrests. He immediately asked about the fate of his little brother, whom he had brought into the network two years ago.

The situation was bleak – Henk and Nijs van den Dool had been sentenced to death and were awaiting execution at The Hague.[12]

Christiaan, consumed by guilt, was desperate to return to his family in Rotterdam, where he could at least try to make amends for what had happened. Plenty of his friends told him not to go as Giskes would undoubtedly have circulated his name among his network of V-men. With customary bravado he brushed their concerns aside and left the pregnant Gilou at the hotel and returned to Rotterdam on the first train out of Paris.

By the time he reached the Lindemans house it was dark. His mother and father, gathered in the gloom of their hall, kissed their son.[13] They hadn't seen him for so long and they had so much to tell him. But all they could talk about was Henk. Did Krist have any news?

Christiaan caressed his mother's furrowed brow.[14]

According to interviews with Lindemans' family by the French writer Anne Laurens after the war, Christiaan rashly promised, because he had no answers to the questions: 'We will get him out.'

Then he puffed out his chest, exuding a confidence he didn't feel:

'I know what I am saying. Everything is ready. We have our plan. The English are marching with me. If we want, we could empty the prison and all the prisons in Holland, but we won't do that. It is not yet the right moment. We cannot save Henk this time, but he will come out, Mummy, I promise you. Don't cry any more, you mustn't cry. I'm not scared you see, for it is the Germans who are scared of me. They have nicknamed me King Kong because they think I am a sort of Superman.'[15]

Mother Lindemans' face crumpled; she couldn't bear losing another son to the war.

'Chris, Chris, my son, be careful. What are you going to do?'

In his anguish he told his mother: 'Don't try to understand, Mummy, it is too dangerous … believe me, have confidence and don't ask any questions.'[16]

But Christiaan Lindemans didn't have a plan. Nor did he believe the English 'were marching with him'.

Lindemans felt he had helped enough Allied airmen back to England to feel he was justified in asking London for assistance. But after Englandspiel it was plain to see that British intelligence and its SOE were impotent against the Germans. The British were finished in Holland.

It was becoming more and more dangerous for Christiaan Lindemans to remain in Rotterdam. Giskes' men were everywhere. The net was closing on the Dutch resistance fighter.

Lindemans left for Paris, where he planned to lie low and try to raise enough money to bribe the Germans into releasing his brother. He couldn't stay with Gilou as this was the first place the Germans would look for him. There were of course enough women who would willingly hide him until the heat was off. But Giskes and Ridderhof would be following up each of the links in the escape line.

On reaching Paris, Lindemans sought refuge with Freule von Vredenburgh[17] in her house on the Rue de l'Université. Lindemans still didn't know whether the aristocrat who had given so generously to resistance funds was Dutch or Belgian. But he must have believed he could trust her. It was here he was contacted by Max Goudriaan, a communist resistance worker whom he knew from Overschie, near Rotterdam. Goudriaan was not part of the usual networks that Lindemans dealt with but Christiaan must have trusted him. Goudriaan took his orders from Moscow and he wanted Lindemans to meet an important resistance leader who he said might be able to help his brother. The man was the head of a communist resistance network in Paris, an agent who operated a printing press and was well placed to assist him in his quest to save his brother.[18]

At the end of the war, MI5 compiled a lengthy report on Lindemans. The report does not say what happened during this meeting and it remains a mystery.

But a week later, Lindemans left Paris for Brussels with 5,000 French francs he said were given to him by von Vredenburgh.

There, he sought out a V-man who had caused him considerable trouble over the years. He had an important proposition he wished to put to him.

It was turning dusk when Hermann Giskes left the Hotel Metropole in Brussels on an evening towards the end of February 1944 for a meeting with a 'British agent'. He had plenty on his mind. Englandspiel had run its course. More troubling were the five SOE prisoners who had escaped. Reports had reached him that Berlin was looking to blame someone for the escape of the prisoners. That someone was Giskes, although it was Schreieder who had direct responsibility for the security of captured agents. To make matters worse, the Abwehr had just been abolished and his old boss and protector, Admiral Canaris, was weeks away from an arrest which would culminate with him being hanged from a hook and executed as a traitor to the Nazi cause in the most barbaric fashion a year later.[19]

Giskes desperately needed a new breakthrough or else face transfer to the Russian front, or worse.

He entered the office of the Abwehr in central Brussels[20] and acknowledged Hauptmann Walter Wurr and the loyal Willy Kup, who acted as Giskes' eyes and ears. Sitting next to Kup wearing a wide grin on his face was Cornelis Verloop, 'Satan Face'.[21] All three were well known to Giskes. But the other member of the party was not.

'The man towered a full head above all of us,' Giskes later wrote in his diary. 'Standing before me was an athlete with the head of a child.'

There was no mistaking King Kong – the legendary Dutch agent.

Giskes began: 'May I ask you to explain what brings you here?'

Lindemans replied in fluent German: 'If I am not mistaken I am speaking to the head of the German counter-espionage. I wish to address my proposal to him alone as I do not expect to get satisfaction from anyone else ... I am Christiaan Lindemans of Rotterdam and I have worked for the English Secret Service since the beginning of 1940. For the last six months I have brought in my youngest brother to assist in getting English airmen out of the country. He has been discovered, arrested by the SiPo (SD), and is now on the sentence of death pronounced by a German military court.'[22]

Lindemans spoke clearly and confidently, seemingly unbothered that what he had already admitted was enough to see him suffer the same fate as his brother.

'I feel myself responsible for my brother's fate, since it was I who introduced him to this work. If you can arrange to have my brother freed, I am ready to hand over the whole of my knowledge of the Allied secret services. I know the underground from the North Sea to the Spanish Frontier. You may assume that after five years of work for the Allies I have experienced contacts who will be of great value to you.'[23]

Giskes was intrigued by the force and effrontery of this giant of a resistance fighter.

'But I must specify one condition,' continued Lindemans. 'I'm aware of the methods which the German military counter-espionage is accustomed to use, in contrast with those of the secret field police and the SiPo. That is why I have come to you and not to the police. I could not imagine that you would proceed to make mass arrests of all my friends. But that is not the main point. The decisive factor is whether you can give me your word that my brother Henk Lindemans will be set free.'

Lindemans placed his fists on the table like a pair of blacksmith hammers as he waited to hear how Giskes would respond.

'I do not know your brother's case. If he has been sentenced simply for a crime of helping prisoners to escape, I think I can promise you that we can have him set free. I will go into the matter at once. If you can satisfy me that you are playing us no tricks and if the information which you give us proves that you are the man you make yourself out to be, you may rely on it that your brother will be free in a week at the latest.'[24]

Given the deteriorating relationship between Giskes and the SD it was a rash promise, but Giskes was being thrown a lifeline and no doubt felt he had no choice but to promise Lindemans what he asked for. What Lindemans appeared to offer could be even bigger than Englandspiel. There were, however, one or two nagging doubts. Henk had been arrested in October. It was now nearly April. Why had the giant resistance leader waited five months before reaching out to him? And why hadn't the SD already carried out the execution?

Lindemans got up from the table. He seemed agitated and began purposefully striding up and down the room.

Giskes listened in astonishment as Lindemans poured out his feelings to the Germans: 'For the past five years I have been impelled by a single thought – to do my most for the Allied Secret Service, without thought of thanks or reward. Now I've been met with ingratitude, mistrust and betrayal. If you only knew how many weaklings, place seekers and collaborators, who have used their connections with the Germans simply to enrich themselves, and are now starting to come over to us because they believe that the defeat of Germany is imminent. If you knew this you would understand me better when you realise why I have come to you.'[25]

Lindemans appeared swept up in the emotion of the moment:

'The men through whom we carried on the resistance during the first years of the occupation have nearly all gone – dead, arrested or just disappeared. Of the remainder there are only a few whom I can trust. Leave them in peace. I will guarantee that in due course you will learn a great deal about the plans of the underground and of London. Hand me over my brother and then make use of me as seems best to you. King Kong as they call me is friend or foe. I should like to be your friend from today. I have often heard and always believed that those who work conscientiously for you are treated properly. As regards confidence I have had enough experience to know that there is no such thing as half confidence. That goes for me too – all or nothing. I shall show you that King Kong can be relied on and what it means to have him for a friend.'

As a final sign of his good faith, the giant agent lifted up his brown briefcase and emptied the contents on to the table.

Giskes could make out Wehrmacht ID cards, SD passes, Todt travel permits, thick wads of German, Dutch, Belgian and French banknotes. Lindemans then unclipped a 9mm German pistol and placed it on top of the pile of documents and contraband.[26]

Lindemans watched the incredulous expressions on the faces of the German intelligence men as they pored over his collection of spy 'toys'.

All at once, Lindemans gathered up the articles from the table, saying he had an urgent appointment. Giskes checked his watch – it was 9pm. He had been listening to King Kong for almost three hours.

Three days later, Giskes was back at his office at the Abwehr headquarters in Holland. An excited Walter Wurr knocked on his door. In his hand the German officer held a large folder containing the first intelligence briefing by Lindemans.

The resistance leader had delivered on his promise. 'The report,' said Giskes, 'amounted to a convincing picture of every kind of clandestine activity in the Western occupied areas. Dozens of important courier lines, complete with their safe houses, methods of contact, passwords and frontier crossing points, several hundred names and cover names of paymasters, pay offices, couriers and agencies of all kinds belonging to various secret organisations formed the mosaic of seditious activity such as we had never before been able to acquire through penetration from the outside.'

Giskes claims that he then 'set in motion' measures for the release of Henk Lindemans, who he says was to have been sent to Germany to join a labour camp. But Dutch court records show that Henk Lindemans was not released until mid-June,[27] long after Lindemans had already started handing over his intelligence to the Germans.

Giskes called Wurr and Kup into his office and told them only the three of them were to have contact with Lindemans, who was given the code letters CC. No one else was to know of his existence.

Because much of the information related to names and addresses in Paris where Lindemans' escape line was based, Giskes enlisted the help of Helmut Knochen, who headed the SD in the French capital.

Giskes' intelligence breakthrough could not have come a moment too soon for the Germans. It was an open secret that the Western Allies were on the verge of crossing the English Channel to open up the long anticipated second front. The question was where – and when?

Giskes' first task was to cross-check the resistance information supplied by Lindemans while also instructing Willy Kup and Cornelis Verloop[28] to keep Lindemans under close surveillance while Giskes worked his way through the dossier.

Lindemans had always resented the way the middle-class, university-educated members of the resistance looked down on the uneducated King Kong.[29] So this was a chance to settle scores. Among his list of resistance workers were rivals in his network and at least two of his lovers who had threatened to tell Gilou about their relationship.[30]

Lindemans had become aware that Gilou, who was now also living in Paris, had formed a close friendship with another Dutch resistance man by the name of Victor Swane.[31] So Lindemans also decided to allow the Gestapo to sort out this part of his messy love life for him. It was to backfire in the most terrible fashion.

In the early hours of 9/10 March 1944, a squad of SD officers entered the Hotel Montholon near the Rue La Fayette.[32]

All the guests were ordered to assemble in the hall. Among those standing in their night clothes were Victor Swane, Agnès de

Beaufort and her husband Jan, Baron van Boetzelaer, who helped finance a Lindemans escape line. Standing next to Swane was a young French woman. Her name was Gilou Letuppe.

When the SD searched Letuppe's handbag they discovered identity cards in three different names. In her room they found the stamps of the Kommandantur (headquarters of the Paris SD), fake travel passes and workers' cards, which Letuppe had stolen from Todt the day before. Under her bed they also found three revolvers and a box of cartridges.

Letuppe and the other guests were led away to waiting cars and at 10am the following morning; Letuppe was dragged to the sixth floor of the Kommandantur.

The pregnant Letuppe refused to cooperate or answer any of the questions. In testimony after the war, she said she was interrogated between 10am and 11pm every day: 'They slapped me in the face with such force that I fell out of my chair. They whipped me with a rubber tube across my face.'[33] Swane did not survive the war and died in Buchenwald concentration camp. Letuppe was taken to Fresnes Prison in Paris.

Lindemans had been out of Paris on the night of the raid, helping Giskes, Wurr and Kup locate resistance workers on the escape route through Bordeaux towards the Pyrenees.

According to one of the resistance fighters who was with Lindemans, when told the news about the arrest of his wife at the Montholon Hotel, he was so shocked he began trembling 'like a reed in the wind'.[34]

Another said: 'He was a confused, unhappy boy, half mad with grief, incapable of reasoning, ready to clutch any straw of hope, to do anything to save his brother and his girlfriend.'[35] For the next nights and days, Lindemans lost himself in a series of drinking binges. When he sobered up, he had just one thing on his mind – to see Giskes.

The German officer remembers Lindemans' visit to his office, which he recorded in his diary: 'He arrived very cast down and asked me to set free his wife … Generally speaking, women were Lindemans' weak spot and it was the only sphere of activity in which he had to be warned to be careful.'[36]

Giskes claims that he arranged for Gilou to be released immediately. But prison records show that she was only freed when Paris was liberated by the Americans six months later. Her ordeal at Fresnes continued right up until her release. Letuppe told the Nuremberg War Crimes trial:[37] 'I was thrown into a dungeon without a mattress, without a blanket and for four days I had no food or drink. On the fourth day, they came to fetch me for questioning. I had 24 interrogations all with torture and always with handcuffs and my hands behind my back.

'Each time I came back with my face more swollen. Faced with my silence, they threatened to shoot me. But because I didn't talk, they placed me incommunicado in a cell for six months.'[38]

It is hard to know whether Giskes, working with Helmut Knochen, head of the Paris SD, held Letuppe as leverage over Lindemans[39] or even if he used torture to extract corroborating information from her. It seems likely that as one of Canaris's Abwehr men and outside his Dutch sphere his influence was weak. He will have been further hampered by his need to keep Lindemans secret from his 'colleagues' in the SD, because by this stage in the war he may well have felt that this new stream of intelligence was keeping him alive.

Lindemans kept talking. And in the next few weeks, Giskes estimated that the Dutchman betrayed 267[40] resistance fighters, escape line contacts and girlfriends. No one was safe, and he even betrayed his wealthy benefactor Freule von Vredenburgh, who had helped him when he needed help most, as well as the two resistance workers who spent the night trying to console him when he first discovered Letuppe had been arrested.[41] Lindemans' intelligence undoubtedly handed the Abwehr a vital advantage in the war against the resistance in France, Belgium and Holland, just when the Allies were relying on them to support the coming invasion. Once the American, British and Canadian troops landed in Europe, these resistance fighters were expected to come out of the shadows to take part in surveillance and sabotage operations. Giskes' hard-won reputation as a spymaster had won the Nazis an unexpected advantage in one of the crucial theatres of the last months of the war.

Chapter 6

Cornered Traitor

Two of the escaped SOE agents, van Rietschoten and van der Giessen, now emerged from the shadows. In April 1944 they received the good news that London had agreed to send a submarine to Zeeland for their exfiltration.¹ All they needed now were travel permits for the hazardous journey to the pick-up point.

The local resistance had promised to organise their safe passage and had made arrangements for the two agents to be photographed for their German identity cards.² Unfortunately, the man in charge of the operation was Christiaan Lindemans and Lindemans handed the pictures to Hermann Giskes, who immediately recognised them as the two Haaren escapees.

Just a few weeks earlier, Giskes would have seen this as a way of decisively restoring his reputation in the eyes of Berlin. But with Lindemans as his agent he decided against arresting the men. He reasoned that the intelligence they could give to London was no more damaging than that supplied by Ubbink and Dourlein and that by letting the British rescue operation go ahead, Lindemans' credibility in London would be given a huge boost.³

Lindemans radioed London to fix the date for the rendezvous with the submarine. All was going to plan until with two days to go, Lindemans turned up at Giskes' office with the news that London had arranged for the Dutch agents to take possession of a secret consignment of Leica film that had been acquired by SOE/SIS agents operating across the Low Countries. This material had been given the highest priority from London.

No matter how much Giskes wanted his own deception plan to succeed, he knew he could not risk the film reaching London.

On 5 May 1944, Lindemans and the two escaped Dutch SOE men set off by train from Rotterdam heading towards Zeeland, but at Roosendaal, west of Breda, they were stopped at an SD control. Lindemans faked surprise and assured them that once the papers were properly checked, they would be able to resume their journey.[4]

Instead, they were told they were to be taken by car to a nearby SD office. Van der Giessen suspected something was up and tried to wrestle the gun from the guard sitting next to him, but was immediately knocked out by a pistol butt to the head.[5]

A few hours later, Giskes was in possession of the British intelligence and the two escaped agents were back in Haaren.

When the Germans developed the 30 films, Giskes now understood why the British were prepared to send a submarine to pick up a pair of lowly SOE operatives. Giskes recalled in his war memoir:

'In them a complete picture of the enemy's intelligence targets laid before us. We were accustomed to come across good work in the way such reports were prepared – the training in England saw to that – but in this case especially they had worked with an accuracy and efficiency which we had not previously encountered. Particularly worthy of note was an almost complete picture of the secret weapon sites in Holland.'[6]

The secret sites to which Giskes was referring were the V1 'doodlebugs' launched from bases in France and Belgium and the more deadly V2 rockets that were eventually unleashed against Britain in September from The Hague. The V1 and V2 were Hitler's wonder weapons that he believed would bring the Allies to the negotiating table should their armies ever manage to cross the Channel.

Thanks to Lindemans, the secret of their locations would not now leave continental Europe.

In England, however, the build-up to D-Day continued at pace. But while the Allies' planners had good intelligence reports on the German military presence in France and Belgium, the intelligence picture in Holland was worryingly opaque.

SOE decided to send five more replacement agents to Holland. They were to be led by Nicolaas Celosse, who had been rushed through training, completing only two practice parachute jumps. Nevertheless, his instructors described him as: 'a fine student … who would have been classed Grade One if completed the remainder of the course.'[7]

Celosse was assigned the code name FARO and was accompanied by Harry Seyben, agent Ping Pong, a committed communist, Tony Cnoops and Huub Sanders (WT operator).[8] Their initial mission was to make contact with RVV and CS-6 so that both resistance organisations could receive orders from Allied High Command ahead of the planned D-Day landings.

Celosse's orders read: 'When the full scale invasion of Europe takes place the priority of targets will be: 1) road and rail communications, 2) telecommunications. It is essential you should NOT take action before we give you a specific order because: i) a landing on the continent may not necessarily mean full-scale invasion. ii) only the Allied High Command can assess at what stage of invasion operations your action will provide the most valuable contribution to the war efforts of the Allied forces.'[9]

On 1 April 1944, Lindemans was back in Holland, staying with friends in Amsterdam.

That same evening, the four Dutch SOE agents, led by Nicolaas Celosse, had landed on the Wieringermeer polderland, at the northwest corner of the Zuider Zee.

Celosse had orders to make contact with RVV and CS-6 but was acutely conscious that both organisations were suspected of being partially penetrated by the Germans. So after lying low for several days, it must have come as some relief that his wife was able to put the group in contact with his old friend from CS-6 days, Christiaan Lindemans.[10]

Lindemans had arranged a car in which he ferried Celosse and the other agents around Amsterdam. The group's first operation was to assist the RAF in the bombing of Dordrecht power station and they spent several days surveying weaknesses in the building's air defences.[11]

Lindemans was torn as he was close to Celosse and overcome by guilt, he decided to drive to the headquarters of the Abwehr for a showdown with Giskes.

The German intelligence chief was now living in a Dutch country house on the outskirts of Driebergen.

As soon as his German orderly had shown Lindemans into the large drawing room, Giskes sensed the giant Dutch spy was uneasy.[12]

Giskes recalls in his memoir that he offered brandy and cigarettes, which Lindemans declined.

'I did not like his attitude – he was morose and incoherent. I was even less happy when he drew his 9mm Colt, which Willy [Kup] had given him some time before.'[13] Lindemans placed his elbows on the table, fixed Giskes with one of his menacing glares and began loading the pistol and repeatedly clicking the safety catch.

Giskes knew Lindemans' reputation as 'le tueur', the killer, and wondered if he was to be next.[14]

Concealing his unease, he got up and walked slowly towards his desk, opened a drawer and produced a US Army issue 12mm pistol.

He walked back to where Lindemans was sitting and gave it to him, enquiring whether he had ever handled such a weapon before. Lindemans put down his own gun and started playing with the bigger pistol Giskes had given him.

'If you like, Willy will get you one,' Giskes said, while explaining the weapon's specifications and firing power in every detail. Lindemans let Giskes take back the American pistol, although the German was careful to leave it in the middle of the table between them. The ploy worked. Lindemans left Driebergen without a shot being fired, but nor had he mentioned to Giskes the arrival of Celosse's team.

While he had managed to protect the group from the scrutiny of the Abwehr, the SD, the secret police force led by Schreieder, were still unaware of Lindemans' special relationship with Giskes. This was partly because, in the aftermath of the Haaren escapes and the end of Englandspiel, the Nazi security and intelligence chiefs were no longer on speaking terms.

Schreieder had his own spies and informants, just as devious as Giskes' V-men.

One of them was Ellie van der Werff, an attractive girl from Rotterdam, who knew Harry Seyben in Rotterdam before he had left for England to join the SOE.[15] Her real name was Betty (Betje) Wery, a Jew who had betrayed many Jews to the Germans. In April 1944 she was working for Devise Anschutz Kommando (Foreign Exchange Protection Commando), an SD agency that targeted the wealth of the Untermensch.[16]

When Harry Seyben appeared in Rotterdam, she suspected he had been sent by the British and reported these suspicions to Schreieder. One night, Ellie and Harry went out to the bars of Rotterdam[17] and using cash supplied by Schreieder proceeded to get very drunk, ending up back at the house where Seyben was staying. There, Betty let in a squad of German soldiers, easily overpowering the drunken Seyben.

Two days later, Lindemans received a telephone call from Wery, who told him she had news about Harry and he must meet her at Devisenschutzkommando in Parklaan, Rotterdam. Lindemans suspected a trap and armed himself with two pistols that he concealed in his jacket pockets.

When he arrived, he was shown to Wery's office, where she told Lindemans she could reach Harry. 'She attempted to ring up Harry,' Lindemans later told MI5 interrogators, 'but each time there was no reply. Suddenly a door opened and a man in plain clothes was aiming his revolver at me. I attempted to draw mine but he shot me in the chest.'[18]

Lindemans fell to his knees, before collapsing forwards. One of the SD men searched his jacket pockets, pulling out an Abwehr identity card. Only then did it dawn on them they may have shot one of their own agents. The bullet had missed Lindemans' heart but glanced his right lung. If he was going to survive, he would need emergency hospital treatment. Giskes and Kup had him taken to a local hospital, from where he managed to get a message to a communist cell[19] operating in the city, who were in contact with Nicolaas Celosse and the rest of the SOE agents still at liberty.[20]

A few days later, Lindemans was transferred to Zuidwal Hospital in The Hague[21] to convalesce.[22] One afternoon, Lindemans awoke to see Celosse, his brother Jan and a group of communist fighters standing at the foot of his bed, brandishing machine guns.

The resistance men had had no trouble in disarming the guards and freeing Lindemans. Once they had safely transported the wounded leader to a secure house in the city, Celosse telegrammed London informing his SOE handlers of the latest developments, including Seyben's arrest, the involvement of 'van der Werff' and the successful operation to rescue Lindemans.

But Schreieder had placed Lindemans and the hospital under surveillance. The German security chief now knew about the SOE mission and Lindemans' involvement. He wasted no time in closing it down.

On the evening of 18 May, an SD unit raided the Celosses,[23] seizing SOE agent Tony Cnoops.

The SD men waited upstairs with Cnoops, arresting in turn each of the other members of the group as they returned to the house.

It was all too easy for Schreieder, who hoped he could restart the Englandspiel without Giskes' help.

Celosse and Cnoops refused to play ball with the Germans and were sent to join the rest of the SOE prisoners in Haaren. Huub Sanders, the wireless operator, was forced to send messages back to

London but did so by including security warnings that alerted the British to the fact he was in German hands.[24]

The SD operation finally ended the already strained relations between Giskes and Schreieder. Giskes recalled: 'The experience only proved afresh that the former fruitful cooperation with the SD/SiPo was finally at an end. It had deteriorated to a gulf of mutual mistrust and antipathy which simply could not be bridged.'[25]

Giskes was also certain that Schreieder had deliberately targeted his agent, King Kong.[26]

A fortnight later, Giskes and his staff were transferred to Brussels to take over Abwehr operations in Belgium, nearer to where German military intelligence expected an Allied landing. Major Ernst Kiesewetter was left in charge of IIIF Holland.

Giskes set up his temporary headquarters in the Hotel Metropole. Belgium was much more unruly than Holland and Giskes describes the situation in some parts of the country as 'verging on civil war'. The German intelligence officer had no contacts or informants with the underground and 'the number of ambushes, attacks and incidents involving the use of explosives by the Belgian and northern French underground increased slowly but steadily in April and May … Bloody affrays in which Abwehr officers and GFP officials were shot to bits increased in number and forced us to take additional security measures.'[27]

Yet the main mission ordered by Berlin remained the same – find the date and location of D-Day (or Day-X as it was known to the Germans).

After the arrest of Celosse and the rest of the CS-6 group, the wounded Lindemans knew it was only a matter of time before Schreieder and the SD tracked him down to The Hague and no longer sure he could trust Giskes, King Kong made plans to seek help outside Holland.

He arranged a car to drive him across the Dutch/Belgian border to the Château de Battel near Malines (Mechelen), owned by one of the leaders of the Witte Brigade, a wealthy seed merchant.[28] Here, the merchant's daughter, Ellie Zwaan, nursed Lindemans back to health.[29] Lindemans made a remarkable recovery and even in his convalescent state managed to seduce the young art student,[30] taking all her jewels and some of her father's cash to fund what he promised was an important 'underground organisation' with which he had become involved.

By now, Giskes had tracked down Lindemans and knew he needed to win back his trust, so he sent Willy Kup to give him 100,000 Belgian francs and 1,000 Dutch guilders.[31]

Giskes also authorised Kup to promise the Dutchman that should the Germans win the war, he would be gifted the ownership of a chain of brand new garages.[32]

By the time Lindemans made contact with Giskes again, he had recovered sufficiently to have spent most of the Giskes cash on bribes and lavish entertainment in the Brussels nightclubs.

Yet the Abwehr chief was still pleased to see him: 'I heard to my relief a week later that CC had arrived back in Brussels. The man was capable of the most improbable surprises. You could always remember when you had last seen him but it was quite impossible to rely on when or whether one would see him again.'[33]

Lindemans based himself in the Hotel Royal Nord in Brussels, but for security reasons frequently moved locations. During this time he renewed his acquaintance with a well-known Belgium resistance fighter called Jimmy Hendrickx and resumed his affair with 'Johnny', who was now secretary to Dr Brucker of the Todt Organisation.

Reassured that he had Giskes on his side, Lindemans was leading an increasingly debauched, reckless and callous lifestyle.

When he tired of Johnny he replaced her with a Belgian woman called Mia Meersman, whom he had met in the Royal Nord bar.[34]

Meersman was 25 years old, 5ft 4in tall, very attractive, and always dressed in black. Lindemans' multiple double dealings in espionage and on the black market called for a more methodical approach to his work. So he employed Meersman as his personal secretary.

Lindemans was infatuated by the 'ravishing' Meersman,[35] and he showered her with the jewellery given to him by the Countess Zwaan. This would turn out to be a betrayal King Kong would live to regret.

Chapter 7

Invasion

Giskes knew the resistance organisations in France, Belgium and Holland were waiting for the signal to rise up as soon the order was given for Allied forces to set sail for the Continent. Giskes says the Germans focused on deciphering the dozens of coded messages broadcast by the BBC to the resistance to try to unlock the secret of 'Day-X'.[1]

The German intelligence chief wrote in his diary: 'A successful landing would be irreparable unless it could at once be thrown back into the sea by superior forces.'[2]

There was also a human source of whom Giskes had high hopes of delivering Day-X:

'We were hoping that we could introduce Lindemans into sufficiently close contact with the operational headquarters of the enemy Secret Service to give us timely information of the time and place of Day-X. Giskes ordered CC to establish closer links with the leaders of the Witte Brigade, the Flanders-based resistance group that had posed the greatest threat to the German occupation of Belgium and the one with the closest links to London. After the arrest of its founding leader, former teacher Marcel Louette, in May 1944 the Brigade was headed by the young and charismatic Urbain Reniers, who had already proved himself to be a brave and daring resistance fighter.[3]

In March, Lindemans travelled to Brussels to speed up the supply of weapons from Belgium to Dutch resistance groups who were in desperate need of guns and explosives.[4]

Lindemans immediately hit it off with Reniers, perhaps recognising a kindred risk-taking spirit. Through Lindemans and Reniers, the link between the RVV and the Witte Brigade was cemented.

Giskes continued to impress upon Lindemans the importance of penetrating the Belgian underground and the Allied networks that were being readied in advance of the invasion. Kup issued him with four different phone numbers to contact his Abwehr minders.[5]

In Brussels, news had spread of Lindemans' miraculous escape from the clutches of the Gestapo, enhancing his reputation among the Witte Brigade. Although there were murmurings among resistance circles that King Kong may be playing both sides.

However, Urbain Reniers was pleased to renew his working relationship with the Dutch resistance fighter who seemed to have nine lives.

At this stage of the war, Lindemans' loyalties appear to have been split between his German spymasters and the resistance groups who were fighting for a free socialist post-war Europe. He claims to have warned Reniers that the Germans had broken the British codes and penetrated nearly all the resistance groups in Holland, including CS-6. Reniers didn't know of course that the enemy's success was partly the result of King Kong's treachery.

At the same time, Lindemans set up meetings with various resistance workers and escape line contacts at bars, cafes and churches. Before each appointment he rang one of the numbers Willy had given him. In the next few weeks, dozens of members of the resistance and acquaintances of Lindemans – many of whom had crossed him, stood in his way or disrespected him – were picked up by Giskes and his men.[6]

Lindemans' double dealings were about to be brought into sharp focus by the arrival of the Allies on the Continent. The Dutch agent had managed to establish from his contacts in the resistance that the landings were planned for May/June, but like many spies feeding the Germans with intelligence he had been led to believe that the Allies' chosen landings site was on the Norwegian coast.[7]

Hitler received the news of the Allied landings six hours after the first troops hit the beaches of Normandy. His staff were under strict instructions not to disturb his morning slumber. Even then, Hitler and his generals believed the attack was a feint and the main assault was to take place at the Pas-de-Calais, where Hitler's Panzer units were preparing to throw the Allies back into the sea. It wasn't until 4pm that afternoon that Hitler released two divisions of Panzer Group West, the 12th SS and Panzer Lehr, for deployment to the Normandy coast.

Four days after D-Day on 10 June, Aart van der Giessen and Jan van Rietschoten were taken from their cells at Haaren Prison, marched through the main gate and put up against a wall and shot. They were among 50 Dutch SOE agents executed as a result of Englandspiel.

While the British and Americans were fighting their way out of the Normandy bocage, Christiaan Lindemans remained in Brussels, where he had established himself as the leader of a well-organised resistance operation. He made two hotels the headquarters of his network in the heart of the city from where he supplied weapons and men to groups all over Belgium and France.

His mistress and secretary, Mia Meersman, was given her own office in the Royal Nord Hotel, where she worked full-time fielding phone calls and providing the paperwork and documents for Lindemans' various enterprises.[8] At the nearby Siru Hotel, Lindemans had taken over one of the upper floors and installed his own staff. The hotel was kept under a 24-hour watch by eight of his men, all armed with sub-machine guns. According to a German SD report, it was here that he hosted meetings with representatives of other Belgian, French and Dutch resistance groups: 'The care with which Brandt [the alias Lindemans used in Belgium] works is also shown by the fact that he has rented the rooms to the right and left of his Room 605 in the hotel and thus provides for his own security. Besides, the people who sleep on the same floor are mostly those who are in contact or indirect touch with Brandt.'[9]

Lindemans, who had taken to wearing a rudimentary metal bulletproof vest, made use of the Royal Nord bar to entertain his contacts during drunken, raucous evenings. In one night he spent 15,000 francs on women and drinks while hosting German officers and business contacts. More money was spent on bribing representatives of the Todt Organisation. Once inside the doors of these two grand hotels, King Kong believed he was untouchable. The Germans noted: 'In the evenings they were most often in the Bar Royal. Anyone bringing material to Brandt, or wanting anything from him, came there. When he knew enough he withdrew and asked the barmaid to throw out the Germans.'[10]

Lindemans had built a reputation as an efficient and ruthless assassin, and he kept photographic records of everyone he had 'liquidated'. The hits usually took place outside cafes or on bridges, and involved drive-by shootings from armed men firing from official 'mail or B.D.T.' vehicles.[11] It seems clear that not all of these were resistance operations. Some will have been the settling of scores and others contracted hits, undertaken for money.

The records of these killings were entrusted to Meersman, who locked everything in a secret room adjoining Lindemans' own hotel suite. The group's weapons were supplied by Jimmy Hendrickx, who maintained an arms dump in Vilvorde, a few kilometres north of Brussels. Female couriers, including relatives of Gilou Letuppe, brought the guns into the city when they were needed for an operation.

And Lindemans kept in touch with the Holland network through his brother Jan, who became a regular visitor to Brussels.[12]

Hermann Giskes and the Abwehr turned a blind eye to their agent's activities, confident that King Kong was making inroads into the Belgian underground network.

Ignorant of his links to Giskes, the local SD had taken a very different view of Lindemans and his resistance group.[13]

Lindemans had grown closer to Meersman, with whom he shared all his secrets, although not his true identity. One evening after a drunken night in the Royal bar, the Dutchman took Meersman back to his room and drunkenly suggested that he was neither working for the Germans nor the British and that as well as fighting in Holland, Belgium and France he had also 'worked in Russia' and that he was 'directly responsible' for a mysterious organisation he called 'Inter.Serve'.[14]

Giskes also began to receive reports that his maverick agent may not be who he seemed and had gone native. After the initial bout of intelligence handed over to the Abwehr, Lindemans had offered very little and still appeared to be working closely with the resistance.

To assuage these concerns, Lindemans was able to report to Giskes that he was making good progress in infiltrating the Belgian underground.

The failed July 1944 plot to assassinate Adolf Hitler had finally tipped the scales in the political battle in Germany. Canaris, who had been deposed as head of the Abwehr in February, was now actively accused of treason by Himmler. The Abwehr was finally abolished and Walter Schellenberg was put in charge of all foreign military intelligence for Nazi Germany.

Giskes, who now found himself reporting directly to the kinds of party members he had spent years working to avoid, was under intense pressure from Berlin to demonstrate that his trust in Lindemans was paying off. When he told his superiors about the Witte Brigade and its legendary leader Urbain Reniers, Giskes was ordered to arrange an assassination.[15] And who better than 'le Tueur' himself to undertake this mission.

So Giskes sent Lindemans to find his Belgian resistance comrade and eliminate him.[16]

Reniers and his Witte Brigade were based in Antwerp, where they were in the midst of preparations to oust the Germans once the Allies had broken out of Normandy and were closer to the city.

Rumours of King Kong's double dealings had reached Reniers and Reniers carried out some further due diligence to make sure his incredible stories checked out. All the results came back positive but he still decided to test Lindemans by sending him on a sabotage mission: 'I gave him the job of destroying the railway between Malines and Termonde. This he did.'

Reniers was still not completely satisfied, sensing there was something not quite right about the giant Dutchman, although he couldn't put his finger on what it was that troubled him. He later told MI5: 'I never had entire confidence in Chris ... [but] he never betrayed me and whenever he was with me his behaviour was always correct.'[17]

Reniers decided to give Lindemans another mission, more dangerous and involving a return to Brussels to carry out the execution of Prosper de Zitter – an extremely unpleasant character, a convicted rapist and fraudster before the war, who was masquerading as 'Captain Jackson', a Royal Canadian Air Force airman on the run.[18] He was perhaps second only to Lindemans in terms of the scale of his betrayal of his fellow countrymen and women.

In the end, Lindemans decided against carrying out this assassination too.

Perhaps part of the reason for his disinclination to kill was a suspicion the Gestapo were watching him. Betrayal was now a constant concern and so he stepped up his security and started sleeping away from the hotel.[19]

Those who were closest to him and shared his secrets presented the greatest threat. Mia Meersman knew almost everything about Lindemans' business – where he stored his forged identity documents, the photographs of his victims, the names and numbers of the many people who contacted him at the hotel and where he stored and how he couriered his weapons – and Lindemans began to wonder if she had become a liability.

Meersman sensed Lindemans' attitude towards her had changed. She had been around him long enough to know how dangerous that could be. When Lindemans' affections were transferred to another woman he had met in the Royal bar, she knew it was time to leave.[20]

Margaret Albrecht was a 22-year-old German actress who used the stage name Akke Volges. She had also been an enthusiastic member of the Hitlerjugend and was dating a string of German officers and businessmen based in Brussels. She soon fell under the spell of King Kong and Lindemans moved in with her in a suite of rooms in the Rue de Villian, which he had rented.

That still left him with the problem of Meersman. Lindemans started making it known that he no longer wanted her around and began threatening her when she spoke back to him. One morning, Meersman and Lindemans were together at one of his associates' apartments in Brussels. She later reported to the Germans: 'I was with Brandt early on Saturday. He trained his pistol on me, then swore to me by his child that he would not kill me.'[21]

News of the Allies' advance on Paris had reached Lindemans in Brussels and raised the prospect of the liberation of the city and with it the release of Gilou Letuppe. Lindemans had already tried to secure his 'wife's' release by using a very well-connected socialist called Maurice Vos, who was living in Paris.[22] He had given Vos 5,000 French francs with which he approached Baron van Heemstra, Audrey Hepburn's grandfather, who had promised to use the francs to bribe the Gestapo.[23] Instead, Lindemans claimed, van Heemstra was working for the SD and pocketed the money for himself.

Lindemans knew if the Germans put up a fight, the prisoners held in Fresnes would be in grave danger, especially those like Letuppe who had already been condemned to death. Her life had only been spared because she was pregnant with their second child. Now the child was born there was no reason not to carry out the execution. Lindemans concocted an audacious plan to try to break his 'wife' out of prison before the Allies arrived and asked Jimmy Hendrickx to bring some guns into town.

The mission was undermined from the start. Margaret Albrecht's links to Lindemans had been reported to the Gestapo by one of her spurned German lovers. She was summoned to the SD headquarters in Brussels and warned her relationship with Lindemans meant she was considered an enemy agent. To save herself she was told to report everything she could find about King Kong and his resistance contacts. In one of her SD reports, later found by British soldiers in Brussels, she said Lindemans had been sent from England and his leadership of the resistance had 'wide ramifications'.[24] Her SD handlers suspected that he had a wireless with which he was in contact with England.

On the afternoon of the Fresnes Prison mission, the SD raided the Royal Hotel and arrested Jimmy Hendrickx and other members of the resistance group. Lindemans had been tipped off and was away from the hotel when the German squad cars arrived outside. After the war, evidence emerged that Lindemans had informed on his own mission.

Field Marshal Montgomery's Anglo-Canadian 21st Army Group finally broke through the German defences at Caen in the first week of August. Linking up with American armies near Falaise, the Allies encircled and destroyed the main German force, Army Group B, taking 50,000 prisoners. It was the decisive battle in the Normandy campaign, forcing the remnants of German Panzer units to retreat across the Seine. Montgomery ordered his armour divisions to give chase in the hope of catching and completing the destruction of the enemy in the open country before they had a chance to cross the Rhine.

The Allied advance was so rapid that the British tanks covered 250 miles in four days. For the first time since D-Day, the Allies could see a direct route to Berlin. With the retreating Germans in disarray, newspaper headlines speculated that the war would be over in weeks. The Allies could at last contemplate the defeat of Nazi Germany and turn their thoughts to the post-war settlement. While the Western Allies charged across northern Belgium to the Dutch border, the Russians were still fighting far to the east in Ukraine.

Chapter 8

Crossing the Line

On 22 August 1944, Bletchley Park picked up[1] an unusual message sent by German intelligence HQ to field units in the Belgian theatre of operations. Its source was a proven V-man and the subject of the top secret message read 'enemy intentions'. The decoded Abwehr report stated there had been an important meeting of the Belgian resistance leaders in Liege between 12 and 15 August. The V-man had tried to get there but had suffered a motorbike accident en route.

A second report by the V-man dated 21 August revealed that the German agent had held 'a discussion with three English officers including the man employed by England for directing armed rebellion in Belgium'.[2] This British officer had arrived in Belgium on 8 August with full powers to take over leadership of the Belgian resistance.

The Abwehr report added: 'The enemy is planning the dropping of great numbers of parachute troops in the assembly areas of the insurgents (Maas line).'[3]

The 'proven V-man' was identified by the code name CC, the cipher Hermann Giskes had given to Christiaan Lindemans.

The intelligence gathered by Lindemans, and picked up by Ultra, undoubtedly referred to Operation Comet, a planned British and Polish air assault on the Maas and Rhine bridges. The parachute brigades waiting in England were stood up and then stood down on at least three occasions as the British military chiefs worried about contrasting reports of the strength of the enemy during August and early September.

Such was the speed of the Allied advance that the German front line was in a state of flux, a situation that Giskes described as one of 'impending catastrophe'. The German retreat threatened to turn into a rout. In this atmosphere, SD concerns about Giskes' loyalties and Lindemans' failure to assassinate Reniers had to be put to one side because despite his misgivings, Lindemans was the Abwehr's most effective agent with a unique ability to operate behind enemy lines.

The German intelligence officer later reflected: 'Whether CC would ever be able to carry out the task which I had given him was as dark and uncertain as everything else in these mad days. We knew that Brussels and Antwerp were in a fever to greet the victors. So why should CC not now fight once again openly on the side of the enemy? What had defeated Germany still to offer him other than the certainty of being shot once his connection with me was discovered? What could I still offer him – I, a small Kommando leader in a hopelessly beaten army?'[4]

According to Giskes: 'I had given Lindemans his instructions for the future in Brussels before my departure for Lüttich. He was to remain behind in the city and establish contact with the intelligence of the advancing English army immediately after the occupation of the capital. His active work as an enemy agent since 1940 and his connections with the underground ought to speak well for him and should soon bring him into contact with the right quarters. We agreed that he should get himself employed by the English as a forward agent, so as to enable him to get back to us through the lines at the earliest moment possible.'[5]

The French 2nd Armoured Division under General Philippe Leclerc reached the gates of Fresnes Prison on 24 August 1944. After a day of heavy fighting with many casualties on both sides, the French liberated the prison, freeing hundreds of French resistance workers and British SOE agents. Among them was Gilou Letuppe, who returned to the family home near Lille, where she was reunited with her two daughters. Henk Lindemans had also been released from Scheveningen Prison, the Oranjehotel, in June. The Germans no longer had any hold over King Kong and yet he continued to work for them. Giskes had every reason to be mystified.

It was at this moment that Lindemans decided to make direct contact with the British.

While London was aware of a resistance leader called King Kong, all that British intelligence knew of him were the many stories contained in the reports from agents returning from occupied Europe. But among the senior Dutch staff working with the Allies was a very familiar and welcome face, a man whose life Lindemans had saved in the Pyrenees eight months earlier.

Kas de Graaf had been made head of Dutch security and had travelled with Prince Bernhard, the leader of the Dutch ground forces, as the 21st Army advanced through Belgium.[6] De Graaf was delighted to be reunited with his CS-6 resistance comrade.

Realising his potential value to the next stage of the Allies' campaign, the liberation of Brussels and Antwerp, Lindemans was taken to the office of Commander Philip Johns, head of the Low Countries section of Special Forces.[7]

On 25 August, Lindemans crossed the lines again, to pay one last visit to Hermann Giskes in Brussels. The city was in chaos as the Germans made their final preparation for withdrawal.

Lindemans told him of intelligence which 'indicated that the main thrust of the Allies was directed at the Dinant area, with the intention of advancing via Namur in the direction of Eindhoven so as to seize the river crossings at Nijmegen and Arnhem. The subsequent attack would follow from a bridgehead thrown across the Rhine and the Waal down to Ijssel and towards the German North Sea coast.'[8]

Giskes immediately radioed the intelligence to No III Headquarters West in Luxembourg.

They were delighted with the report as it gave them vital warning of the 'actual development of Allied attacks in the next three weeks'. Giskes told Lindemans to lie low in Brussels and await the arrival of the British.

Field Marshal Bernard Montgomery's Anglo-Canadian 21st Army Group reached the outskirts of Brussels on 3 September and then pressed on for a full assault on the city. The Household Cavalry on the British left and the Grenadier Guards on the right led the way with the Welsh and Irish Guards following close behind. Resistance fighters suddenly appeared on the streets of the Belgian capital and began engaging the German defenders in fierce firefights.

Among them was the unmistakable figure of Christiaan Lindemans ignoring Giskes' warning to lie low. In one action he relieved a group of Belgian policemen who had turned on their German masters and were involved in a shoot-out with a unit of SS soldiers. The police officers were trapped in their headquarters in the Rue des Croisades, where they were pinned down by a German machine-gun position. The soldiers lobbed several grenades into the building, killing one of the Belgians. Lindemans arrived in the nick of time with his own machine gun and attacked the German position, killing two and wounding two more of the Germans, and allowed the trapped policemen to break out.[9]

That evening there were joyous celebrations as Brussels residents welcomed the liberating force of British soldiers. Lindemans joined the celebrations and carried on toasting their new-found freedom into the night.

The next morning, Lindemans left Brussels for Antwerp, where Reniers was mounting a skilful defence of the docks against German sabotage crews sent in to render the docks inoperative.

Giskes had also been sent to Antwerp to lend a hand in bolstering the defences.

The German intelligence officer recalled in his diary: 'As we started out at about 1700 on our journey to Antwerp, a thick cloud of black smoke was standing above the lofty Brussels Palace of Justice. The mob had broken in for the purpose of burning the records of the police and of the Belgium Courts of Justice. Looting was in full swing.'

Both sides appreciated the strategic value of the port to the Allies, who were now overstretched, running low on both fuel and military supplies. Eisenhower had tried to impress on Montgomery the importance of opening up the port to Allied shipping, telling the British commander: 'I insist upon the importance of Antwerp. As I have told you I am prepared to give you everything for the capture of the approaches to Antwerp, including all the air forces and anything else you can support.'[10] The Germans had fortified the estuary with heavy coastal batteries on Walcheren Island that prevented Allied ships from approaching the Scheldt.

When the Sherman tanks and 25-pounders of XXX Corps arrived on the outskirts of Antwerp, led by the swashbuckling British general Brian Horrocks, the Germans initiated plans to sabotage the docks.

Giskes was one of them: '... suddenly bullets began to whistle around our ears as we got to the middle of the large canal bridge in Antwerp harbour. Invisible marksmen, concealed in the large warehouses on the south bank, had the bridge under fire. Groups of civilians and scattered German soldiers on the North Bank were making their escape, springing to their feet one moment and seeking cover the next. We took shelter with the car in a corner among a group of houses on the South Bank ... at the same time English armour had appeared from along the Boom Road and forced their way into the city. We dashed back across the bridge with a wounded hauptman in our car. A demolition detachment was standing ready to blow up the bridge at the first appearance of the English.'[11]

Among the resistance fighters shooting at Giskes was Christiaan Lindemans. According to Reniers, the Dutch resistance man had taken part in the storming of the left bank of the Scheldt, where he had led an attack on a German position, killing at least eight soldiers. Reniers later testified: 'Before the liberation of Antwerp, Chris had taken part in various actions in which he had distinguished himself with his bravery.'[12]

Reniers' men managed to defuse the German charges and kept the SS units suppressed with fire, unable to carry out their mission to disable the docks and bridges. It was a major coup to capture the port intact and Lindemans had played his part.

But the British failed to capitalise on this Belgian resistance's success. There was nothing to stop XXX Corps, after taking Antwerp, from driving the additional 20 miles north and cutting off German positions along the inlet to the port and encircling the 86,000 German troops still holding this part of the harbour approach.

The failure to secure the port from German artillery fire meant Allied shipping would be prevented from using Antwerp for two more months. But Montgomery had set his sights on a grander prize: the bridges across the Rhine. The last great obstacle on the road to Berlin.[13]

At the spearhead of the British and Canadian breakout of Normandy were a number of special forces units, some deployed deep inside enemy territory. One of them was Intelligence School (Western European Area) no. 9 (IS9), whose primary role was to liberate captured POWs, often working alongside the Special Air Service (SAS) and local resistance groups. IS9 (WEA) comprised two field sections, one headed by Major Airey Neave, the veteran Colditz escapee, and the other by a young British captain called Peter Baker.[14]

After the capture of Brussels, IS9 set up headquarters in the Hotel Metropole, vacated just days earlier by Hermann Giskes and the rest of the local Abwehr.[15] The Hotel Metropole was also the temporary quarters of Prince Bernhard, head of the Dutch Armed Forces and a close friend of Philip Johns, chief of special forces for Belgium and Holland,[16] privy to the top-secret British plans for coordinating the resistance groups.[17] Brussels was engulfed by a spirit of premature triumphalism and almost anyone in an Allied uniform could expect to be stopped, smothered in kisses and doused in champagne. It was an atmosphere that did not serve the best interests of military discipline. Edgar 'Bill' Williams, Monty's chief of security, reported that British intelligence in Belgium had been dangerously infected by complacency, its officers 'too busy partying' before the war had been won.[18]

The war was far from won, but Montgomery had persuaded the Allies' supreme commander, General Dwight D Eisenhower, to launch a narrow thrust through the Netherlands and into northern Germany, bypassing the main enemy defences of the Siegfried Line.

The daring plan was high risk but offered the ultimate prize of defeating the enemy in one brilliant tactical manoeuvre. The operation was to be a combined airborne and tank thrust. It remains the largest airborne operation in global military history and is to this day one of the most talked about operations of the Second World War. This was Operation Market Garden.

Its objective was to establish an Allied salient into German territory with a bridgehead over the Nederrijn (Lower Rhine River) and to open the road to the Ruhr industrial region and on to Berlin. This was to be achieved by two operations: seizing nine bridges with combined US, British and Polish airborne forces (Market) followed by British armoured units coming on behind to drive over the bridges (Garden). Key to its success were the final bridges at Arnhem and that relied on a British armoured column charging the 64 miles from the Dutch–Belgian border to Arnhem in four days. The German army was thought to be so badly damaged by the fighting in Normandy and continual air attacks that they would be unable to stop the British tanks.

Operation Market Garden is often seen as a plan hatched to serve Montgomery's ambition to secure his reputation as the greatest

Allied general of the war. But it was its geopolitical urgency which was the reason why Churchill backed it so heavily in the face of some considerable scepticism by the Americans who favoured fighting on a broader front.

Market Garden was finally given Eisenhower's blessing[19] on 10 September with the first paratroopers to be dropped over Holland seven days later. Montgomery had given the 'Garden' job to his best tank commander, Lieutenant General Brian Horrocks, a veteran of El Alamein.

After Englandspiel, the British knew they could not rely on agents operating from inside Holland. There were even intelligence reports of some Dutch communities, near the German border, still showing strong Nazi loyalties.[20] Nor would it have escaped the British that the Dutch had raised five infantry regiments to serve with the SS.[21] Nevertheless, Commander Philip Johns had the task of liaising with the Dutch underground in support of the offensive.

Johns knew he urgently needed a trusted agent to cross the lines and enter Eindhoven to warn the resistance of the forthcoming attack so that they were ready to help the Allied troops when the time came.

Johns consulted his friend Prince Bernhard. Bernhard believed the secret operation would give his country its first high-profile role in the war and he was determined that the chosen agent should be a Dutch national. He told Johns he had a man in mind who had proved himself to be a loyal and courageous agent in a number of resistance operations against the Germans.[22]

This man, said Bernhard, was 'absolutely outstanding' and his name was Christiaan Lindemans. Bernhard, through de Graaf, was already well acquainted with Lindemans, who held a legendary reputation among the Dutch and Belgian resistance and had been appointed a member of his staff with the temporary rank of captain.

Johns put Peter Baker in charge of the mission and told him to locate the Dutchman immediately. Baker had arrived in Normandy a few days after the landings and had already taken part in a number of rescue operations of Allied airmen behind enemy lines.

It wasn't hard for Baker to track down the resistance fighter. Lindemans, dressed in his captain's uniform, had acquired a chauffeur who drove him around Brussels in a black LaSalle.

Chapter 9

A Spy Too Far

Captain Peter Baker[1] had taken a room in the Hotel Metropole[2] in Brussels, which he was using as his headquarters.[3] It was here that he assembled his team for the Eindhoven mission – a couple of British soldiers and a Belgian named Lucien de Ness who was to accompany Lindemans across the lines and a French lieutenant attached to British special forces, Charles Muller. Lindemans was given his final instructions and a new call sign alias for the mission, 'de Vries', as well as issued with the British code word 'Toulouse'.[4]

The British lorry headed out of Brussels in the direction of the Dutch border. Mechanical problems soon forced Baker to make a detour via Diest, where Lindemans was able to find the parts to repair the lorry. The party continued to Bourg-Leopold, where they joined a Dutch guide called De Weiss and a British patrol of 14 men under a Major Ross. The patrol escorted the agents as close as possible to the front line without drawing unwanted attention from the Germans and then parted company. From here, Lindemans and de Ness continued across the front line alone.

What happened next is uncertain. Lindemans claimed that the two men were caught in a German ambush in which de Ness, who Lindemans later told the British was working for the Germans, was mortally wounded.[5] But IS9 chief James Langley believed Lindemans murdered him.[6] What isn't in dispute is that Lindemans was alone when he gave himself up to a German patrol from the 1st Parachute Company at Hertogenbosch.[7] He said he was an Abwehr agent on a secret assignment for 'Dr German', the rather unimaginative code name for Hermann Giskes. The officer leading the patrol immediately drove him to the country mansion in Vught, where the German general Kurt Student[8] had set up his headquarters. It is worth noting that Student probably knew more about airborne operations than any other soldier serving in the Second World War. It was Student who had commanded the Fallschirmjäger, the first German paratroop force, and he who had led the first ever large-scale air assaults on The Hague in May 1940 and on Crete a year later. The historical consensus outside of Holland tends to downplay the significance of Lindemans' treachery. Not only does that view tend to overlook Lindemans' previous briefings to Giskes weeks earlier, but what is also undoubtedly true is that there was no one he could have now handed this information over to who was better equipped to make use of it.

Lindemans met Student's intelligence chief and passed on detailed accounts of British armour positions, including 300 Shermans preparing to move against Eindhoven on 17 September.[9]

Lindemans also outlined what he had found about the airborne element of Market Garden from his time with Philip Johns, Peter Baker and Kas de Graaf.

Student's intelligence chief then telephoned FAT 365 in Driebergen to inform the Abwehr that their agent had miraculously reappeared and what he had to say could be of vital importance. Richard Christmann – who was now a full Abwehr officer – was immediately dispatched to collect Lindemans.[10] In Driebergen he was met by Major Ernst Kiesewetter, who had replaced Giskes as Abwehr chief in Holland. It was now the evening of 15 September – two days before the start of Operation Market Garden. Lindemans was taken to an office with Christmann and Kiesewetter, who were fully occupied in the next 36 hours debriefing the agent. According to Christmann: 'CC told me about the situation in Antwerp and also that the port was hardly destroyed. CC further reported that he had succeeded in getting American and British officers to talk about a big aerial landing to take place on the 17/18 September. CC gave us the positions of 400 heavy guns. From 16 September, all the Dutch special troops [Dutch resistance] were to be mobilised. The aerial landings were to take place in the Eindhoven, Nijmegen and Arnhem ... with the goal to drive a wedge into the German front, to reach Bremen.'[11]

This information was dutifully passed on to General Christiansen, the head of the German army in Holland, Kurt Student and the OKW in Berlin.[12] In fact, an Ultra decrypted intercept[13] on 15 September had picked up Lindemans' initial intelligence report sent on by Christmann. The intercept made clear that a 'concentrated Allied airborne assault was now expected at Eindhoven through to Arnhem'.[14]

When the Dutch resistance man later arrived at Driebergen on the 15th, Major Kiesewetter had appeared sceptical of Lindemans' intelligence.[15] After all, he had not had any dealings with Lindemans before and was not sure how much he could trust the information of an agent who had suddenly appeared at his headquarters after crossing the enemy line. Many officers in Ernst Kiesewetter's position would have been sceptical. But the scale and precision of Lindemans' betrayal drew him in. If true, it represented a major intelligence breakthrough that had the potential to, if not change the course of the war, at least slow it down.

It was so exhaustive it included detailed instructions for sabotaging Antwerp docks, the whereabouts of 21st Army British headquarters and the routes the Allies were using to send agents into occupied territory.[16]

Lindemans also gave away the identities and addresses of the British intelligence special forces officers in Brussels, including Captain Baker.

The Germans had been expecting an attack into Holland. Allied reconnaissance flights and bombing attacks on the 16th were interpreted by the Abwehr as indicators of an imminent assault on the Rhine.[17] Lindemans' intelligence indicated when to expect the landings and gave them details of some of the forces they would be facing.

Yet Kiesewetter's lukewarm reaction meant the German High Command remained unconvinced by what Lindemans had risked so much to tell them. The one senior Abwehr officer who could vouch for CC had been kept in the dark. Kiesewetter, perhaps jealous of his predecessor's success, didn't tell Hermann Giskes about the reappearance of Lindemans at Driebergen until after the battle.[18] Instead he reported directly to Berlin.[19] Nevertheless, not all German units ignored the warning. The auxiliary troops of the SS School Arnhem took up positions in anticipation of an attack near Arnhem.[20] The Holland Militia were stood up and warned of an imminent attack.[21] Kiesewetter, to cover himself with the OKW in Berlin, also sent a 'hulptroopen', a unit of German auxiliary troops, to Arnhem. According to Christmann they would both turn out to play a key role in fighting the British 1st Parachute Brigade at Arnhem three days later.[22]

Other deployments were fortuitous. The 9th and 10th SS Panzer divisions, which had received a hammering in Normandy, had escaped through the 'Falaise gap' between advancing Allied armies in Normandy and been sent to the Arnhem area for refitting. This was not based on any intelligence.

Following his 36-hour debriefing by Kiesewetter and Christmann, Christiaan Lindemans was driven back to Eindhoven, still in German hands, and told to fulfil the original mission he had been given by Captain Baker and report back to Kiesewetter anything more he could find about the enemy's plans.

King Kong's sudden appearance in Eindhoven after so long away in Belgium aroused suspicions. One of the resistance fighters thought Lindemans' picture had been published in the underground press 'Signalementblad', which carried photographs of Nazi agents.[23] These suspicions were hardened when Lindemans bizarrely claimed to hold the rank of Lt Colonel in the Witte Brigade and that he was a graduate of Delft University. Neither claim was true.

The resistance men drew their weapons and arrested the Dutchman, throwing him in a coal cellar in a house opposite the police station, where they intended to keep him until the British arrived.[24] He wouldn't have to wait long.

The early morning mist of 17 September clung to the landscape, cloaking the British countryside in an ethereal veil. On airfields dotted across southern England, the engines of 1,544 air transport planes and glider tugs spluttered into life. The Market element of Operation Market Garden, carrying the first lift of 20,000 parachute and glider troops over the Channel and North Sea into occupied Holland, was under way.[25]

German intelligence had partly benefitted from Christiaan Lindemans' reports that had first warned of a frontal armour attack from the British bridgehead as long ago as August and as recently as two days earlier when he told Student's intelligence chief of the British tanks about to move on Eindhoven. And an Ultra intercept featuring Lindemans' report from the morning of 15 September when he visited Student's headquarters shows the Germans were expecting XXX Corps' advance towards Eindhoven.[26]

According to the Dutch security and intelligence historian Bob de Graaff: 'As Student lacked reconnaissance facilities, Lindemans' information about the concentration of Allied armoured divisions preparing for a northward thrust was very welcome. As a result of this intelligence fresh anti-tank battalions were moved north and were able to hold up the Allied ground offensive for 10 to 15 hours.'[27]

Thereafter, progress was stop and start and the advance units of the XXX Corps didn't reach the approach road to Eindhoven until late afternoon the following day, 18 September. While Horrocks waited to give orders for an all-out assault, intelligence reached him from inside the city. One of the local resistance leaders had crossed the lines with a map locating the positions of the German defensive guns around Eindhoven.

The atmosphere in Eindhoven had been tense ever since earlier in the day when three British scout cars had raced through the centre of the city, halted and then turned around and raced back across the lines, encountering no resistance. This daring reconnaissance dash put the German garrison on a state of heightened alert while encouraging the resistance groups, anticipating the main attack, to come out of the shadows and on to the streets.

One such band of fighters was a group led by Eddy Verkaik, 34, a relative of the author, who had been preparing and desperately hoping for this moment since the German occupation four years ago. Eddy, an Eindhoven office clerk and regional chess champion, was not a natural fighter but he was determined to play his part in the liberation of Holland from the Nazi overlords. He had already helped to hide Allied pilots and carry out a number of sabotage attacks. His group, loosely attached to the KP organisation, kept a cache of weapons and ammunition in the city's Augustine monastery, which they had recently moved to a garage in the centre of the city. Word had reached Eddy that the Allies would soon be launching their attack. On the morning of 17 September, Eddy appeared at the home of one of his comrades 'looking like a balloon', his coat stuffed with hand grenades.[28]

The Nazis, aware of the overwhelming force of British armour poised outside Eindhoven, retreated to the outskirts of the city.

A ragtag unit of 60 Germans, some of them from Kampfgruppe Walther who had ambushed the British tanks the day before, set up a defensive position in the woods of the Leenderheide to the south of the city.

In the afternoon, Eddy Verkaik, wearing a white armband distinguishing his resistance group from other units in the city, led 20 of his men to the German positions. Having established contact with the enemy commander, he asked permission to meet the Germans to arrange their surrender. But as he walked down the road with his white flag in his hand, the Nazi lieutenant pulled out his Luger and shot him down, severely wounding him in his left shoulder. The Nazis had no intention of surrendering to Dutch civilians and had lured Eddy into a trap. The enraged KP fighters called in reinforcements and launched a ferocious assault on the Germans using Eddy's grenades to great effect.

The enemy lost six of their soldiers before deciding to abandon their position. Eddy Verkaik survived his wounds and after the war became a leading figure in socialist politics.

By 7.30pm the city was in British hands, triggering wild celebrations that swept up the British tank crews.[29]

Among the liberating force was Captain Peter Baker. He had spent an unsuccessful evening looking for the special agent he had sent into the city on 15 September.

It was Eddy Verkaik who told Baker that Lindemans was a prisoner of the resistance.[30] Baker was furious.

The British officer demanded that they release his agent, complaining: 'You've kept one of my best men in prison.'[31]

The Dutch refused, saying they had uncovered evidence that Lindemans was a German agent. They had searched him and found a German pass in the name of Kiesewetter and a German newspaper. Baker swept the damning evidence aside, claiming it was all fake and that in any case he had checked with Prince Bernhard's headquarters, who had already given Lindemans the all-clear. Lindemans was freed but still a suspect among the Dutch and Baker continued to come under pressure to have him arrested. In the end he sent Lindemans back to Brussels under escort for interrogation.[32] Lindemans' war appeared to be over.

Operation Market Garden was about to enter its key phase. Everything depended on capturing and holding the bridges for the

British armour to race across towards their final object at Arnhem and the Zuider Zee. The Allies hoped surprise would be their best weapon.

At Best, 12 kilometres north of Eindhoven, as in many other places, the airborne troops would meet unexpected resistance. Brigadier General Samuel Lyman Atwood Marshall, the US Army's chief combat historian during the Second World War, concluded in 1950: 'On the night before the air drop (16 September), the enemy suddenly shifted 1,800 Infantry along with supporting artillery into the town of Best, just north of Eindhoven. We had expected only a platoon there and the surprise nearly brought off a second Arnhem disaster along the Wilhelmina Canal. We have long wondered why this happened, but not been able to find the answer. And now it seems likely that the terrible fight at Best was a gift from Lindemans.'[33]

As the fighting ran into the second day, the battle was confusing and fast-moving. Reliable hard intelligence was difficult to come by – for both sides.

Operation Market Garden was now hanging by a thread.

Heavy fighting around Nijmegen meant the US 82nd Airborne Division supported by the tanks of XXX Corps were unable to capture the two bridges over the Waal River until the afternoon of 20 September. It required a daring river crossing by the Americans costing many lives. Despite the heavy sacrifice, the Allies' advance was delayed by nearly 36 hours.

The first lift of British paratroopers arrived on their drop zones to the west of Arnhem as planned on 17 September. They were mostly unopposed and the battalions were formed up in good order and ready to march on Arnhem by 15.30.

According to Richard Christmann, some enemy units opposing these British paratroopers were in possession of Lindemans' intelligence report and so already knew the thrust and direction of Operation Market Garden.[34]

One of these battalions was SS Unteroffizierschule Arnheim. This SS NCO school was led by an experienced SS Colonel Hans Lippert, and belying its name was one of the few effective units commanded by General Christiansen. Most of its soldiers had already completed one year's service and all had served on the Russian front.[35] After the Allies' breakout from Normandy, Lippert had been directing defensive positions on the Waal crossing, waiting for the Allies attack, 40 kilometres west of Arnhem.

The German commander later wrote: 'During the midday meal at my command post I heard a terrific droning noise from aircraft engines. It was about 1300 hours. As I came outside to work out where the noise was coming from I saw hundreds of aircraft with escorts heading westwards. Looking through my binoculars it was possible to make out that the doors were open and an airborne landing was about to take place.'[36]

Lippert concentrated his resources on disrupting and capturing the British landing zones needed for flying in reinforcements. The fighting was desperate on both sides as the British fought off several concerted attempts to encircle them.

Lippert was assisted, with mixed results, by a Dutch SS Surveillance battalion of Dutch Nazi recruits (Wach Battalion 3), stationed in Amersfoort north of Arnhem and commanded by SS Captain Paul Helle.[37]

Christmann claims this 600-strong unit, made up of Dutch criminals, collaborators and ultra Nazis, was also aware of Lindemans' intelligence.[38]

Lippert was not the only German commander to inflict heavy casualties on the British. On 4 September, Sturmbannführer Sepp Krafft's SS Panzer Grenadier Depot and Reserve Battalion 16 had been called up from the coast to strengthen the German defences. Krafft's machine gun, mortar and flame thrower units were ordered to take up positions around Oosterbeek and 'prepare for and attack air landings' as well as 'to defend the ferries and the bridge over the Rhine at Arnhem'.[39]

On 17 September at 12.30, before the Allied paratroopers had reached their landing zones, Krafft ordered the battalion to stand to and brought back his men from Arnhem to join his main force in Oosterbeek. An hour later, British paratroopers were reported dropping around Wolfheze, two to three kilometres west of the 16th. Krafft ordered a machine-gun unit to attack the airborne landings, inflicting many casualties, while the bulk of his force formed a blocking line in front of the British. Very quickly Krafft had worked out, or been warned, that the enemy's ultimate goal was to form a bridgehead at Arnhem for the Allied armour advancing through Nijmegen. Krafft's job was made easier after the capture of a British officer who, strictly against orders, had brought plans for the British airborne battalions' routes from the landing zones to Arnhem.[40] There is no doubt that had it not been for the presence of Krafft's battalion, the British 1st Airborne Division would have been able to reinforce the bridge at Arnhem. After the battle, Krafft's commanding officer, General Hans von Tettau, claimed Krafft's actions 'had decided the fate of Germany'. And Major General Robert 'Roy' Urquhart, who commanded the British 1st Airborne Division, said the 'redoubtable' Krafft and his battalion had done 'more than any other German to delay us'.[41]

But Krafft could not prevent one British battalion from securing its objective.

By following the river road, Colonel John Frost's 2nd Parachute Battalion had slipped through the German defensive cordon and reached the bridge at Arnhem, capturing the northern end. He was only supposed to hold it for two days but courageously fought on for four, towards the end without food, water or ammunition, before finally surrendering in the face of overwhelming odds in tanks and artillery.

Market Garden was a decisive and very unlikely victory for the Germans, coming as it did less than a month after the catastrophe of the Falaise pocket. Until Arnhem, the Allies had almost uninterrupted success in vanquishing the German armies. The Allies enjoyed superior manpower and firepower as well as complete dominance in the air. After sweeping the Germans aside in Normandy and then chasing them through Belgium back to Holland, it seemed unthinkable that the Nazis would be able to reverse these setbacks by defeating a combined airborne and land force of almost 100,000 men supported by hundreds of tanks and artillery.

More than 10,000 Allied paratroopers paid the ultimate price fighting for the Dutch bridges. British and Polish losses were between 11,000 and 13,000 dead or wounded and 6,450 captured. The American losses totalled 3,996 dead, wounded or missing, and German casualties were between 7,500 and 10,000. Dutch resistance fighters and civilians suffered more than 500 dead or wounded.

Market Garden was a daring plan that threaded beads on to a strung-out necklace of armour and firepower. Everything had depended on surprise and a rapid and coordinated deployment of paratroopers and tanks. But it failed at the last hurdle.

Churchill's and Montgomery's dream of reaching Berlin before the Russians was dead in the water. The war would not be over before Christmas. There would be eight more weary months of hard fighting before the Allies would be able to declare victory in Europe and instead of Montgomery riding into Berlin at the head of a British Army, it would be Marshal Zhukov, the Russian general, who claimed the German capital as Stalin's trophy.

In the days after the battle, Montgomery outrageously claimed that Arnhem was 90 per cent successful on the basis that the Allies had made advances into Holland which they had held – these were around the bridges taken by the Americans. Montgomery could never understand how he had thrown away such a superior military advantage over the retreating German forces and complained in his memoirs: 'Berlin was lost to us when we failed to develop a good operational plan in August 1944, after the victory in Normandy.'[42]

Yet most British historians have argued that Montgomery's plan was inherently flawed and bedevilled by disastrous setbacks in the field. Some claim the deteriorating weather was the decisive factor, others the faulty British radios or the failure to understand intelligence and surveillance reports that revealed the presence of the refitting panzers. Most agree that the plan was just too ambitious and for it to succeed, it required everything to go right on the day.

Not all Germans involved in the battle accept this as the complete explanation of the defeat of such a mighty Allied force.

Richard Christmann, who was captured after the war, told his American interrogators that Christiaan Lindemans' intelligence had been decisive: 'The SS School Arnhem (Lippert) and the Holland Militia (Helle) were ordered to be ready. Without the presence of these troops in the Arnhem area, the aerial landing on 17 September would have succeeded.'[43]

In 1986 he repeated this claim to Dutch historian Frans Dekkers,[44] adding: 'He [Lindemans] was very heated and rushed. He started immediately to recount. "There was an Allied invasion", he said. He had managed to make contact with a few officers in the Allied headquarters at Hotel Metropole in Brussels. They had informed him about the invasion and showed him a large map on the wall that outlined the invasion plan.'

In truth, Lindemans' reports had helped to confirm what German intelligence had been anticipating in the days leading up to Market Garden.[45]

General Christiansen did expect airborne landings, but only in conjunction with an assault from the sea. Intelligence obtained by the Luftwaffe Third Fighter Division, based at Deelen, just north of Arnhem, was more confident and more accurate. A few days before 17 September, it had recorded in the Division war diary that 'a parachute landing in our area is expected'.[46]

The commanding officer of the 9th SS Panzer Division had been ordered by Heinrich Himmler 'a few days before Arnhem' to put his 39 tanks and 500 Waffen SS soldiers into 'immediate fighting condition' in case of a Dutch uprising. This was very close to what Lindemans had told Kiesewetter about Baker's instructions to the resistance to stand by to coordinate their attacks with the main landings on the 17th.[47]

Intriguingly, this report of a timely intervention by Himmler was corroborated by one of his staff after the war, who recalled how Himmler had received intelligence from a Dutch agent a few days before Arnhem. Felix Kersten, who had loyally served Himmler as his personal masseuse and adviser, said that in December 1944 the Reichsführer-SS had confided in him how he (Himmler) had received 'reliable information' before the Allied landings from a Dutch officer who had crossed the lines. Himmler is reported to have said: 'I will be eternally grateful to that fine Dutch officer.'[48] Had Kiesewetter's report about Lindemans' intelligence been read and acted upon by the head of the Waffen SS?

There is further evidence that the Germans had been preparing to defend against an airborne assault.

As soon as Montgomery's 21st Army Group came to a temporary halt at the Albert Canal and the Schelde-Maas Canal, the German commanders began to game plan the enemy's next move. On 14 September, Field Marshal Model's intelligence chief at Army Group B drew up an imaginary order issued by General Eisenhower for the next stage of the Allies' advance. It predicted a ground assault in the direction of Eindhoven, cutting off the German forces on the Scheldt, followed by a 'large scale airborne landing by the 1st Allied Airborne Army north of the Lippe River in the area south of Munster for a date as yet unidentified'.[49] It was an uncannily accurate assessment.

On 15 September, Heinrich Himmler sent a telexed message to General Hanns Rauter, head of the SS in Holland, asking him to report to Model.[50] During their conference, Hanns Rauter asked Model if he had taken any precautions against an Allied airborne attack. Hours earlier, Rauter's subordinate Schreieder had lunched with Kiesewetter when they discussed the significance of Lindemans' report. According to Dutch intelligence reports,[51] Rauter was so concerned about the imminent prospect of an airborne assault that he placed Sepp Krafft's battalion in the Oosterbeek area on standby to repel the Allied attack. It was this order that meant Krafft was able to react so quickly on 17 September when the British began their march on Arnhem.

Yet it has never been established whether Rauter's prescience was based on Lindemans' report. After the war when Rauter was asked why he had discussed the plausibility of airborne landings with Model in the Arnhem area, close to where Model's HQ was based, 48 hours before the start of Market Garden, Rauter said it was merely precautionary.[52]

To varying degrees, Hermann Giskes, Gerhard Huntemann, Ernst Kiesewetter and Richard Christmann all believed Lindemans betrayed Arnhem. Many more former Dutch resistance leaders and modern-day politicians still hold Lindemans accountable for the military failure at Arnhem in the last year of the war and for the German reprisals that followed.

Nevertheless, what you have just read is the generally accepted narrative. Lindemans worked for the Allies and fought heroically for the Dutch before he then turned traitor after his brother and then his girlfriend were arrested by the Nazis.

But there are aspects about the legend of King Kong that simply do not ring true. There are German officers[53] of the Abwehr and Dutch V-men who believe Lindemans was working for the Germans long before he went to Giskes with his offer of betrayal. Could he have been turned by the Germans after his capture and imprisonment by the Gestapo in France as long ago as 1941? Was his subsequent work with the resistance really only a hall of mirrors?

Could that chase through the bars of Paris to try to assassinate 'George' Ridderhof have been a charade to boost his credibility with de Graaf, who was to prove so crucial to his credibility later? At the same time, Hermann Giskes could never understand why King Kong returned to the German fold in September 1944 when the writing was so clearly on the wall for the Nazis and anyone who collaborated with them. Neither was MI5 and IS9 ever able to explain why Lindemans had risked his life fighting and killing Germans with such enthusiasm in Antwerp and Brussels while he was supposed to be working for Giskes.

Lindemans maintained that he had betrayed his countrymen because his brother and 'wife' were prisoners of the Germans. But Lindemans began his collaboration months after Henk was imprisoned and before Letuppe was arrested and when he carried out his greatest act of betrayal both of them had been set free. The Nazis had no hold on Lindemans whatsoever when he crossed the lines two days before the start of Operation Market Garden.

There is then perhaps more to Lindemans' treachery than meets the eye. It begs the question who was he really working for and who else might have benefitted from the Anglo-American (and Polish) failure at Arnhem? The answers to these questions would not only explain the contradictions of Lindemans' espionage but perhaps open up a more far-reaching and chilling interpretation of his motives and casts him as a much more important figure in the closing chapter of the war.

The Germans were certainly the battlefield victors of Arnhem but they were not the ultimate beneficiaries. The 11th-hour temporary reversal in fortune of the Western Allies at Arnhem, halting the Anglo-American inexorable march towards Berlin, played directly into the hands of the Russians. Both Churchill and Stalin knew whoever reached the German capital first would be able to seize the geopolitical initiative in setting the terms of the post-war settlement and the consequent division of Eastern Europe.

A SPY TOO FAR

Lindemans' perplexing story of betrayal contains several clues which point to who he believed his true masters to be. These clues were ignored by both the British and the Germans. For that story to be told we now need to go back to the start of the war and tell the story of Market Garden from a British perspective, because however big Lindemans' betrayal was, the greatest traitors lay in London.

Operation Market Garden. The Western Allies' audacious plan to land 40,000 paratroopers and glider troops (Market) behind enemy lines to capture the bridges over the River Rhine. The air landings were supported by an armoured thrust of Sherman and Cromwell tanks of XXX Corps (Garden) that was to 'drive like hell' from the Belgium-Holland border to link up with British paratroopers at Arnhem, 60 miles away. The ultimate objective was the outflanking of the Siegfried Line and the occupation of the Ruhr, Germany's industrial heartland, before taking Berlin. (CAB 106 962 – front cover of file 21 Army Group "Operation Market Garden" Secret)

TOP SECRET

M.I.5 INTERIM INTERROGATION REPORT.

NAME: LINDEMANS.   CHRISTIAN NAMES: Christiaan Antonius.

ALIASES: Christian BRAND: (given to LINDEMANS in Holland, beginning of
         1944 by ROELOF, a nephew of Dr. van der NAGEL. Resistance
         Group, as name LINDEMANS was well known to Germans.)
         LINDEMANS was also known to German I.S. under this name.

KING KONG: Nickname given to him about 10 years ago by his rowing
           trainer. Latterly, LINDEMANS had used this name when sending
           messages to the Resistance Group.

de VRIES: Name given him by Capt. BAKER to hide the identity of
          both LINDEMANS and BRAND.

SPY NAME: CHRISTIAN (sometimes known as BRAND).

Date and Place of Birth: 24th October 1912. Rotterdam.

Nationality: Dutch.

Occupation: Motor mechanic (working under his brother JAN).

Date of arrival at Camp 020: 3rd November 1944.

Height: 6' 0½"
Build: Thick set and very heavy build.
Hair: Brown.
Face: Full, short straight nose.
Physical
Peculiarities:
    Paralysis of left arm.
    Entry and exit of bullet wound, left thorax.
    4 gold teeth upper jaw.
    9" scar on left thigh.
    Suffers from epilepsy.

Last Permanent Address: Westzeedyk 21, Rotterdam.

Languages: Dutch. French; German (both good) English (slight)

MI5 file on Christiaan Lindemans. The swashbuckling, stone-hearted double agent known as King Kong who betrayed 267 resistance workers, including many of his friends and lovers. (The National Archive, KV-2-237 p 7/8)

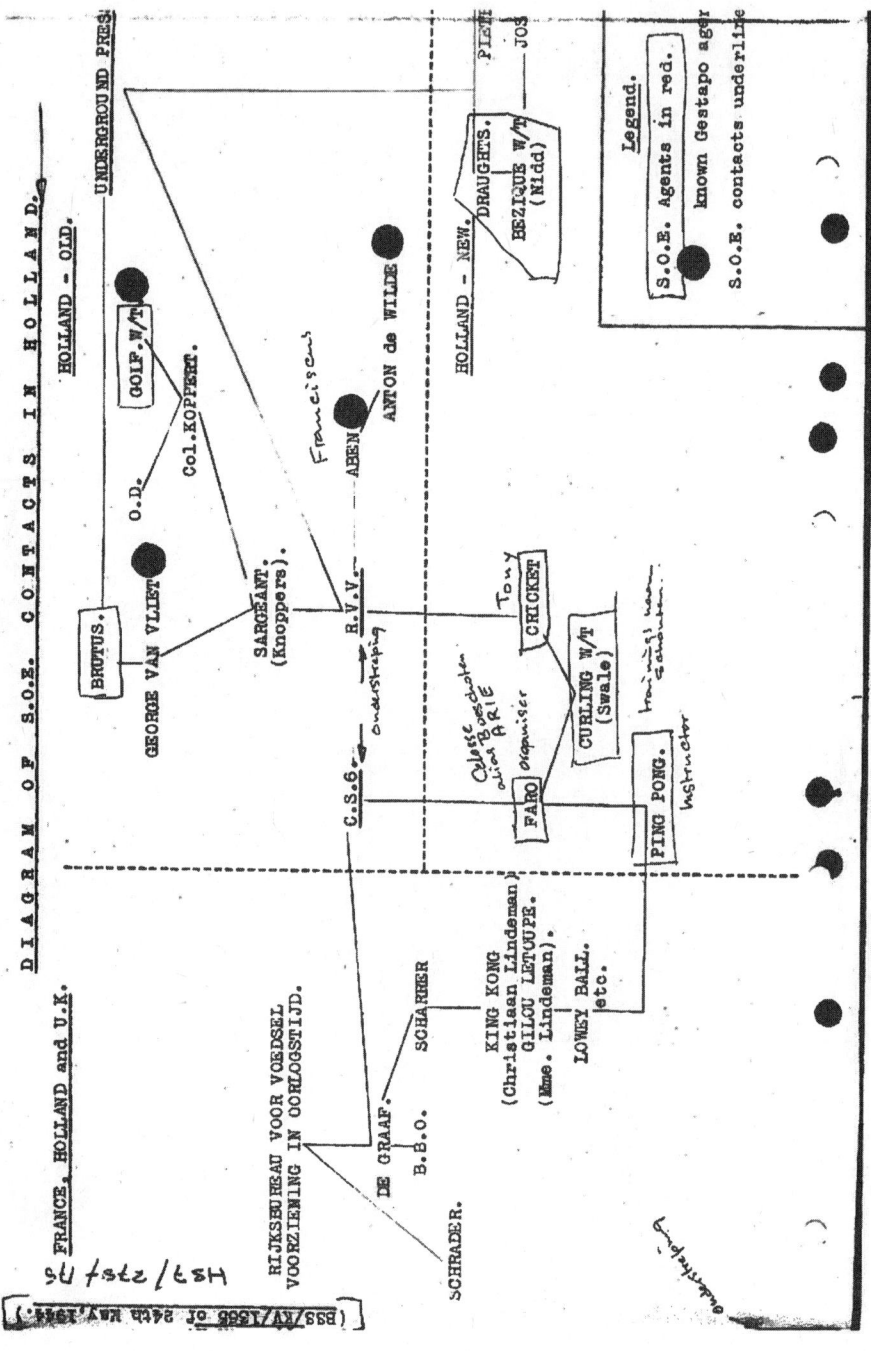

The King Kong network. Special Operations Executive (SOE) in Holland was blown by the German Englandspiel which ended in the capture and deaths of 50 Dutch agents. By 1944, communists had infiltrated the SOE Dutch network, at the heart of which was Lindemans and his wife Gilou Letuppe.
(Nederlands Instituut voor Militaire Historie)

> The following if a report given to us by "CC":
>
> "In BRUSSELS, "CC" immediately got into contact with a British Captain BAKER who had his office in the Hotel Metropole 4th floor. His office was called H. S. G-2 Section (or similar). Captain BAKER brought "CC" to Allied Headquarters in ANTWERP, believed to be in Hotel Central. There, "CC" received orders to go through the front to EINDHOVEN in order to notify the Philips electrical plant that the liberation can be expected in a few days. From 16 September 1944 all the Holland special troops were to be mobilised in order to prevent a destruction of the Holland industry by the German troops. "CC" then told me about the situation in BRUSSELS and ANTWERP and also that the post of ANTWERP was hardly destroyed. "CC" FURTHER REPORTED THAT HE SUCCEEDED IN GETTING AMERICAN AND BRITISH OFFICERS TO TALK OF A BIG AERIAL LANDING, TO TAKE PLACE ON THE 17TH TO 18TH SEPTEMBER 1944. "CC" GAVE US THE EXACT POSITION OF ABOUT FOUR HUNDRED (400) HEAVY CANNONS. THE AERIAL LANDING WAS TO TAKE PLACE IN THE EINDHOVEN, NYMEGEN AND ARNHEM AREAS. IN CASE OF SUCCESS OF THIS LANDING, SEVERAL OTHER LANDINGS HAVE BEEN PLANNED IN THE AMERSFOORT OSTRAND AD ZUIDERSEE AREAS, WITH THE GOAL TO DRIVE A WIDE WEDGE INTO THE GERMAN FRONT, TO REACH BREMEN. "CC" also precisely reported which ones of the locks in the part of ANTWERP had to be destroyed, (through sabotage) in order to make the port unuseful for the Allies. He furthermore described to us the exact routes on which the Allies would send their Agents in o the German occupied territory. On all these reports I made up two (2) summaries that same night. One report covered all general information and the second covered the prospective aerial landings. The second report was already in the hands of:
>
>   a. The 1st Parachute Company the morning of 16 September 1944.
>   b. A. O. I, XV
>   c. The staff of W. B. N. (Genral CHRISTIANSEN)
>   d. With special courier to IKH Berlin. He notified department did not know and were guessing if there was any truth to the prospective aerial landings and refused to send troops for counter messages. Only the auxiliary troops, police, SS School ARNHEM, Holland militia and other troops were ordered to be ready. WITHOUT

Statement of Abwehr officer Richard Christmann. He collected Lindemans from the General Kurt Student's headquarters in Vught on 15 September 1944 and drove him to Abwehr headquarters, where the Germans spent 36 hours debriefing their star agent before the start of Operation Market Garden. CC was the codename given to Lindemans by Abwehr spy chief Hermann Giskes.
(The National Archive, KV-946 p.21)

PART TWO
THE BRITISH

Dramatis Personae

Anthony Blunt: Polymath, scholar, traitor. A Russian spy from the thirties, he played a central role in British intelligence in the Second World War and went on to become Surveyor of the Queen's Pictures.

Kim Philby: Fellow traitor to Blunt. One of the Cambridge spies.

Jane Archer: At the start of the war, the only female MI5 officer. Her textbook debrief of Krivitsky set the standard for years to come and she was arguably the greatest single thorn in the side of the Cambridge spies.

Felix Cowgill: Ex-Indian police, he joined MI6 tipped for a top job, but his abrasive manner and concerns at Soviet penetration of the secret services meant he was sidelined.

Walter Krivitsky: NKVD defector who warned of Soviet penetration across all levels of British society, including the secret services. He was never taken seriously enough and was murdered in 1941.

Guy Liddell: Affable and shrewd head of counter-intelligence for MI5. A diarist and talented cellist, he was Blunt's greatest ally and mentor.

Herbert Hart: MI5 colleague of Blunt's, a fellow investigator into the identity of Josephine.

Frank Cervell: Loose-lipped, aristocratic Swedish air attaché.

Karl Heinz Kraemer: Tall, tennis-playing Abwehr officer based in Stockholm. The conduit for Josephine.

Walter Schellenberg: Nazi spymaster, mastermind of Venlo, who protected Kraemer and received the Arnhem warning.

Guy Burgess: Close friend of Blunt and one of the Cambridge Five.

Ivan Chichaev: NKVD Head of Station, he set up Pickaxe and went on to become the head of Atomic Espionage.

Boris Krotov (aka Kreshin, real name Boris Krötenschield): Blunt's NKVD handler in London in 1944/45.

Leo Long: Blunt's sub-agent working for military intelligence with Montgomery's army in France and Belgium.

Chapter 10

The Second Arnhem Warning

At midday on 16 September 1944, a teleprinter at the German Foreign Office in Berlin clattered into life. It was a message[1] marked KR Blitz ('decisive for the outcome of the war') from the Abwehr's spymaster in Stockholm with an urgent communication from his most valued agent, a shadowy source deep in the heart of the British state, known to him only as Agent Josephine.

The message contained a warning of a massive Allied attack due to take place the following day and was so detailed and accurate it was unlike anything Berlin had ever received before.

The message began:[2] 'The Allied Supreme Command intends airborne operations in the environments of Arnhem, Tilburg and Eindhoven. Aim of the operation is to enforce the crossing of the Rhine. The Allied units consist of the 1st British, 82nd and 101st USA Airborne Divisions, all of them will start from England. The operation will be carried through between Sunday [17 September] and Thursday.'

This was the Allies' most closely guarded secret – the correct dates, configurations of the three airborne units and final targets – of Operation Market Garden. Even so late in the day, only a tiny handful of Allied generals were privy to that level of operational intelligence. How had Agent Josephine got hold of such highly classified material?

The 'Josephine' report was forwarded to Walter Schellenberg,[3] head of the SD, and in September 1944 the 'absolute master of all

Nazi intelligence'. Schellenberg immediately recognised its importance and sent it on to Wehrmachtführungsstab, Oberkommando der Wehrmacht (OKW), the German High Command, who circulated it among the German generals defending Holland.[4]

'Josephine's' warning arrived in Holland as the armada of Allied aircraft, carrying the first lift of 35,000 paratroopers, was crossing the Dutch border to take part in Operation Market Garden and came at a vital time in the battle, when the Germans, who lacked reconnaissance, were blind to much of the British and American movements. Above all, the knowledge that the key strategic aim of the entire operation was to capture the bridges at Eindhoven and Arnhem was invaluable.

General Kurt Student, head of the German 1st Parachute Army that met the brunt of the Allies' attack around Eindhoven, later said: 'Better than anyone else I knew that airborne troops are at their weakest during the first few hours and that rapid and decisive action on our part was called for.'[5] Josephine's intelligence allowed that to happen.

The day before, on 15 September, Josephine had also issued a more general warning highlighting a British Army advance 'on a broad front as far as the Meuse (Maas) and if possible even as far as the Waal by 24 September. After that the employment of powerful airborne forces in Eastern and Northern Holland and the German frontier region is planned [to] eliminate German river positions in the rear.'[6]

The British later admitted this was 'unpleasantly near' to Arnhem.[7]

Josephine even neutralised MI5's own double agents who had been sending deception intelligence saying that any airborne attack in Holland would be a dummy run and the real target was Scandinavia.[8]

On 17 September, the German High Command issued a briefing to field commanders:[9] 'In connection with the air landings which have taken place, particular attention is deserved for an agent's report which has only just come in and predicted these air landings correctly. ... The agent above considers that reports, particularly

THE SECOND ARNHEM WARNING

emanating from diplomatic circles, about landing intentions against Norway and Denmark are deliberate camouflage.'

When Walter Schellenberg was interrogated by MI5 at the end of the war,[10] he emphasised how it was Josephine's intelligence that helped the Germans 'appreciate the serious intention of the landings' so that he could 'stress to the staff concerned the seriousness of the position'.[11]

To add to the mystery, Josephine's advance warning of the air landings at Arnhem had evaded all the usual Allied intercepts[12] and monitoring of the diplomatic and Abwehr communications out of Stockholm. It even slipped the watchful attention of the MI6 agent working as a teleprint operator[13] in the German embassy who collected secret teleprint messages sent to Berlin.

One of the most senior German commanders to receive the Josephine report was General Wilhelm Bittrich, commander of II Panzer Group, the 9th and 10th Panzer Divisions, which were to have such a decisive role in the battle.

The unexpected contribution of these two SS units is widely credited with playing a decisive role in the defeat of the British, American and Polish forces.

Bittrich said that he was first alerted to the air landings at 'noon' on 17 September 'by the Luftwaffe communications network at my command post at Doetchingen'.[14] He said 'a report, transmitted by the air force installation at Doetinchem, indicated that Arnhem–Nijmegen was the point of main effort of the airborne operations.'

An hour later, Bittrich said he 'alerted' both SS Panzer divisions.

Bittrich was the first German commander on the afternoon of Sunday 17 September to conclude that the airborne landings were intended to capture the Dutch bridges. He sent the 10th Armoured Division 'Frundsberg' to face the American airborne troops of the American 82nd Airborne Division at Nijmegen. The more lightly armed 9th Armoured Division 'Hohenstaufen' was tasked with stopping the British at Arnhem.

After the war it was left to Field Marshal Bernard Montgomery to reflect on the devastating impact the two SS armoured divisions had on the outcome of the battle: 'The 2nd SS Panzer Corps was refitting in the Arnhem area, having limped up there after its mauling in Normandy. We knew it was there. But we were wrong in supposing that it could not fight effectively; its battle state was far beyond our expectation. It was quickly brought into action against the 1st Airborne Division.'[15]

Montgomery does not mention Josephine in his memoirs nor is it known whether he was ever told about the Arnhem warning sent from Stockholm to Berlin at the start of the battle.

The mystery is that Josephine has been almost entirely forgotten and that without specifically researching the betrayal of Operation Market Garden she would not have come to light. You will not read about Josephine in any of the major histories of this most storied of Second World War operations. Yet Walter Schellenberg, the Nazi's most senior spy by the end of the war was, when interrogated by Allied intelligence, explicit that he was convinced the Josephine intelligence helped the Germans work out Allied intentions in the crucial first hours of battle.

Indeed, Josephine barely even merits a mention in the intelligence histories of the Second World War, and yet she had been supplying the Nazis with high-grade intelligence since at least 1943. So highly regarded was this source that Josephine material was regularly read verbatim by Hitler himself, as well as Field Marshal Alfred Jodl, Chief of the Operations Staff of the German High Command. Even more mysteriously, there appears never to have been a British intelligence investigation into Josephine's betrayal of Arnhem. How could it be possible for such a significant intelligence breach to be so forgotten? To answer that we need to answer the biggest mystery of all: who was Agent Josephine?

Chapter 11

Bombed Out

There is a pretty drive down from The Hague which passes a quiet hamlet near the city of Venlo on a winding road through pine woods just inside the Dutch border with Germany.

On 9 November 1939, a car carrying two British MI6 officers stopped at an inviting red-brick cafe encircled by a veranda with a sloping roof. Behind it a large garden with swings and see-saws was laid out to entertain the children of families who'd come to hike and cycle through the wooded lanes and tracks that criss-crossed this peaceful corner of the Dutch countryside.

Two hundred yards farther down the road, a Dutch customs house with a black-and-white-painted barrier marked the frontier with Nazi Germany.

A tall German standing on the verandah waved at the driver of the car and his two passengers to come inside the cafe. This was Walter Schellenberg, just 28 years old, but a fiercely ambitious officer in the SD, who had invited the British officers to this meeting which they thought was with renegade Wehrmacht generals opposed to Hitler.

As they stepped out onto the gravel a large open-topped sedan sped around the corner and came to a screeching halt, blocking the entrance to the car park.[1] Four men in black leather raincoats jumped out, waving pistols. Two more on the running plate of the vehicle brandished machine guns and fired warning shots over the top of the British car.

The two hapless British intelligence officers had no choice but to surrender and were marched at gunpoint across the border, prisoners of the Nazis. Duped into believing they would be meeting anti-Nazi Wehrmacht generals plotting to depose Adolf Hitler, the gullible MI6 men instead found themselves kidnapped by the Nazis. The Venlo incident, as it became known, was a humiliating catastrophe for the British secret services.

Five months later, Hitler would even refer to it when justifying the invasion of Holland, claiming it proved the British were involved in a plot to assassinate the Führer.

The spies captured at Venlo were Major Richard Stevens, a chubby 44-year-old former Indian Army officer with no espionage experience, who was head of the SIS station in Holland. He was accompanied by Captain Sigismund Payne Best, a secret service veteran from the First World War, who was friendly with the Dutch royal family.

Neither was any match for Walter Schellenberg, who was even more delighted to discover that the British were carrying a list of all MI6 agents operating in Europe. Fearing Gestapo torture, the two MI6 agents gave up many more British secrets. The perfectly executed German sting was an intelligence disaster from which the British would take years to recover.

The Secret Intelligence Service had come into being just before the start of the First World War.[2] Its headquarters in Broadway Buildings, 54 Broadway, near St James's Park underground station, was a British state secret and its 'tap on the shoulder' recruitment policy relied on a small pool of candidates drawn from England's finest public schools with a smattering of ex-colonial policemen to add a dash of professionalism. It had scored some notable successes during the First World War but by 1939 was a poorly funded, incoherently structured institution, run as an old boys' club rather than a well-oiled spying machine.

The intelligence debacle at Venlo was only part of MI6's troubled start to the war.

Stalin, who regarded Britain as a more natural enemy than Germany, was in receipt of intelligence that convinced him that British foreign policy was committed to provoking a war between Russia and Germany. To him this made perfect sense – members of the British Cabinet, most notably Winston Churchill himself, had argued for crushing Bolsheviks in the civil war that followed the revolution and had been actively adversarial towards the Soviet Union ever since.

MI6 comprehensively failed to appreciate the Russian leader's enmity and were blindsided when, on the night of 23/24 August 1939, Germany and the Soviet Union secretly signed a non-aggression agreement, the Molotov–Ribbentrop Pact. The two dictators not only agreed that they would not attack each other, they secretly arranged for the occupation and division of the countries that lay between them. Germany claimed western Poland and part of Lithuania. The Soviet Union would occupy eastern Poland, the Baltic states and part of Finland.

One week later, Hitler ordered the invasion of Poland and on 3 September, Britain and France honoured their undertaking to the Poles and declared war on Germany. Within days, Stalin followed suit, taking the Red Army into Poland, occupying the Baltic states and attacking Finland.

The Russian leader hoped to quietly consolidate his eastern conquests while the two imperialist nations locked horns in a war in the West. He had not reckoned on the fighting spirit of the Finns, who mounted a heroic defence of their country.[3]

However, despite Allied support for the Finns, it was only a matter of time before sheer military might tipped the war in the Soviet Union's favour.

And by early February 1940, the Finnish Army was exhausted and their defensive lines eventually overrun. Outside help never materialised. Finland was forced to sign the Treaty of Moscow on 12 March 1940, ceding 11 per cent of their territory to the Soviet Union.[4]

In Britain, the utopian appeal of international communism still held sway among many sections of British society, despite Stalin's alliance with the Nazis. For them, Russia's aggression against its Scandinavian neighbour was justified as the necessary growing pains of a new political ideology that promised better and fairer lives for all.

The imperialist slaughter of the First World War was still fresh in the minds of millions and the 1929 crash, just three years after the General Strike, saw capitalism facing its greatest test, a crisis that shook the West's economic system to its foundations, with reverberations that were still being felt ten years later. Above all, communism offered a counterpoint to the fascism that had emerged in Germany, Italy, Spain and even parts of Britain.

Reports of the purges and terrors inside communist Russia as well as the appalling tragedy unfolding in Ukraine, where millions were dying of starvation, were all too readily dismissed as fake news, the propaganda of the decaying old world order.

By 1939, membership of the Communist Party of Great Britain had risen to a record 50,000, significantly more than the 30,000 or so who were reported to be members of the British Union of Fascists.[5]

Membership was strong among the young privately educated intelligentsia, and Cambridge University was to prove particularly fertile ground.

Anthony Blunt, Kim Philby, Guy Burgess, Donald Maclean and John Cairncross may all have gone to different public schools, but they moved in similar circles and shared a radical and treacherous outlook.

Using their public school and university connections, the Cambridge spies effortlessly secured jobs at MI5, MI6, the Foreign Office and the BBC.

In Anthony Blunt, the Soviets found an intellect (he got into Cambridge on a maths scholarship), talented linguist and networker whose discretion and Protestant work ethic surpassed the other

Cambridge spies. Blunt, the son of a well-connected Hampshire vicar and a third cousin of Queen Mary, attended Trinity College and became a leading member of the Apostles, the self-selecting secret society of Cambridge University. He stayed on to continue his studies after graduation before taking up a position as a Cambridge don. It didn't take long for the Russians to find him and recruit him. Blunt was spotted by Theodore Maly, given the rather unimaginative code name 'Tony' and began working for the Russians in 1934,[6] shortly after or during his visit to the USSR in the same year.[7] Blunt's visit to Russia accompanied by like-minded Cambridge students opened his mind to a more liberated, even avant-garde society where homosexuality was for a while tolerated. It was a far cry from the class-ridden and sexually repressive world he inhabited back in England. After Cambridge Blunt joined the Courtauld Institute, where he established himself as a leading Marxist art critic.

Like many of his contemporaries, he was frustrated with Britain's policy of appeasement towards Hitler. His background gave him the perfect cover to become a leading talent spotter for the NKVD, the all-powerful People's Commissariat for Internal Affairs and precursor of the KGB.

Blunt is alleged to be the 'first man' and to have recruited Guy Burgess,[8] (rather than the other way around), Donald Maclean and the so-called fifth man, John Cairncross, although Kim Philby is also likely to have started to work for the communists while in Vienna in 1933. When the war started, Blunt applied to join the Intelligence Corps in the British Army. The vetting process drew attention to his interest in Marxism. The 32-year-old spy, who had been careful to avoid joining the Communist Party of Great Britain,[9] was able to successfully plead youthful intellectual exuberance and he was duly appointed[10] and sent to northern France in command of No. 21 Field Security Unit.[11] There he came in contact with Kim Philby, working for *The Times* as an accredited war reporter during the so-called Phony War before the Germans swept through Poland and the next year France in 1940. It was during this period in France that Blunt claims he first told Philby he was working for the Russians, although it seems likely they were already aware of each other. They shared a mutual friend in Victor Rothschild.[12]

During this period, Philby established contact with leading members of Russia's European spy network of illegals known as the Rote Kapelle (Red Orchestra).[13] They were contacts who would prove useful to him later in the war.

The spies were together in Boulogne in the early summer of 1940 when Hitler's panzers drove the British Expeditionary Force back towards the French coast. Both must have questioned their allegiance to the Soviet cause after news of the Molotov–Ribbentrop pact. At the same time they must have been keenly aware that their value to the cause they were later willing to risk so much for was at that point negligible. We will never know what the two young men discussed in the cafes of Boulogne as Britain teetered on the edge of defeat in those first few weeks of real war. What we do know is that within weeks of their return, Blunt had joined MI5 and Philby MI6.

Blunt knew a formal application would set in motion security checks that would reveal his communist affiliations so he had enlisted fellow Apostle Baron Victor Rothschild, who was already an officer, to have a quiet word on his behalf.

In the same vein, Kim Philby joined MI6's D (for destruction) section after his father took Valentine Vivian, the deputy head of MI6, to dinner at his club.

British intelligence was badly shaken after the catastrophe of the Venlo incident the year before. Morale was low and years of underfunding meant it was ill-prepared to take on the challenges of the war. In Britain's darkest hour it was a case of all spies to the pumps; between 1939 and 1944, SIS was to grow in size tenfold so it is perhaps not surprising if the vetting was rudimentary.

As if to prove that point, among the fresh intake for MI5 and MI6 were two Dutch recruits newly returned from Holland. Folkert van Koutrik and Bill Hooper had both worked for the German Intelligence Service in Holland and had both been implicated in the Venlo disaster the year before.

Anthony Blunt's first posting was to D Division,[14] military security, based at Wormwood Scrubs in West London. The grim Victorian prison was the newly appointed headquarters of MI5, the home security agency tasked with the job of hunting the spies, saboteurs and fifth columnists threatening the country in the wake of the defeat of the British land forces across the Channel. A series of interconnecting, cramped cells was home to 35 male officers (and one female) and 103 female secretaries and registry staff who were pitting themselves against Nazi infiltration of wartime Britain.[15]

Blunt made short work of getting himself transferred from this intelligence backwater to B Division, responsible for counter-espionage also in the Scrubs, where he immediately made an impression on MI5's chief of counter-intelligence, Guy Liddell.

Liddell, a rare non-Oxbridge and non-public-school-educated[16] outlier in MI5, had earned a wartime commission as well as a Military Cross in the First World War and then spent time in the police before joining MI5, spending the years before the war helping to mastermind the hunt for Bolsheviks across Europe, while warning politicians of the dire intentions of the Comintern's plan for world communism. He had also, in 1936 on a trip to the USA, provided Herbert Hoover with information which gave the FBI their first major international intelligence case, breaking up a Nazi spy ring. Over the years, Blunt was to cultivate the socially ambitious Liddell assiduously. It was a relationship which would yield him astonishing results.

Blunt was tall with a long chin and a serious demeanour that belied his 32 years. No one seemed to care that he had been an avowedly Marxist art critic before entering the service. It was more important that he seemed the right sort. It also can't have hurt that he was dauntingly intelligent and ferociously hard-working.

Such was his reputation as an art historian that Blunt was invited to Blenheim Palace – MI5's country headquarters after Wormwood Scrubs was bombed, the family home of the Dukes of Marlborough and birthplace of Winston Churchill – to give staff lectures on the building's collection of paintings.[17] Liddell, a talented cellist, admired Blunt's aesthetic credentials and often accompanied him on trips to the West End sale rooms. In turn, Blunt played up to Liddell's social and artistic pretensions.[18]

Liddell made Blunt his personal assistant and came to increasingly rely on the younger officer. In a matter of weeks, Blunt had gone from being an anonymous junior military intelligence officer to become the indispensable right arm of the British spy chief leading the nation's counter-intelligence against the Germans and the Russians. It was a huge boost to Blunt's standing and Liddell's track record before the war sniffing out Bolsheviks lifted him above suspicion. Indeed, Blunt, Liddell, Philby, Rothschild and various other like-minded members of the security services gathered themselves together into what they called 'the group' meeting in the 'magnificent' surroundings of Tomas Harris's house in Chesterfield Gardens where they existed in what Philby would describe as an 'atmosphere of haute cuisine and grand vin'.[19]

On 24 September 1940, a little more than three months after Dunkirk, Guy Liddell met his new PA at the Reform Club in central London for a spot of dinner. They were joined by Blunt's friend and fellow NKVD agent Guy Burgess, who was then working for the BBC. Blunt was trying to recruit him to MI5 and was hoping a meeting with the head of B division would improve his prospects of a job.[20] The subject of their conversation is not recorded in Liddell's diary, probably because after he left the Reform Club that evening the Luftwaffe began dropping bombs on the capital: 'Just as I was going away at about 11:30,' wrote Liddell, 'a Molotov bread basket descended. Three incendiary bombs fell just inside Pall Mall and all sorts of people were rushing about in dressing gowns with bags of sand. By the time I got into the Mall, the whole of St James's Park was lit up as if by Roman candles.'[21]

But the real damage was further afield than St James's.

When Liddell arrived for work the next morning, he discovered the German bombers had targeted the MI5 office in Wormwood Scrubs. 'I found,' wrote Liddell, 'that part of the registry had been burnt by incendiary bombs and all the card indexes had been destroyed. Mercifully we had had it photographed. Some 1,000 files had also been destroyed.'[22]

The very existence of MI5 and its card registry of individual 'subjects of interest' was a state secret and the location of its headquarters known only to its members and a handful of ministers, so the bombing of Wormwood Scrubs and MI5's headquarters in London was a major success for the Nazis.

But what were the Germans doing bombing an out-of-the-way West London prison? It was hardly an important target. Was it just luck that the Luftwaffe had hit the secret site of Britain's home security agency?

Some inside the building suspected the Luftwaffe was acting on inside intelligence.

Oreste Pinto, an Anglo-Dutch officer who worked with Blunt and Liddell and who crops up later in this story, was to point out that:[23] '... Wormwood Scrubs was dive-bombed. It seems more than a coincidence that the Luftwaffe should adopt the one method of ensuring that a particular target should be hit when to all the world, apart from the select few, that target was merely an ordinary prison. I am certain in my own mind that the secret had leaked out and the raid was a deliberate attempt to smash the nerve centre of MI5.'[24]

Who could have been responsible?

There were three MI5 officers who had a motive to betray the location of MI5's top secret temporary headquarters. The German spies Bill Hooper and Folkert van Koutrik were two of them. Blunt, a Russian spy, was the third.

However, German agents such as Hooper and Koutrik, now working for MI5 and MI6, had lost the ability to get in touch with their Abwehr handlers. That was not the case with the Russian spies. Even though, in 1940, the Nazis and the Soviets were allies, the Soviets retained a strong diplomatic presence in London. Was this Blunt's way of announcing to his Russian handlers that he had arrived and that he was to be taken seriously?

We may never know, but what is certain is that Blunt will have had good reasons for helping to destroy the MI5 Registry and its card index to cover up his and his fellow spies' communist links.

Moscow's instructions to its agents in 1940 were very clear: 'Imperialist war must be gradually converted into a civil war, that no steps should be taken to oppose a German landing in this country since a short period under a Nazi regime would be the quickest way to bring about a Communist revolution.'[25]

Liddell, meanwhile, was oblivious to the enemy within. His anti-Bolshevik focus was naively restricted to the propaganda efforts of the members of the Communist Party of Great Britain employed by the Ministry of Information film unit. When he got home from the bombed-out Scrubs that evening, he wrote: 'It is really rather a waste of time, our vetting people from a communist angle if these individuals continue to be employed. If they were doing a really useful job of work it might be worthwhile stretching a point, but since all the work coming from that department [Ministry of Information film unit] in connection with films is so obviously useless I should have thought that a change would be advantageous.'[26]

The irony is that just a few months before the Scrubs was bombed, MI5 had been directly warned about the extent of Soviet penetration of Britain's security apparatus.

On 19 January 1940, the Russian spymaster who had been responsible for counter-intelligence and sabotage operations across

Western Europe braved the U-boats of the Atlantic and arrived in Liverpool from America aboard the *Duchess of Richmond* ready to brief British intelligence. Walter Krivitsky had fled to the West two years earlier after discovering he was to be the next target in a Stalin-orchestrated purge of the Russian intelligence services. Thanks to Krivitsky, MI5 had been able to arrest Soviet agent John Herbert King, a cipher officer working in the Foreign Office whose details had been passed on to MI5 via the Americans the year before. On 18 October 1939, King had the dubious distinction of becoming the first Second World War spy to be convicted in Britain. He was tried in secret in Court 1 at the Old Bailey and sentenced to 10 years imprisonment for breaching the Official Secrets Act 1911. During the investigation it emerged that King had taken industrial quantities of Foreign Office documents from the Code Room to a flat in Buckingham Gate, where his NKVD handlers had set up a photographic centre for the purpose of making copies of the British secrets. Some of King's material was deemed so important it was shown to Stalin and included a verbatim account of a meeting between Lord Halifax and Adolf Hitler in 1936.[27] The Russians passed on much of King's intelligence to the Germans, hoping to stoke tensions between the two European powers.[28]

Despite this proof of Krivitsky's bona fides, King's criminal conviction seemed to satisfy MI5 that they had caught and dealt with the entire Russian threat to British security.[29]

Once he was in London, Krivitsky was debriefed over three weeks at the Langham Hotel in London by Jane Archer, MI5's sole female officer. It was later described by historian Christopher Andrew as 'the first really professional debriefing of a Soviet Intelligence officer on either side of the Atlantic'.

In one session, at which spy chiefs Valentine Vivian (MI6) and Brigadier Oswald Harker (MI5) were present, Krivitsky disclosed that both services had been infiltrated by a sophisticated network of Russian agents.[30] He said King had been recruited by a Dutchman called Henri 'Hans' Pieck, a well-known commercial artist, who under his cover as an official courier of the Dutch Ministry of Foreign Affairs made frequent trips to London. Pieck, he said, had recruited many other agents operating in London, including Bill Hooper, who had also been selling secrets to the Germans. Hooper, whom the British had failed to suspect of being a German agent,[31] was also a Russian one.

He had been taken on to MI6's books by Nicholas Elliott, who headed up MI6's Dutch section, and worked down the corridor from Kim Philby.[32]

Hooper would turn out to be the first, but not the last, treble agent of the Second World War.

In March 1941, MI5 received a report about how Bill (Jack) Hooper had been the victim of a blackmail attempt by a conman, whose métier was stealing suitcases. Hooper's suitcase contained a document linking him to 'Soviet espionage'.[33] During the investigation it emerged that Hooper had a younger brother, Herbert Hooper, who was working for MI5. In May 1941, Herbert was moved to head up the Dutch Country Section in MI5, E1a in E-Division. The Hooper brothers, now fully embedded in the counter-intelligence operations against Nazi Holland, were described by MI5 as being 'unusually devoted to one another'[34] but it was only after the war that the agency discovered what the brothers had actually been up to.

Liddell asked Anthony Blunt to investigate any possible Soviet ties to the Hoopers, but within a few weeks the Soviet agent had reported back, giving the brothers a clean bill of health. Most shockingly, Krivitsky had told MI5 there was a sleeper cell of British NKVD agents working in London with access to the highest classification of secrets.[35] He said one of the Soviet sleepers was 'a Scotsman of good family, educated at Eton and Oxford ... working in a senior position in the Foreign Office.'[36] Another was a young English aristocrat, who was a journalist who had worked for a British newspaper during the Spanish Civil War. The man was a friend of the agent in the Foreign Office. With the benefit of hindsight, it seems incredible that Guy Burgess and Kim Philby were not identified, but the reality was these descriptions led to numerous suspects in the security services. Certainly Kim Philby presented himself as a happily married man with little interest in politics and whose wife was expecting their first daughter, Josephine.

Krivitsky had risked his life to warn the British and Americans of the threat from Stalin. MI5's Jane Archer reported that he 'cannot however emphasise too strongly that since 1935 Stalin has regarded the Soviet as in a war position'[37] and 'his point is that the Comintern no longer has any genuine interest in the needs of the British working class and that the Communist Party organisation is merely a Russian agency superimposed upon extreme left-wing opinion in order that it may be used as a weapon to assist Stalin in his aggressive military policy'. In February 1940, these were messages that the British and American spy hierarchy were woefully underprepared[38] to accept, and less than a year later Krivitsky would end up dead in a Washington DC hotel, murdered by the NKVD.

It is indicative of the threat that the Russians perceived Krivitsky to be that Anatoly Gorsky, the man who ran the Cambridge spies in London, was recalled to Moscow in March only to return in November, after Krivitsky had left the UK.

At the same time, Jane Archer, who would continue to be a thorn in the side of the Cambridge spies for years to come, found herself drummed out of MI5 for publicly calling the then acting Chief, Brigadier Harker, 'incompetent'.[39] It is unclear what this incompetence was, although Liddell records in his diary that he regarded the charge as justified if undiplomatic. It seems likely that it relates to Krivitsky and the report she had circulated at the end of April 1940. The report was hugely sensitive and yet a copy appears to have found its way into the hands of Guy Burgess, who shortly afterwards fled the country with Isaiah Berlin on a madcap scheme to journey to Moscow, overland, via America. The pair only made it as far as Washington before Burgess was sent ignominiously back. That and his subsequent erratic behaviour saw him lose his position at MI6, but given that he was to panic and bolt again in 1951, it seems reasonable to wonder if he thought Krivitsky's testimony about aristocratic Etonians was too close for comfort.

Certainly it seems likely that Archer, who described Krivitsky as a 'keenly intelligent, widely read and cultured man', liked and admired him and would have been horrified if the assurances she had made that MI5 would look after Krivitsky were not kept. It was an affair which would rumble on. As late as November 1946, Philby was writing letters about the whereabouts of Krivitsky's secretary.[40]

After the war, Blunt and the other Cambridge spies tried to mitigate their treachery by claiming they were passing on secrets to help one of Britain's allies. But up to June 1941, Blunt, Philby and Burgess had knowingly given away key intelligence to their Soviet handlers who were allies of the Nazis and so were directly harming the British war effort. For example, Burgess and Philby passed on to Moscow a list of names of all the SOE officers, foreign agents and secret details of the operational structure of the SOE agency.[41] Who is to say how many Allied lives were endangered or indeed lost because of their treachery?

Chapter 12

Red Orchestra

In 1940, the Russian secret service was well resourced, had no qualms about acting outside the law and could rely on the ideology of international communism as its recruiting sergeant. For the NKVD, the actions of a few young upper-class idealists in all but defeated Britain must have seemed a long way down their list of priorities. They had a spy network that stretched right across Europe and for them the focus was on those countries such as France where revolution was a more realistic goal. But by the end of 1940, all of that was about to change.

At Bletchley Park, the British government's secret cryptography establishment 50 miles north of London, a small group of cryptanalysts had made a major breakthrough in decoding intercepted messages that had been encrypted by German operators using electrical cipher machines, the most important of which was the Dutch-designed Enigma machine. The flood of decrypted high-grade military intelligence which began to pour from Bletchley Park was code-named Ultra (as in 'Ultra Top Secret').

In February 1941, the code breakers at Bletchley decoded intelligence that showed Hitler was amassing what would eventually be three million German troops at the Soviet border in preparation for Operation Barbarossa, the Nazi invasion of Russia.

It would prove to be the turning point in the Second World War and Winston Churchill seized on the intelligence as a way of bringing Stalin into the conflict on the side of the British. In fact, Churchill had already anticipated Hitler's move, confiding in his close friend, the South African Jan Smuts, as early as June 1940: 'If Hitler fails to beat us here he will probably recoil eastwards. Indeed he may do this without attempting an invasion [of Britain].'[1]

On 3 April 1941, he wrote to Stalin setting out the German military movements and exact current positions, adding: 'Your excellency will readily appreciate the significance of these facts.'[2]

Churchill's warning fell on deaf ears.

Instead, Stalin regarded the prime minister's secret correspondence as part of a perfidious British plot to pit Russia against Germany in a war that would annihilate the two powers, leaving Britain in command of the battlefield and dominant over Europe.

There was evidence to support such a thesis.

As recently as November 1939, after the Russian invasion of Finland, Churchill broadcast to the nation: 'Many illusions about Soviet Russia have been dispelled in these first few weeks of fighting in the Arctic Circle. Everyone can see how communism rots the soul of a nation – how it makes it abject and hungry in peace and base and abominable in war.'[3]

Stalin's scepticism of Churchill's motives was further supported by sound secret evidence, largely supplied by his agents in London. Pavel Sudoplatov, the man in charge of the operation to assassinate Trotsky and one of Stalin's most trusted spy chiefs, wrote that: 'Philby had reported plans of the British cabinet to stimulate tension and military conflict between Germany and the Soviet Union to distract the Germans and bring about their defeat.'[4]

Philby's intelligence about Britain's true intentions was backed up by a Soviet agent who had secured an even more critical position in the heart of military intelligence, John Cairncross, another Cambridge graduate and gifted linguist and mathematician, had been taken on as an analyst at GC&CS, Bletchley Park in Hut 3, working on ULTRA ciphers.[5]

Said Sudoplatov: 'We received further reports from Cairncross and Philby of British activity to stimulate fear among the German leadership that the Soviet Union was coming into the war. There were also reports of increased serious contact between British and German informal representatives in search of peaceful solutions to the European war.'

Pavel Sudoplatov told Stalin that any attack by the Germans 'depended on a rapprochement with the British because they [the Germans] could not risk fighting on two fronts.'[6]

Then, on 10 May 1941, a Messerschmitt 110 carrying Rudolf Hess arrived in Scotland. It was left to Nazi intelligence Chief Walter Schellenberg, the mastermind of the Venlo trap, to inform Hitler, incorrectly, that Deputy Führer Rudolf Hess had been long under the influence of the British secret service. Stalin was told the same thing by Philby and Blunt, stoking Stalin's fear the Germans were close to signing a secret peace pact with the British. These fears were amplified by the fact that Moscow was in receipt of secret reports of the UK's Joint Intelligence Committee, the body responsible for the main British intelligence assessments, that concluded Hitler was *not* preparing an invasion of the UK. This flatly contradicted what the British were telling Stalin through official channels.

The Russian leader found it easy to convince himself of the duplicitous intentions behind the Churchill warning. Other intelligence was not so easily brushed aside. Moscow's most trusted spy cells in continental Europe were flashing red.

Leopold Trepper, the chief conductor of the Red Orchestra, reliably reported the year before that the Germans had abandoned plans for any invasion of Britain.[7]

As early as May 1940, he had sent a detailed report to the Soviet military attaché Ivan Susloparov in Paris naming June 1941 as the date chosen for the Nazi attack on Russia.

Trepper later lamented: 'He who closes his eyes sees nothing, even in the full light of day. This was the case with Stalin and his entourage. The generalissimo preferred to trust his political instinct rather than the secret reports piled up on his desk.'[8]

On the evening of 21 June, Alfred Liskow, a German communist deserter, crossed the lines and informed the Soviets that an attack would commence at 04:00. Even then Stalin chose to ignore the intelligence.

German forces commenced the invasion of the Soviet Union with the bombing of major cities in Soviet-occupied Poland and an artillery barrage on Red Army defences along the entire front.

The initial momentum of the Nazi ground and air attack completely destroyed the Soviet military organisational structure, paralysing every level of command and control from the infantry platoon to the Soviet High Command in Moscow.[9] By mid-July, the German forces had advanced within a few kilometres of Kiev, encircling the Ukrainian capital on 16 September.

Despite Stalin's mistrust, Russia now found itself an ally of the British against the Germans. To Stalin it was only ever an alliance of necessity that the Russian leader intended to exploit in the long-term interests of his post-war ambition for a pan-Soviet empire.

In this endeavour, Moscow was grateful that it could now call on its agents secretly recruited in Britain before the war and the highly effective communist-led resistance cells already operating in German-occupied Europe.

Trepper and the other continental communists had a long track record of service to the USSR, but the Russian spymasters in the Kremlin could never quite fathom why this cross section of the British *haut bourgeoisie* would turn against their own country. Despite voluminous intelligence reports sent from London to Moscow, the Kremlin still decided to err on the side of caution and keep the British spies at arm's length. Indeed as late as 1943 the NKVD were mounting round-the-clock surveillance on the Cambridge spies, so convinced were they that it was all an elaborate deception on the part of the British secret services.

Nonetheless the German invasion of Russia changed the political landscape and created an urgent need for intelligence about their new Allies in the West.

The Cambridge spies themselves were delighted by Barbarossa as it meant they were no longer conflicted by the Soviet treaty with the Nazis. Blunt wrote in his memoir, made public in the British Library in 2009,[10] that the Germans' attack on Russia 'brought a profound sense of relief'.

They could also rely on the support of Pavel Sudoplatov who had been made deputy director of the NKVD. Sudoplatov had convinced his Kremlin bosses, Pavel Fitin and Lavrentiy Beria, that after distancing itself from the Cambridge ring in the wake of the Krivitsky defection in 1939, it was time to reactivate what would become the Soviets' most important Western spy network: 'we had to risk compromise and get our networks running again.'[11]

Chapter 13

Red Alert

Winston Churchill knew he had to take the fight to Germany by creating a new secret force he named the Special Operations Executive (SOE), which adopted the work of MI6's underperforming Section D (for destruction) of SIS and two other secret guerilla and propaganda warfare units. Churchill rallied the new agency to his cause of 'setting Europe ablaze' by recruiting and training men, and later women, and dropping them behind enemy lines to blow up railway infrastructure, munitions factories and carry out assassinations.

Heading up Churchill's new agency was an Old Etonian socialist, Hugh Dalton, a bisexual Cambridge graduate. 'Comrade Hugh'[1] was stuck-up, irascible and a hopeless administrator who turned out to be a disastrous choice to lead Britain's new clandestine fighting force.

There is no strong evidence that Dalton was in the employ of the Soviets but that didn't matter because two of the British officers responsible for the training of the new recruits, Kim Philby and Guy Burgess, were.[2]

Neither were vetted but had been appointed solely on the recommendations of old school friends and family contacts. The selection of Burgess was particularly egregious as he had been rejected for a teaching job at Eton after the school had contacted Cambridge seeking a reference only to receive the reply: 'I would very much prefer not to answer your letter.'[3]

At Section D, Philby and Burgess had written the SIS syllabus for the new cadre of agents being trained at Brickendonbury Manor near Hertford and then the SOE training camp at Beaulieu in Hampshire. Burgess was the spy school's political adviser offering guidance on how to work with communist resistance groups in Europe. Part of his instruction even included screenings of the Soviet film featuring the heroic revolt of the crew of the battleship *Potemkin*. At Beaulieu, Philby instructed the agents on the workings of the Abwehr and the various resistance movements active in Europe.[4]

After Barbarossa, Churchill and Stalin, erstwhile bitter ideological adversaries, now sought common cause against Hitler. Stalin desperately needed arms and raw material to help stem the Germans' seemingly inexorable march towards the gates of Moscow.

On 7 July, Churchill ordered the British ambassador in Moscow, Stafford Cripps, to begin discussions with the Russian leader for a treaty of mutual assistance. On 12 July, an Anglo-Soviet treaty was signed in the Russian capital to fight together and not make a separate peace with the Nazis.

Under a further lease agreement, 3,000 RAF Hurricane fighters, aircraft the RAF could scarcely afford to give away, were shipped to Russia, along with guns, tanks, clothing, rubber, engines, trains and much more material aid.[5]

Stalin still chided Churchill that he would have preferred Spitfires.

Part of the Moscow agreement[6] also provided for the active cooperation between the SOE and Russian special forces who would be permitted to work out of England. These Russian missions were code-named 'Pickaxe' and relied on the RAF to drop Russian, 'sabotage' teams deep into enemy territory. From the outset there was a mismatch in expectations. The Russians saw sabotage less in terms of blowing up bridges than in terms of the political 'decomposition' of their enemies as Walter Krivitsky had spelled out 18 months earlier.

However, this arrangement gave the NKVD and the GRU, Russian military intelligence, an official presence in London that could be used to secretly support the 'illegal rezidentura' that was already running as many as 40 British communist spies including the Cambridge Five. Station chief and head of the Pickaxe mission in London was the 'legal rezident' Colonel Ivan Chichaev, an experienced foreign intelligence officer who had been running an underground communist network of agents in Stockholm, where he had been station chief.[7] Chichaev reported to Viktor Lebedev at Kremlin Centre, not the Moscow ambassador in London. Lebedev in turn answered to Pavel Sudoplatov.[8] The NKVD presence in London was no longer secret.

The War Office, carefully briefed by Moscow, told MI5 to expect the arrival of Chichaev[9] and 12 other Russians on 18 November 1941 with the added rider: 'no inquiries to be made of Chichaev'.[10]

Chichaev and his wife and son were put up at a grand house at 54 Campden Hill Court, Notting Hill Gate while his two-man staff stayed at the nearby but less salubrious 3 Addison Road, where they operated a wireless transmitter in direct and secret contact with Moscow, all financed by the War Office.

To add to the bizarre fact that SOE were now committed to training and infiltrating Soviet agents into Western Europe, a further decision was taken to neither intercept nor make any attempt to decrypt any secret Russian radio communications. In fact, Churchill had ordered MI5 and MI6 not to conduct any anti-Soviet operations.[11] How this decision was reached is unclear, but it doesn't take too much to imagine that it was news that will have been welcomed by both Blunt and Philby.

Guy Liddell was understandably uncomfortable about the arrival of the Soviet mission. Only the year before, MI5 had drawn up contingency plans for the expected war with Russia and Liddell had ordered his officers to make preparations for the internment of all prominent Soviets living in Britain. He was immediately suspicious of Chichaev. An MI5 check uncovered a photograph of the Russian spy chief in England before the war registered under an alias living as an English student at 'the London Polytechnic'.[12]

Liddell, no longer so dismissive of the communist threat as he had once been, wrote in his diary: 'There is no doubt that the Russians are far better in the matter of espionage than any other country in the world. I am perfectly certain that they are well-bedded down here and that we should be making more active investigations. They will be a great source of trouble to us when the war is over.'[13]

Under the terms of the 'Pickaxe' missions, the SOE Russian officers were trained at Beaulieu separately from the other agents and partly under the tutelage of Kim Philby and Guy Burgess.[14] The Kremlin gave them false identities, and their real names were never disclosed to the British.

Neither was SOE allowed to know the nature of the Russian missions so that the RAF essentially performed the role of a covert 'travel agent' for the NKVD.[15]

In return, London sent just one man to Russia, Major George Hill, who was promptly seduced by a Russian agent and became an unwitting stooge for the NKVD against the British.

Liddell wanted to order a round-the-clock watch on the Russian NKVD officers but SOE forbade it, arguing that it interfered with the terms of the agreement with the Kremlin.[16] Undeterred, Liddell called on Russian-born MI5 agent Klop Ustinov, the actor Peter Ustinov's father, to befriend Chichaev, but despite initial success, protest soon filtered back from Moscow and Liddell was reprimanded.

He had to settle for an unofficial report on Chichaev that read: 'This officer was a subordinate of General Nicholas in the Soviet subversive organisation. He is about 42, probably of Siberian stock and of Jewish appearance, and is inclined to be effeminate with a passion for roses, one of which he usually carries in his pocket. He drinks little and has a dislike for vodka ... Unlike all the other Russians who had learned English in America he has no nasal accent.[17]

Among the contingent of NKVD agents who had arrived in Britain were Ivan Danilov, 31, Anna Frolova, 25 and George Robigot, 40.[18] All three were working-class French communists who fled to Russia at the start of the war.[19]

On 3 March 1942,[20] they arrived at RAF Tempsford and boarded a converted Whitley bomber from which they parachuted on to a drop zone in Montpellier, where they were met by a reception committee organised by the 'chief conductor', Leopold Trepper.

Robigot was not a Russian saboteur at all but a well-known French communist politician called Raymond Guyot,[21] who had been sent by Fitin and Sudoplatov to establish a communist government in France after the war. Guyot's presence among the Pickaxe agents should have raised suspicions among the British about the real purpose behind the Russian missions. Frolova, whose real name was Francine Fromont, was to act as Guyot's radio operator.

From his contacts inside Todt, the German military construction company, Trepper learned a great deal about where and how the Wehrmacht was concentrating its resources, valuable intelligence for the Soviets. These were the same German networks and contacts exploited by Christiaan Lindemans, who was also using the cover of Todt construction sites and labour camps to ferry his human cargo across Europe.

In June 1942, two more replacement NKVD agents were dropped in occupied Europe. They were the Dutch father and son Wilhelm and Nicodemus Kruyt, who had moved from Holland to Moscow before the war. Kruyt senior was a church preacher who claimed to have been on personal terms with Lenin.[22] He was supposed to play a similar role to Raymond Guyot by helping to establish a Russian-friendly government in Holland after the war. However, he was betrayed a few days after being dropped in Belgium, arrested by the SD and executed the following year. His son, who had a Dutch identity card in the name of Jan Schouten, landed in woods near the town of Harderwijk, a few miles north of Arnhem, and managed to escape the attention of the Germans, successfully making contact with the editor of the Dutch communist newspaper *De Waarheid*.[23] Kruyt junior sent a message to the Russian station in London informing them of his safe arrival, although complaining SOE had mixed up the luggage belonging to the father and son.[24]

Before Kruyt left for Holland, Liddell had risked taking a closer look at the young Dutchman and arranged for his personal belongings to be searched.[25] Liddell, who knew Kruyt only as Frederick Schmidt, discovered his real name and that the Russians had given him addresses in Holland and Belgium. After making a safe landing, Kruyt was met by NKVD agent Bart Rissouw (Sizauw), the *De Waarheid* editor. Nico Kruyt went on to establish himself at the heart of the Dutch communist group led by Daniel Goulooze and used the WT code name Herman (the same as Wenzel).[26]

He lived with another NKVD agent Anna 'Puck' Voute, who hid him in her flat. Voute was the sister-in-law of Edith Tudor-Hart, the woman who had helped recruit Philby as a Soviet agent in the 1930s[27] and acted as an intermediary for Anthony Blunt and Bob Stewart, the Comintern worker and secretary of the Communist Party of Great Britain control commission.[28]

This was clear evidence, should more have been needed, that the Rote Kapelle, the Kremlin web of agents, saboteurs and political activists on continental Europe, were closely interlinked with their British brethren of communist spies. Liddell's concerns about Chichaev and Pickaxe had turned out to be well founded.

There was a ruthlessness about the Soviets that the British could neither match nor understand.

An MI5 report sent to Liddell after one NKVD agent had perished in an aircraft accident near Tempsford described how the supposedly 'effeminate' Chichaev, who so loved roses, had insisted on visiting the crash site and 'turning over the charred remains' of the corpse so he could be sure of the man's identity and that the British hadn't replaced the body with a double: 'On both sides there is a great deal of suspicion,' an MI5 minute of the time noted. 'Moreover SOE also take the view that the Russians are more concerned in establishing long-term Comintern men in Europe than short-term tactically important subversive agents and saboteurs.'[29]

The Kremlin sent 34 NKVD agents to London under the terms of the SOE agreement, and 25 were parachuted into Europe by the RAF. Three were killed or presumed dead and six returned to Russia. Even before Operation Barbarossa, members of the Red Orchestra were being hunted down by the Nazis, but thanks to the British it was able to replenish its complement of agents under the Pickaxe progamme.

On 30 December 1942, Guy Liddell received reports that a tracking van of the Radio Security Service had picked up 'illicit wireless signals near the Russian Embassy six days in a row'.[30]

MI5 knew that Russian embassy staff were in contact with Moscow but these new signal readings indicated freelance NKVD radio operators were working outside the embassy, sending back coded messages to the Kremlin.

Liddell suspected that the Soviets had agents based in London of whom MI5 was completely ignorant.

One of them was sitting in a room down the corridor from Liddell's new and rather swish office in 58 St James's Street, the former London offices of Hollywood film producers Metro-Goldwyn-Mayer.[31]

These modern offices were MI5's central London headquarters, handily situated close to Section V (international counter-intelligence) of MI6, just down the road.

For Blunt and Philby this was a godsend. Blunt later wrote that 'cooperation was essential,'[32] but of course both spies circumvented the barriers that kept the two agencies apart in the name of wartime security.

In 18 months, Blunt had progressed from Liddell's PA to a senior officer in his own right. He was now also working closely with Dick White, head of German counter-intelligence.

Blunt told his NKVD handlers: 'White asked me to investigate the question of diplomatic communications which had not up until that time been studied systematically by MI5. Each country section was naturally interested in its own particular diplomats, but there was no section to study the problem as a whole. I had to therefore start from the beginning.'[33]

Any documents that he couldn't remove from an embassy site he photographed using his trusty second-hand Leica camera.[34]

Until now the snooping on embassies had been the business of SIS.

Blunt reported how he had begun to get hold of diplomatic bags that were being sent abroad with couriers by intercepting them at the ports without anyone noticing.

'This works particularly well,' he told Moscow, 'with the Spaniards and Portuguese who go out from Poole or Bristol to Lisbon ... the immediate project I am working on is to get a good agent inside the Swedish legation.'[35]

Blunt was even prepared to exploit his, then still illegal, homosexual relationships to further his espionage.

Among Blunt's lovers was a 23-year-old aspiring ballet dancer from Gateshead called Jack Hewit.[36] A working-class son of a metalworker, Hewit's father forbade him to take up a ballet scholarship and so Hewit ran away to London, where he first met Guy Burgess while dancing in the chorus of *No, No, Nanette*. He was first Burgess's partner before transferring his affections to Blunt.

Blunt encouraged him to join the Royal Artillery and then exploited him as his own agent, twice intervening to prevent him being called up for active service.[37] Blunt's principal use for Hewit was to entrap suspected fifth columnists and foreign diplomats working for the Germans.[38] Hewit would casually drop into conversation that he worked for a secret department in the War Office and then wait to see who took an interest.

Among Blunt's other close contacts was Wolfgang zu Putlitz, a German diplomat who defected to the British. After the war it was claimed that Putlitz, who became one of Blunt's lovers, was also working for the Soviets.[39] At this time, Blunt and Burgess[40] also brought the Kremlin agent Eric Kessler, a Swiss diplomat, into the MI5 fold and gave him the code name Agent Orange. But the icing on the cake was the Hungarian Andrew Revai,[41] agent Taffy, who was the leader of the exiled Free Hungarians in London and a Soviet plant.

Blunt's influence across British intelligence was about to deepen. In the spring of 1942, MI6 and MI5 agreed to confront the sensitive and mutually damaging issue of the sharing of very secret intelligence that had been a running sore between the two agencies since the start of the war.

Under the existing intelligence sharing protocols, all data traffic relating to MI6 had to go through Section V's small team of SIS officers led by the fiercely territorial Felix Cowgill, who liaised with their sister agency at MI5. But the demands of the war had brought a 'landslide' of requests that inevitably meant much intelligence sharing was being done outside the official channels of Section V. A serial offender was Kim Philby, who liked to forge back channels of communications with MI5 officers he had befriended. Of greatest concern to Sir Stewart Menzies, head of MI6 and known as 'C', was the unrestricted access to the new streams of classified intelligence generated or acquired by his agency. This included the Ultra secret intelligence gathered by the code breakers at Bletchley Park, other cipher traffic and 'special material' picked up from the mailbags and wireless communications of the foreign embassies abroad.

Menzies instructed Valentine Vivian to write to Liddell on 20 May informing the head of MI5's counter-intelligence branch that he had come up with a solution.[42]

'C' suggested the best way to resolve the problem of 'under the table' intelligence sharing was to select a trusted member of MI5 and designate them the point of contact with MI6. This officer would be able to restrict access of the very sensitive material on a need-to-know basis only. The officer Menzies and MI5 chief, Sir David Petrie, chose for the role was the pleasingly efficient Anthony Blunt.[43] The Soviet agent now stood at the crossroads of British intelligence, entrusted with its most valuable secrets.

In Nazi-occupied Europe, the non-British Soviet agents were also getting to grips with their new predicament.

At the heart of the Rote Kapelle, or Red Orchestra, was its chief conductor, GRU officer Leopold Trepper. The Polish-born communist had been active in Palestine against the British mandate helping to incite an Arab uprising before the war. In 1936 he was sent to France to serve as the Kremlin's technical director of Soviet intelligence in Western Europe, where he began recruiting more agents for his network. He was assisted by another GRU officer, Anatoly Gurevich, a Ukrainian from Kharkiv, whom Moscow assigned the code name Kent, the name of a fictional British agent character in a book that Gurevich had read when he was a boy called *Diary of a Spy* by N G Smirnov. Gurevich based himself in Brussels, where he posed as a wealthy Uruguayan ballroom dancer called Vincente Sierra. Both Trepper and Gurevich took their orders from Ivan Susloparov, the Soviet military attaché in Paris.

Before the war, Trepper had set up a French business called the Foreign Excellent Raincoat Company, which he used as cover for his network of secret agent 'raincoat salesmen'. It was this network that was in touch with his fellow Polish communists working with the French resistance group in Lille, where Christiaan Lindemans had made his new home.

Trepper's contacts did not stop at the Channel. Between 1937 and the summer of 1939, he made four or five visits to the UK.[44]

MI5 reports show that in the UK he met at least four Soviet agents, one with the code name 'Jean' and another 'the Professor'.⁴⁵ Trepper also made contact with the husband-and-wife communist couriers Franz and Germaine Schneider, who worked the Channel crossing, carrying intelligence from London to the Russian embassy in Paris.

It was only after the war that Britain's home security agency found evidence of Trepper's links to Harry Pollitt, the General Secretary of the Communist Party of Great Britain. However, it was Trepper's involvement with an Englishman 'who spoke fluent French' that demonstrated the length of the Kremlin's reach into communist circles of Britain.⁴⁶

The Francophone Englishman could have been any one of the members and associates of the British Communist Party, but it is worth noting that Blunt had switched to French from maths at Cambridge and spoke it as a second tongue.

Chichaev's arrival at the head of the Pickaxe mission, and the entirely one-sided intelligence arrangement between the British and the Russians, combined with NKVD infiltration of the British intelligence services gave Stalin an unparalleled window into the thinking and military planning of his old foe. It meant the Russian leader had a far better understanding of the war in the West than Churchill or Roosevelt did of the war in the East.

It was only long after the war that it fully dawned on the British spy chiefs they had been willing pawns, trainers and travel agents in the Kremlin's plan to subvert democracy in Europe.⁴⁷ They might have found out sooner had it not been for Kim Philby and Anthony Blunt, the British section of the Red Orchestra, who spent the war, and several years after in Philby's case, covering up the true identities of the Russian agents, their whereabouts and the real purpose of the Pickaxe missions. The Cold War had started on the day Hitler invaded Russia, years before Winston Churchill was to give it a name.

Chapter 14

Agent Josephine

On 2 September 1943, Guy Liddell wrote in his diary of a meeting with 'C', Sir Stewart Menzies, Valentine Vivian, deputy head of MI5 and himself. At this meeting, C questioned the two MI5 men about 'certain messages emanating' from a 29-year-old air attaché at the German embassy in Stockholm[1] by the name of Karl Heinz Kraemer. The messages were from an agent unknown to both Liddell and Vivian, Agent Josephine, who appeared to be working inside the UK. Their embarrassment at the fact that neither man had heard of Josephine was mitigated by the fact that in Liddell's own words, 'everything was being done to keep the information away from us'[2] by MI6's head of V section, Lt Col Felix Cowgill.

Cowgill had received the Josephine intelligence via the Americans who had an agent[3] working in Switzerland, a German diplomat called Fritz Kolbe, who on 19 August[4] reported it to Allen Dulles, later a Cold War director of the CIA. Cowgill had also been approached by Kolbe with the Josephine tip-off but had rebuffed him as he suspected the German of being a double agent.

Cowgill was determined that MI5 should not find out about Josephine and tried to keep the new intelligence under wraps. This was too much for Jane Archer, now working for MI6, who in defiance of her boss[5] passed on the secret information to MI5.[6]

The famously thin-skinned and difficult Cowgill had joined the service in 1939 after 12 years in the Indian Police. On joining he had been tipped to take over from Vivian in the deputy chief role, but able though he was, he lacked interpersonal skills and had irritated many of his colleagues by the jealous way he controlled access to the Bletchley Park ULTRA decrypts, which were his special area.

The first Josephine transcripts sent by OSS to Cowgill were alarming as they reported on the Salerno Landings in Italy with some accuracy.[7] 'Diplomatic channels' were immediately suspected as being the source of the leak, although the intelligence was later downgraded by MI5 as being reports based on newspaper cuttings. Nevertheless, any notion that the OSS agent was a German plant was quickly dispelled and Liddell made sure that proper efforts were taken to establish the diplomatic traffic between London and Stockholm on the key dates.

But as 1943 drew to a close, the British code breakers at Bletchley Park deciphered reams of new intelligence reports sent from the German embassy in Stockholm[8] covering very detailed information about aircraft production in the UK and the deployment of British airborne parachute divisions.[9]

These reports all had the German code names 'Josephine' and 'Hector', two agents operating from Britain and both seemingly 'run' by Kraemer. There was much fluttering in the SIS dovecote when Bletchley Park decoded a secret teleprint sent to Berlin from 'Josephine' reporting on a secret War Cabinet meeting between Stafford Cripps, brought back from Moscow to be Minister for Air Production, and Ernest Bevin, Minister of Labour, in which they had a heated argument about a serious hold-up in the production of Lancaster bombers.[10] Josephine's report was alarmingly close to the conversation which had in fact taken place and was followed by other reports detailing British criticism of American policy and Roosevelt's military staff. The Germans appeared to have at least one source right at the heart of the Allied war effort. The question was who?

For Vivian and Liddell the Josephine reports were uncomfortable reading. By this stage of the war, MI5 were of the view that there was not a single German agent in Britain who had not either been arrested or turned by them to work against the Nazis.

Finding Agent Josephine was therefore an absolute priority and Sir David Petrie,[11] head of MI5, asked Guy Liddell to investigate. Liddell – who noted in his diary that 'throughout the year the intelligence situation in Stockholm was a growing concern for SIS and MI5. The Abwehr had a number of diplomats in their pockets and the Russians had been steadily building up their resources in Sweden' – decided[12] to bring in Herbert Hart, one of the Oxbridge academics recruited by MI5 to bolster the department's capacity for analytical examination of the mountain of documentation acquired by MI5 since the start of the war. Hart, who until the war had been working as a Chancery barrister, shared an office in Blenheim Palace with Anthony Blunt.

In 1941, Hart had married Jenifer Fischer Williams, a high-flying civil servant[13] who was a member of the Communist Party of Great Britain and had once been in contact with Arnold Deutsch, one of the Soviet spymasters responsible for recruiting the Cambridge spies.

Hart and Liddell now decided to bring in Blunt to help with the investigation in the hunt for Josephine and Hector. Coincidentally, Blunt was already involved in an MI5 deception operation with a British agent also codenamed 'Josephine'.[14]

Soon afterwards, Hart formally instructed Blunt in the German Josephine case, writing: 'Please see the enclosures to Cowgill's letter ... Some of the sources purport to emanate from diplomatic sources in this country.'[15]

Blunt's enquiries began with the MI5 registry, which held the names and details of thousands of 'subjects of interests', and soon turned up an intriguing lead. A German called Karl Heinz Kraemer had visited London just before the start of the war and stayed at 9 Sussex Place in central London. SIS were able to source a picture of Kraemer and passed it on to Hart who arranged for it to be shown to Mr and Mrs Donnet, the owners of the boarding house that Kraemer had visited.[16]

They were able to confirm it was the same Kraemer.

Mr Donnet, a retired cavalry officer from the First World War, described the young German as an 'important fanatical Nazi' who appeared to be in the UK on some sort of mission.

Towards the end of July 1939, said Donnet, Kraemer received a telegram which caused him to leave London in a 'frightful state, shaking and nervous'.[17] A check on passenger lists revealed that Kraemer had in fact left Britain on a ferry from Harwich on 28 August, bound for the Hook of Holland, a mere three days before the start of the war.

Kraemer had been in Britain for three months although the exact nature of his mission remained a mystery.[18] A few weeks later more light was thrown on the subject when Blunt and Hart were able to link Kraemer to three German agents who had secretly landed by seaplane in Scotland in September 1940.

The agents, Karl Theodor Drücke, Werner Waelti and Vera Erikson, were part of the Abwehr's ill-fated Operation Lena to send penetration agents to Britain in support of the planned German invasion Operation Sealion.[19]

Vigilant Scottish police arrested Drücke and Erikson at Portgordon and Waelti later in Edinburgh after they tried to buy train tickets to London.

All three claimed to be refugees who had escaped from Nazi-occupied Europe and were going to London to report to the appropriate immigration authorities. Their stories quickly unravelled when the police found that Drücke and Waelti were carrying weapons – German-made Mauser HSc self-loading pistols. Shortly afterwards, coastguards recovered the Luftwaffe rubber dinghy they had used to row ashore.[20]

The Nazi agents were handed over to Lt Col Robin 'Tin Eye' Stephens, the fearsome commander and chief interrogator of

Camp 020, the Combined Services Detailed Interrogation Centre (CSDIC) at Latchmere House, a large Victorian residence set behind a barbed-wire security perimeter fence in the middle of Ham Common in West London. Stephens, nicknamed Tin Eye because of a permanently attached monocle, was half German but zealously hostile to anyone not British. He had a record of breaking down even the most hardened spy.

But after several weeks of interrogation and a number of interventions by the medical orderly, Stephens could not break the obstinate Werner Waelti.[21] It was at this point Liddell decided to employ the more subtle talents of one of his other interrogators.

Major Oreste Pinto was a veteran interrogator. Born in Holland, he had married a British national after the First World War before settling in London, living with his teenage son.[22] Despite his immense talents (Eisenhower later described Pinto as 'the greatest living authority on security'),[23] his dubious business transactions and predilection for going easy on attractive female suspects meant that he was never fully trusted by the MI5 hierarchy. Nevertheless, his talent could not be ignored and MI5 had called him up to help in the sifting of thousands of refugees who were flooding into Britain in 1940. Pinto spoke five languages and like Anthony Blunt, had a near-photographic memory. But it was his ability to drag the truth from the most obstructive enemy agents that had brought him to Liddell's attention. Three German agents had already been executed on the basis of confessions extracted by Pinto.

While Stephens demanded that every suspect should be questioned 'at the point of a bayonet',[24] Pinto liked to put the individual at a false sense of ease. In October 1940, Oreste Pinto sat down with Werner Waelti in an interrogation room at his South London offices[25] and offered the young agent a cigarette.

Pinto recalled in his memoirs[26] after the war that Waelti, who was actually a Dutchman, 'did not look like a very dangerous figure, sitting opposite me, hunched up and apprehensive. But then spies very often don't look sinister; it is their ability to blend with the crowd that makes them dangerous.'[27]

'It was,' he continued, 'of the utmost urgency to find out all that Waelti knew. Were they [the three German agents] just random shots fired off by German intelligence?'

Or were they were part of a bigger operation hoping to establish contact with a network of Nazi agents already in place planning attacks?

It turned out to be the former and Waelti was later convicted for spying under the Treachery Act and hanged at Wandsworth Prison. Drücke met the same fate. But Pinto helped Erikson, a 28-year-old former ballet dancer and aristocratic beauty, escape execution. She ended up playing ball with her interrogators. She confessed that her real name was Vera Starizky, born in Siberia, who admitted to being a Russian agent before the war.[28]

Pinto took a keen interest in the slim, raven-haired agent, and MI5 decided to turn Starizky and try to use her against the Germans. And so Starizky became the first female triple agent of the war. Whom she was really working for was anyone's guess.

There was, however, an important piece of intelligence she gave up to MI5 that would greatly assist the British in their enquiries into the Josephine and Hector case.

Starizky disclosed that the addresses in West London supplied to the German agents before the operation were given to them by Dr Karl Heinz Kraemer.

So, when Blunt and Hart started their investigation into Kraemer two years later, Pinto, blessed with his photographic memory, assisted by the detailed records kept in the Registry, was able to recall that Kraemer had stayed at Sussex Place, a road off Sussex Gardens, when he was visiting London and it was this which meant MI5 were able to positively identify Kraemer so quickly.

Thanks to Pinto, MI5 was able to link their Kraemer in Sussex Gardens to the one who had been involved in Operation Lena and was then transferred to Stockholm to head up the Abwehr operations in Sweden in 1942. Kraemer's name also cropped up as one of the German intelligence officers identified in 1940 by Agent Snow, helping to send German spies to England under Lena.[29] MI5 was closing in on the German spymaster who appeared to have unrestricted access to Britain's top military secrets.

With the assistance of Section V, SIS's counter-espionage division where Kim Philby was also making a name for himself, the British quickly discovered Kraemer kept a large house in Stockholm which he shared with his wife and three children. He worked as an air attaché at the German embassy in Stockholm but was in fact head of the Abwehr I Luft and had a direct line to Walter Schellenberg. The tall and good-looking Kraemer maintained a grand and high-spending lifestyle, enjoying a number of adulterous affairs and driving a range of fast cars, which made life difficult for the SIS team in Stockholm who had the job of following the flamboyant spy and were often simply unable to keep up. The Kraemers' inexplicable wealth and haughty manner made them unpopular among the other German embassy staff.

In the second half of 1943, Kraemer was a prolific agent, churning out industrial quantities of intelligence reports relating to British and American interests all over the world. He had his fingers in many pies and contacts in almost every embassy in the Swedish capital. But it was at the Swedish defence offices where Kraemer concentrated his efforts, cultivating a series of girlfriends who had access to senior Swedish military and government staff.[30]

Kraemer was now considered by Berlin to be the Abwehr's most valuable spy, a man whose intelligence was read by the Führer. Nevertheless, his success meant that some of his more jealous colleagues wondered if the reason his intelligence was so good was that he was working for either the British or the Russians or indeed if he was simply making it all up from things he read in magazines and newspapers. Meanwhile, Kraemer continued to tell his bosses in Berlin that his best agent, Josephine, was a society hostess living in London.[31]

Chapter 15

Secrets of D-Day

On 20 March 1944, MI5 appeared to have made a breakthrough in the Josephine investigation. MI5 officer Robert Seeds[1] reported a contact with a woman called Mary Josephine Owen, an Austrian who had married a teacher at Malvern College. Seeds wrote to Guy Liddell saying that Owen had recently returned to the UK after internment in the Middle East, where she had been 'spreading propaganda on behalf of the enemy as apparently one of an organised group during Rommel's advance on Cairo.'[2]

Owen had continued to show 'pro-Nazi attitudes' during her internment but was now free and back living with her husband in the UK. Most concerning of all was that Mrs Owen 'sought out the company of military officers, one of whom is now working in the War Office transport department who is in her financial as well as her amorous debt'.[3]

What linked her to Kraemer was the fact that Josephine Owen was also a close friend of a pro-Nazi Swedish minister in Hungary from whom she was in receipt of correspondence via Swedish friends living in London, who in turn were in 'undercover touch' with Stockholm.

Seeds said he was very concerned by the way she had been granted her freedom in Britain and was 'now working for the international Red Cross in a not wholly unconfidential position'[4] and no one seemed to be taking any notice of her.

Liddell told Blunt to follow up the lead.[5]

It looked promising. There were a number of Josephine reports relating to troop and transport movements in Liverpool and Bristol, which were first transmitted by Kraemer on 24 June 1943. Owen arrived in the UK on 6 June and then travelled from the Clyde to Farnham in Surrey.

Seeds concluded: 'It seems quite possible that she passed through and spent the requisite number of days in Liverpool and Bristol,' adding, 'it is perhaps significant here that Josephine has ignored Liverpool and Bristol in her intelligence apart from this first message.'[6]

Further investigations showed that the 'continental backgrounds' of Owen and 'Josephine' matched and that Owen had many contacts with fairly 'senior officers and officials'.

Seeds also suspected that Owen was operating a wireless transmitter set from her home in Farnham.

Hart, however, was far from convinced that they had their woman. In fact, he wrote to Seeds saying he had established from alternative intelligence sources in France that Josephine was in fact a man. Seeds vehemently disagreed and wrote a two-page memo discrediting the misgendering theory.[7]

Then around the same time, MI6's man in Stockholm, Peter Falk, managed to secure the services of Kraemer's Stockholm housekeeper, who had taken a sharp dislike to the grand Mrs Kraemer. Under instruction from Falk she had used a pat of cold butter to make a mould of the key used by Kraemer to lock his office safe.[8] Falk had measured this up and sent the exact schematics of the key to Herbert Hart in London, who had arranged for MI5 boffins to make a replica which was duly sent back to Stockholm. It fitted like a glove.

Inside the safe, the housekeeper recovered a piece of paper with the name and personal details of a woman called Irene Ward. Enquiries in London revealed that an Irene Ward had been turned down for a job with MI5 because of her poor typing and shorthand skills.

The housekeeper said Kraemer treated the Ward piece of paper with 'extreme secrecy and care'.[9]

MI5 now had another suspect: the disgruntled MI5 reject Irene Ward.

Both investigations soon fizzled out. Neither suspect had anything like the access to the kinds of high-quality and wide-ranging top secret intelligence that Josephine was passing on.

The pressure was now on Blunt and Hart to get the investigation back on track and find the Nazi spy.

A year before, in 1942, MI5 had put Anthony Blunt in charge of one of the most closely guarded secrets of the Second World War: XXX (Triplex, regarded as so sensitive that it is still classified as secret) – the illegal extraction from diplomatic bags of any and all secret information passed from embassies representing neutral and Allied countries and their governments at home.[10] These diplomats had regular confidential briefings by the Chiefs of Staff and also had some access to British military facilities. Most, if not all, of them were also engaged in their own espionage, on each other as well as their British hosts. Despite the huge breach of diplomatic protocol it represented, Triplex was a sensible precaution in a time of war. It was just unfortunate that the man they gave the job to was Anthony Blunt. It further cemented his extraordinary oversight of all secret activity in the United Kingdom during the war.

In the closing months of 1943, his work with Dick White had paid off and Blunt was able to tell Moscow: 'I have spent a good deal of my time arranging for various kinds of most secret documents to come through me. I get in the ordinary course of my job the deciphered diplomatic telegrams, the diplomatic telephone conversations and the product of the various agents in the embassies.'

Tellingly, he informed his handlers: 'I have also managed to get myself in touch with Robertson [TA Robertson], who runs the double agents over the question of putting over false information through diplomatic channels. In this way I can usually get an idea of what is actually planned and what is being put across as cover.'[11]

Blunt began to take a closer look at the diplomatic pouches that were ferried between London and Stockholm by the Swedish Air and Naval Attachés based in London and his investigation revealed a duplication of the material being leaked by Josephine[12] and Hector. He reported back to Liddell and White that both Swedish attachés, Major Cervell (Air) and Count Johan Oxenstierna (Naval), 'were up to no good' and linked the Josephine (air force) and Hector (naval) leaks to the two diplomats.[13] Blunt's human intelligence source in the embassy was a female agent codenamed Lemon, whom he had recruited from the Swedish staff.[14] Blunt's charm, when he chose to project it, also worked on women. In the MI5 office the secretarial staff likened him to the matinee film idol Leslie Howard. Agent Lemon was Susan Maxwell, widow of Colonel Somerset Maxwell, killed at El Alamein fighting with Montgomery's 8th Army.[15]

Blunt told Moscow: 'Her value is she knows some of the Swedish diplomats ... she used to have a boyfriend there, Knut Wijk, from whom she got a certain amount of gossip.'[16]

It looked as if Blunt had at last found the source of the leak. Although MI5 was unable to prove that either of them were working for the Germans, the matter was considered so serious that the troubling case of 'Josephine' was finally raised with Churchill.[17]

The prime minister was told in an MI5 briefing: 'A document recently captured from the Germans showed that the enemy was unusually well informed about production figures of aircraft construction in Great Britain. The German report was evidently based on a large number of sources, some of them emanating from neutral air attachés in London ... For example, most secret and sensitive sources recently provided information that the Swedish air attaché, Major Cervell, had sent back long, well-compiled reports on air matters that included detailed information on types of aircraft, general facts on tactics etc ... We know him to have reported that he had "precise details on the production of fighters and bombers in the UK".[18]

MI5 also noted that Cervell visited RAF fighter and bomber stations, where he picked up more sensitive combat-related intelligence.

The report concluded: 'There is, unfortunately, very clear evidence that information reaching Stockholm reaches both the Germans and the Japanese.'[19]

What Churchill knew so did the Soviets, who had been carefully briefed about the progress of the Josephine investigation by Blunt.[20]

Back in Stockholm, Peter Falk, the SIS officer who had recruited the Kraemers' housekeeper, had made another breakthrough. The housekeeper had now found inside the safe other papers[21] written by members of the British Cabinet and War Office. A separate set had been taken from the Quebec talks in August 1943 when Roosevelt and Churchill had met to discuss plans for the prosecution of the war. Falk realised that these 'Josephine' papers were extraordinarily sensitive original minutes of the conversations between the two Western leaders, 'material that affected the entire war effort',[22] and included the Western Allies' views on Stalin, terms for a possible peace with the German High Command and the future arrangements for the occupation of Germany after the war. Whoever had leaked them must have held a very senior position in Whitehall indeed. Knowing that he could not risk the usual Foreign Office channels with such explosive documents and fearful of further leaks, he decided to return at once to London and deliver them in person.

On the evening of 23 December 1943, Peter Falk walked into the cathedral of Whig grandeur of the Reform Club. He had given his coat to the porter and been shown a seat upstairs in the library. A few minutes later, Anthony Blunt walked in and shut the door behind him. Falk laid out all the documents before Blunt, telling him what he feared most of all was the Allied secrets falling into the hands of the Soviets.[23]

According to Falk – who described this incident in his unpublished memoir – Blunt began by suggesting that the documents were fake. When Falk insisted he knew they were not and repeated his fears about the Russians getting hold of them, the unflappable Blunt uncharacteristically lost his temper: 'I can categorically assure you there is no cross knowledge.' He told Falk, 'The Soviets know nothing about this; they're only interested in the timing of the second front.'[24] Nevertheless, it was clear to Falk[25] that someone who had access to Roosevelt and Churchill's private conversations, or at least first-hand reports of them, was passing them direct to Kraemer.

Steadying himself, Blunt gathered up the papers to look at them more closely later on and took Falk into dinner, in the course of which he managed to reassure him that he would take care of the 'Josephine' leaks as he was certain that the Swedes were responsible for the breaches of security.

Among the other sensitive papers in Kraemer's safe were reports that detailed how Heinrich Himmler and Walter Schellenberg had held secret talks in Stockholm, where they discussed working with the British in return for immunity from prosecution after the war. This was information Blunt knew would feed Stalin's paranoia that Britain and Germany would reach a separate deal and turn on him.

There is no record of whether Blunt passed on Falk's documents and suspicions to his MI5 superiors. It seems very likely that he didn't. In the 1970s (the report is undated), MI5 continued to be so worried about Josephine that they commissioned a 300-page report from SIS officer Patricia McCallum, who had served in the registry during the war. This report, quietly transferred by MI5 to the National Archives in 2003, mentions the cutting of the key and Kraemer's housekeeper, but mysteriously makes no mention whatsoever of Falk's name or of his meeting with Blunt so it would appear that there was no official record of this meeting. We do know that when Falk tried to raise the matter of the Kraemer material with his SIS boss he was warned to keep quiet. He later discovered the source of the warning was Anthony Blunt.[26]

Guy Liddell's diary only says Blunt had now successfully traced the Josephine leak to the Swedish air attaché in London, Frank Cervell. Blunt wrote to SIS baldly stating: 'The source of information is to be found with the Swedish Military Attaché in London.'[27]

As far as MI5 were now concerned, the identity of Josephine had been established. The only question was whether to expel Cervell and Oxenstierna. Blunt was able to persuade his superiors that it would be far more useful to keep them in London, where they could continue to be used as conduits for MI5-sanctioned intelligence to be fed to Kraemer.

MI6 wanted to take more robust action and approach the Swedes to have Kraemer kicked out of Sweden. When Sir Stewart Menzies came up with a plan to flush out Cervell by planting on him 'rather hot' material, Blunt poured cold water on the idea by arguing[28] that Cervell was only interested in military aircraft production figures.

Somehow Kraemer got wind of the plan to expel him from Sweden and told[29] Hans Schaefer of the Deutsche Lufthansa: 'I know that the British are trying to get rid of me. I do not mind as I have one very good friend in the Swedish Foreign Office.' This conversation was relayed back to Falk in Stockholm, who passed it on to Herbert Hart in London.[30]

Liddell, who now believed he had shut down Josephine, had more pressing matters with which he wanted Blunt to concern himself.

Blunt remained in firm control of the diplomatic communications emanating from the neutral embassies. He wrote in his memoir, published in 2009: 'With the prospect of the invasion of Europe the question of possible leakage was even more crucial than before. We had by then established a fairly good control over the communications of most of the neutral missions through which information was likely to be passed to the Germans.'

Blunt's work on Triplex and his management of the embassy agents was also well known to the Russians. An NKVD report held in the Moscow archive said: 'TONY meets these agents and manages and directs them. He obtains material, some of which he passes to us, but he does not tell us in detail about his work.'[31]

In Blunt's desperation to please his Russian employer he had no qualms about putting agents' lives at risk.

One Kremlin-bound report contained the identities, descriptions and code names of many of the MI5 agents working out of the London embassies, including the loyal Mrs Maxwell and an agent called 'Sevat', whom White had planted among the entourage of Prince Bernhard.[32] Under Liddell's recommendation, Blunt was next appointed to the ultra-secret Twist committee, an inter-departmental committee responsible for the deception of the enemy in the run-up to D-Day, and directly answerable to the Chiefs of Staff. Blunt's role on the committee was the 'dissemination of disinformation through MI5 channels in London' by exploiting his unique access to the diplomatic bags.[33]

By early 1944, Blunt was not only the point of contact for most intelligence shared between MI5 and MI6 and responsible for the oversight of diplomatic correspondence, he was now *ordered* to plant intelligence material among the Triplex diplomatic correspondence.

Churchill and the Joint Intelligence Committee were told: 'Steps are already being taken to supply certain attachés and heads of missions with misleading information. This will help to some extent to distort the intelligence they supply.'[34]

Blunt must not have been able to believe his luck and informed his Soviet handlers that he 'conducted this work outside the MI5 network and is not accountable to superiors in the Service in this regard'.[35]

And with Cervell now widely accepted as Josephine within the service there was little to concern him, even if he knew that story was unlikely to withstand the coming months.

In the weeks before D-Day, MI6 were able to report that the Germans were desperate for more intelligence, especially about D-Day. But Kraemer's sources were no longer delivering the goods, so much so that he was reduced to filing intelligence reports culled from Western newspapers freely available in Stockholm. By April 1944, MI5 concluded that Josephine's reports had been rendered 'wholly inaccurate'[36] and were no longer a threat to Allied operations. It appeared as if Blunt had been correct about Cervell.

Yet Kraemer's star remained high.

His importance to German intelligence-gathering was affirmed by Schellenberg when he came to assess the capabilities of the Stockholm operation in 1944. An audit of the Abwehr officers working out of the Swedish capital revealed that some of his agents were work-shy or hoping to see out the remainder of the war quietly in neutral Sweden. One intelligence officer hadn't made a single intelligence report since he had been stationed in Sweden. He and four others were recalled to Berlin. But Schellenberg said of the German air attaché: 'Kraemer and his two assistants [Josephine and Hector] have done good work in the British/US field.'[37]

One of the reasons the Abwehr chiefs had such unbending confidence in Kraemer was that they were able to check the accuracy of his reports against one of their other star agents operating out of London. His name was Roman Czerniawski, a Polish officer who had been attached to French intelligence in 1940, when after the German occupation he set up a resistance organisation. He was betrayed and captured by the Gestapo and tortured into working for the Abwehr. In fact, Czerniawski had long been working for the British (code name BRUTUS) and was an integral part of Operation Fortitude, the deception plans in the run-up to D-Day and which fell under the oversight of the Twist committee.

As the days ticked down towards the biggest amphibious landings in history, security surrounding the operation took on paramount, and often paranoid, importance. Only a handful of military planners knew the date and true location of the invasion and the identity of the units to be used in Operation Overlord. During this tense period, code breakers at Bletchley Park decrypted an intercepted message sent by teleprinter to the Foreign Office in Berlin that threw the D-Day planners into panic.

The secret message identified the formation and location of the 2nd Tactical Air Force, a newly founded RAF group made up of units from Fighter Command and Bomber Command that was intended to support the Allied armies during the invasion.[38]

The message had been dispatched from Stockholm and the sender's code name was 'Josephine'. Karl Heinz Kraemer appeared to be back in business and Josephine was once again sending shockingly accurate intelligence.

In the run-up to D-Day, the objectives of Blunt and the rest of the British Soviet spies were broadly in line with those of the Western Allies – to establish a second front in Europe.

The Soviet leader's calls on Churchill and Roosevelt to open the second front and alleviate the pressure in the East were becoming deafening. It seemed to matter little to him whether the British or Americans were ready. Indeed in a moment of pure hypocrisy, Ivan Maisky, the Russian ambassador to London, and Molotov, the Foreign Minister, had demanded the British open up a second front within just eight days of the alliance between communist Russia and Nazi Germany ending when Hitler launched Operation Barbarossa.

Whether the Western Allies succeeded or were pushed back into the sea didn't really matter to Stalin. The landings would force Hitler to transfer divisions from the Eastern to the Western Front, enabling Stalin to launch his planned decisive Red Army offensive and begin the final thrust towards Berlin.

It was a reminder that he still firmly believed the British were as much a threat to communist Russia as the Nazis.

This view was partly informed and encouraged by Anthony Blunt and Kim Philby, who passed on a welter of anti-Russia briefings and documents to their Soviet handlers. One NKVD report based on the Cambridge spies' intelligence sent to Stalin suggested the British and Americans were so concerned about the threat of Bolshevism in Europe that they wanted to open the second front nearer Russia rather than in France and postpone the landings to later in the year. A diplomatic intelligence note sent by Blunt read: 'to eliminate the Bolshevik danger, the Americans are planning to build an army of ten million men to guarantee a democratic Europe.'[39]

In fact, this was deception intelligence deliberately fed by the British to Portuguese and Swiss diplomats intended to disguise the Allies' real D-Day plans. Churchill, who was yet to divulge to Stalin the date and location for D-Day, had to reassure the Soviet leader that the invasion would be in northern France and very soon.

Nothing, however, could allay Stalin's paranoia. On 19 May 1944, Anatoly Gorsky, the NKVD joint head of the London *residenzia*, ordered Blunt and the other spies to 'focus their attention on the uncovering of British deception activities in regard to the Soviet Union, on which we do not possess any intelligence information so far.'[40]

But they were unable to, for the simple reason that there weren't any.

Nevertheless, Winston Churchill was aware that the war would take on a different dynamic once British forces had a foothold in France.

As the clock ran down towards D-Day, British intelligence belatedly attempted to confront the question of the Soviet threat in a post-invasion European landscape.

An intelligence document[41] dated 6 June 1944 and entitled 'SIS plans for Anti-Soviet Operations' at last confirmed to Stalin that the British had begun an all-out counter-intelligence war with Russia. The document emphasised that the post-D-Day geopolitical landscape anti-Soviet operations were to be conducted in 'absolute secrecy' and 'have to be completely different in nature from those we ran against XK [Soviet Russia] before the war'.[42]

Blunt and Philby made sure that Stalin was sent these reports of SIS's counter-intelligence call to arms against the NKVD that envisioned activating agents across Europe to penetrate Soviet intelligence, although SIS still refused to countenance any operations on Russian soil.[43]

The authors of the report said that to 'eliminate any suspicion, the head of the section working against XK must have excellent cover'.[44] In a sense they were right, because the person chosen was Kim Philby.

Yet, for now in 1944, the start of the fifth year of the war, Anthony Blunt was the most important British spy serving Soviet interests.

Aside from his official roles, Blunt had also recruited his own agents and was running a sub-spying operation outside MI5 that he could use to serve both British and Russian interests. One of his key agents in military intelligence was another Cambridge graduate whom Blunt had recruited to the Soviet cause. Leonard Long was the son of an East London carpenter who had won a place at Cambridge in the 1930s. Long, the first and only non-public schoolboy in the Cambridge spy ring, was an idealist from a working-class background who saw Russian communism as the best route to ending the English class system. When Long told Blunt he had access to intelligence analysis based on Ultra, the Soviets were able to know not only what the Germans were planning on the Western Front but also how the Allies interpreted that intelligence. In this role, Long, and therefore Blunt, now also had access to the most secret intelligence derived from decoded intercepts decrypted at Bletchley Park.[45] Blunt milked him for all he was worth, providing the Russians with a valuable window into German operations.

Meanwhile, Churchill's focus on the threat to the security of D-Day was more directed towards the French. When he discovered that De Gaulle's French National Committee had a number of communist members who would be involved in invasion planning, he summoned Petrie and Menzies to Downing Street to see what could be done. The security and intelligence chiefs persuaded him that they had systems in place to deal with any possible penetration of the security apparatus. Churchill later told Duff Cooper: 'I suppose you realise that we are weeding remorsefully every single known Communist from our secret organisations.'[46]

The Supreme Headquarters Allied Expeditionary Force (SHAEF) was located in a central London red-brick building called Norfolk House, close to the offices of MI5 in St James's and MI6 at 54 Broadway[47] and 14 Ryder Street, where SIS Section V (counter-intelligence) was based. There was keen competition among the young officers of MI5 and MI6 for a plum posting at the newly created entity. Selection was, as usual, a matter of whom one knew. One of the first through the doors of Norfolk House was Christopher Blunt, brother of Anthony, who was a principal officer in the censorship department. Not long afterwards, his brother Anthony followed him through the door.[48]

SHAEF personnel directories reveal that it was British officers who dominated and controlled the Supreme Allied Command's intelligence establishment in the run-up to D-Day.[49]

Kim Philby was not one of them.[50] Strangely, perhaps because he was so focused on his own intrigues inside MI6, Philby was not privy to the deception plans for D-Day, which underscores that at this stage of the war it was Blunt not Philby who was at the heart of NKVD operations in London.

But Blunt now had prime access to the secrets of the most critical operation of the Second World War. If he knew the timing and location of Overlord then so did Stalin. In fact, on 6 May, Blunt passed on[51] a 'complete copy of the entire deception plan' devised as part of Overlord. At this stage of the war, Soviet interests were undoubtedly best served by the success of an Allied landing in northern France. But Stalin had been briefed that D-Day was an extremely risky operation that had as much chance of failure as it did of success.[52]

As part of Fortitude, Blunt was able to play a crucial role in the deception of German High Command.

Hugh Trevor-Roper, the historian who was working for MI6 counter-intelligence during D-Day, said of the Kremlin's intentions at the time: 'If the Russians had thought they could win the war on their own we would have been butchered on the beaches. I don't know if Blunt was told and don't know if he would have dared to leak it.'[53]

Patricia McCallum's report in the 1970s fails to establish the identity of Josephine. But it also makes repeated reference to 'Maj. Blunt' as if he was merely another MI5 officer when by the 1970s the SIS hierarchy knew full well that Blunt was a Soviet spy after his 'confession' in 1964. Perhaps it seemed not to make sense that Blunt would pass on secrets to the Germans. How would that help Russian war aims? But given that the two most significant lines of inquiry of the McCallum report, D-Day and Market Garden, show Josephine operating in ways that clearly align with Stalin's war aims, the suspicion that Blunt most certainly did know and was prepared to 'leak it' becomes unavoidable.

For Stalin the main focus was how his troops in the East could capitalise on the distraction and the expected redeployments of the Wehrmacht armies once Overlord was under way. Yet there were genuine security reasons for not letting the Russians into the D-Day secrets. The code breakers at Bletchley had obtained evidence from the Ultra intercepts that German intelligence had broken some of the Soviet ciphers.[54] Anything the Western Allies told the Soviets was at risk of being picked up by the Germans – and the Cambridge spies must have known this.

Anthony Blunt's role at SHAEF was to help in the principal deception operations that would convince the Germans that the Allies were planning a landing in the Pas-de-Calais. He worked closely with Czerniawski, aka Brutus, run by his old friend Tomas Harris (a fellow member of 'the Group'), and Garbo, run by Christopher Blunt's close acquaintance Lord Astor,[55] who were sending false information to the Germans about Allied forces being built up in Kent as part of a mythical, non-existent force called FUSAG (First United States Army Group).

This gave Blunt the opportunity to combine his expertise in planting misinformation in the secret diplomatic communications of the foreign embassies and his new role at SHAEF in helping to play back[56] the double agents. To assist him in getting close to the Swedish delegation in London, Blunt had tasked Jack Hewit (Agent Dumbo) with befriending the chauffeur working at the Swedish embassy.[57]

Kraemer's 'Josephine reports' to Berlin therefore included a good deal of deception material that mirrored the intelligence sent by double-cross agents Garbo and Brutus, who had until then been regarded as the crucial players in the deception of German High Command; indeed after the war, Colonel Roger Hesketh, a key member of the deception team who wrote a report on the D-Day leak, expressed his dismay and bafflement at this discovery: 'we had no idea that Kraemer was playing with our toys' he wrote plaintively.[58]

Meanwhile, Blunt, supported by Hart, assured Liddell that Kraemer was merely copying Brutus and Garbo intelligence reports, repackaging them and presenting the intelligence as his own.

The Germans were of course still using Brutus to help cross-check the accuracy of Josephine.

On 1 May 1944, Brutus's Abwehr handler asked about a Josephine message: 'Is there a 9th and 19th Air Support Command in the 9th American Air Force?'[59]

Brutus replied on 5 May: 'The 9th Air Support Command is concentrated in the Kent area which is to be its theatre of operations, on aerodromes between Ashford and Tonbridge.'

The US 9th Air Force, commanded by Lieutenant General Lewis H Brereton, would play a key role in softening up the enemy before the invasion of Normandy and supporting ground forces on D-Day and helping to make possible the rapid advance through France.

Contrary to reports by Kraemer and Brutus, the Air Force command centre was actually in RAF Middle Wallop in Hampshire and its aircraft took off from air bases in Hampshire and south-west England.[60] Josephine was precisely mirroring the wider Fortitude deception material and it was this which so astonished Hesketh immediately after the war and was apparently still causing MI5 to scratch their heads 30 years later.

Chapter 16

War of Spies

The Operation Fortitude deception plan, involving a mass of false communications by a vast network of agents run by MI5 and MI6, had been a spectacular success. The Abwehr and the German High Command remained completely deceived by D-Day who believed that the location for the landings was to be the Pas-de-Calais. The Abwehr's own star spy, Karl Heinz Kraemer, played a crucial role in this deception. In fact, Kraemer sent more reports from Josephine supporting the Pas-de-Calais invasion plan than Garbo and Brutus combined.[1]

In the critical hours and days after the landings, Josephine continued to play a key part in the Allies' deception by providing intelligence that told the Germans that Normandy was only a feint and that the real target were still the beaches further down the coast.[2]

Kraemer may have even single-handedly saved D-Day in the vital days that the Allies were securing their bridgehead in Normandy and when they were most vulnerable to a German counter-attack. It was well known that in the hours after the invasion, the Germans ordered their armoured reserves to the landing sites. However, this order was swiftly reversed and between 8 and 10 June, the Germans held back waiting for what they thought would be the main invasion force. After the war, Colonel Hesketh investigated what had changed the Germans' mind about committing the reserves. According to Hesketh, Field Marshal Alfred Jodl, who was responsible for routing the most important intelligence to Hitler's office, attributed Kraemer's Josephine intelligence, rather than Garbo's, as being the most influential in holding back the panzers.[3]

The deception was so convincing that for several weeks after D-Day, as many as 22 divisions of the German Army held their defensive posture at Pas-de-Calais.[4]

Germany had 1,400 tanks in theatre at the beginning of the Normandy invasion. Roughly 400 were south of the Loire with Army Group G. Of the balance remaining in northern France, fewer than 400 saw any action within the first 48 hours of the Allied operations.

Despite this, Josephine's role in the D-Day deception plans has been largely airbrushed from history. Jodl's observation that Josephine was more important than Garbo was dismissed by Col Hesketh's research[5] into Fortitude after the war which claimed Kraemer had simply copied the intelligence from Garbo's reports. However, MI5's much more comprehensive investigation into Josephine released more than 30 years later came to a rather different conclusion.

MI6's Patricia McCallum[6] found that the Josephine material on the D-Day orders of battle must have been obtained independently from Garbo and Brutus, most likely in her view from Kraemer's Hungarian sources based in Lisbon and Madrid. The Germans had also taken steps to ensure that Kraemer did not see the Garbo and Brutus intelligence in case he was tempted to copy it. She said this proved conclusively that Cervell could not have been Kraemer's source, adding rather tellingly: 'One thing is certain. Had Josephine been a real agent she would have had to be a member of the deception staff! In no other way could her message have been based on Fortitude material.'[7]

* * *

Leopold Trepper and Anatoly Gurevich, the two Rote Kapelle agents, had now been captured by the Germans, but were able to continue feeding the Kremlin useful intelligence even though they were Nazi prisoners. In an elaborate game of Funkspiel, both agents tricked the Germans into believing they had swapped sides. The Germans were so taken in by them that Gurevich had even persuaded his Nazi handlers to pay his son's private school fees and Trepper was so trusted that he was allowed out for escorted shopping trips.[8]

On 13 September 1943, Trepper slipped his guards during a visit to a Paris pharmacy. His first port of call was Charles Spaak, a communist member of his network and the brother of the Belgian prime minister. Trepper had hidden a large metal box crammed full of dollars and false identity cards.[9]

From an address in Paris he arranged for Spaak's wife to send an urgent message to the Soviet embassy in London: 'Am alive will soon meet, Otto.'[10] Adding: 'I will be at the church every Sunday between 10 and 11am.'[11]

Trepper was now taking his orders directly from the NKVD in London, where station chief Ivan Chichaev coordinated Soviet efforts against both the Nazi and the Western Allies in Europe.[12]

Chichaev was at the heart of a highly organised and sophisticated espionage and counter-espionage operation. The embassy was run by a cadre of NKVD officers who employed 40 local British staff. Chichaev oversaw a steady flow of secret Soviet agents travelling between Sweden and London.[13] There were also satellite offices scattered across the capital, some known to British intelligence and some not. Chichaev could call upon an unknown number of agents to carry out Moscow's bidding, among whom the best known were the Cambridge spies, but the truth was there were many more, perhaps hundreds of British and foreign diplomats, spies, couriers and cut-outs working for the Soviets. There were similar operations in Stockholm, Berne, Madrid and Lisbon – all supporting each other in an all-out intelligence war against the West in 1944.

Stalin still believed that the British and the Nazis were conspiring against Russia and would eventually settle their differences in order to defeat the Bolsheviks.

One NKVD agent reported back to the Kremlin 'that the German Foreign Office in Berlin had made contact with the Western Allies and Ribbentrop personally was handling the negotiations.'[14]

Although this was untrue the arrival of the Allies on the Continent had transformed the face of the war. From a Soviet perspective the worst possible outcome now was a peace deal between Hitler and Russia's Western Allies.

Anthony Blunt's earlier intelligence from Kraemer's personal safe, alluding to secret negotiations between Himmler and the British taking place in Sweden, made such a scenario even more credible in the eyes of the Kremlin.

Stalin, careful not to let his mask slip, sent a telegram to Churchill on D-Day congratulating him on his success, proclaiming: 'History will record this deed as an achievement of the highest order.'[15]

This was faint praise indeed.

For Stalin, Overlord was always going to be too little, too late.

The Russian leader had been planning a D-Day of his own. As we have learned, he hoped the Allies' landings in Europe would force Hitler to divert large numbers of divisions from the Eastern Front to face the invaders from the sea. He waited in vain for two weeks, during which time barely a tank was sent west, before launching Operation Bagration, named after the Russian general who had helped defeat Napoleon. In manpower and resources, Bagration dwarfed Overlord and destroyed 28 of 34 divisions of Hitler's Army Group Centre, completely shattering the German front line. It was the biggest defeat in German military history, with around 450,000 German casualties and trapping a further 300,000 more German soldiers.

A few weeks later, the Lvov–Sandomierz Offensive allowed Soviet forces to recapture Belorussia and Ukraine within its 1941 borders and set the Red Army on the road to Warsaw and Berlin.

Meanwhile, the Battle of Normandy was developing into a bitter, hard-fought campaign. The bocage landscape of small fields separated by thick hedges and narrow sunken lanes gave defenders the advantage. Casualties – especially among the infantry – were heavy, leading to fears of an attritional stalemate reminiscent of the First World War.

On 12 July, Churchill wrote to Stalin: 'The fighting is very hard and before the recent battles, for which casualties have not yet come in, we and the Americans had lost 64,000 men. However, there is every evidence that the enemy has lost at least as many and we have besides 51,000 prisoners in the bag. Considering that we have been on the offensive and had been landing from the sea I consider the enemy has been severely mauled. The front will continue to broaden and the fighting will be unceasing.'[16]

On 24 July, he wrote again: 'I have just returned from three days in Normandy. Our advances have not been as fast or as far as I had hoped, but the weather has prevented on most days the use of our superior air power and has gravely impeded operations.'

Stalin exhorted Churchill to make even greater sacrifices: 'You tell me about the planned new offensive in Normandy. If launched it will be of tremendous importance in the situation in which Germany finds herself and will make Hitler's plight pretty sore indeed.'[17]

With his allies bogged down in a war of attrition in the West and southern England facing its first barrage of 'doodlebug' flying bombs, one of Germany's new range of superweapons, Stalin looked forward to a triumphant march into the heart of Germany.

Stalin's Red Army was in the driving seat and the Soviet leader could now turn his mind to the shape and control of postwar Europe.

Sudoplatov recalled Leopold Trepper to Moscow to reappraise him of the military and geopolitical situation and to receive his new orders.[18]

At the same time, Anatoly Gorsky, Blunt's Russian handler, was posted to America to become the first secretary of the Russian embassy in Washington. The Russians had been reluctant to disturb Gorsky in London while Blunt was working at the heart of the SHAEF headquarters.[19]

After D-Day the MI5 officer returned to his normal duties.[20]

Blunt's replacement handler Boris Krotov[21] was determined to drive the Cambridge spies into making even greater betrayals of their country in line with Russia's post-war geopolitical ambitions.

In London, Anthony Blunt's access and influence had received a final, extraordinary boost when he was put in charge of the selection and editing of MI5's monthly written briefings for Winston Churchill covering British intelligence operations in every theatre of activity. It was a role that gave him unrestricted access to MI5 and MI6 files as well as being the controlling hand on what Winston Churchill knew about Blunt's own operations. The document was delivered in person by Petrie for the sole eyes of the prime minister.[22]

The intelligence historian and spy writer, Nigel West, summed up Blunt's new role: 'Few spies in history could have ever been presented with such a spectacular opportunity to call for files or question colleagues and demand briefings on topics that would otherwise be completely outside the ambit of their duties. Quite simply, Blunt, who had been a Soviet agent since 1934, was granted a licence to delve into just about any operational issue that caught his interest.'

However, when Petrie handed over the sixth, and most up to date, report to Churchill, one subject was conspicuous by its absence. There was no reference to 'Josephine', a case that still preoccupied MI5 and whose leaks were a cause of serious concern for the military planners. According to West, the 'passage was removed from the report's final version'.[23]

It can be no accident that one of the officers in charge of the investigation into Josephine had omitted it from the official MI5 report sent to Churchill.

And it is easy to understand why Blunt didn't want to draw Cabinet attention to his involvement in the sensitive case. Blunt had almost complete control over the investigation into Josephine and the German air attaché Karl Heinz Kraemer. The fewer questions asked about its progress, or lack of progress, the better.

But 'Josephine' was still very much in the minds of the military planners. After D-Day, intelligence would continue to play a key role in the final defeat of Germany. In the summer of 1944, it was crucial that the enemy was kept guessing as to how the Western Allies intended to deliver the *coup de grâce* against the Nazi forces opposing them in northern Europe.

Among those attached to Montgomery's headquarters at the 21st Army Group was Leo Long, the British intelligence officer serving with MI14, the directorate that was responsible for analysing the strength and deployment of the enemy. Long's deployment to the front line gave Blunt, who remained in London passing on and manipulating intelligence from all his other sources, a fly-on-the-wall view of the British military's progress in Belgium and when Long moved to SHAEF in Paris, his help may have proved crucial in Agent Josephine's greatest betrayal.

Chapter 17

Bridge of Spies

In the aftermath of the victory at Falaise, the Allies' breakout from Normandy was explosive. The Germans were forced into a disorganised retreat as Allied air and land power finally began to tell. Churchill and his most senior general in the field, Bernard Montgomery, wanted to maximise their hard-won initiative and saw an opportunity to deliver a final blow to the enemy. The result was a daring plan to drop 40,000 parachute and glider troops in Holland to secure the bridges that would open the path to the German interior, the industrial Ruhr and on to Berlin ahead of the Russians.

The race to Berlin made Operation Market Garden a critical moment in the war.

Churchill had at first been cautious about Montgomery's plan, but the rapid advances of the Red Army after Operation Bagration had forced him to upgrade the threat from the east. There were also reports of Russians operating deep in German-held territories, including Romania, Bulgaria and Yugoslavia, conspiring to impose Soviet-friendly governments.

In August, the South African leader Jan Smuts, one of Churchill's closest confidants, wrote to the British prime minister, reflecting the fear that Russia represented a serious threat to the Balkans, most notably to Greece and Turkey, where Britain's own interests lay.[1]

At the same time, SIS was at last waking up to the reality of a post-war Soviet-dominated Europe. In September, Colonel Valentine Vivian, deputy head of SIS, tackled the communist (XK) problem head-on, alerting[2] the Cabinet to Soviet infiltration operations in France and Italy and the scale of the counter-intelligence task against the Russians. He warned that the Russians had known all about Allied operations, including Operation Torch, the invasion of French North Africa in 1942, through contact with 'British officers' who he believed were still in position.[3] While the Russians might have been trusted not to jeopardise these operations in 1942, after D-Day the political landscape was very different. He was forced to remind the government that SIS had not recruited a single new agent in Russia since the start of the war to combat the Soviet threat.[4] The fact that they had agreed with the Russians not to send any SOE operatives into Eastern Europe while funnelling dozens of Soviet operatives into Western Europe cannot have been an irony lost on him.

Explaining the dangers posed by the 'stagnation' in Russian counter-intelligence operations, Vivian reported on 6 September 1944: 'It must be borne in mind that Communism has not been a current SIS target since 1939. We have gradually lost practically all our special agents who were at one time particularly effective and in addition the war has deprived us of our links with various official sources from which we used to get valuable intelligence.'[5] In short, nothing had been done to counter the emerging Soviet menace. Vivian concluded: 'The fact remains that we have not taken effective steps to get our house in order, either at home or overseas, or to grapple appropriately with solving a problem that will almost certainly be one of the most important tasks of the future SIS.'

The unpalatable truth was that in 1944, SIS had not got a single agent operating in Moscow and now Vivian and some of his colleagues feared the chickens were coming home to roost.

Vivian warned his political masters that they could not wait until the war was over before doing something about it. The time to act was now: 'The moment when local governments will begin to be restored in the liberated countries, when resistance movements with a heavily Communist flavour may exert a decisive influence out of proportion to their real national significance, and when underground groups supported or directed from Moscow and run by covert or overt Soviet organisations abroad may lead to the creation of governments totally unrepresentative of the wishes of the majority, may even provoke civil war and postpone indefinitely the restoration of law and order. It may be we have already missed the opportunity to shed light, successfully, on this vital stage in history. We must therefore realise that we have to make at a minimum certain decisive efforts to save the situation by urgent creation of an organisation overseas.'[6]

Vivian explained that 'Russia already controls the most important sectors of the resistance movement in Yugoslavia; it also exerts a measure of control over the movement in Greece, and it is possible that the Bulgarian Communist Party, which Moscow has always rated as the most effective party outside the USSR, is the main driving force behind the anti-fascist movement in Bulgaria. Romania will be an easy victim of Soviet psychological warfare as soon as the time is ripe. Russia can always count on the inherent hostility of the Balkan people towards the Axis dictatorship and on the outstanding victories of its forces on the battlefield.'

Vivian's final recommendation was for the immediate reactivation of Section IX, the counter-Soviet intelligence department that he now said should be led by a senior and effective officer.

In September, Stewart Menzies, head of MI6, called Kim Philby into his office to inform him that he was to be the officer to take charge of section IX.[7]

Philby's appointment was the culmination of a long and ruthless campaign by the Soviet agent to demolish the prospects of the man best qualified for the job – Felix Cowgill, the man who had first got wind of Agent Josephine a year and a half earlier. Cowgill, unable to resist the influence of Blunt and Philby as well as the rest of 'the Group', promptly resigned.

Next on Philby's hit list was Jane Archer. She had been forced out of MI5 after Krivitsky in 1940 but had not forgotten what the Russian defector had told her about the Russian double agents. In January 1945, she had been ordered by Valentine Vivian to transfer to the newly revamped section IX under Philby. She suspected at least one of the new team might be a Soviet agent. She ended up plumping for the wrong one – Colville Barclay.[8] Philby was sufficiently spooked to make a request to see the files relating to Krivitsky and Soviet agent John King to make sure there was no incriminating detail that might come back to bite him.

Philby wrote in his memoir that immediately after being made head of section IX, 'I was in the middle of my recruiting campaign when Vivian told me that Jane Archer had become available, suggesting that she would make an excellent addition to Section IX. The suggestion came as a nasty shock, especially as I could think of no plausible reason for resisting it. After Guy Liddell, Jane was perhaps the ablest professional intelligence officer ever employed by MI5. She had spent a big chunk of a shrewd lifetime studying communist activity in all its aspects. It was she who had interrogated General Krivitsky, the Red Army intelligence officer who defected to the West in 1937, only to kill himself a few years later in the United States – a disillusioned man. From him, she had got a tantalising scrap of information about a young English journalist whom the Soviet intelligence had sent to Spain during the Civil War. And here she was plunked down in my midst!'

As with anything Philby writes it needs to be treated with great care, not least because Krivitsky was in fact murdered by the Russians. One also wonders if Vivian was manipulated into placing Archer in Philby's power. Certainly he swiftly moved against her. Liddell records in his diaries, in an entry dated 6 September, a very short time after Philby was made head of section IX:

'Lunched with Jane (Archer) – she will lose her pensions if not reinstated. Certainly it would be a scandal if after her many years of service she was given nothing.'

It is not clear to what this refers, and Archer was to return to MI5 and go on to play a crucial role in the unmasking of the Cambridge spies. Nevertheless, her time at MI6 was over, so within days, Philby, no doubt assisted by Blunt, had disposed of the two greatest threats to revealing their true identities.

For Moscow it was nothing less than the seizure of control of the British counter-intelligence operations against Russia and gave Stalin a critical window into Britain's real attitude towards the Soviets at perhaps the most important moment in the war.

Stalin was partly acquainted with Allied double dealing after intelligence reports leaked to the Kremlin revealed the Western Allies had now deliberately halted the supply of vitally needed armaments and explosives to the Red Army.

According to Yuri Modin: 'Stalin was beside himself with rage. He calmed down, however, when he learned via Burgess and Philby this was a deliberate decision on the part of the Allies. Clearly they were unwilling for the Russians to move forward into Germany too quickly. Yet again, advanced intelligence enabled Stalin to make decisions without awaiting the pleasure of our allies.'[9]

The month before, the world had a bitter foretaste of how the Soviets would trample over the democratic rights of the peoples in countries conquered by the Red Army.

On 23 August 1944, King Michael of Romania, supported by all major parties, launched a *coup d'état*, overthrowing the pro-Nazi government. The coup facilitated the advance of the Red Army into Romania. An armistice signed three weeks later, on 12 September 1944, was on terms dictated by Moscow, with 160,000 Romanian prisoners forced to march to remote detention camps located in the Soviet Union. One third of them perished en route.

On 8 September, Soviet forces crossed the Bulgarian–Romanian border and overthrew the Bulgarian government after taking strategic points in Sofia and arresting government ministers. A new government of the Russian-controlled Fatherland Front was installed on 9 September.

To counter the communist threat, the Western Allies knew they would have to respond immediately.

By now Montgomery had persuaded Churchill that Market Garden would put the British at the head of an army entering Berlin before the Russians.[10] Roosevelt and Churchill, anticipating a quick and decisive victory after the D-Day breakout, even planned to host Stalin at The Hague at a conference to dictate terms for the settlement of the end of the war.[11] Such confidence for a quick victory was supported by the initial reception given to the first Allied troops crossing the German border in September near Aachen, who the BBC reported had been welcomed with flowers.[12]

The Russians were making plans of their own to bring some Soviet influence to bear in anticipated defeat of the German army in the West.

British intelligence was aware of Russian agents working inside the Metropole Hotel, Brussels, who had been openly approaching British officers for intelligence.[13]

Before Captain Peter Baker and Christiaan Lindemans had crossed the Dutch border in September 1944 to undertake their mission to Eindhoven, the young British captain had to take care of another matter threatening the British operational security.

A force of Georgian Russians, who had been co-opted into the Wehrmacht and deployed as part of the defending force on the Dutch section of the Atlantic Wall, had made contact with SOE and were making preparations to overthrow their German masters.[14] London had encouraged them to strike quickly in support of the Allies' advance, but Stalin had countermanded the order, telling them to stay put.

Instead, they joined Belgian communist resistance groups. Baker complained that along with a squad of British soldiers he was now responsible for 233 Russians. 'They had somehow accompanied the advancing British through Belgium and now wished to operate in Holland,' he wrote in his autobiography after the war.[15]

What London couldn't know was that Moscow had redoubled its intelligence operations on the Continent in anticipation of a German defeat before Christmas. The call went out to the Rote Kapelle to prepare for the next phase of the war, one that would be fought in the West.

Pavel Fitin, the NKVD's chief of intelligence, instructed the London rezidentura to heap rare praise and money on Anthony Blunt.

The British spy responded: 'It is difficult to say how proud I feel that work which I have been doing has been of value to the struggle against fascism ... the proof that it is worthwhile will, I hope, provide stimulus to producing better results. That greater possibilities of useful work will develop I have no doubt, but this will give me renewed energy for pursuing them since I now have positive evidence that the work is valuable.'[16]

On 22 August 1944, the London rezidentura was told to make even further efforts to engage Blunt and the rest of the Cambridge spies in Soviet operations.[17] The strain on Blunt was beginning to tell. The NKVD files reveal that Krotov had reported to the Centre: 'He may be nervous but he has such a colourless, typical English face, that it is hard to notice it. When he is nervous, he drinks.'[18]

Three weeks later on 15 September, Blunt attended a meeting with the London rezident. According to the NKVD files, the British agent told his handlers he wanted out and that he had handed over his final secret documents.[19]

Why Blunt wanted to leave MI5 at this critical point in the war, when the Russians and British were in touching distance of victory, the file does not say. What could have happened, or what could Blunt have been asked to do, to make the British spy feel so strongly that he could no longer serve both MI5 and communism?

Chapter 18

Arnhem Betrayed

On the evening of Friday 15 September, two days before the start of Operation Market Garden, Karl Heinz Kraemer, the German air attaché and Abwehr agent based in Stockholm, received a letter in his diplomatic baggage from Agent Josephine containing 17 microdot documents – secret documents photographed using a microscope to reduce them to the size of a typewriter's full stop.

What Kraemer discovered the next morning when he had magnified and decoded the report was unlike any intelligence he had received before. It contained very detailed military information about Market Garden and he was also able to report that the 1st British Airborne Division was in 'sealed camps'.

The German intelligence officer later told MI5:[1] 'I knew what it meant to keep airborne units in "sealed camps" and reported this very important information to Berlin as quickly as possible.'

Kraemer, knowing that the landings were to start the following day, had made it clear that his intelligence was for Schellenberg's urgent personal attention. Kraemer was able to act so quickly because he had been given vital authoritative context for the Arnhem intelligence on 13/14 September when he received a separate report telling him that an airborne landing in Holland was imminent and giving the exact locations in England of the 1st British, 82nd and 101st US Airborne Divisions, the three paratroop divisions to be deployed in Operation Market Garden.[2]

When he was interrogated after the war, Kraemer claimed that he had been sent the second, more detailed, Arnhem warning from a Hungarian diplomat called Josef Fuellop based in Madrid, the same source who had fed[3] him details about D-Day. From Madrid, claimed Kraemer, the microdot photographs had been sent by Hungarian diplomatic bag to the Hungarian legation in Berlin. Here, they were placed in a new envelope and sent by the Hungarians to the German embassy in Stockholm, where Kraemer had collected them.

Kraemer believed the intelligence had come from a source of Fuellop's in England.

But due to a 'technical hitch', Kraemer's report of the Allies' overall battle plan sat unattended in the teleprinter office of the German Foreign Office and did not reach German military intelligence headquarters in Berlin until 17 September – the day Market Garden began. Why it was not sent on immediately has never been explained.[4] But as soon as he got it, Schellenberg acted at once, so nevertheless it reached Wehrmachtführungsstab, Oberkommando der Wehrmacht (OKW), soon after the first Allied aircraft crossed the Dutch coast[5] and gave the Germans an extraordinarily accurate grasp of the overall objectives of Market Garden.

Kraemer had also taken the precaution of warning the Germans of the Allied deception plan to trick the enemy into believing there were to be follow-up sea landings in Holland, Denmark and Norway.[6] A German intelligence report at the time of the battle read: '*The confirmation of the forces engaged, namely so far about three airborne divisions, shows that they are composed of two battle-tried American airborne divisions (82nd and 101st) and the 1st English airborne division in action for the first time, to which the Polish and Dutch parachute units which are also engaged... the fact that the only two battle-tried American airborne divisions were dropped in front of the English sector makes it seem improbable that a second large scale airborne operation is planned for the American sector. Rather we deduce that the main effort of the whole operation lies in the sector of the second English army. According to our present picture of the battle the main objective of the Airborne operation is the capture of the crossings along the Eindhoven to Arnhem line in order to facilitate a quick thrust by the main forces of the 2nd English Army through Holland the former bridgehead at Arnhem. This confirms the intention already suspected to cut off the German forces in Holland and at the same time to win a base from which to continue the operation east of the Rhine.*'[7]

General Wilhelm 'Willi' Bittrich commanded II SS Panzer Corps, which included the two key 9th and 10th Panzer Divisions during the battle. After the war he told the Dutch officer Lieutenant-Colonel Theodor A Boeree, who was asked by the Dutch government to investigate the Arnhem betrayal: 'Both divisions had received extensive specialised training in opposing airborne landings ... which we had been expecting.'[8] Field Marshal Walter Model, commander of Army Group B, had issued an order on 11 September to be aware of airborne landings and after the 9th SS Panzer Division arrived in Holland their commanders were told to 'prepare stand-up units' to defend against Allied paratroopers.[9]

Bittrich did not say why they had been 'expecting' airborne landings. They were a reasonable tactical assumption, but Christiaan Lindemans' warnings about the abortive Operation Comet one month earlier may also have played a role. Bittrich also admitted to Boeree he had 'heard rumours about the Lindemans betrayal' two days before the start of the landings.[10]

The German general said[11] that he was first alerted to the air landings at 'noon' on 17 September 'by the Luftwaffe communications network at my command post [II Panzer Corps HQ] at Doetinchem'. He said shortly after the first message was received, 'a second report ... indicated that Arnhem–Nijmegen was the point of main effort of the airborne operations.'

The significance of the timing given by Bittrich for this first alert on the day of the attack is that at 'noon' on 17 September

1944, the British and American paratroopers had not crossed the North Sea and were still en route to their landing grounds. Could it be then the Luftwaffe warning had come from Schellenberg[12] in Berlin, based on Kraemer's detailed report that had arrived the previous day? Boeree, who did not know about the Kraemer warning, dismisses the disparity by suggesting Bittrich had simply muddled up his timings.[13] Bittrich never clarified why he gave this time or upon what intelligence sources the Arnhem warning to his headquarters was based.

The official German report[14] from Bittrich's headquarters says that first alert actually arrived at 13.30 hours when the HQ of II Panzer Corps received a notification of air landings via the Fliegerdienststelle (Flight Advisory Service) close to Doetinchem. But just one and a half hours later at 15.00, the II Panzer Corps HQ was visited by Field Marshal Walter Model (fleeing from his own headquarters that was at risk of being overrun by British paratroopers), who personally discussed the situation with the commanders of the corps after new intelligence had arrived. Shortly afterwards Bittrich was able to tell one of his officers: 'The British intend to bridge all the gaps between their frontline and the Reich.'[15]

It therefore seems likely that the Kraemer intelligence did reach the German commanders at the front as the British battalions were still mustering on the landing zones.

The first Arnhem leak through Christiaan Lindemans was limited in that he may not have known the ultimate objective of the Allies' forces was the bridge at Arnhem. Kraemer's report not only independently verified Lindemans' intelligence, but it gave the Germans this vital piece of the missing intelligence jigsaw. It meant Model and Bittrich were swiftly able to make sense of the battle and deploy their forces accordingly. The battered 9th and 10th SS Panzer Divisions were located north of Arnhem on the Veluwe, where they were to rest up and be reequipped.

Christiaan Lindemans. Legendary resistance fighter known to the British and Germans as 'King Kong'. (Alamy Stock Photo)

Operation Market Garden: the Allied air armada arrives over Holland.
(Gamma-Rapho via Getty Images)

German units on the edge of the drop zone open fire on paratroopers from 4th Para Brigade arriving in the second lift. The Germans had been expecting an air landing. (Getty Images)

Gilou Letuppe. Nightclub singer, spy and wife of Christiaan Lindemans. (McMaster Uni, Canada)

Double agent Mia Meersman. She claimed to have warned British intelligence about Lindemans before Operation Market Garden. (Lukas/Maria De Meersman)

From left to right: resistance fighter Jimmy Hendrickx, 'Johnny', King Kong's German mistress who worked for the Nazi construction agency Todt, and Lindemans, with his arm raised. (National Archives (KV-234))

Eddy Verkaik leading his resistance fighters through the streets of Eindhoven after British and American troops liberated the city on 18 September 1944.
(Regionaal Historich Centrum Eindhoven)

  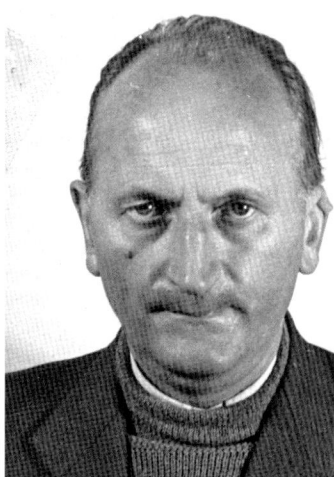

From left to right: Cornelis Verloop, aka 'Satan Face'; Captain Peter Baker of IS9; Hermann Giskes, Abwehr spy chief in Holland.
(credits: National Archives (KV2-139) / John Calder publishing / National Archives (KV2-962))

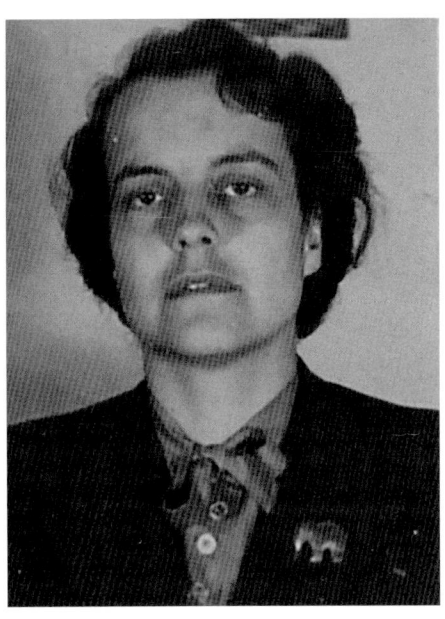

Nazi spymaster Karl Heinz Kraemer (above) and his assistant and mistress Nina Siemsen (left). Kraemer was Germany's most important agent of WW2 whose reports were read by Adolf Hitler. Kraemer codenamed his source in London, 'Josephine'. MI6 suspected Josephine of being a mole at the heart of the British government.

(National Archives (KV2-151) / National Archives (KV-2-154))

British traitors Anthony Blunt (agent Tony) and Kim Philby (agent Stanley).
(Chris Ware-Keystone-Hulton Archive-Getty Images / Hulton-Deutsch Collection-CORBIS-Corbis via Getty Images)

Ivan Chichaev, the shadowy head of the Soviet station in London. Stalin had everything to gain from the Western Allies' defeat at Arnhem. Eight months later, the Red Army won the race to Berlin, and an Iron Curtain plunged the world into a Cold War. (National Archives (KV2-3226))

Top, from left to right: Capt Kas de Graaf, aide to Prince Bernhard and friend of Christiaan Lindemans. Jane Archer, MI6 officer and thorn in the side of the Cambridge spies. Col Robin 'Tin Eye' Stephens, the fearsome interrogator of Camp 020, who extracted confessions from Lindemans and Kraemer. (unknown / Family Archives / unknown)

Bottom, left to right: Commander of 30 Corps Lt Gen Brian Horrocks, Field Marshal Bernard Montgomery and Prince Bernhard consult over plans for an air landing in Holland, September 1944. Captain Guy Liddell, MI5's head of counter-intelligence, who worked closely with Anthony Blunt. Pavel Sudoplatov, Stalin's specialist assassin and Kremlin spy chief. (Alamy Stock Photo / Bettmann/Getty Images / Sovfoto/Universal Images Group/Shutterstock)

At the start of Operation Market Garden, their units were scattered across Dieren, Zutphen, Apeldoorn and Brummen, all no more than a 20-mile ride from Arnhem. The strongest part of the 9th SS Armoured Division, the SS Panzer Aufklärungs Abteilung 9, was at Hoenderloo, 12 miles north of Arnhem.

As the Allied air armada was passing into Dutch airspace, its commander Walter Harzer was presenting a Knight's Cross to the unit commander Hauptsturmführer Viktor Gräbner. Harzer recalled: 'When the Knight's Cross was awarded, the first landings of paratroopers and gliders were observed. It could not yet be concluded that this was a major action. We therefore enjoyed our lunch in peace.'[16]

But when he got the call from Bittrich, this all changed. Harzer immediately ordered Gräbner to advance to Arnhem and Wolfheze with his unit of 500 men and 40 armoured vehicles. Harzer himself drove back to his headquarters in Beekbergen to send all units of the division to the landing sites.

The immediate deployment of Harzer's troops meant that the Germans held a strong line of defence by the early evening of Sunday 17 September 1944, running from Amsterdamseweg, north of Oosterbeek, to Lombok on the western fringes of Arnhem. Only the area around the St Elisabeth Gasthuis hospital and the road hugging the river into Arnhem were undefended. It was through this gap that the 2nd Battalion led by John Frost was able to slip undetected along the riverside road towards the Rhine Bridge. But due to the 'lightning-fast' reaction of parts of Harzer's division and by the even quicker response of Sepp Krafft and his Battalion 16th, the other thrusts (1st and 3rd Battalions) of the British advance towards Arnhem were halted just a few hours after the airborne landings had begun.

In the days that followed, the 9th SS contained the British at the Arnhem bridge and drove back the main force from Oosterbeek, where the Germans used their superiority in artillery and mortars to break the British resistance.

Bittrich was able to dispatch the 10th SS Division to Nijmegen, which arrived just in time to prevent the American 82nd from making an early crossing of the River Waal (the Dutch branch of the Rhine). Major General Roy Urquhart, who led the British 1st Airborne Division, described Bittrich's decision as 'immense foresight' and one that meant the more mobile elements of the division were able to 'help repel the first tentative American thrust at Nijmegen Bridge'.[17]

Urquhart attributed Bittrich's 'foresight' to a story that the Germans had acquired Market Garden plans from a dead American paratrooper captain whose Waco glider had crashed near Vught.[18] These plans[19] were limited to the US 101st objectives and were only recovered from the glider on the evening of 17 September and did not reach Bittrich until 19 September.[20]

Just as at D-Day when it was the combined effect of Garbo with Josephine that proved so telling, the combination of Lindemans with Josephine gave the Germans a window into Allied planning. It also allowed them to dismiss British deception signals being sent by controlled agent Brutus warning the Germans that the air landings were only a precursor for major sea landings on the Dutch coast.[21] In this respect Josephine's credibility really mattered. Alfred Jodl, who considered Josephine more reliable than Garbo, passed Kraemer's reports directly to Hitler.[22] Oberingenieur Dietrich Schwenke, a senior member of the German diplomatic staff, thought his information to be so good that he eventually concluded Kraemer must be working for the British.[23] Certainly it remained a mystery to both the Germans and the British how the Josephine intelligence had reached Kraemer in Stockholm.

Market Garden had only been given the green light on 10 September and battle orders were not handed to the commanders in London until two days later. Horrocks only shared his orders with his tank commanders the day before the attack. It would have been almost impossible for this intelligence to travel so circuitously between London, Madrid, Berlin and Stockholm and back to Berlin in just three days.

There was another reason why Kraemer's own account of the source of his intelligence didn't make sense. Kraemer had a few weeks earlier become so infuriated with Fuellop's 'fabricated' reports that he had to be persuaded by another Abwehr officer 'not to abandon the source altogether'.[24]

It is much more likely that the microdots were planted in the diplomatic mail by someone with access to both the highest-grade British intelligence and the diplomatic courier mail system. A Sweden ABA regular air service between RAF Leuchars in Scotland and Stockholm's Bromma airport that ran throughout the war and ferried diplomatic bags between the two countries in a matter of hours was the subject of many MI5, MI6 and Abwehr penetration operations.

Master of the diplomatic courier routes, as head of Triplex, was Anthony Blunt. He had almost complete control over the snooping of the embassy mailbags and wide access to the files on GC&CS's diplomatic codebreaking and the resulting decrypts – known in Whitehall as the 'Blue Jackets' or 'BJs' because of the distinctive blue files they were circulated in. Through his investigation of the Josephine leaks he had been able to closely follow Kraemer's activities for months. And through his contact with Peter Falk, the MI6 officer in Stockholm, he also had excellent access to the German air attaché's personal office. Blunt could also call upon the well-placed contacts of Colonel Ivan Chichaev, the head of espionage operations in London, who between 1939 and 1941 had been stationed in Stockholm, where he had helped build up a Soviet spy network.[25]

The British knew all about microdots as this was the means of communication the Abwehr chose to keep in contact with their agents, many of whom had been turned against their German handlers. The Russians knew even more as they had developed the technology and used it throughout their European residenzia.[26]

Blunt was MI5's foremost expert[27] on microdots, or 'duff' as they were referred to inside the service, and was called upon by SIS to decipher their more difficult microdot cases. He used his second-hand Leica camera to make microdots of every secret document he could lay his hands on that he thought might be useful to the Soviets.[28]

Blunt's fellow Kremlin spy, Kim Philby, was head of SIS's operations in the Iberian Peninsula, where Fuellop was based and from where he gathered his intelligence.

Blunt's partner in espionage accepted[29] the war was effectively over by the end of 1943 and his new orders from the Kremlin were much more about slowing the Allies' advance on Berlin than defeating the Germans.

Philby[30] had experience of running agents trusted by Hitler who could whisper into the Führer's ear and so would have been on hand to assist Blunt in routing a planted intelligence leak like that of Arnhem. Philby had been monitoring Fuellop, part of a cell[31] of Hungarian intelligence officers and agents working for both the Abwehr and Russian intelligence since 1943 when Fuellop had based himself in Madrid and Lisbon, the two cities where Philby controlled a number of agents.

Fuellop, who used the English alias Emory Philips, would have been of particular interest to Philby. According to the MI5 files he spoke with an 'Oxford English' accent[32] and had spent many years as a diplomat in Washington before the war. He was also amenable to bribes and tended to work for the spymaster with the biggest wallet.

In a joint intelligence operation with MI5, Philby had even passed a detailed description of Fuellop to London[33] but declined to hand over a photograph of the Hungarian.

In September 1944, just days before Arnhem, Fuellop mysteriously left[34] Spain to pay a visit to Lisbon, a city often visited by Philby on MI6 duties.

There was something else that was odd about Kraemer's Arnhem report – it had evaded[35] all monitoring of the enemy's intelligence reports sent from Stockholm and so was not picked up by Bletchley Park decrypters who would have been able to decipher the intelligence. Had the Allies decoded it on 16 September when Kraemer sent it, Montgomery might have been forced to stand down Market Garden. Section V of MI6 had the job of collecting copies of teleprinted messages and passing them back to London. But from August 1944 until January 1945 there had been an intelligence blackout.

For one leading British intelligence expert, Kraemer's Arnhem leak has raised too many unanswered questions.

After the war, Professor Harry Hinsley, the Bletchley Park code breaker and the official Second World War British intelligence historian, smelt a rat. He wrote: 'Even if Kraemer's general truthfulness is accepted, as the operation [Market Garden] was only authorised on 10 September and the date for it was not fixed and formation commanders in England were not briefed till 12 September, it is very hard to believe that the information could have reached Stockholm via the Iberian Peninsula in three days ... probably because his account was not available until sometime after the event (Arnhem) no formal inquiry was carried out.'[36]

What Hinsley doesn't appear to have known was that the Kraemer warning may have arrived in the nick of time, just as the air armada passed over Holland. Nor does he seem to be aware that between 1943 and 1945 an investigation was being carried out into Josephine. And although Hinsley reviewed the secret MI5 files in the 1980s and 1990s, he didn't appreciate that investigation was being handled by a Soviet agent – Anthony Blunt.

Just after the defeat of Operation Market Garden, at the end of September 1944 Anthony Blunt met his Soviet handler Boris Kreshin in London. The Russian wanted to pass on that Moscow was especially delighted with their English spy and Kreshin took great pleasure in reading out a commendation sent from the Kremlin to Blunt. It was accompanied with a £100 payment, worth about £6,000 today. Until then, Blunt had always been careful not to accept money from the Russians as he always maintained his treachery was motivated by political ideology. This time he gratefully accepted the cash.

On 2 November 1944, Blunt, having overcome his wobble of 15 September, wrote a letter to the Centre effusively thanking his Moscow spymasters for the money and praise. 'Dear Comrade,' Blunt began. 'Once again how to thank you for your most generous premium which is not only gratitude in itself, but is above all valuable as an encouragement to me to think that my work has been of use to the cause. If my contribution has really been of value, I can only say that a great part of the credit must go to our friend Max [Boris Krotov] without whose patience and unfailing understanding in my difficulties which [inelligible word], the work could never have been carried out so successfully. Now that victory seems at last to be in sight, I can only hope that I may be able to continue to be of use, though I feel that the opportunity will be less in the future.'[37]

The official narrative around Blunt, put forward by him as well as MI5 and the British government, is that while he was in a legal sense a traitor, he only passed over technical intelligence documents and did nothing to cause harm to any Allied soldier or citizen.

And yet no spy in history has been as well placed as he was so it seems highly unlikely that the Russians would have used him for the kinds of unimportant work he claims he carried out. Certainly his superiors in the British secret service held him in the highest regard and from what we know his Russian ones did too so it makes no sense that he did so little. The full case for whether he really was Josephine will need to wait until Part Three of this book when we examine the role he played in the interrogation of Kraemer at the close of the war and the way in which Christiaan Lindemans became a kind of part bogey man, part lightning rod, distracting all attention from the potential betrayal of one of the most iconic and emotive Allied actions of the Second World War. One thing is certain: a number of senior German, British and Dutch intelligence officers knew that Market Garden had been betrayed. The questions we then have to answer are: why is it that there was never a proper inquiry into that, and why the identity of Josephine was allowed to remain a mystery that has faded into the obscurity of the archives?

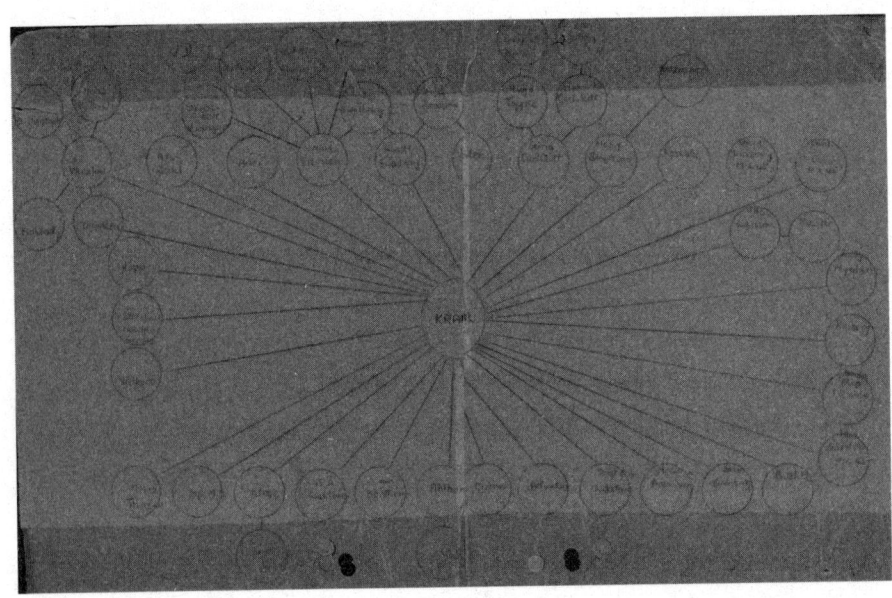

The Kraemer network as drawn up by MI5. From his base in Stockholm, Karl Heinz Kraemer was at the centre of a pan-European web of double agents and intelligence sources. MI5 suspected Agent Josephine could be Air Vice Marshal Leslie Brown or an advisor to Cabinet minister Sir Stafford Cripps.
(The National Archive, KV-2-149 (2) p.40)

APPENDIX III

THE "ARNHEIM REPORT"

KRAEMER

That Kraemer sent an advance warning of the Arnhem airborne operation (MARKET GARDEN) is beyond question (see main narrative pp 38-34). How he got the information is another matter. In view of the continuing interest in the possibility of an Arnhem leakage, it is perhaps worth quoting the statement he wrote about it while at Camp 020.(1)

"A. 1. My information given to I/Luft Berlin, at Saturday before the actual landing of airborne divisions in Holland, which took place on Sunday (approximately 16.9.44), called in my former statements 'the Arnheim Report'. I confirm my former statements.

" 2. Approximate contents of the Report.
The Allied Supreme Command intends airborne-operations in the environs of Arnheim, Tilburg and Eindhowen (Note: I am not quite sure if Eindhoven was mentioned).

Aim of the operation is to enforce the crossing of the Rhine.

The Allied units consist of the 1st British, 82nd and 101st USA Airborne Divisions, all of them will start from England.

The operation will be carried through between Sunday and Thursday (Note: In the information the figures of the dates of the two days were mentioned).

" 3. Source of the Report.
I had got the report sub 2 from FULLEP in the form as given above without further comment and without further reference to the original source. The report was sent to me by diplomatic mail, which arrived at Friday night (Sept. 14th ?) I had a look on the mail the same night and found that the mail consisted of 16 or 17 microdots; in the night and on the following morning, Saturday, I read through the reports and found on one of the microdots the 'Arnheim' information. Immediately I gave the information to the Air Attache's teleprinter office with the order to forward it to Berlin I/Luft as 'KR-Blitz', the signification for the most urgent importance of a message. Conform to the original message and as usual in the case of FULLER-intelligence, which dealt with strategic matters, I chose the cover designation 'Zuverlaessiger V-Mann' (Reliable agent).

Patrica McCallum's Arnhem report was part of the 1970s MI5 investigation into Josephine long after the trail had gone cold. Was it commissioned by the security and intelligence services as a pre-emptive strike for handling the fall-out of the outing of Blunt in 1979? (The National Archive, KV-2-153 (2) pp 68,69)

MI6 believed Kraemer was lying to cover up for a Whitehall mole. After Kraemer was brought to London in May 1945 for interrogation, his interrogators said he told a 'clever fabrication of untruth.' (The National Archive, KV-2-149 (2). P84.)

MI6 warned Blunt that the Nazi intelligence chief, Walter Schellenberg, believed Josephine/Kraemer was working for the Russians. (The National Archive, KV-2-151 (2) p50.)

MI5 officer Major Michael Ryde reported that Kraemer may have been 'working unconsciously or consciously for the Russians'. (The National Archive, KV-2-149 (1) p33.)

Sir Edward Blanchard Stamp (who also led the investigation of Christiaan 'King Kong' Lindemans and after the war became a High Court judge) told Col 'Tin Eye' Stephens, head of Camp 020, that one explanation for why Kraemer was not telling the truth about Josephine's identity might be because he was working for the Russians. Dated 12 June 1945. (The National Archive, KV-2-149 (1) p44.)

A few days later, Blunt takes control of the Kraemer investigation. Dated 7 July 1945. (The National Archive, KV-2-150 (1) p.41)

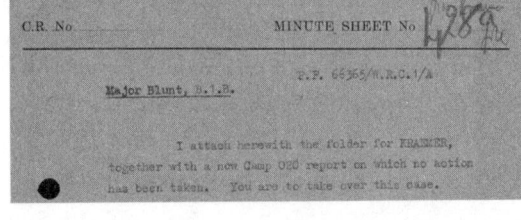

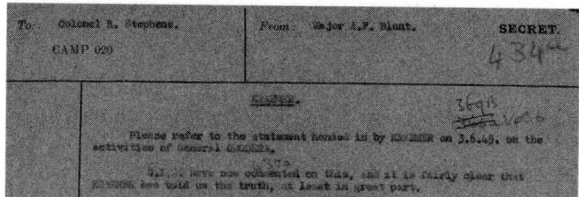

Above and below: Blunt informs Stephens that he believes Kraemer 'in great part' and 'in general' is telling the truth. Dated 7 July 1945. (The National Archive, KV 2/150 (1), pp.40.41)

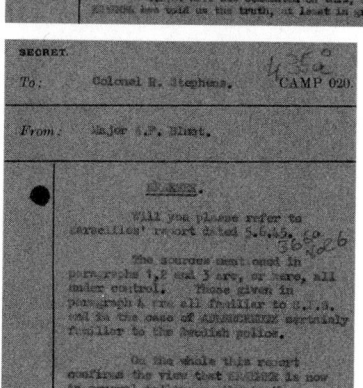

In a top-secret memo to MI6, Blunt plays down Kraemer's espionage and says enquiries linking Josephine to Moscow are 'flogging a dead horse.'
(The National Archive, KV-2-150 (1) pp.19, 20. 15.7.1945.)

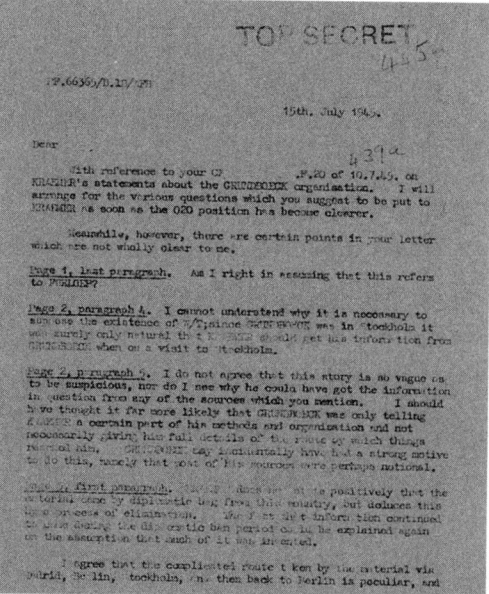

PART THREE
THE RUSSIANS

Dramatis Personae

Anthony Blunt: Polymath, scholar, traitor. A Russian spy from the thirties, he played a central role in British intelligence in the Second World War and went on to become Surveyor of the Queen's Pictures.

Kim Philby: Fellow traitor to Blunt. One of the Cambridge spies.

Jane Archer: At the start of the war, the only female MI5 officer. Her debrief of Walter Krivitsky set the standard for years to come and she was arguably the greatest single thorn in the side of the Cambridge spies.

Oreste Pinto: Hugely capable, if morally somewhat shady, Dutch intelligence officer.

Robin Stephens (aka Tin Eye): The slightly cartoonish (the tin eye refers to the monocle he always wore) head of interrogation for MI5.

Leo Long: Blunt's sub-agent working for military intelligence with Montgomery's army in France and Belgium.

Prince Bernhard of the Netherlands: German 'Ex' Nazi, leader of the Dutch military, protector of Christiaan Lindemans, he went on to become a founder member of the Bilderberg Group.

Kas de Graaf: Security chief of communist-run CS-6 resistance group. Lindemans saved his life. He escaped to England and went on to play a prominent role in Dutch security.

Henk Lindemans: Christiaan Lindemans' younger, favourite brother and a member of the Dutch resistance.

Gilberte Letuppe (aka Gilou): Christiaan Lindemans' long-suffering wife. Resistance fighter and nightclub singer.

Cornelis Verloop (aka Satan Face): Dutch ex-French Foreign Legion, Abwehr V-man and thoroughgoing rat.

Peter Baker: Special forces officer attached to Intelligence School 9 (W.E.A.) reporting to Airey Neave. He was to play a mysterious role in the downfall of Lindemans and went on to have a chequered post-war career.

Joseph Fuellop: Hungarian spy in Spain with a cut-glass English accent. He worked closely with Kraemer and was repatriated in 1946 and subsequently disappeared.

Chapter 19

Operation Tolstoy

As midnight approached on 7 October 1944, Squadron Leader Bill Fraser was in the cockpit of his Avro York LV-633 at RAF Northolt just 11 miles west of central London making final checks. Developed from the more famous Lancaster, the York was Britain's most advanced long-range four-engine aircraft. Bigger and faster than its illustrious cousin, the York's wings housed seven internal fuel tanks carrying 2,478 imperial gallons of aviation fuel.

Fraser knew he would need every drop to complete the journey he had painstakingly charted over the previous days. The RAF crew was under strict orders to say nothing of their mission. Indeed, Fraser and his navigator had been ordered to plot two flight paths: the secret real one and another to deflect unwanted attention from Britain's enemies. The flight manifest listed the York's VIP passenger as 'Colonel Kent' and the mission's code name was given as Operation Tolstoy.[1]

A convoy of cars drove down the main runway and pulled alongside the spluttering aircraft and his passengers began to disembark.

There was no mistaking the portly figure tightly gripping the sides of his favourite grey Homburg hat against the backdraught from the York's propellers.

'Colonel Kent' was Winston Churchill and LV-633 was *Ascalon*, Churchill's personal aircraft named, appropriately enough, after the sword St George used to slay the dragon.

Ascalon had been especially adapted for the prime minister. It had a telephone for talking directly to the flight crew, a well-stocked drinks cabinet and a table with an extra-large ashtray. There were Pullman-style sleeping bunks for 10 passengers, a lounge and a small conference room where the prime minister held mid-air meetings. It even had an electrically heated toilet seat, though after one sitting Churchill had complained that it was too hot and ordered it to be disconnected.

Fraser must have been feeling nervous. This would be the RAF officer's first flight as captain of the *Ascalon* and it was well known that Churchill disliked new faces.

To complicate matters even further, Fraser had been told that because of the prime minister's high blood pressure he must not fly above 8,000 ft for any prolonged period.

Churchill's blood pressure had every reason to be high. Just weeks earlier his intention had been to summon Stalin to a summit at The Hague. But, with the failure of Market Garden and the fear that the Western Allies would not reach Berlin before the Russians, he was now going cap in hand to the Russian leader.

Britain had gone to war over Poland. Five years later, the people of Warsaw had bravely risen up against their Nazi overlords. In August 1944, fighters of the Polish Home Army (Armia Krajowa) emerged from their hideouts in the city's attics, cellars and sewers, and caught the Germans by surprise. The Poles had timed their attack to coincide with the arrival of the Soviet armies on Poland's borders. For nearly 60 days, the battle raged with the heroic under-gunned Poles holding out against the armoured units of the SS.

Churchill sent frantic telegrams to Stalin urging him to come to the aid of the beleaguered Poles. But the Russian leader held his troops back and allowed the Germans to gain the upper hand. In desperation, Churchill had authorised the RAF to drop supplies to the Polish resistance, but most of the cargo fell into German hands and the week before the prime minister left for Moscow, Churchill received the news he had been dreading. The Poles had unconditionally surrendered. Hitler immediately ordered the slaughter of nearly 200,000 resistance fighters and civilians.

When Soviet troops finally 'liberated' Warsaw in January 1945, Poland's capital was 'a vast desert of hollow-shelled buildings and rubble'.[2] The Nazi annihilation of the Polish Army and the Warsaw resistance movement had eliminated all possible military and intellectual obstacles to communist rule. Joseph Stalin's ruthless playbook was plain to see.

British intelligence reports indicated Stalin had similar plans for Hungary, Bulgaria, Romania, Yugoslavia and even Greece.

Churchill had appealed to Roosevelt for American support over Poland. But Roosevelt had made it clear that he felt it was not in US interests to become embroiled in European post-war power struggles. Churchill was increasingly convinced that the Americans underestimated the Russian threat.

It was true that Roosevelt was personally relaxed about communism, seeing it as a problem confined to distant, foreign countries. The historian David Reynolds says when it came to the Soviet Union, Roosevelt 'knew little and feared even less'.

In a private message to Churchill on 28 September 1944, FDR reminded the British prime minister of the need to keep the Soviets onside, while making a case for bringing the Soviet Union into the circle of 'civilised nations': 'We are all in agreement as to the necessity of having the USSR as a fully accepted and equal member of an association of the great powers formed for the purpose of preventing international war. It should be possible to accomplish this by adjusting our differences through compromise by all the parties concerned and this ought to tide things over for a few years until the child learns to toddle.'[3]

In the face of such high-minded patronising nonsense, the British prime minister felt he had no choice but to reach out to Stalin and suggest a bilateral summit. The failure at Arnhem meant the Soviets were able to dictate the terms of any meeting and Stalin replied to Churchill, welcoming the invitation, but said that his own doctors had warned him his health made it impossible for him to travel. Churchill agreed at the last minute to come to Moscow.

The two leaders promised to keep President Roosevelt fully abreast of the talks while he fought the 1944 presidential election. Roosevelt had been reluctant to support the bilateral talks and remained secretly concerned the British and Americans were pursuing divergent interests. He told his ambassador in Moscow, Averell Harriman, to keep a watching brief and sent a secret telegram to Stalin saying: 'I'm firmly convinced that the three of us, and only the three of us, can find resolutions to the questions. In this sense, while appreciating Mr Churchill's desire for the meeting, I prefer to regard your forthcoming talks with the Prime Minister as preliminary to a meeting of the three of us, which can take place any time after the elections here as far as I'm concerned.'[4]

Ascalon was damaged on landing to refuel in Cairo so Churchill flew the final stage of the journey in a second York which carried the Foreign Secretary Anthony Eden and his closest military advisers, General Ismay, Chief of Staff, and Field Marshal Alan Brooke, the Chief of Imperial General Staff. It was a sign of how seriously Churchill took this summit. These were the most important people in the country and the risk of putting them all into the same plane, let alone flying them unguarded into the hands of Stalin, was an extraordinary roll of the dice. It had all been very last minute. Alan Brooke records in his diary[5] on 1 October that the 'PM suddenly informed us that he and Anthony Eden were off to Moscow on Saturday next and that he wanted me to come with him!!'

Brooke had been at Churchill's side the last time they met Stalin in Moscow in 1942, when he described the Soviet leader as having an 'unpleasantly cold, crafty, dead face, and whenever I look at him I can imagine his sending off people to their doom without ever turning a hair.'[6]

OPERATION TOLSTOY

Shortly after midday on 9 October, Churchill and his retinue arrived in the city and Moscow's streets were adorned with military souvenirs: captured Tiger tanks, artillery pieces and even downed Messerschmitt 109 fighters had been dragged into the centre of the capital for its citizens to openly gawp at and jeer.

Churchill's staff were dispatched to the famous National Hotel and given rubles and instructions about how to negotiate the city and notes on the character of the 'war-weary but battle-hardened' Muscovites.[7] The National's hotel management and clerks all spoke excellent English and were all employed by the People's Commissariat for Internal Affairs, better known as the NKVD, the Soviet secret police.

The British prime minister was driven to the same Moscow dacha he had stayed at in 1942, the last time he was in the Russian capital when the two Allies were united in their war against the Nazis. Its rooms were also stuffed full of secret microphones listened to by NKVD officers stationed in a nearby house.

The British leader was determined to 'strike while the iron was hot'.[8] In the early evening, he dined with his foreign secretary in his private quarters and then sent Eden off to lay the groundwork with Molotov, Stalin's foreign affairs negotiator. Eden told Molotov that Churchill was ready 'to review the world scene' with Marshal Stalin.

The official British records of what transpired at the 1944 Tolstoy Conference, the Tolstoy Files, are held at the National Archives in Kew.[9]

At 10pm, Churchill was driven to the Kremlin for his first meeting with his Russian host.

When the two leaders met, Churchill handed Stalin a signed photograph of himself in return for one of Stalin the Soviet premier had sent Churchill a few days earlier. Stalin's welcome was fulsome and very shortly the two leaders and their foreign secretaries, together with two interpreters, were alone in a Kremlin ante-chamber sitting around a table laden with caviar, vodka and oversized Cuban cigars.

In his Second World War memoir, Churchill says he sensed the moment was 'apt for business' and impressed upon Stalin how they could save themselves months of wasteful diplomatic cabling if they could reach agreement over Europe. Stalin replied that he was ready to discuss anything. Churchill opened proceedings by introducing the 'tiresome' question of Poland's independence which he said the British people wanted to settle favourably as it was Polish sovereignty that had brought Britain into the war. The two leaders agreed that this was best done by flying the Polish leaders from London to join them in Moscow.

Then the British leader turned to the question of the Balkans, offering to give the Soviets almost free rein in Romania in return for a similar British free hand in Greece. Stalin accepted the argument that Britain should be allowed to be the dominant sea power in the Mediterranean, something that could not be secured without influence in Greece.

With the talks proceeding at lightning pace, Churchill seized the initiative, conspiring with Stalin over how to bring about a deal in the absence of the Americans. According to the Tolstoy files he told the Soviet leader: 'It would be better to express these things in diplomatic terms and not use the phrase "dividing into spheres of influence" which might shock the Americans. But as long as he and Marshal Stalin understood each other he could explain matters to the President.'[10]

Churchill recalls in his memoirs that he then took a piece of paper from the table and asked: '... how would it do for you to have 90% predominance in Romania, for us to have 90% of the say in Greece and go fifty-fifty about Yugoslavia?'[11]

While the British offer was being translated, Churchill began scrawling out more percentage shares for the divvying up of the rest of the Balkans.

Romania = 90% Russian and 10% The Others.

Greece = 90% Great Britain (in accord with USA) and Russian 10%.

Yugoslavia = 50–50%.
Hungary = 50–50%.
Bulgaria = 75% Russian and 25% The Others.

'I pushed this across to Stalin,' Churchill wrote in his memoirs, 'who by then had heard the translation. There was a slight pause. Then he took his blue pencil and made a large tick upon it, and passed it back to us. It was all settled in no more time than it takes to set [*sic*] down.'[12]

The piece of paper was left in the centre of the table. There was a long silence, finally broken by Churchill: 'Might it not be thought rather cynical if it seemed we had disposed of these issues, so fateful to millions of people, in such an off-hand manner? Let us burn the paper.'

'No, you keep it,' replied Stalin.

Pleased with his handiwork and Marshal Stalin's agreeable mood, the prime minister pressed on to discuss the settlement of Germany. Stalin wanted the execution of 1.5 million Nazis while Churchill said it was better to kill as many as possible on the field of battle[13] and 'use the Gestapo and Hitler Youth to rebuild Germany to teach the German people that it was more difficult to build than to destroy'.[14]

The British leader told Stalin that his recent meeting with Roosevelt indicated that the Americans would support 'hard' terms but may not be persuaded by arguments for a 'harsh' settlement against the German people.

Churchill moved the discussion to a more global view. On 18 September, Roosevelt had invited Churchill to his family home in Hyde Park, New York, and confided in the British leader that scientists were close to developing an atomic bomb. America was on the precipice of becoming the world's first true superpower. Churchill was left in little doubt that Washington would oppose a British return in the Far East because the Americans intended to end the war as the dominant power in the region.

The British prime minister, who considered the new wonder weapon to be just a 'bigger bang', was determined not to be pushed around by his American ally, nor give up a single British territory.

In Moscow he sensed an opportunity to use Stalin to help bolster the British Empire. And so he suggested that they might be able to do a deal over the potentially wealthy oil states neighbouring the Soviets in the Middle East. With Stalin in such a receptive mood, anything seemed possible to Churchill.

The next morning Churchill drafted an upbeat message to Roosevelt telling him of the 'extraordinary atmosphere of good will' he had encountered in Moscow.[15]

A better reflection of his true state of mind might be found in a curious rant Brooke records towards the end of their trip where Churchill inveighs against the possibility of Montgomery having a parade in the Mall. In typical soldier fashion, Brooke puts this down to the egotism of politicians, but Churchill must have been feeling the deep sting of having to go cap in hand to Stalin because of the failure of Market Garden. Blaming Montgomery must have seemed like the natural thing to do. What he didn't know was that Market Garden had also been betrayed by the very person who wrote his security briefings.

Stalin, on the other hand, did. He must have relished the fact that not only were British and American forces bogged down in Holland with little hope of a breakout before Christmas, but that it was his security services who were at least partially responsible.

It was all too easy for Stalin to go along with the British proposals because he had been assured by his generals that within a few short weeks the Red Army would be in complete control of the battlefield in the East. His spies and double agents working in London and Washington had also told him what Roosevelt had confided in Churchill a few days earlier – that the Americans were close to developing an atomic bomb.

In May 1944, efforts by the Soviets and the leading Danish physicist Niels Bohr to pool their knowledge had been rebuffed by Winston Churchill.[16]

'Churchill,' said Pavel Sudoplatov, 'was horrified, and urged all efforts to be taken to prevent Bohr from contacting us. If the development of atomic weapons had been left totally to the scientists, they might have changed the course of history.'

It was John Cairncross, the so-called fifth man recruited by Anthony Blunt at Cambridge, who had first alerted Moscow to the Western Allies' nuclear weapons programme as early as 1941.[17]

In February 1944, Stalin appointed Pavel Sudoplatov to head up Department S, the Soviet agency in charge of atomic espionage.[18]

Stalin, more than all of the three Allied leaders, understood that the world power who possessed a nuclear weapon would be able to dictate the terms of peace. The fact that his two Allies had chosen not to share their secret weapon with him was clear evidence of their bad faith.

Stalin therefore had no intention of surrendering to Churchill's demand for Polish independence. He had already authorised plans for the installation of a Soviet government in Warsaw. Nor was he willing to go ahead with any of the other political and military commitments discussed with Churchill. Indeed, that piece of paper with Stalin's blue tick was very nearly as useless and misleading as the one Chamberlain had waved on his return from Munich five years earlier. Churchill, one suspects, knew this.

Chapter 20

To Catch a Traitor

By 1944, Major Oreste Pinto, the Dutch intelligence officer, had established himself as one of MI5's premier spycatchers. Since his early success in breaking the Abwehr-sent agents of Operation Lena, seven more foreign spies unlucky enough to encounter the Dutch interrogator had been hanged at Pentonville Prison.

Pinto had command of a section of 'examiners', specialists in counter-espionage, seconded to the Dutch Security Service at 82 Eaton Square.[1]

It was Pinto who had suspected that the Luftwaffe's Stuka bombing of Wormwood Scrubs at the end of 1940 must have been the result of a security leak. But his suspicions were not taken seriously. There were two likely reasons for this. One was his appearance: his diminutive stature and Iberian extraction always marked him as foreign.

The second reason, and perhaps more telling, was his somewhat suspect private life. In 1943, Guy Liddell warned him that if he wanted to be promoted he would have to apply for British citizenship. Reluctantly, Pinto made the application[2] to the Home Office, who commissioned a police report which uncovered some unhelpful facts. Pinto had separated from his wife but was now living with the married wife of a London stockbroker. More relevant was the fact he was a declared bankrupt as a result of being sued before the war by German businessmen who had contracted with Pinto to help them form companies in Britain. Pinto had pocketed their fees and done nothing to honour the contract. The police described this as a very good example of the 'English fraud'. In 1943 the Home Secretary wrote to Pinto refusing to make him a naturalised British citizen.[3]

Pinto had also clashed with the Dutch leadership in London, who he said exuded a stench of appeasement. This was exemplified by the Prime Minister Dirk Jan de Geer, who had chosen to return to Holland in August 1940 so he could lead a collaboration with the Nazis. An equally serious question mark hung over the loyalty of the Dutch Queen's son-in-law Prince Bernhard, de facto head of Dutch military forces. Bernhard, who remained in London, was a German national who had signed up with the Sturmabteilung (SA), the paramilitary wing of the Nazi Party, before marrying the Queen's daughter. He was now directing Dutch military operations from a grand house in Piccadilly.

* * *

Oreste Pinto arrived in Belgium as head of the Dutch Counter-Intelligence Mission attached to Supreme Headquarters Allied Expeditionary Forces (SHAEF), in charge of a staff of eight investigators whose job it was to sift the spies and saboteurs from the genuine refugees and freedom fighters.[4]

There was no love lost between Pinto and Kas de Graaf, Prince Bernhard's aide-de-camp and new operational head of the Bureau Bijzondere Opdrachten (BBO, 'Office of Special Assignments').

Pinto harboured deep reservations about de Graaf from the moment he had arrived in England with the help of Christiaan Lindemans in February 1944. One MI5 report[5] suggested de Graaf may be an Abwehr agent, he had certainly been head of security for CS6, a communist resistance group, and yet here he now was working for the Dutch royal family.

De Graaf countered Pinto's suspicions by accusing him of sexually exploiting women. It was an accusation that de Graaf had been unable to fully make stick. Instead he resorted to characterising the experience of female suspects who had been interrogated by Pinto as being 'Pintoed'.[6]

Pinto set up his headquarters at a detention camp just outside Antwerp, a sprawling facility contained by barbed-wire fences guarded by Allied troops and holding hundreds of potential suspects subject to security vetting. Pinto observed: 'Civil control was almost non-existent, since many members of the police forces and local authorities who had acted during the German occupation were either discredited or in hiding. Looting, famine, revolt were the grisly camp-followers of the war. The Germans had not been slow to exploit these circumstances and had left behind them spies and saboteurs to continue the war from the rear of the Allied lines. Everything was in confusion and many civilians were making the most of their opportunity to pay off old scores and to indulge their wants free from police control.'[7]

One afternoon, Pinto was alerted to a commotion at the main gate. A man in a Canadian Army officer's uniform was arguing with the sentry on duty and was refusing to take no for an answer.

Major Pinto marched over to the gate: 'Towering over the sentry on duty was a giant of a man. Well over six feet in height. He was disproportionately broad with a massive chest that strained and threatened to split his khaki shirt. His biceps bulging against the sleeves of his jacket seemed to be as big as an athlete's thigh. He must have weighed nearly 18 stone, but he was hard and solid all over, like a great monolith of a man.'

Stuck in his leather belt were two steel knives, a long-barrelled Luger pistol with marksman's sights was strapped to his right hip and a Schmeisser sub-machine gun was slung across his chest. His pockets bulged with hand grenades.

But that was not all – on each arm was a young Dutch girl who he said he was 'rescuing' from the camp after a sentry had challenged him over the custody of the girls.

Pinto immediately recognised the name King Kong, the daring leader of the Dutch resistance forces whose brilliant and brave exploits were revered across Belgium and Holland.

He was not impressed:

'He had no right,' recalled Pinto, 'to come swaggering into my camp. To pick up a couple of girls and remove them before they have been screened by the proper authorities. Let him by all means be a hero in his own sphere, but here he was trespassing.'

In his war memoirs,[8] Pinto recalls shouting: 'Come here – you.'

Lindemans turned round, blinked and shrugged off the girls.

He tapped his chest with a forefinger. 'Were you talking to me?'

'Yes, you. Come here.'

Before Lindemans spoke, Pinto touched the three gold stars on Lindemans' sleeve.

'By what right do you wear those? Are you a captain, and, if so, in what army?'

Lindemans, not used to being challenged, growled back at Pinto: 'I wear these three stars by authority of the Dutch Interior Forces – the underground!'

'Really? And who are you?' Pinto fired back with mock naivety.

'Me?' shrugged Lindemans. 'Who am I? Why, Colonel, everyone knows who I am. I live at Castle Wittouck, headquarters of the Dutch resistance,' pausing before adding: 'I – I am King Kong!'

'The only King Kong I ever heard of,' Pinto replied softly, 'was a big stuffed monkey.'

For a moment Pinto was worried that he may have pushed the Dutch fighter too far, and he records that he unobtrusively slid his hand inside his jacket towards the Walther automatic pistol he carried in his shoulder holster.

Yet Lindemans seemed unsure how to respond. The two men stood staring at each other. Sensing he held the advantage, Pinto carried on his baiting of Lindemans: 'As you do not hold the rank of captain in the Netherlands Army, you are not entitled to wear the insignia.'

And with one hand he ripped off the cloth band with the three gold stars from Lindemans' sleeve.

Pinto expected King Kong to lash out in an uncontrollable rage.

Instead Lindemans stepped backwards, his expression having turned to that of an errant schoolboy caught out by the teacher. Finally, mustering his self-respect, he shouted: 'I shall make a formal complaint of your treatment at Castle Wittouck.'

In Brussels, Pinto had no trouble tracking down people who knew Christiaan Lindemans.

'I found the problem was not so much locating men and women who had known Lindemans intimately,' said Pinto 'but fobbing off the dozens who claimed intimate knowledge of him.'[9]

Eventually, Pinto found a reliable witness, a Belgian resistance fighter who had accompanied King Kong on a sabotage mission to blow up a bridge.

The man told Pinto how a team of eight resistance fighters had arrived and begun planting demolition charges. The resistance fighter took off his beret to reveal to Pinto a scar on the side of his head.

'How did you get that?' Pinto asked.

'I was just bending down fixing the fuses to the charges under the bridge stanchion when, just like that …' he snapped his fingers quickly once, twice, thrice, 'bullets began to crack all over the place. Somehow the Nazis had got wind of our plan and had set an ambush. The sudden shock knocked me off the bridge into the river and luckily I had the presence of mind to stay under the water until the current – it was very fast just there – pulled me out of sight of their guns.'

He told how the Germans picked off the other fighters on the bridge, one by one, with sniper rifles 'like knocking tins off a wall'. He and Lindemans were the only survivors.

When Pinto enquired how such a large target as Lindemans had managed to evade the bullets, the Belgian replied: 'King Kong – our leader – he was magnificent! He got away right from under their noses. Every man hit – and there were eight of us – except King Kong. They couldn't hit him. What a man! He was born lucky, that one.'

Pinto weighed up the evidence: 'Here was the famous resistance leader on the one hand,' he considered. 'The man whose daring, giant strength and romantic affairs had made him the darling of all patriotic Dutchmen and almost equally popular with his Belgian comrades. A born leader who had done the Nazis much damage and who had risked his life repeatedly for his country. On the debit side were four strange facts which did not yet add up to any conclusion. He had been strangely apprehensive when I had tackled him over wearing insignia of rank to which he was not entitled … The Gestapo had released his brother and girlfriend [Gilou had in fact been released by the Americans] from captivity. It was not like the Gestapo to lose the opportunity of avenging themselves [even indirectly, on one of their most hated enemies]. The third and the fourth facts were that on at least two separate occasions, someone had obviously betrayed a resistance raid to the Gestapo sufficiently far in advance for them to plant a careful ambush. In each case the only common factor who had escaped was the leader, King Kong.'[10]

The evidence was by no means conclusive but it was building into a very interesting case. Pinto plied the Belgian resistance man with more red wine.

'They say that King Kong has an eye for the ladies,' Pinto remarked casually.

'Oh yes, sir, there they speak the truth! He is très gallant – not a girl who would not give anything to feel those big arms around her. I tell you, the pretty heiress who lives in the big chateau on the hill beyond Laeken – they say she gave all her jewellery, her family heirlooms, for his resistance group war funds.'[11]

Pinto wasted no time and drove to the chateau home of Ellie Zwaan.

Zwaan confirmed to Pinto the story about how she had handed King Kong her family jewellery to help fund the resistance. She told Pinto she now regretted doing so as she believed Lindemans had taken the jewellery for himself. When Pinto asked why she thought this, Zwaan explained: 'I do not like saying so because he is such a brave man and he has done such fine things for Belgium. But one day I saw a girl in town wearing one of my emerald pendants. She was not a respectable girl and the pendant belonged to my mother.'[12]

Ellie Zwaan first thought Lindemans must have sold the jewellery to finance his operations, but when she approached the woman about the provenance of the pendant the girl proudly told her that Lindemans had given it to her as a gift. After making further enquiries, Zwaan discovered another woman had also been treated to her jewellery.

Pinto asked whether she knew the names of the two women.

The first was called Margaretha Delden and the second was Mia Meersman. Zwaan was particularly bothered by Meersman, whom she suspected of having an affair with Lindemans. But when she challenged[13] Lindemans about this he told her that he had in fact murdered Meersman for being a spy.

Pinto tracked down Meersman to an apartment in the centre of Brussels only to discover that he was too late and she had fled the city a day or two earlier in fear of her life.

Fearing the worst, he then raced across town to Margaretha Delden's address.

'The door was heavily bolted,' recalled Pinto. 'We had no search warrant but there was no time to observe niceties. We smashed the door in and burst into her room and found her lying on her bed.'

Pinto took a few minutes to take in the scene: 'She must have been a pretty girl but poison does not improve one's features. Her face was a mottled colour, like those marbled endpapers one sometimes comes across in old books and ledgers. Her lips were a ghastly magenta and were stretched in a mirthless grin. She was still just breathing when we found her but she died in hospital that afternoon without uttering a word.'

Hanging from her neck was Ellie Zwaan's pendant.

'Lindemans was to be strongly suspected as a traitor,' Pinto wrote, 'But this one inexplicable fact seems to disprove his guilt … the inescapable fact that he had himself been wounded, shot through the lung and then captured by the German security police.'

Eventually Pinto concluded that in light of all the damning evidence, Lindemans being shot by the Germans was in fact 'the perfect answer to anyone who might suspect him of being a traitor'.

Pinto decided the time had come to call in King Kong for questioning. He first wrote to Col James Langley, the head of IS9 (WEA), warning him that he believed Lindemans to be a German agent and was in the process of gathering evidence against him.[14] Then he sent a message to Prince Bernhard's headquarters at Castle Wittouck.

'Lindemans was supposed to have reported me for my cavalier conduct in ripping off his badges a few days before,' Pinto remembered. 'Needless to say he had not acted on his threat. Instead I mentioned that I wanted the opportunity of a talk with him but was careful not to reveal the main purpose behind my wish. Lindemans had many friends in high places, as was natural for so famous a resistance leader, and I dared not risk the possibility of some casual remark or deliberate tip warning him of my real purpose. So I merely left word that he was to report to me at 11 o'clock next morning at the Palace Hotel Brussels, where SHAEF officers,[15] myself included, were billeted.'

Pinto was not the only Allied officer suspicious of Lindemans. Peter Baker had also now picked up talk that King Kong had been seen in company of the Gestapo before the liberation of Brussels.

'Three times I referred his credentials back to Prince Bernhard's headquarters. The third time I was rudely told to stop doubting the loyalty of one of Queen Wilhelmina's most gallant fighters.'[16]

On 15 September, two days before Market Garden, Oreste Pinto arrived early at the Palace Hotel for his reckoning with Lindemans.

An hour passed and Pinto began to wonder whether he had perhaps misjudged his quarry: 'Was he so confident in his reputation and the friendships he enjoyed with the politically powerful that he would deliberately disobey a specific order?'

It was 1pm when the silence in the lounge was finally broken by the arrival of his old adversary.

Kas de Graaf offered an insincere apology to Pinto for keeping him waiting, before informing him: 'Lindemans cannot keep the appointment. He's had other orders.'

Pinto asked: 'Other orders; whose orders?'

'Lindemans,' said de Graaf[17] in a reverent tone, relishing the impact of the news he was about to impart, 'left this morning on a very special mission.'

Chapter 21

A Traitor Betrayed

In the nick of time, Christiaan Lindemans had evaded Oreste Pinto and managed to cross the front line and make his report to the Germans.

When he reappeared in Nazi-occupied Eindhoven, his loyalty was immediately questioned by the local resistance leaders. A search of Lindemans and his belongings had turned up a German newspaper and a pass made out in the name of Colonel Kiesewetter. Lindemans was able to offer up plausible explanations for both articles, but nevertheless he was held and word was sent back to the British.

Bafflingly, Lindemans' superior officer Captain Peter Baker by now shelved his previous doubts and seemed convinced of the Dutchman's innocence. But under pressure from the other Dutch resistance members he had reluctantly agreed to place Lindemans in the custody of Lt Col Maurice de Rome, head of Canadian special forces.

Once again, Lindemans found himself having to account for his charmed life in battle, suspect contacts and a bulging bundle of incriminating evidence.[1] Lindemans fended off hours of questioning by portraying himself as a resistance hero who had saved the lives of many Allied airmen. He told de Rome he began working for the British secret service in Rotterdam in 1939 when he reported to a 'Mr Sandwich', 'Eddie Allen' and 'Mr Lord'.[2] No records of any of these men have ever been found.

De Rome was wholly ignorant of the history of British intelligence operations in Holland and lacked any witnesses to contradict Lindemans' version of events. Nevertheless, he still felt uneasy about the Dutchman and decided to pass him on to Prince Bernhard's headquarters for further questioning.

Lindemans arrived at Castle Wittouck on 23 September[3] and was greeted by his old friend Kas de Graaf, who had been pressed by Oreste Pinto to interrogate Lindemans and in a four-page report dated 26 September 1944, de Graaf insisted he had spoken to Lindemans at length, putting to him all Pinto's concerns: 'After having talked with Chris Lindemans for a long time, I have come to the conclusion that he cannot distinguish right from wrong (literally does not know what is a mistake). He is and always will be slightly fantastic and I am firmly convinced that the anti-social element in his psychological makeup disturbs the balance of his mind. He has always been accepted as 100% trustworthy by the Belgian and Dutch organisations. ... He must always remain under someone else and under no account be given authority over a group. O.K. as a subordinate officer.'[4]

After clearing Lindemans, de Graaf took it upon himself to accuse Oreste Pinto of sleeping with a known SD agent, Akke Volges, asserting: 'He [Pinto] arrested her after which he gave her a Pintoing.'[5]

Akke Volges was the stage name for the actress and part-time Gestapo agent Margaret Albrecht, better known to Dutch security services as a 22-year-old mistress of Christiaan Lindemans.

Finally free from Pinto, Lindemans was now made liaison officer between Prince Bernhard and the resistance forces of the Netherlands.[6] Lindemans based himself at Prince Bernhard's headquarters at Castle Wittouck, where he worked with de Graaf and the Canadians on an infiltration mission, establishing a chain of informants inside Dutch-occupied territory.[7]

By all accounts, Bernhard relished having the huge resistance hero on his staff, parading him in front of visiting dignitaries and seeking his advice on matters of insurgency and counter-espionage. One report even has him sitting on Bernhard's bed while the Prince was shaving.[8] Undeterred, Oreste Pinto continued to press his case with SHAEF.

'Most [British] senior officers dismissed my suspicions as being utterly fantastic. To accuse the famous resistance leader of one of our Allies of being a traitor was not only absurd but was really in doubtful taste.'

Pinto was forced to pursue the case alone. The trail took him to Eindhoven, where Lindemans had been detained by the resistance.

On 26 October, he was contacted by a British captain who had arrested a suspected Abwehr agent,[9] a Dutch ex-Legionnaire who had been placed in an interrogation cell.

In his autobiography *Spycatcher*,[10] published just after the war, Oreste Pinto recounted in great detail his encounter with the Dutch traitor.

Pinto says that after finishing with the suspect, he stood up and began dusting cigarette ash from his uniform.

The man's eyes were closely trained on the interrogator's.

'Am I to be shot?' he enquired. 'I have a young wife in Amsterdam, sir, a good Dutch girl. She is innocent, I swear it.'

'So?' replied Pinto. 'We do not propose to shoot your wife. We are not like your German masters.'

Desperately, the man tried another tack. 'I will give you valuable information, sir – in return for my life.'

'You fool,' responded Pinto impatiently. 'Any information you have can be extracted from you before you are shot. It is a simple and painless process.'

The traitor gave a wan but sly smile: 'You can make me tell what you think I should know but you cannot find out those facts which you do not suspect I know.'

'Well, my young philosopher, what do you know?'

The young Dutchman bartering for his life was none other than Cornelis Verloop, Satan Face. He leaned forward and slowly began to recite the names and descriptions of all of Pinto's intelligence staff. When he could see he had the attention of his interrogator, he started to dissect the 'network of our counter-espionage system in Belgium and the Netherlands'.

Pinto was unable to stop himself from demanding: 'Who told you all this?'

The transfer of power from interrogator to suspect was palpable. It was now Verloop's turn to sit back in his chair. He waited for Pinto to take his own seat again before surrendering his source: 'Colonel Kiesewetter of the Abwehr told me. In the Abwehr headquarters at Driebergen. But who told Colonel Kiesewetter is my secret. Do you wish to make a bargain, sir?'

Pinto may have been alarmed but he was also very tired. In the past few weeks he had dealt with scores of double-dealing collaborators and spies.

As Pinto describes it, he had reached the bottom of the barrel of this trade in human treachery.

'I had seen many men fight for their lives like cornered rats, prepared to sacrifice employers, country or friends to save their own skins, but somehow I could not stomach this last case of sordid bargaining.'

Pinto took his Walther pistol from its holster and pointed it at the prisoner: 'Come along, Verloop. I have had enough of your scheming. You are a traitor and you are not going to add to your treachery by bargaining with me. Your Nazi friends made the rules for this game. I didn't. So let us play the game their way. Who told those facts to Colonel Kiesewetter?'

'In exchange for my life, sir ...'

Pinto jerked his pistol forward. 'Get up.'

Without any staff or transport, the colonel decided to march Verloop back to the military prison at the other end of the city. The night was dark and Pinto pointed his pistol at Verloop's back so that he could keep the suspect in front of him at all times.

Pinto hoped a troubled night in jail would make the prisoner more cooperative.

But Verloop misread Pinto's intention and became convinced he was about to be executed.

'Wait,' he gasped.

'I'll tell you. Don't shoot. It was Chris Lindemans, King Kong. He told Colonel Kiesewetter.'

Pinto leaned forward and prodded Verloop with the muzzle of his pistol: 'Did King Kong betray Arnhem to the Nazis?'

Verloop, who had worked closely with Lindemans and who was at Driebergen when King Kong brought in his intelligence from the Allied lines, nodded. He could not speak until he had slipped his tongue over his dry lips and then the words came tumbling from him. 'Yes, he told Colonel Kiesewetter on 15 September, when he called at Abwehr headquarters. He said that British and American troops were to be dropped.'

'Did he say where?'

'Ja. He said that a British airborne division was waiting to be dropped on Sunday morning beyond Eindhoven.'

Pinto writes that he lowered his pistol and coldly considered the damning testimony that he knew would nail the giant traitor he had been trailing all these weeks.

Verloop once again misread the pause and fell to his knees: 'You won't shoot me now, will you? I've told you what I know.'

'I won't shoot you myself,' replied Pinto, 'but I can't speak for the Army. A court martial will decide your fate. Now stand up and let's go.'

* * *

On 10 October, Christiaan Lindemans, cleared by Dutch security over allegations that he was working for the Germans, co-opted a Dutch SOE agent, Sergeant Cornelis Goorden, as his personal driver and headed off to Brussels to make sure he did not miss out on the spoils of liberation. After King Kong had gorged himself on women, caviar and champagne, Goorden drove on to Lille, where Lindemans was finally reunited with Gilberte Letuppe and their two children. Later that day, Lindemans told Goorden to drive him to Paris for a rendezvous with a mysterious agent called Maurice de Vos, who lived near the Champs-Élysées. Earlier in the year, Lindemans had entrusted de Vos with 50,000 francs in a failed bid to secure the release of Gilou Letuppe from the Germans.

De Vos, a socialist member of one of Lindemans' escape lines, possessed a radio transmitter he used to contact someone in Britain. It would later emerge that MI5 had no record of de Vos or his mystery contact, but the communist cells of northern France were known to be in radio contact with Moscow via London. Throughout all his dealings with the resistance during the war, de Vos remained a constant fixture in almost all of Lindemans' escape lines. He was the one resistance leader Lindemans never crossed or ever betrayed to the Germans.

In Brussels, Pinto, armed with Verloop's testimony, raised the alarm with SHAEF. But after making enquiries at Château Wittouck, the Dutch spycatcher discovered that Lindemans had eluded him and once again crossed the front line. Unable to contain his rage, he barged into the Dutch officers' mess.

'I could not control myself,' he wrote in his memoirs. 'I trembled with a white-hot anger that left me speechless ... Notwithstanding my frequent warnings, King Kong had been allowed to go on a secret mission behind the enemy lines where he could do most damage to the Allied cause ... Nothing could undo the tragedy of Arnhem but at least I could put an end to Lindemans' treachery.'

Chapter 22

Caging the Gorilla

A little over two weeks later, on the morning of 28 October, Christiaan Lindemans' black Cadillac LaSalle pulled up in the grand forecourt of Château Wittouck.

Wearing full battle dress, Lindemans bowled into the main entrance and was ushered up the grand staircase into a private room at the top of the mansion. In his hand was an invitation from Prince Bernhard, who said it would be his greatest pleasure to have the honour to award Lindemans a medal for his service to the Dutch resistance. Lindemans paced around the baroque-decorated salon, where he impatiently waited to be called to the private ceremony.

In a room opposite, Major Alfred Vernon Sainsbury was also waiting. Sainsbury was in charge of security and counter-intelligence liaison for all special forces detachments in 21 Army Group.[1] An excellent skier, horseman and marksman, Sainsbury had been specially chosen for this most difficult and delicate assignment.[2]

It was Pinto's idea to put Lindemans at his ease with the promise of a medal, as he knew this would appeal to his 'collossal ego'.[3]

At 15.15, Sainsbury ordered five well-armed military policemen to apprehend the traitor.[4] The soldiers burst into the room with their weapons drawn, pointing at the bemused Lindemans, who was standing in the middle of the floor. For a moment there was a stand-off as the British soldiers waited for King Kong to make his move. But Lindemans offered no resistance and, according to Oreste Pinto, who insisted on being present during the arrest, the resistance leader was then 'lamb-like shorn of all his weapons'.

Pinto later wrote: 'There were no handcuffs in Holland big enough to clamp round his mighty wrists so instead his arms were lashed with steel-cored rope.'

Lindemans was transferred to St Gilles Prison, a mock medieval nineteenth-century chateau in Brussels. Sainsbury's initial report was passed on to MI5 Defence Security Office in the Belgian capital.[5] The senior MI5 officer in Brussels telegrammed Guy Liddell in London outlining the immediate problem presented by Lindemans: 'XB [counter-intelligence] potentialities of this case appear likely to be of considerable importance. King Kong is a X [enemy spy], stated to have betrayed more than 100 Dutch patriots during his many trips across the lines. This appears borne out by the fact that nearly every resistance or escape organisation with which he has been connected has been betrayed. In view of his close association with Bernhard's Headquarters and the fact that his Dutch staff is notoriously indiscreet, it is feared that King Kong may have given the Germans valuable military intelligence.'[6]

The MI5 office in Brussels was not equipped to undertake a full interrogation of Lindemans, whom they described as a 'particularly tough character'. Pinto expected to carry out the questioning, but the MI5 officer told Liddell: 'Personal enmity between KK and Pinto makes it undesirable for the latter to interrogate. Most important that KK should be interrogated as soon as possible on what military information he has passed to the Germans. Clearly he will have to be broken before this can be obtained. Therefore recommend that he's sent to UK for expert interrogation.'[7]

On 2 November, the prisoner, under the cover name of Mr Christopher Van Dam, was flown to RAF Northolt London.[8]

Lindemans was no longer the 'lamb' he had been upon his arrest. The American escort reported 'trouble en route' and were unable to use a pair of outsized handcuffs to contain him. When he arrived at Northolt he was fully bound.[9]

From there he was met by a military detachment and two officers from Scotland Yard, who described him as being in a 'truculent mood'. They escorted him to Latchmere House, Camp 020, the detention and interrogation centre for captured Nazi agents.

Lindemans was stripped, given a full body search and issued with prison-standard flannel trousers, hessian shirt, a coat, each with a distinguishing six-inch diamond-shaped piece of white cloth sewn on to a prominent part of the clothing – denoting his status as a prisoner awaiting interrogation. He was photographed, medically examined and then placed in a cell on his own. The prison officers were under strict instructions not to talk to him or answer any of his questions.[10]

Guy Liddell gave Colonel 'Tin Eye' Stephens the task of overseeing the interrogation. Stephens had been warned that Lindemans would be a tough customer, perhaps his toughest yet, but he was relishing the challenge.

By the time Lindemans had arrived in Ham, his addresses in Brussels had been thoroughly searched and all his personal effects and paperwork sent on to the UK. The search team recovered more than 50,000 Belgian and French francs stuffed into envelopes and securely kept in a dead box.

In a briefcase marked 'Lindemans 2' there were two loaded automatic revolver magazines, a stopwatch marked Berlin, a Kodak camera, 13 white pills and a white metal signet ring inscribed with the words 'toujours fidele' [always faithful].[11]

The contents of Lindemans' Brussels filing cabinet, so carefully administered by Mia Meersman, had the names and addresses of hundreds of people Lindemans had come into contact with over the last four years.[12] Among them were cut-outs, couriers, resistance fighters and Allied officers. Even the London home address and telephone number of Peter Baker.

But nothing among the many documents conclusively proved that Lindemans was working for the Germans.[13]

MI5 would have to rely on the testimony of Cornelis Verloop, the Dutch traitor, who had been flown from Brussels to Camp 020 ahead of Lindemans.

Stephens had nothing but contempt for 'Satan Face', whom he described[14] as a 'cunning, treacherous and avaricious scoundrel without shame, scruple or humanity'. Stephens said Verloop told his story of 'betrayal and deceit with the air of a man recounting heroic deeds'. Verloop was as much hated by the Germans as he was by the British. In one of his last acts of treachery he had written to Berlin telling Walter Schellenberg that Hermann Giskes and his NCO Willy Kup were in a homosexual relationship (outlawed in Nazi Germany).[15]

According to Verloop, Lindemans had been spying for the Germans since at least March 1944 and had betrayed 267 people, many of whom had been arrested and executed by the Gestapo.[16] It was treachery on a breathtaking scale.

But the most pressing question facing Liddell and Stephens was what current Allied military secrets Lindemans had given up to the Germans.

There was particular nervousness around the exact location of Monty's headquarters in Eindhoven because King George VI was shortly due to visit him in Holland. This meant Stephens did not have the luxury of letting Lindemans stew for a few days; the interrogation had to start immediately.

Stephens, who described Lindemans as an 'obstreperous giant',[17] maintained he never laid a hand on any of the detainees in his charge, but after the war he faced a court martial for professional negligence and disgraceful conduct. (He was eventually acquitted.)[18]

Yet Lindemans presented Stephens with a unique difficulty. The prisoner began to suffer a series of epileptic seizures, forcing Stephens to abandon the interrogation until the prisoner had been seen by the camp doctor. The epilepsy, the doctor diagnosed, was genuine and was linked to the brain injury Lindemans suffered during his motorcycle accident in Holland before the war.

Because of the pressure to complete the interrogation as quickly as possible, the doctor agreed to administer Luminal, which suppressed the epilepsy.

Stephens had made much more progress with Verloop, who was being interrogated in the nearby cell and who repeated what he had told Pinto: that Lindemans had passed on intelligence to the Germans about Market Garden two days before the airborne landings and the start of the ground assault towards Eindhoven.[19]

He also said Lindemans had given detailed information to the Germans about Oreste Pinto and Peter Baker.

Armed with these lines of inquiry, Stephens decided to start the questioning. However, he found that the Luminal prescribed by the doctor had transformed the violent Lindemans into a sedated zombie, again forcing him to halt the interrogation.

Stephens finally began his interrogation at 21.00 and stopped at 23.50, noting in his report: 'he proved extremely difficult and no admission of any kind was obtained during the first hour.'[20]

Stephens later noted: 'It was the first and last interrogation carried out under a drug. It was certainly the wrong drug for intelligence purposes as it had a steadying effect. Lindemans, hour after hour and day after day, was obdurate.'[21]

Then on 6 November, the British officer had a breakthrough, obtaining a limited confession that Lindemans agreed to sign.[22]

Stephens sent an urgent and rather unsatisfactory report to 21st Army Group: 'Lindemann [sic] has signed confession to espionage on behalf of the Germans since June 1944. He has given Germans information on British troop movements and resistance activities. Motive was Germans promised to release wife and brother from prison. He does not respond to questions regarding whereabouts of C-in-C and HQ 21 Army Group and my impression in interrogation is that he does not know. Lindemann [*sic*] was however at Eindhoven on October 5th – 12th and again on October 18th. If HQ were established at Eindhoven at these times it is likely it was the talk of the town. The case is extremely difficult as Lindemans has been violent and thrown an epileptic fit. He is consequently under Luminal treatment and reactions under interrogation are regarded with reserve. The denunciation by Verloop is substantially accurate.'[23]

Having established Lindemans' guilt, the spotlight immediately fell on Kas de Graaf, who had three times cleared him of any treachery.

Prince Bernhard was told to relieve the Dutch officer of his command and send him back to Britain, where he could do no further damage. Bernhard reluctantly agreed. De Graaf was replaced by 'Jack' Herbert Hooper as Bernhard's new head of security and in charge of the vetting of agents.

Hooper of course was the younger brother of the NKVD and Abwehr triple agent Bill Hooper. De Graaf was guilty of showing blind loyalty to Lindemans, but nobody had bothered to ascertain where Jack Hooper's true loyalties lay after he had left Holland for England in 1940.

The fate of Captain Peter Baker was much more troubling. Four weeks earlier on 10 October 1944, Baker crossed the front line by canoe over the River Waal in an attempt to meet up with resistance groups to begin the rescue of hundreds of Market Garden troops trapped behind German lines. He was accompanied by the American war hero Private Theodore 'Ted' Bachenheimer, known as the 'GI General' from the US 82nd Division, who had won honours fighting in Anzio and Sicily.[24] Both men remained behind the lines working with the Dutch resistance to locate British and American soldiers still trapped after the defeat of the landings. On the night of 16/17 October, the farmhouse in which they were staying was raided by a German patrol. Four resistance fighters were shot on the spot and the farm was burned down. Baker and

Bachenheimer had been betrayed. Baker was brutally interrogated and sent to a POW camp while Bachenheimer was executed with two bullets to the back of the head.

On 11 November, Stephens extracted a second confession in which Lindemans admitted that Baker had sent him to Eindhoven and that he had passed on details about the British captain to Richard Christmann: 'At Driebergen I gave the name of Captain Baker to a German lieutenant. The day of this was about 15 September 1944. I told the Germans that I worked as Captain Baker's chauffeur. I said that Captain Baker's headquarters would be in Eindhoven and that we had come from Diest. I drove a black private car for Captain Baker but I did not tell the Germans this.'[25]

Yet he still refused to acknowledge his role in Market Garden, beyond saying that Baker had sent him over the lines to Eindhoven when he had been picked up by a German patrol.

When Stephens put the Arnhem allegations to Lindemans he claimed 'that much of the information he gave to the Germans was deliberately false'.[26]

Lindemans was, however, willing to give up more names of the people he had betrayed, including Audrey Hepburn's grandfather, Baron van Heemstra, several women resistance couriers, many escape line members and his close friend Jimmy Hendrickx. He admitted taking 80,000 francs from Ellie Zwaan and spending a large chunk of it on his new lover, Mia Meersman, who he said he knew was an SD agent.[27] He also confessed to giving up two British agents, 'Aspateros' and 'Victor', to Richard Christmann.[28]

The investigation appeared to have run its course. Then Liddell obtained from Bletchley Park the decrypted message sent by Hermann Giskes on 28 August revealing Lindemans' involvement in passing intelligence about a British airborne operation.

In his interim report on the case, Liddell wrote: 'An ISOS trace shows almost undoubtedly that he attended a meeting where agents from this country disclosed to the Dutch resistance movement the possibility of parachute landings in the Maas area. This was fairly late in August and was probably part of the plan to seize the Arnhem bridgehead.'[29]

The ISOS message in fact referred to Operation Comet, the forerunner of Market Garden. The real value of the new intelligence about King Kong was that it proved the Abwehr agent had been holding out about the depth of his involvement with the enemy.

'If he is lying about this material matter then he has probably lied in other respects,' Liddell concluded in his interim report on the interrogation.

Stephens sent his own message to 21st Army Group requesting answers to questions about Lindemans' contact with British special forces and the Dutch and Belgian resistance. He also circulated 12 copies of Lindemans' photograph.

He asked three questions:

'When the three British officers handed over the plans to chosen resistant chiefs in Liège on 22 August 1944, was Lindemans one of these chiefs?

'Was the Arnhem plan matured by 22 August 1944?

What were the full circumstances of Captain Baker's disappearance?'[30]

After three weeks of interrogation and field investigations, Stephens was still unsure how much more Lindemans would be able to tell them, reporting to MI5 and 21st Army Group: 'On the one hand there was the unsupported denunciation by Verloop. On the other hand his [Lindemans' MI5] file and all his documents were clearly in his favour. Indeed they showed a long history of excellent service on behalf of the resistance movement in Holland. There was the added complication that this man appears to be persona grata with Prince Bernhard.'

Liddell knew that the secret of Lindemans' betrayal of Arnhem would most likely be found in the contacts he had with agents he *hadn't* turned over to the Germans. Crucially, Liddell wanted to know what Lindemans was doing in the weeks after Market Garden when he returned from the German lines and had been given the all-clear by de Graaf.

The key to Lindemans' whereabouts and activities in October before his arrest lay with his driver, Sergeant Cornelis Goorden, who had recently returned to Britain. Liddell traced him to a Dutch army training camp in Wolverhampton and pulled him in for questioning.

Goorden's account of Lindemans' activities after Arnhem opened up a whole new line of inquiry.

Liddell wrote: 'Point is given to the foregoing remarks by the report which has only just been received of the interrogation of the chauffeur Sergeant C Goorden, which shows that Lindemans omitted to give the particulars of some of his movements; omissions which may have great significance. In this connection we suggest that attention should be given in the field to the question of whether Lindemans had an opportunity to pass information to the enemy on any three of the occasions when agents were conducted by him with the intention of passing them into enemy held territory.'[31]

Of these, it was Lindemans' visit to Paris to visit Maurice de Vos which most troubled Liddell. De Vos was known to have a wireless transmitter, not one that he used to contact the Germans, one that he used to send secret communications to an unidentified destination in London.

'The visit to Paris referred to by Goorden,' deduced Liddell, 'opens up a new line of inquiry but we have not so far obtained any indication at all that Lindemans had any other means of communication.'

MI5 was unable to establish to whom de Vos was transmitting or why Lindemans considered it so important to visit the Dutchman at this critical time in the war.

On 12 December, Winston Churchill was officially informed about Lindemans in the monthly update on the work of the Security

Service. The report made only a brief mention of the German spy who had been given the code name King Kong. There was no reference to his role in Arnhem and the number of people he was alleged to have betrayed was downgraded from 267 to just 40. Neither did the report say that Lindemans had been working for British special forces. Instead it said he had 'obtained his post on Prince Bernhard's staff' and 'appointed by the prince as liaison officer with Dutch Forces of the Interior'. The author of this innocuous version of events was Anthony Blunt.[32]

Chapter 23

Betrayal of the Bulge

In light of the Allies' defeat at Arnhem, Adolf Hitler now clung to the idea he could salvage something from the war and ordered a massive counter-attack in the West. On 16 December 1944, 410,000 soldiers, 1,400 tanks and 2,600 artillery pieces supported by over 1,000 combat aircraft achieved complete surprise in a German attack through the Ardennes. Hitler expected his forces to drive a wedge between the American and British forces that would allow fast-moving Panzer divisions to reach the coast at Antwerp, entrapping Montgomery's 21st Army Group in Holland. It would have been a repeat of the feat his armies had managed four years earlier in the Blitzkrieg victory during the Battle of France.

The German leader hoped he could split the Allied forces and compel the Americans and British to settle for a separate peace, independent of the Soviet Union. Success in the West would give the Germans time to deploy their new 'super weapons' of flying bombs and rockets as well as concentrate resources against the advancing Red Army in the East.

But right from the start the offensive, which became known as the 'Battle of the Bulge', played into Stalin's hands by diverting substantial resources from East to West. The Russian leader must have been delighted by the Führer's plan, which practically guaranteed the Red Army's arrival in Berlin before his British and American allies.

The brunt of the German attack in the West fell on largely untested American units, who dropped back in confusion only to make a rousing last-ditch defence, supported by Montgomery's XXX Corps, who had held on to key bridges on the northern banks of the Rhine, which blunted the German advance and eventually ended the Battle of the Bulge.

The initial element of surprise achieved by the Germans raised questions about the failure of Allied intelligence obtained through Ultra to warn of Hitler's intention. It was apparent from October 1944 that the Germans had begun to suspect the security of their Enigma machines had been compromised.

While Bletchley Park had picked up and misinterpreted some German messages during the Bulge offensive, it had been noticeable that the enemy had relied much more on landline communications and tightened security over intelligence passed through the Enigma machines. Had the Germans already worked out the British had cracked their codes?

According to Anthony Cave Brown, the historian and friend of Kim Philby, it was Christiaan Lindemans who had alerted the Germans to Ultra and the existence of the code breakers at Bletchley Park.[1]

Cave Brown says it was during Lindemans' 15/16 September visit to Driebergen that he also passed on what he had gleaned about Ultra from his British intelligence sources rather than his contact with Prince Bernhard, who Cave Brown says would not have been told about Ultra.

Joseph Stalin waited until 12 January, when the German push in the West had been reversed and the two armies had fought themselves to a standstill, before launching his own new offensive in the East. He wrote to Churchill, telling the British leader that he had brought forward the Vistula–Oder Offensive to 'render assistance to the glorious forces of our Allies'.[2] The truth was that, having stood back and watched Hitler weaken his Eastern Front defences by the withdrawal of the Panzer Armies (5th and 6th) to fight in the West, the Russian leader's decision to attack was taken purely in support of his own war aims.

Meanwhile, Winston Churchill was facing down a communist insurgency in Greece, where he had given British troops orders to fire on revolutionary groups who were attempting to impose a communist government on the newly liberated population. British soldiers and bombs killed hundreds of armed communists and unarmed Greek civilians.

The British action was condemned more by the Americans than by the Soviets. Greece was a British 'sphere of influence' agreed by Stalin and Churchill at the Tolstoy Conference in October.

Churchill secretly wrote to Field Marshal Jan Smuts on 22 December: 'Greece has proved a source of endless trouble to me, and we have indeed been wounded in the house of our friends. With this new chance, communist and left-wing forces throughout the world have stirred in sympathy, and our prestige and authority in Greece has to some extent been undermined by the American press ... but if the powers of evil prevail in Greece, as is quite likely, we must be prepared for a quasi-Bolshevized Russian-led Balkans peninsula and this may spread to Italy and Hungary. I therefore foresee great perils to the world in these quarters, but I'm powerless to do anything effective without subjecting the government to great stresses and quarrelling with America.'[3]

On 31 January, British code breakers at Bletchley Park deciphered a message sent by German intelligence warning of a planned Anglo-American offensive between Venlo and Aachen, a preparatory step before the crossing of the Rhine.[4]

The Abwehr intelligence was entitled 'American offensive plan' and its author's identity was code-named Peterson Hasso. It began: 'After talks with 05[5] (between 22 and 24 January) who has recently been in London I learned that the offensive plans of the Allies has changed in the last three weeks. The changes [are] chiefly due to the astonishing success, in SHAEF's eyes, of the Soviet Offensive. They were informed that the Germans would be able to hold the Soviet Offensive on the German frontier. As a result of a personal request from the Whitehouse, Eisenhower is preparing to mount an offensive within four weeks at the most ... the English are fully supporting this plan of Eisenhower's for military and political reasons. This attack is to be expected from the northern sector of the Aachen bulge on the north of Venlo ... The withdrawal of German units from West to East has been observed by '05' [code number for one of his sources]. This weakening is a decisive moment in which Eisenhower may carry out his plan.'

Peterson Hasso also identified each of the British and American units to be involved in the operation. It was followed by further reports giving more details of the 'Anglo-British' offensive.[6]

Peterson Hasso was another code name used by Karl Heinz Kraemer.

Harry Hinsley, who worked at Bletchley Park at this time, later described the Hasso reports as 'disturbingly accurate' and looked 'uncomfortably like a reference to Operations Grenade and Veritable.'[7] At the time, SHAEF regarded the intelligence as 'very dangerous'.[8]

The 'Rhine' leakage was not so easily dismissed as previous Josephine material. These latest reports posed a real threat to ongoing Allied operations and also highlighted Anglo-American concerns about Soviet advances.[9] Guy Liddell said the leakage was so accurate that it had to be regarded as 'dangerous.'[10]

Kraemer had even picked up on claims of tension between Montgomery and Eisenhower which, although dismissed as nonsense by the MI5 analysts in London, were in fact true and had been a running sore between the leader of the Allied forces and his deputy since before the Arnhem operation.[11]

It was also noticeable that Kraemer's reports tended to exaggerate the strength of British and American equipment and forces on the Western Front, encouraging Hitler to transfer troops from the Eastern to the Western Front.

The Americans had by now come to believe that Kraemer's Arnhem and Rhine reports were anything but 'lucky guesses'.

Lieutenant General Lewis Brereton, head of the 1st Allied Airborne Army who had organised Market Garden, was increasingly worried that there had been a security breach that had betrayed the Allied operation to the Germans. He wrote in his diary: 'The enemy espionage system in France is giving us serious concern. Intelligence reports that it has captured a document which indicates the enemy has correct information about the proposed Operation Naples II, a landing across the Rhine at Cologne – had the correct area and date.'[12]

There was another, far more sensitive, reason why the Americans were worried by Kraemer. Intelligence had emerged that showed Kraemer had tipped off[13] Berlin and presumably his close associate, the Japanese military attaché in Stockholm, Onodera, about the American landings in the Philippines. Additionally, the Americans were concerned that Onodera had got hold of very accurate intelligence about US aircraft carriers.[14]

The date of the Philippine landings, 20 October, had been shared with the British during a meeting with American Joint Chiefs at the Octagon Conference in Quebec between 12 and 16 September.

The Americans categorised Kraemer as the highest paid German spy who had delivered the important 'scoops' of Arnhem and the Philippines.[15] But they had also noticed that Kraemer was funnelling a 'great deal' of Russian intelligence to Berlin.[16]

The Office of Strategic Services (OSS), the American intelligence agency and forerunner of the CIA, had recently taken custody of a German diplomat based in Sweden who had worked closely with Kraemer and had convinced the Americans that Kraemer's contacts were genuine and based in Britain.

Hauptmann Peter Riedel, a pilot and aeronautical engineer, claimed to be horrified when he discovered the extent of the atrocities committed by the Nazis and had offered his services to the OSS in Sweden. During his interrogation by the Americans, Riedel said that although he was sure before D-Day Kraemer's reports were fabricated or based on published defence material, after D-Day the intelligence was very accurate and was taken so seriously by the OKW that it was passed directly to Adolf Hitler.[17]

According to the OSS report, Riedel partly based his assertion of Kraemer's credibility on the strength of his report on the Arnhem landings, which he said had triggered a 'furious' response when Berlin had realised it had been received, and ignored, a day before the start of Operation Market Garden.[18] Riedel told the Americans he was convinced Kraemer had a well-connected source based in London. But he said he had also seen secret Russian intelligence reports in Kraemer's office which he could not explain.[19]

On 22 March, another alarming Kraemer message was picked up by an SIS agent in Stockholm. This time it described an operation to cross the Rhine using a combination of the 6th Airborne Division and a direct assault by units from the 21st Army Group in the Wesel area. The source of the intelligence was given as Air Vice-Marshal Brown. Such was the level of concern that the War Office immediately alerted 21st Army Group and SHAEF.[20]

Blunt's colleague Herbert Hart, who was asked by SIS to assess the accuracy of the report, played it down by saying Kraemer had not properly located the 6th Airborne Division whereas if AVM Brown had really been the source, the error would not have been made. He concluded that Kraemer had been working off 'guess work' that he said was a 'practice of agents who are trying to build themselves in the eyes of their masters'.

Blunt himself said Kraemer's messages were 'unlikely to tell the Germans much that they did not know before, but they may, in spite of this, of course constitute a leakage'.[21]

This was not an argument that SHAEF found particularly convincing and so launched its own investigation.[22]

SHAEF's 'veracity checks' on Kraemer's Rhine messages found that the thrust and much of the detail was accurate and that there was nothing to disprove that AVM Brown had been the unwitting source.

Sir Stewart Menzies, the head of SIS, who funnelled all the decoded Kraemer intelligence to MI5, felt moved to write to Blunt and Hart: 'I still feel that we are not justified in assuming that Kraemer invented or intellectually deduced this information. He may have done, but when you recall that Kraemer is reported to have given Berlin prime warnings of the Arnhem airborne landing and as far back as 20 February received information that the 6th Airborne Division was to take part in a British Second Army offensive with the special task of securing a bridgehead east of the Rhine in the Eimerich Wesel area, I consider that there is at least a 50/50 chance that he has one real-world place source apart from his many others (the majority of whom are probably notional). I would be grateful for your comments.'[23]

Karl Heinz Kraemer did not ever send another piece of credible intelligence to Berlin.

Chapter 24

Confessions of King Kong

On 13 November 1944, a German intelligence officer crossed the Siegfried Line near Saarbrücken. His name was Carl Marcus, a successful lawyer and an aide to Walter Schellenberg and Schellenberg's intelligence adviser, Kurt Jahnke. Marcus had lived in Holland before the war and after joining the Abwehr helped lay the groundwork for the invasion of the Netherlands in 1940.[1]

He told the French that he had an important message which he could only deliver to Sir Robert Vansittart,[2] the shadowy British diplomat who ran agents across Europe.

The Foreign Office sent senior MI6 officer Frank Foley to interview Marcus in Paris. What he had to offer was a peace deal – in return for lenient treatment of Marcus and Jahnke after the war.[3] But neither Marcus nor Jahnke had the authority to make such a deal.

Instead Marcus was given the code name 'Dictionary' and brought back to England, where he was interrogated by officers from Section V of MI6.[4]

SIS interrogators extracted two important pieces of intelligence from the German officer.

The first concerned the close links which had formed between the NKVD and the German intelligence security services. According to Marcus, the Soviets had infiltrated the Abwehr, the SD and the Gestapo. He also claimed that Schellenberg was using informal diplomatic channels in Stockholm to speak to the Kremlin.[5] Marcus reported the Russians had completely infiltrated the Hungarian secret services years ago.

He said many German intelligence officers, like Heinz Pannwitz, who ran the Gestapo unit against Rote Kapelle, realised they stood a better chance when the war ended by siding with the Russians.

Summarising the typical German officer's attitude he explained: 'The Russian system, these men are convinced, is dependent on the use of a secret police and who, they ask, should fulfil this role if not themselves? The great majority of these men are experts who will not mind obeying orders whatever the authority that gives them and whatever the political system that they are expected to serve. Naturally it is accepted that the Russians will liquidate those Gestapo men who have ill-treated Russians during the German occupation of part of the Soviet Union. This however affects very few members in Amt IV.'[6]

Stalin was made aware of the Marcus defection almost immediately when a report of his interrogations was sent to Major Blunt at B1B.[7]

The second part of Marcus' intelligence report was even more disturbing.

It related to Holland and Operation Market Garden. Marcus disclosed that the Abwehr controlled two agents: one unidentified agent working as a senior officer among Prince Bernhard's staff and another close to Queen Wilhelmina's government in London.[8]

According to the MI6 report, Marcus claimed the Germans 'became aware of the British plans to land airborne troops at Apeldoorn and Arnhem from intelligence gathered from Dutchmen. As a result, the Germans placed a company of SS Jagdverband [Waffen SS, mostly Dutch special forces soldiers] in English uniform at Apeldoorn and Arnhem and in the background there was a heavily equipped SS mobile unit. These men were all in position eight days before the airborne landings.'[9]

Marcus was very damning of the Allied operation saying that the British paratroopers at Arnhem were poorly equipped. Their jump boots, he claimed, 'were not strong enough, causing many broken ankles and knees while some of the paratroopers had no knives or pistols'.

Finally, he said the Germans considered the tactics adopted in the landings to be outdated, long rejected by its own parachute corps under the leadership of General Kurt Student.

The new intelligence about Arnhem reignited interest in Lindemans, who was still being held at Camp 020. Allegations about Dutch traitors close to Prince Bernhard and the Dutch government fed British prejudices about the 'leaking' Dutch camp at a critical moment in the war – the Allies were preparing a new offensive to break through the German lines with all-out assault across the Rhine.

Liddell once again pressed for more help from the field so MI5 could step up their interrogation of Lindemans. Twenty-first Army Group HQ had become uncharacteristically reticent about the case and MI5 soon discovered that Monty's staff were no longer interested in Lindemans in the same way they were when he was first captured. It left Stephens in a difficult position as he once more tried to break King Kong and get to the truth behind the betrayal.

Stephens later wrote: 'A greater measure of cooperation in the field would have helped to clear important details of this case but for one reason or another this was not forthcoming.'[10] Nevertheless, Stephens' perseverance paid off. Towards the end of December he succeeded in obtaining a third confession[11] from Lindemans, who agreed to sign a statement to the effect that he had passed on military intelligence to the Germans at the time of Arnhem. But he still refused to give any details of the intelligence or, more importantly, from whom or where he had obtained the information.

Stephens had one last interrogation trick up his sleeve. He decided to place Lindemans in the same cell as Verloop and Tony Damen, the Abwehr agent who had betrayed Verloop to the British in Eindhoven.

He told Liddell: 'All three men have several reasons for lying: each has to a greater or lesser extent acted as stool pigeon and each suspects the other two of filling that role; each aims at being sent back to work for the Allies; each has private feuds both with the other two and with associates elsewhere, and is more than prepared to black another's character in his own personal interest.'[12]

But when Oreste Pinto found out about Stephens' interrogation ploy, he voiced strong objections, warning that the three traitors would use the time together to corroborate their stories.[13]

Stephens felt he had no choice. And on 18 November, he wrote: 'If I have not yet plumbed the depths of human degradation I am at least near it.'

His gambit did succeed in loosening Lindemans' tongue.

The Dutch spy agreed to make a full confession about his 15 September mission, admitting for the first time that he had been taken to the headquarters of General Student at Vught, where he had first passed on his intelligence about the coming attack.[14] From there he was driven by car to Driebergen, where he was interviewed by Major Kiesewetter. Stephens wrote:[15] 'Lindemans admits that he gave the German officer information about the numbers of British troops and tanks he had seen ... The following day he was taken back to the region of Eindhoven in a car driven by Arnaud [Christmann], a man working with the German intelligence service at Driebergen. His instructions were to re-cross the Allied lines and proceed to Brussels and then find out where the certain acts of sabotage are being carried out by stay-behind agents as ordered; the password was "Bonnifacius". He was expected to report back in the course of a week or so.'

Lindemans also disclosed that his mission to Eindhoven had a second part: to warn the resistance of the imminent Allies' attack and to contact the directors of the Philips electrical works about secret intelligence on the V2 rockets.

Lindemans told Stephens that he knew from the Germans all about the V2 project and was able to disclose that the weapons each weighed 12,000 kilograms and had a range of 700 kilometres. He supplied details of the launch sites in the Marlot district of The Hague.

Lindemans said he had been told of a far more deadly and even more secret weapon that the Germans had been working on – 'an atomic bomb that burns and destroys everything in a radius of 500 yards'.[16]

But Stephens, who could not have realised the significance of this intelligence relating to what was then an unknown technology, dismissed Lindemans' claims: 'For what it is worth, Lindemans states the effect of another invention, the "atomic bomb", is to dehydrate living bodies, reducing them in size.'

The 020 commandant believed he had finally broken his man: 'This man is a thug. He has certainly betrayed his countrymen and it is probable he has betrayed Allied personnel. Although Lindemans stoutly denies this under interrogation it is possible he has betrayed operational plans to the Germans. The obvious disposal is death.'[17]

Lindemans' case had turned into a political hot potato. The reputation of King Kong as a colourful Dutch resistance hero and his connections to Prince Bernhard meant a public trial in England was out of the question.

At the same time, the failure of Arnhem had triggered vicious Nazi retributions and a winter famine in German-occupied Holland in which 20,000 people starved to death.

Stephens later said: 'If Lindemans was guilty of Arnhem then his name will reek to the end of time.'[18]

Lindemans' treachery was also a significant embarrassment for the British. At every stage of his betrayal of Market Garden he was an agent attached to a British special services unit and sent across the lines by a British officer who had released him from detention by the Dutch resistance in Eindhoven.

At the end of December, Lindemans was flown back to Allied-occupied southern Holland, ostensibly so he could be tried for treachery by his countrymen. Instead he was detained indefinitely in Breda Prison, his identity and crimes a closely guarded secret.

The man who had most to lose from a public trial was Prince Bernhard, who had been so comprehensively beguiled by the giant resistance fighter. He embarked on a discreet lobbying campaign to clear his name of any association with Lindemans and particularly the allegation that the Arnhem betrayal originated in his headquarters.

On 2 February 1945, his close friend Commander Philip Johns went to see Guy Liddell in London. After a convivial dinner with Johns, Liddell wrote in his diary that Bernhard had told Johns there were two rumours circulating about the German-born prince: one that he led a dissolute lifestyle which he could laugh off and another, much more serious, allegation that he had passed on information to King Kong that had led to the betrayal of Arnhem.

'I told Johns,' wrote Liddell, 'that I was aware in Dutch circles there was a belief that Lindemans had betrayed Arnhem. We had told Dutch security, but as a result of our inquiries there was no possible foundation for the belief. I'd never heard any suggestions that Bernhard, the former Nazi, was involved. I agreed that we would do our best to counteract such rumours in Dutch circles.'[19] This, as Liddell well knew, was completely contrary to the evidence obtained from the prisoners at Camp 020.

Bernhard's secret lobbying had achieved the result he intended.

Oreste Pinto, who had been recuperating from exhaustion, returned to Holland to continue his work as head of the Netherlands counter-intelligence mission attached to SHAEF.

A few days after his arrival he was called to SHAEF headquarters, where he was personally commended by Dwight D. Eisenhower for his work on the Lindemans' case.[20]

Such high praise from the leader of the Allied forces encouraged Pinto to establish his own headquarters in Breda, south Holland, where he could keep a close eye on 'King Kong'.[21]

Yet Pinto was no nearer to seeing Lindemans in the dock to be held account for his betrayal. The British had washed their hands of him and the Dutch authorities and Prince Bernhard had no appetite for a public show trial before the end of the war. Perhaps the world would never know of the evil of King Kong and the 267 SOE agents, resistance workers and couriers who were alleged to have died as a result of his treachery: 'When I read the list of names, many of whom were known to me and some indeed being my good friends,' said Pinto, 'I vowed that I should not rest until Lindemans had got his desserts.'[22]

The climax of Lindemans' treachery was the betrayal of Arnhem. Pinto believed that the Dutch people should know the truth no matter how distasteful: 'Most Dutch people did not yet know why Arnhem had failed. They had been taught to blame the weather or "the luck of the game" or Field Marshal Montgomery's recklessness in mounting a daring operation without sufficient resources at his disposal. They did not know that one of their own countrymen had betrayed the battle before it started. It seemed that as long as Lindemans could be kept obscurely in jail – and there appeared to be no time limit to this – they never would know.'[23]

Then on Saturday 17 February 1945, the *Daily Mirror* ran a front-page story claiming that a dangerous Dutch officer had betrayed Arnhem and was being held in the Tower of London. Apart from the reference to the Tower of London, other details of the story were true and although Lindemans was not named, the subsequent press coverage ran all over the world and put the spotlight on the failure of Market Garden.[24]

Pinto says he didn't know how the media picked up on the story, although he acknowledged there were journalists asking questions in Breda.[25] It's quite likely the wily security chief fed the story to the media, ensuring public interest in the case, but shifting the attention from Breda to London.

In Whitehall, the newspaper stories were deeply problematic.

CONFESSIONS OF KING KONG

The *Daily Mirror* and *Sunday Times* had published further details of the betrayal linking 'the spy' to Prince Bernhard. Liddell had a meeting with Edward Cussen, head of legal at MI5, and discussed trying to shut down the story by bringing prosecutions against the *Mirror* editor and its owner. But it emerged that due to a misunderstanding, the official censor had approved the story before publication.[26]

The Foreign Office was contacted by Prince Bernhard demanding the British government issue a statement that Lindemans had not been on the Prince's staff and confirming he was engaged by British special forces when he carried out the alleged betrayal.[27] This triggered a flurry of confidential memos sent between MI6, MI5, MI9 and SOE as each agency tried to distance itself from any association with Lindemans.

One from SOE to SIS read: 'The report of the arrest of Lindemans appeared in the Daily Mirror newspaper of 17 February. It is inaccurate in a number of respects particularly; a) Lindemans is not a Dutch officer; b) he did not occupy a position of trust in the underground movement; c) he had no advanced knowledge of the Arnhem attack. This report was elaborated in the Sunday press with reference in some cases to King Kong's presence at Prince Bernhard's headquarters as a member of his staff. This is also untrue.'[28]

MI5 and MI6 continued to put pressure on the newspapers not to publish Lindemans' name or the people he had given away.

The press was briefed along these lines,[29] and largely it stopped the story going much further, although of course by now it was widely known in Whitehall that Lindemans had held a position on the Prince's staff, was working with British special forces, and at the time of Arnhem had, by his own admission, betrayed the landings. Nevertheless, the government had, for the time being at least, killed the traitor of Arnhem story.

It was a British cover-up designed to keep Bernhard onside and support the war effort in Holland, which heavily relied on the

Prince as head of the Dutch army and 12,000 irregular, armed resistance fighters.[30]

But the cover-up was even more important to Britain's strained relations with the American military, who already blamed the Arnhem fiasco on Monty and Horrocks' XXX Corps, who were respectively accused of championing a hare-brained plan and not being aggressive enough in pushing through to Arnhem. Had the Americans found out about the Lindemans' story they could have added to the British charge sheet a catastrophic security failure that may have cost the lives of hundreds of American servicemen.

Should it have emerged that the Arnhem traitor was recruited by British special forces and sent across the lines under escort before betraying Market Garden, the disclosure would have threatened future joint operations. After the war the American generals in the field wrote disparagingly about how Arnhem was a wholly British defeat. In a letter[31] to Cornelius Ryan, the Irish-American author of the book *A Bridge Too Far*, Jim Gavin, commander of the US 82nd Airborne Division, wanted it made clear that the Americans secured all their objectives and held on to their bridges.[32] Arnhem was a British, not an American, blunder.

Ryan agreed, pointing out the British had been complacent and had arrived in Holland 'packing golf clubs and dinner jackets'[33] in anticipation of the victory celebrations. Although that fails to take account of the fact that Gavin's own indecisiveness has also been much of the focus for why Market Garden failed.

* * *

On 20 February 1945, a special forces conference held at SFHQ in London had finalised the details for a new offensive to be launched against German positions in Nazi-occupied north Holland. The conference report noted that Bernhard was very anxious about the communist elements within the Dutch resistance movement.[34]

Chapter 25

Josephine in Chains

On 11 May 1945, Anthony Blunt and Leo Long met Guy Liddell for lunch at the Reform Club in central London.[1]

Long had recently been promoted to the British Control Commission in British-held territory in Germany, where he exercised a senior role overseeing the security and interrogation of prisoners who had fallen into British hands.[2] Long impressed Liddell with his assessment of the security challenge facing the British occupation, telling Liddell that the Americans 'were not really tackling the problem' while the German population greatly feared the Russians.

Long, a Russian agent himself, even reported how one German woman mistook him for a Soviet officer and, expecting to be raped, 'implored him to shoot her'.

There were two groups of Germans who the NKVD was extremely keen should not fall into the hands of its Allies. The first was the nuclear and rocket scientists that Stalin had ordered Pavel Sudoplatov to round up and transport to new laboratories in Russia. The second was the Abwehr officers and agents whose secrets about the Western intelligence services the Soviets were keen to unlock.

The day after Long and Blunt lunched with Liddell, one of these Abwehr officers was captured in a small office at Flensburg, a town at the northern tip of Germany that was serving as the newly established 'German Foreign Office'.[3]

A British special forces unit based in Denmark tracked down the spy to the Nazi outpost where he was roused from bed. The indignant German, who was with his loyal secretary, protested that he had not been allowed to change into his air attaché uniform and afforded the respect of his diplomatic office.

The officer in question was Karl Heinz Kraemer, who had at the last minute escaped Stockholm for Denmark with his wife and secretary before the Swedes were able to take the trio into custody.

Former MI6 officer Patricia McCallum, who was entrusted with investigating 'Josephine' 30 years later, says that MI6 had been attempting to manoeuvre Kraemer into being arrested by the Swedish police, which would have put him into MI6 custody but somebody had tipped him off and he fled to the Danish border and into the arms of MI5.

On 17 May 1945, Kraemer, still dressed in civilian clothing, found himself standing before interrogators in a room at Camp 020.

In front of him sat Colonel Robin 'Tin Eye' Stephens assisted by Major Michael Ryde, the MI5 B1A officer assigned to the case. Ryde had been one of Eddie Chapman's (Agent Zigzag) case officers and had a reputation for being a tough operator who had tried to have Chapman cut loose from MI5 when he caught him dabbling in his old criminal ways.

'His reception at Ham,' said Stephens,[4] 'was noisy and shattering. Disillusioned but soured, he yielded his personal history and some knowledge only grudgingly. There were reticences and there were half-truths.'

It was a dramatic moment. MI5 had at last laid their hands on the Nazi's top conduit for British intelligence in the Second World War. Where every single other Abwehr network had been rounded up and either arrested or turned in the first weeks of the war, Kraemer had emerged in mid-1943 with a source (or sources) which had repeatedly astonished intelligence officers with their detail and accuracy. Herbert Hart described[5] Josephine's material as 'the best illicit intelligence derived by the enemy from this country which I have seen'. Some appeared to be verbatim records of conversations

JOSEPHINE IN CHAINS

that had taken place at the very highest levels and with only a tiny number of people present. At last, MI5 had the opportunity to solve what at the time must have appeared the last great mystery of the war. Who in Britain was betraying their country to the Nazi cause? And doing so in the final months of the war after Germany had all but lost the war and when the risk of exposure must inevitably be so great and any possible reward so negligible?

In the weeks after the end of the war, Camp 020 was a veritable rogues' gallery of Nazi intelligence officers, but for the British the star attraction of the several dozen they held was the enigmatic attaché from Stockholm who had done so much damage to the Allied cause.

Kraemer spent the first weeks of his interrogation claiming that while he gathered his information from a wide range of sources, his principal source was the Japanese Military Attaché Colonel Onodera Makoto. As Onodera (as he is referred to in the files) was also head of Japanese Intelligence in Western Europe, this had a certain plausibility. But it was not the full story. Onodera had simply not been in Europe for long enough and nor were Japanese intelligence networks good enough to have come up with the flood of intelligence Kraemer had been passing on. Above all, the dates did not match. MI6 were able to confirm that Onodera and Kraemer were certainly friendly and clearly cooperated, but further investigation showed that Onodera's reports to Japan containing Kraemer's material were always sent after Kraemer had made his own reports to Berlin.[6]

Major Michael Ryde, part of the counter-espionage section of MI5 still headed by Guy Liddell, directed the initial interrogations with Tin Eye Stephens. Kraemer, who was described[7] by his fellow German officers as 'self-confident and rather conceited', was proving a tough nut to crack ...[8]

Ryde decided to up the stakes and began lobbying for what is described in the files as a 'blitz'. It's not entirely obvious what this is, but it was clearly not a course of action to undertake lightly. Stephens noted that 'if a blitz is to be successfully carried out, the 020 interrogators themselves must be convinced they are on sure ground.' One can imagine that in 1945, after six long years of war, Camp 020 notions of enhanced interrogation will have been pretty robust. In any case, the blitz went ahead and the interrogation of Kraemer entered its critical phase.[9]

It was now late June and Kraemer had been at Camp 020 for over a month of what was already intense pressure. There were suggestions that he had been commandant of a concentration camp in Hamburg at one point and even though these were unfounded, he can have been under few illusions that he was fighting for his life. The blitz yielded results, because 'under pressure'[10] the interrogators got their break and Kraemer suddenly changed his story. All of a sudden he began to talk[11] about a Hungarian businessman, a naturalised Swede by the name of Antal (or Anton) Grundboek. Grundboek, who had died the year before, was a millionaire businessman with extensive links, not only to Swedish high society (he had invested in the business of Raoul Wallenberg, the Swedish businessman who rescued thousands of Jews from Nazi Hungary) but with Hungarian intelligence. He is recorded as being close personal friends with both the former and the current head of Hungarian intelligence.

Grundboek, according to Kraemer, had been the connection to a Hungarian network in Spain known variously as the Fuellop/FULLOP network and that had been Kraemer's source for the best of the Josephine material. Grundboek had died of natural causes in March 1944, but he had ensured the pipeline had remained open by putting Kraemer in touch with another Hungarian, a diplomat in Berlin by the name of Janos Horvath.[12] Kraemer would meet Horvath monthly on his regular trips to Berlin, and carry back the Josephine material, which he would then transmit back to Berlin.

The Hungarian connection certainly appeared as if it had some legs. Kraemer's passport detailed his trips across Europe for the whole of the war and he had visited Hungary a considerable amount; five times in 1940 alone. It was at this time that he first met Grundboek,[13] who had been working as an Abwehr agent in Austria before the war.[14] SIS had also seized Kraemer's office accounts in Stockholm that showed Grundboek and later Horvath were the only contacts to whom Kraemer paid substantial sums of money for their intelligence during 1944. The money was apparently funnelled to the Fuellop organisation, the ultimate source of the reports, under the code name 'Siegfried'.

SIS continued to insist that Onodera and Fuellop could not be the ultimate source of the leak, which could only be someone in England. Ryde, still heading the MI5 investigation into Kraemer and until now had rejected the London mole theory, had come round to SIS's view of Kraemer's real sources.[15] Stephens agreed, he wrote in an MI5 memo: 'I am now satisfied that there is the strongest possible ground for thinking SIS were right.'[16]

Then, on 13 June, British interrogators in Germany passed to SIS the product of an interrogation of a high-ranking German official who worked with Kraemer in Stockholm. The German prisoner claimed he had evidence that Kraemer was either 'consciously or unconsciously working for the Russians.'[17] One of the senior MI5 officers, Edward Blanchard Stamp, who saw the interrogation report, suggested to Stephens that this might be the reason 'Kraemer is not telling the truth'.[18] It was an incendiary allegation that, if true, threatened to turn the Kraemer investigation on its head.

It is at this point that Anthony Blunt, who had been hovering in the background, steps in. A letter dated 30 June from Stamp to Blunt confirms 'you are to take over this case'.[19] Almost at once Blunt starts to muddy the waters. Blunt immediately sent an updated report[20] to Stephens setting out the intelligence case against Kraemer. He began by saying that after receiving comment from MI6 on Kraemer's relationship with Colonel Onodera he considered it 'fairly clear that Kraemer was telling the truth' and now believed that Onodera was sourcing his intelligence through an Estonian network in America.

When SIS informed[21] Blunt that Onodera was also receiving his intelligence from sources in Switzerland, the MI5 officer scribbled and signed a note on the case file suggesting Agent Orange be drafted in to work on the Kraemer investigation. Orange was Swiss diplomat Erich Kessler, a Soviet agent recruited to MI5 by Blunt and Burgess, who could be relied upon to support Blunt's finding that Kraemer was telling the truth.

Blunt sent another memo[22] to Stephens describing Grundboek as a 'low grade' intelligence officer, noting that it was 'of course fairly natural' Kraemer would name Grundboek as he is 'already dead and can be safely blown'.

Nevertheless, he professes concern, noting the increase 'in Hungarian Intelligence activity in Sweden' and the importance of examining 'how Kraemer fits the picture'.[23] Horvath drops out of the picture completely but intelligence from Kraemer comes at 'something of a spate'[24] and a flurry of new potential sources based outside the UK are named and then dismissed in rapid succession.

Once again, the investigation into Josephine was leading nowhere, but the question of who and how Arnhem had been betrayed remained the single most urgent question. The British had gathered at Camp 020 dozens of high-ranking German military and intelligence figures. Among then was Walter Schellenberg, the Nazi intelligence chief who had been detained since June 1945.

In a bid to open up the Josephine case, Stephens allowed the Nazi spymaster to associate with Kraemer at the interrogation centre. This failed to make any headway in the case and left Schellenberg questioning whether Kraemer had ever told him the truth about his sources. After the war an MI5 report concluded that Kraemer was as much a mystery to the Germans as he was to the British.[25]

MI5 interrogators decided to refocus their approach and asked Schellenberg whether the Arnhem warning was passed on to OKW

JOSEPHINE IN CHAINS

[German High Command] and what reliability did Amt VI give to the information it received, and how did it dispose of it?

The answer they got was:[26] '... Schellenberg states that the Luft Attaché passed the information to the Luftwaffenführungsstab [German air force command] from whence it was passed to the Wehrmachtführungsstab [Germany army command of the OKW led by Colonel General Alfred Jodl]. As to reliability, the information was received too late for assessment prior to the acts to which it related, though the serious intentions of the landing were appreciated. The information had originally been passed from Stockholm at about 18–24 hours prior to the landing. The information was received by Mil Amt C [the successor to the Abwehr under Schellenberg] some hours after the landing had occurred, and all that Mil Amt C could do was stress to the Staffs concerned the seriousness of the position. The information was also received several hours subsequent to the landing by the Luftwaffenführungsstab from the Luftwaffe Attaché.'

It was imposible to deny that the Arnhem warning represented a serious leak that had found its way on to the battlefield at a crucial time during the battle.

SIS still insisted that Kraemer must have had a real agent in London upon which to base his reports. The increasingly isolated Blunt insisted he didn't.[27]

Blunt's response[28] was to try a new tactic and threaten Kraemer directly by arranging for his wife to be arrested and interrogated by the British.

MI5 had already tried to put pressure on Kraemer via his brother-in-law, who was a British prisoner of war.[29]

In a memo on the case dated 9 September 1945, Anthony Blunt reports some success with his tactic saying Kraemer was so 'devoted' (despite his repeated infidelity) to his wife that he had agreed to name five more sources – four Swedes and one German journalist based in Stockholm. The most interesting new name was

Count Douglas, who Blunt said was the brother of the Swedish Commander in Chief.

In a signed statement[30] Kraemer agreed to say: 'There were other contacts but I can't remember all the names. Of special interest for me were the informations of Douglas which dealt with the military situation in Northern Europe … It was with regard to these reports about the Allied invasion in Europe and possible actions in Northern Europe that I was questioned by Obstlt. Kleyenstüber about the source of these informations. I stated that they came from Douglas, 'I asked him to be careful with the name because of the value of the source.'

Count Carl Douglas would turn out to be yet another red herring. After the war, Douglas[31] went on to enjoy a distinguished career as a Swedish ambassador including a posting in Washington.

Blunt made sure that this latest report on Kraemer with the new named Swedish sources was sent to the American OSS office in Stockholm, much to the irritation of SIS.

Major Paul Mason, who was head the SIS end of the investigation, told[32] Blunt on 3 September 1945: 'I originally had not intended sending anything to Stockholm until we got Kraemer to tell something nearer to the truth.'

He also suggested to Blunt that MI5 properly interrogate Kraemer's secretary, Nina Siemsen, and by the end of the war Kraemer's mistress. 'On many occasions during 1944,' reasoned Mason, 'Kraemer's teleprints were brought to the Air Department by Nina Siemsen. She mentioned that on several occasions she had composed these teleprints herself without Kraemer having seen them. These included reports from Josephine, Hector and '26' [Onodera]. This seems to be a complete contradiction of what she told you in [Camp] 020. It would appear to be worthwhile having Siemsen re-interrogated in Germany, perhaps under somewhat less pleasant conditions than the last time. What is your opinion?'[33]

Blunt wrote back: 'We must now economise man power and focus on getting information about Kraemer's Swedish contacts and

JOSEPHINE IN CHAINS

I do not think that Siemsen will be able to give us anything more than some small arms ammunition which might pick a small hole in Kraemer's defences. My own feeling is that this is not worthwhile and the only technique at the moment is to concentrate on the major issues.'[34]

Except of course Blunt was doing everything he could to ensure nobody was concentrating on the most important issue: how the German air attaché, whose contribution to German intelligence, according to Blunt, had just been filing reports of aircraft production and regurgitated newspaper articles, came into possession of top-secret details concerning Arnhem five days after Eisenhower had given Market Garden the green light.

Blunt decided to review all the teleprints sent by Kraemer to Berlin (translated and supplied by SIS), announcing that he was now sure that Josephine was not a single agent but simply a 'type of intelligence'[35] that Kraemer had gleaned from a variety of sources.

Blunt also deployed his considerable language skills by declaring in a memo to WRC1 (The War Room registry run by MI5 specialising in Abwehr intelligence and Abwehr officers) that he considered the Josephine teleprint messages to be 'seriously inaccurate'.[36]

One obvious question no one could ignore was the role of Fuellop, the agent who Kraemer claimed had sent the Arnhem warning and who had appeared to be the biggest single recipient of the very considerable sums of money Kraemer was claiming from Berlin every month. In reality, Kraemer had no idea what happened to the cash once he had handed it over to Grundboek and later Horvath.

SIS believed[37] that Fuellop, who operated out of Madrid and Lisbon, had very good contacts in the UK 'through Yugoslav and Greek émigrés'.

MI5 interrogators at Camp 020 concluded that the Fuellop/Kraemer route[38] ran 'by diplomatic bag from England to Portugal/Spain', then on to Berlin and back to Stockholm via German diplomatic bag.

In September 1944, Hungarian intelligence had in fact sent[39] an agent called 'Bagyoni' to Stockholm to seek out Kraemer. According to an SIS report, Bagyoni's boss was at this time working for the NKVD. Although Kraemer, it later emerged, thought Bagyoni was working for the British. SIS said Bagyoni feared the Russians more than the Nazis.[40] It should also be recalled that Chichaev, NKVD station chief in London, had been Station Chief in Stockholm before being posted to Britain.

On 20 July 1945, Major Mason, who had been given access to Schellenberg's first interrogation report before he was brought to Camp 020 from Germany, wrote[41] to Anthony Blunt, telling him: 'Schellenberg is of the opinion that Kraemer's intelligence comes from the Russians.'

Blunt's response was to continue to promote the idea that Kraemer's important sources must be Swedish diplomats based in Sweden. He even denounced one Stockholm businessman contact of Kraemer, Henry Wallenberg, as 'highly suspect, if not an active German agent'.

When Janos Horvath reappeared in the picture, Blunt further muddied the waters by suggesting[42] two other 'Horvaths' as being the Horvath named by Kraemer.

Blunt never addressed the possibility of a Soviet link to Kraemer. Nor did he once consider who might have been the source of the Arnhem leak. Yet, the more of Kraemer's espionage history was uncovered, the more uncomfortable it must have been for the Cambridge spy. He was in a truly astonishing position. If Blunt was Josephine, and there can be little doubt at this stage that there are serious grounds for suspecting he was, then not only was he investigating himself in a desperate game of double bluff with a star witness who appears never to have known what was going on, but he had been doing so, one way or another, for the previous two years.

It seems incredible to us now, knowing what we do about Blunt, that none of his colleagues seemed to have the faintest suspicions. In part that is because the two biggest thorns in his side, Jane Archer and Felix Cowgill, had been sidelined. The idea that the high-minded polymath and aesthete, the great star of MI5, could be a traitor was unthinkable. No one even appears to have wondered if his involvement in the botched investigation of Josephine in 1943/44 may have rendered him unfit to lead the investigation a second time. Above all, he was protected by the unthinkability that he, or anyone else for that matter, could have been a Nazi. The thought that Josephine could have been acting on behalf of the Russians was never seriously entertained.

When it emerged that Karl Heinz Kraemer had visited[43] Moscow in 1934/35, Michael Ryde requested[44] the Foreign Office and SIS investigate whom Kraemer had met as well as the nature of his business there. This was the same year Anthony Blunt made his first visit to the Russian capital[45] and the Cambridge spy made sure to bring the focus back to Sweden. He even requested[46] the transfer of the Japanese diplomat Momotaro Enomoto from Stockholm to Camp 020 so he too could be questioned as a potential source for Kraemer.

This line of inquiry also went nowhere.

Blunt maintained control of the interrogation by telling Stephens,[47] who planned to bring in another interrogator to increase the pressure on Kraemer: 'As soon as the officer has taken over the case I think I should discuss carefully with him what questions should be put [to Kraemer].'

But Blunt was unable to entirely deflect Stephens, Ryde and Mason from the most salient aspect of the Josephine leaks – the Arnhem warning of 15/16 September 1944. A close examination of Kraemer's office accounts[48] revealed that just days after the Arnhem defeat, Kraemer paid Fuellop 80,000 kroners (worth £330,000 today), by far the biggest payment made by the Germans under the Siegfried contract.

On 24 September 1945, Karl Heinz Kraemer finally agreed to give a statement (see Appendix 2) disclosing all he claimed to know about Arnhem and the intelligence he sent to Berlin. It was over a year since he passed on his Arnhem warning, yet Kraemer was able to remember the names of the three airborne divisions involved and the exact timing of the landings as well as the operation's objectives.

He said he had been told by Onodera on 14 September that the Allies were planning an 'imminent' air landing in Holland and that the three divisions involved were not in France but England in 'sealed camps'. Kraemer told his interrogators: 'This report of mine arrived in Berlin in due time.'

He said the following evening (15 September) he had received a microdot report from Fuellop inside a diplomatic bag. Kraemer insisted there was no 'reference to the original source' of the intelligence only that it had come via Horvath at the Hungarian embassy in Berlin. He believed it had been couriered from Madrid or Lisbon direct to Berlin and then on to Stockholm.

Kraemer added:[49] 'I had a look on the (microdot) mail the same night and found that the mail consisted of 16 or 17 microphotos; in the night and the following morning, Saturday, I read through the reports and found on one of the microphotos the "Arnheim" information. Immediately I gave the information to the air attaché's teleprinter office (FS) with the order to forward it to Berlin I-Luft as "KR-Blitz", the signification for the most urgent importance of the message.'

Kraemer was unable to explain why the message had not been sent on to Schellenberg immediately which he said meant 'it was received by Abwehr I-Luft only after the actual landing operation had already begun.'

Neither the microdot nor its contents have survived the war, but it must be likely that it was a full report containing detailed battle orders relating to how the objectives of Market Garden were to be secured. If that was the case then even if it had arrived after the start of the landings it would have provided the enemy with a vital tactical plan of how the British and American ground and air forces were to capture each of the bridges between Eindhoven and Arnhem.

Next, the interrogators moved on to Kraemer's Rhine report, which earlier that year had threatened to jeopardise the Allies' major river crossing into Germany.

Kraemer said that he received this intelligence from 'Peterson Hasso', whom he described as 'an exceptionally high quality source in Stockholm, well informed on domestic politics in England. It conveyed detailed and intimate reports on English trends of thought prevailing in the inner circles of the main British parties.'[50]

But Kraemer said he had never met Peterson Hasso. That was because he was concealing from the British the fact he wrote all the Peterson Hasso reports himself.

He later candidly admitted that apart from one possible fleeting occasion in Lisbon, he didn't think he ever met Fuellop or knew where Fuellop sourced his intelligence. This meant that the intelligence that gave away the correct timing and the exact Allied units used in Operation Market Garden had been sent to Kraemer by a man he didn't know while the source of the Rhine leak was supposedly an agent invented by Kraemer.

Kraemer's confession caused Major Paul Mason to write to Anthony Blunt expressing grave concerns about the case. He was particularly suspicious of the route by which Kraemer claimed he received his intelligence via Madrid/Berlin/Stockholm and then back to Berlin. SIS believed Kraemer was lying about this and must have had some other source or route, possibly by WT or diplomatic bag linked to the UK.

Blunt replied:[51] 'I do not agree that this story is so vague as to be suspicious, nor do I see why he could have got the information in question from any of the sources you mention ... Kraemer does not state positively that material came by diplomatic bag from this country, but deduces this by a process of elimination. The fact information continued to come during the diplomatic bag ban period [in the weeks up to D-Day all bags were stopped] could be explained again on the assumption that much of it was invented.'

Blunt insisted that Madrid/Berlin/Stockholm was the more likely route, explaining to Mason: 'Kraemer was presumably greatly concerned to get the credit personally for this information [Arnhem etc.] and if he allowed it to be handed over in Berlin he would have probably lost the credit.'

MI6 remained convinced that the more likely route for Kraemer's intelligence was via London. And analysts working in the War Office had determined that the means of transmission could not be WT or diplomatic bag but by diplomatic cable,[52] a means of communication Blunt knew all about.

Mason then raised Josephine's report about Air Vice Marshal Arthur Tedder's visit[53] to Moscow to set up a secret 'liaison command' between the Soviets and Anglo-American air forces. Mason wanted MI5 to look into whether an enemy agent had got close to Tedder. Blunt could barely contain his irritation: 'Do you really think it is worth flogging this dead horse? It was proved long ago that the story of an agent joining Tedder was a pure fiction and I therefore doubt if it is worth following up the careers of the Air Force officers mentioned.'[54]

Blunt was supposed to have retired from MI5 at the end of summer 1945, but he stayed on to take personal care of Kraemer and the Joephine investigation. On 19 October, MI5 followed up Blunt's detailed instructions and closed the case.[55]

In Patricia McCallum's report, we are told after a little more than five months in Camp 020, Kraemer was flown to Germany, where he was held at the Combined Services Detailed Interrogation Centre (CSDIC), whose security was partly the concern of Blunt protégé Leo Long.

After years of investigation and hundreds of hours of interrogation, British intelligence was none the wiser about the source the German High Command regarded as the agent with the best access to British secrets in the entire war. An MI5 report[56] on

1 December 1945 noted that SIS officer Paul Mason is still 'vainly chasing Kraemer's sources all over Europe' and that Kraemer has 'concealed the knowledge of some of his important sources'.[57]

Despite investigating and dismissing dozens of potential suspects, the idea that Josephine could be a British intelligence officer seems never to have occurred to anyone working for the British. Yet the Germans themselves had not only been alive[58] to this possibility, they had even investigated the allegation that Kraemer was a double agent for possibly the British, or the Russians, or even both, so it seems incredible that there was such collective myopia about this possibility within the British secret services.

As the war drew to a close, Blunt, so confident in his own subterfuge, brazenly told one of his MI5 colleagues that 'it has given me the greatest pleasure to have been able to pass the names of every MI5 officer to the Russians'.[59] When Guy Liddell was informed about the incident in 1945 he simply shrugged it off. If Blunt was willing to betray his own MI5 colleagues to the Soviets, he was surely happy to pass on intelligence about Allied operations to the Germans if his actions could be justified as supporting long-term communist goals. The Kremlin files on Blunt show that the British MI5 officer was the one agent who the Russian 'General Staff' insisted was personally praised by his Kremlin handlers for the work he had done in the war, an act that one KGB officer who had read the files described as 'highly unusual'.[60]

As early as 1948, a young ex-officer, Philip Hay, came to Buckingham Palace to be interviewed for the post of Private Secretary to the widowed Princess Marina, Duchess of Kent, mother of the present Duke. As he walked down a red-carpeted corridor with Sir Alan Lascelles, the King's private secretary, they passed Blunt examining a picture in silence. When he thought they were out of earshot, Sir Alan whispered to Hay: 'That's our Russian spy.'[61]

A number of witnesses had also come forward to warn MI5 that they thought Blunt was at the very least a communist.[62]

* * *

Even before Arnhem, Churchill was convinced the Soviet threat to the Western democracies represented one of 'mortal danger', so that the 'front in Europe should be as far East as possible' and 'Berlin was the prime and true objective of the Anglo-American armies'.[63]

As the gap between the British and American forces in the West and the Russians in the East started to narrow, the Allies' uneasy partnership was growing increasingly strained. This was not just a race for the prize capital city, so much as for the controlling hand in the coming post-war world order.

By early 1945, the Red Army was barely 40 miles outside of Berlin. British-American forces, set back by the failure of Arnhem and the Battle of the Bulge in the Ardennes, still had yet to cross the Rhine. On 28 March, Eisenhower made the extraordinary decision to send a telegram to Stalin reassuring him that Berlin was no longer the Anglo-American objective, and that the Americans would hold their advance at the Elbe River. The Soviet leader acknowledged the concession but of course suspected double dealing on the part of his allies. He replied that Berlin was no longer a Russian priority before immediately ordering a massive Soviet offensive to capture the city by 16 April, just three days later.

Eisenhower's direct approach to Stalin, without consulting Churchill, was an overreach that had trespassed on to the European geopolitical arena and one that deeply angered the British prime minister. In a series of telegrams at the end of March, Churchill fervently objected to Eisenhower's decision – and urged his armies to press on to Berlin.

Churchill wrote to Eisenhower on 31 March: 'If the enemy's resistance should weaken, as you evidently expect and which may well be fulfilled, why should we not cross the Elbe and advance as far eastward as possible? This has an important political bearing, as the Russian armies of the South seem certain to enter Vienna and overrun Austria. If we deliberately leave Berlin to them, even if it should be in our grasp, the double event may strengthen their conviction, already apparent, that they have done everything. Further, I do not consider myself that Berlin has yet lost its military and certainly not its political significance.'[64]

Churchill was also mindful of a 'tragedy' unfolding in occupied Holland, where three million people were facing starvation after transport communication had been cut with Germany. The Allies made plans to send desperately needed aid and demanded the German authorities not to hinder its distribution.

'If however they should refuse,' wrote the British prime minister, 'I propose that we should at this stage warn the German commander in Holland and all the troops under his command that by resisting our attempt to bring relief to the civil population in this area they brand themselves as murderers before the world and we shall hold them responsible with their life for the fate which overtakes the people of Holland.'

Meanwhile, Stalin had hardened his position on Poland and sent a telegram to Churchill, chastising him for allowing the British media to 'fabricate' stories about the Kremlin ordering the murders of prominent Poles, although this was exactly what was happening to the benighted Polish people.[65]

Churchill and Montgomery had not given up on Berlin and now supported Monty's great rival General Patton, who urged Eisenhower to back a daring plan to capture Berlin ahead of the Red Army. Operation Eclipse 2 was to be an airborne assault on the German capital using the 17th Airborne Division, 82nd Airborne Division, 101st Airborne Division and the British 1st Airborne Division, to seize key airports in and around the city. The paratroopers were to hold the ground until Montgomery's 21st Army Group arrived after the crossing of the Rhine. In Berlin, the anti-Nazi Reichsbanner resistance had already identified possible drop zones for Allied paratroopers, and they planned to guide them past German defences into the city. In scale, the planned offensive dwarfed the airborne operation of Market Garden.

But the painful lessons of Arnhem meant Eisenhower, who had received dire warnings of potential massive casualties, rejected another high-risk airborne assault that would have placed Anglo-American soldiers in the direct line of fire of the advancing Russians.

As the Red Army triumphantly marched into what the Soviet press called 'the lair of the fascist beast', posters encouraged troops to show their anger: 'Soldier: You are now on German soil. The hour of revenge has struck!'

In the first weeks of Soviet occupation hundreds of thousands of women were raped by Russian soldiers. A propaganda film about the operation called *The Fall of Berlin* depicted Hitler and Churchill plotting with capitalists to deny the heroic Stalin his victory.

On 2 May 1945, Soviet troops occupied the Berlin Reichstag and planted the Soviet flag on its roof. It was the culmination of a two-week battle for the German capital. Stalin valued the prize so highly he was willing to sacrifice the lives of 80,000 Russian soldiers, a sacrifice that could have been avoided if he had simply waited for the Germans to surrender.

Five days later, German general Alfred Jodl, the chosen representative of the newly established Flensburg government, arrived at Supreme Headquarters Allied Expeditionary Force (SHAEF), located in a converted school in Rheims (now Reims), France, with the proposal of Germany's surrender. Although initially planning to surrender only to the Western Allies, the German emissary had to agree to surrender the rump Nazi forces to all three of the Allies. Eisenhower asked Ivan Alexeyevich Susloparov, the Soviet representative at SHAEF and Red Orchestra spymaster, to sign for the Russian leader.

Susloparov and the Allied commanders waited in vain for Stalin to acknowledge the surrender document. In the hiatus, the German generals agreed to a ceasefire in the West but did not halt the fighting in the East.

Stalin, recognising the extent of his victory, refused to accept the Act of Military Surrender, and demanded another ceremony on

German soil with a more Soviet-friendly text. On the night of 8 May 1945, a second surrender ceremony was held in Karlshorst, Berlin.

The surrender of Berlin to the Soviets gifted Stalin the long sought-after prize of a vengeful boot on the throat of the German people. It also paved the way for Pavel Sudoplatov to round up all the Nazi nuclear physicists he could and bring them to Russia while stretching back to Russia from Berlin, country after country was brought under the yoke of the USSR.

Stalin had waged a total war and had achieved a total victory.

The failure of Market Garden was not simply a military defeat – it was arguably a disaster for the world. While it is likely that had it succeeded, Nazi resistance in the West would have quickly crumbled and German military leaders would have sued for peace, what seems unarguable is that its failure encouraged Hitler into a final deluded belief that he would be able to force a separate peace with the Western Allies which prolonged the war by many months and allowed the Russians to advance hundreds of miles to the West. Before the Second World War had ended, a new war had just begun, a Cold War, which would take the world to the brink of nuclear catastrophe and leave millions of people imprisoned behind an Iron Curtain.

Churchill, more than any other Western politician, knew what had been at stake. In May 1945, the British leader saw the Soviet threat as so acute that he ordered his chiefs of staff to draw up a feasibility study for an attack on the Soviet Union. It was code-named Operation Unthinkable and involved a joint British and American attack on Russian forces in Poland. These plans were only abandoned when Churchill's generals concluded that the numerical superiority of the Russian forces made it too risky. Russian spies of course had already warned Stalin about Operation Unthinkable. The Red Army in Poland had deployed into defensive positions and was waiting for what Stalin believed was an imminent attack.

Chapter 26

Death Throes

The war was over but there were questions about what to do with the thousands of war criminals, spies, traitors and collaborators in Allied hands. War-weary populations across Europe were electing new governments that were looking forwards, not backwards. Most people wanted to forget the horrors and deprivations of the past six years.

Colonel Oreste Pinto was determined no one should forget the treachery of Christiaan Lindemans and the hundreds of victims he had betrayed.

Victory on the battlefield had led to the capture of vital witnesses that would be able to progress the Lindemans case.

The arrests of the Abwehr trio of Hermann Giskes, Gerhard Huntemann and Richard Christmann had given MI5 the chance to collect new intelligence about King Kong and his betrayal of Market Garden.

The first of the three was Giskes, who was interrogated by Captain Robert Maxwell, the notorious British press baron (under the name Captain Stone) in Germany.[1] Giskes later said it was 'CC' (King Kong) who had given away the destinations of the airborne landings, although he could not be sure that the name of Arnhem was mentioned. His number two in Belgium, Gerhard Huntemann,[2] who was present at the time of Lindemans' arrival at Driebergen on 15 September 1944, two days before the start of Market Garden, was sure the Dutch agent had picked up intelligence about the operation from the fourth floor of Hotel Metropole in Brussels, where Captain Baker had a room and a wireless transmitter that was in touch with London.[3] Richard Christmann, who had been sent to meet Lindemans after he crossed the lines on 15 September, was captured by the French[4] and held at Fresnes Prison.

He told US interrogators that Lindemans was working for the British special forces when he had betrayed Market Garden and reported to General Kurt Student and later Major Kiesewetter about the Eindhoven attack from XXX Corps supported by airborne landings around Arnhem.[5]

A fourth and the most senior of the intelligence officers, Walter Schellenberg, was captured in June 1945. He was quizzed about the 'Arnhem warning' that had arrived on the day of the Market Garden landings.

When he said the Kraemer teleprint had been used to confirm intelligence around the Allied objectives during the battle, the amount of evidence in British hands pointing to a betrayal of Market Garden had reached a critical mass. Yet there was little appetite for an official investigation. British military commanders had publicly complained about the failings of the operation including the surprise presence of the two SS Panzer divisions around Arnhem, but this was regarded by the military as an intelligence blunder not an act of betrayal.

Oreste Pinto's repeated requests for a speedy prosecution of Lindemans fell on deaf ears and a criminal trial seemed further away than ever.

Pinto decided to expedite matters by arranging for Lindemans to be transferred to the 'orange hotel', the notorious Scheveningen Prison where the Nazis had caged Lindemans' brother, Henk, and many other resistance fighters.[6] Pinto hoped that the prison's high profile would help keep Lindemans' case high in the public's consciousness.

The Dutch spycatcher decided to pay one more visit to Scheveningen, where so many Dutch men and women had been tortured, many of them as a result of Lindemans' denunciations.

The one-time all-powerful resistance leader had been placed in the hospital wing of the prison, where his epilepsy was being treated.

Lindemans was a shadow of his former self. Incarceration and epilepsy meant his huge muscles had grown slack and stringy. His hair was tinged with grey and his eyes were sunken. Clothes hung limply on his gaunt stature like a scarecrow.[7]

As Pinto approached the fallen giant, Lindemans dropped to the floor, writhing and frothing at the mouth and nose.

Lindemans was as much a prisoner of his debilitating fits as he was the thick walls of Scheveningen. Pinto watched dispassionately, despising him more than ever:

'What mercy could a man expect who had betrayed his own friends for cash, who had cost us seven thousand casualties at Arnhem, and had prolonged a war for perhaps six months more than was necessary? I could feel nothing but contempt.'[8]

But Lindemans, even after a year of solitary confinement, was not without friends. In July the prison authorities received a letter from an Allied airmen who had been made aware of Lindemans' plight. Fred Sutherland, the Dambuster hero who had returned to Canada, wrote to the Dutch authorities explaining how Lindemans had saved both his and Sydney Hobday's life after they were shot down in Holland. Sutherland said he hoped his intervention would spare Lindemans from the gallows.[9]

Back in his own office, Pinto once again attempted to grind the wheels of justice forward and made a special plea to the Dutch intelligence headquarters for full access to the Lindemans' file.

After weeks of stalling, Pinto was finally granted permission to enter the high-security steel room where Lindemans' file was kept. Except all the papers relating to the case had been removed.

'I checked the record index to make sure that the system had not been reorganised in my absence. There was no entry to show that there had ever been a file on the Lindemans case.'[10]

When Pinto made follow-up enquiries, he was told that a senior officer close to Prince Bernhard had recalled the file days earlier. He was never able to track it down.

In October 1945, Pinto was released from the BVD, the Dutch Security Service, and transferred to new duties in Germany. Talk of his seduction of female Nazi suspects and other indiscretions had begun to circulate.

There is a Dutch proverb which says, 'He who wants to beat a dog can always find a stick for the job.'

Pinto later reflected: 'I had long realised that after the arrest of King Kong a stick would be found for me.'[11]

A few weeks later, in spring 1946, British intelligence in Rotterdam reported that a French woman had made three visits to the Russian embassy in the city. The reports were passed to Squadron Leader Douglas G Baber, the RAF security officer at the Netherlands recruitment centre at Ypenburg (The Hague). Baber had been a POW of the Germans when his Whitley bomber was shot down near Ghent in Belgium in 1941.[12]

After liberation he was appointed to the SIS at The Hague.[13]

The name of the woman visiting the embassy rang a bell as it sounded like someone connected to one of the more sensitive cases he had been working on. Gilou Letuppe, remembered Baber, was the 'wife' of the famous Dutch traitor, Christiaan Lindemans. What interest could the Russians have in a Dutch traitor who had been accused of betraying Arnhem?

Baber arranged for all Letuppe's movements to be monitored and, at the same time, using Red Cross contacts at Scheveningen Prison, he obtained copies of all written correspondence between Letuppe and Lindemans.[14] It soon became apparent that the Russians were closely involved with the couple.

In one letter to Lindemans, Letuppe wrote after a recent visit to the Russian embassy: 'I'm a little nervous you know, and don't worry about it. I know what to say, when I'm here.'[15]

The implication was clear to Baber – Lindemans was about to be sprung from prison. The British decided to get to Lindemans first.

In the last week of April 1946, Baber was waiting in the interrogation room at Scheveningen for the prison guards to bring Lindemans to him.

Lindemans appeared paralysed from head to toe so Baber waved the guards away. When the interview door was closed, Lindemans told Baber that he should not be deceived by what he saw: 'I am going to escape from this place in a few days and there is nothing you can do about it.'[16]

When Baber expressed surprise at such an outrageous claim, Lindemans leapt up from his chair and began waving his arms about to demonstrate that he was in fact perfectly fit and not the physical cripple he wanted the prison staff and doctors to believe.

It was an astonishing charade and perhaps one that testified to Lindemans' utter confidence in the Russians' power to free him.

Baber reported all this to MI5 officer E J Corin in London, saying he would try to see Lindemans again as soon as it could be arranged.

Lindemans' escape plans were well advanced. With the help of another prisoner known as 'the Singing Rat'[17] and a 26-year-old nurse called Tine Onderdelinden, who had fallen in love with the Dutch giant, Lindemans used a steel file smuggled into the prison by the nurse to cut through the iron bars in his hospital cell.[18]

The second part of the plan was even more difficult to execute. His cell was many feet above ground level. Having prepared the severed bars so that they could be removed without drawing any suspicion, the three plotters had to devise some means for Lindemans to reach the ground after climbing through the window.[19]

DEATH THROES

There were no convenient footholds or drainpipes down which he could climb, so it was arranged that on the night set for the escape, 'the Singing Rat' would leave a rubber hosepipe hanging out of a storeroom window which happened to be conveniently close to the window of Lindemans' cell.[20] All Lindemans had to do was perch on the windowsill of his own room, swing across until he grasped the hosepipe and then clamber down it.

He reached the ground with ease, but waiting for him at the bottom was a group of guards who had been tipped off about the escape. Lindemans was bundled back through the prison gates and transferred to a much more secure cell with more security-conscious guards.

A few days later, Cornelius Verloop (who was quite possibly the Singing Rat and if so, likely lived up to his name), with the help of an agent inside the prison, made a successful escape from Scheveningen,[21] hopping into a waiting car parked in front of the main wall. He was to be arrested again in 1947, but was never convicted of any crime and is supposed to have continued to work for Dutch and British intelligence for many years.[22] But there were also reports that he had found work with the Russians.[23]

Baber asked one of his officers, Lieutenant Van Dijk, to write to Lindemans offering to do a deal with the Dutchman so the British could 'find out what the Russians wanted'.[24] Baber also asked Lindemans to tell him where his wife was living so they could interview her.

Lindemans appears to no longer have had any faith in the Soviets rescuing him. Perhaps he felt betrayed. Whatever his motivation he wrote back to Lieutenant Van Dijk, saying that the British must not contact Letuppe under any circumstances.

'I received your letter,' he wrote, 'but cannot understand it. You must know that after many tortures by the Germans, she [Lindemans' wife] is very afraid to speak to British or Dutch agents. I have had my chance to escape, but I was waiting for you, because we worked in the same job. I liked the British better than the Dutch therefore I will work. My wife Gilou likes to work with me and nobody else. I suppose that you are afraid that I am working with the wrong organisation, but that is not true, otherwise I would not have told you all these things. If you think you can play with me, then you will lose. I am in your hands now, so do what you like.'[25]

What he didn't let on to Baber was that Gilou was in fact an agent run by the NKVD who had been directly working for the Russians out of the Soviet embassy at The Hague ever since she had been released from the Nazi custody in the summer of 1944.[26]

In May, Baber came to visit Lindemans to see what he had to say. This time the Dutch traitor was ready to spill the beans, not about the Germans, but about the Russians. What he told Baber revealed a deep Soviet penetration of the Dutch state, from the top of government to ordinary members of the police and armed forces. Although Lindemans was willing to name names, he told Baber he would only give the information to the British, because he did not trust the Dutch. Baber reported back to MI5 what Lindemans had told him: 'This information,' he said, 'has been cross-checked from other sources and can be considered very accurate.'[27]

According to Lindemans: 'At the moment in Holland, France and Germany there is a Russian underground organisation involving some of the senior members of the forces and administrations of these countries. The organisation is throughout Holland, endeavouring to get into the organisation all Dutchmen who served with the SS during the war. At the Russian Embassy in The Hague alone are working several Dutch SS men, clothed in Russian uniform, and equipped with Russian diplomatic passes.'[28]

Lindemans told Baber that SS officers who agreed to work for the Soviets are released immediately.

DEATH THROES

Among the Russian agents named by Lindemans was Major Eduard Voorwinden, a Dutch Nazi leader of one of the Dutch Volunteer legions who was in Scheveningen. Lindemans claimed Voorwinden had spied for British intelligence before joining the Nazis and now worked for the Russians inside the prison. He named 10 more agents who held key posts in the Dutch state, including a senior member of the clergy. Baber reported that the Russian intelligence service was so powerful in Holland it had established an 'underground dump of weapons in Rotterdam'.[29]

Yet it must have been the Russians' interest in two well-known British intelligence officers that most worried MI5 and MI6.

Lindemans claimed that the Soviets knew all about Major Richard Stevens and Captain Sigismund Payne Best and their capture during the Venlo debacle. 'The Russian organisation,' reported Baber, 'is searching for these men and it will be interesting to know if anything has been heard of Best.'[30] In fact, both men had returned safely to England after five years in Sachsenhausen and Dachau concentration camps. So why would the Russians have an interest in the two blundering British agents? The reason may have been their involvement with another prisoner who was held with the two British officers in concentration camps in Germany. His name was Yakov Dzhugashvili, better known as Stalin's only son, who was reported to have died after a violent argument with unnamed British officers. Was this the reason the NKVD were so keen to find the British pair?

During his interviews with Baber, it emerged that Lindemans held a bitter and personal animus against a Russian agent named 'Sanders', who was in a senior position connected to the prison. He told Baber in his letter: 'I will not say anything because I promised someone who is now dead to revenge him.'[31] Lindemans said Sanders used the alias Heemstra.

This was Wim Sanders, a controversial figure in Holland, born in Arnhem, who had worked with the Nazis in the deportation of Jews and Jehovah's Witnesses around Twente when he was mayor. But in 1942, Sanders appeared to switch sides and moved to Amsterdam, where he founded the Central Intelligence Service gathering intelligence on SD and Abwehr agents. After the war, Sanders was politically aligned with the communists.

In his letter, Lindemans tried to explain to Baber his motives for turning against the communists: 'You know that I never made a mistake, but I was always working without help. The British Intelligence Service must not forget that I never work for money but really as an idealist.'[32] It is difficult to know what to make of this statement as Lindemans had now betrayed all three major powers in the Second World War – the Western Allies, the Germans and the Russians.

For a man like Lindemans – who demonstrated disturbing psychopathic tendencies – loyalty does not appear to be a trait to which he attached much importance. Yet he did consider himself to be political. Lindemans' ties to the communists stretched back to 1941 when he was working with the Poles in Lille. Later he aligned his resistance activities with the communist CS-6 group, expressing ideological opinions, decrying the betrayal of the Dutch people by the ruling class after the German invasion and then denigrating the rapacious actions of the capitalists who had prospered under Nazi rule.

In his most vulnerable state in Brussels, Lindemans had confided in both his German lovers, Mia Meersman and Margaret Albrecht, that he worked for organisations not connected to the British or the German intelligence agencies. He even told Albrecht that he had been trained in Russia and now worked for 'Rus.Seite' – the Russian Side. It was an extraordinary admission that Albrecht's SD handlers either ignored or deliberately overlooked. The intelligence gathered by the British showed that he was deeply embedded with the Russians in Holland. Ellie Zwaan, his most recent lover, was convinced he had been communist all along.[33]

DEATH THROES

If this was true and Lindemans took his orders from Moscow, then Christiaan Lindemans' detention in Holland posed a direct threat to Russia as his testimony might betray Stalin's role in the Arnhem defeat.

On 18 July 1946, medical staff were called to Lindemans' cell following reports of a 'terrible accident'. Tine Onderdelinden, Lindemans' nurse and lover, was lying on top of his sprawled-out body on the bed. They had both taken an overdose of Luminal prescribed for the treatment of Lindemans' epilepsy. An ambulance took Onderdelinden to hospital, where her life was saved, but delays in the transportation of Lindemans meant he died en route in the ambulance.

In 1946, the Netherlands government established a commission of inquiry that examined allegations of Christiaan Lindemans' betrayal of Operation Market Garden and circumstances surrounding his death.

Oreste Pinto was asked to give evidence and repeated his claim that King Kong's treachery had been responsible for the deaths of the Allied paratroopers who took part in catastrophic airborne landings.

He also accused the Dutch authorities of a cover-up.

But his evidence was tarnished by his personal involvement with female collaborators and spies whom he had interrogated and seduced. Instead the inquiry preferred the testimony of those officers loyal to Prince Bernhard, like Kas de Graaf, who had helped convince some of the commissioners that Lindemans could not have found out about Arnhem from the Dutch.

It was not disputed that Lindemans had crossed the lines on 15 September to pass on intelligence to the Germans, but because no one could say for sure whether he had mentioned the name of Arnhem, the inquiry concluded that there had been no betrayal.

The commissioners had been denied access to all the facts and the British government refused to give permission for any British witness to be questioned in Holland about what they knew of

Lindemans' confessions and their close links to him before Market Garden. Nor did they divulge what they had discovered about the Russian involvement in the case.[34]

When it came to Lindemans' death, the inquiry, by a majority verdict, found that he had taken his own life and ruled out any foul play.

The British and Dutch governments and Prince Bernhard believed they had done enough to ensure the story of King Kong, his mysterious death and his betrayal of Arnhem had been buried for good.

They were not the only ones who had a motive to make sure the truth about Christiaan Lindemans never saw the light of day. The Russians had just as much at stake and they were much better at burying unhelpful news.

In June 1946, a month before Lindemans' body was found in his cell, the *Sunday Express* had reported that a Nazi agent who had sent 83 people to their deaths had been arrested in Paris. His name was Richard Christmann. The English newspaper erroneously claimed that he had been based in England, where he had run an underground network of spies.[35] MI5 knew Christmann very well as his name had cropped up in the investigations of Verloop, Damen, Giskes and Huntemann as well as Lindemans.

Before the British security service could get hold of Christmann, the French had passed him on to the Americans, who quizzed him about Lindemans and Market Garden. As we have heard, Christmann gave chapter and verse on how he had escorted Lindemans through the lines to first General Student's headquarters and then to the Abwehr station in Driebergen two days before the attack. Christmann was not only sure that Lindemans had betrayed Arnhem, he was able to say which German units had acted on the intelligence at the time of the landings. MI5 (now without the services of Anthony Blunt, who had resigned to become Surveyor of the King's Pictures), immediately wrote to MI6 asking for assistance in procuring Christmann so they could scrutinise his intelligence first-hand. The SIS officer in charge of the investigation was Kim Philby.

'Dear Philby,' wrote Major Vesey of MI5, 'The Sunday Express of the 9th June carried a report that Richard Christman [*sic*] has been arrested by the French at Cannes. This individual has been mentioned in numerous 020 reports and is doubtless well-known to you. He was a notorious penetrator of SOE activities in Holland, Belgium and France. At this late date I do not think there is any fresh information that he can give us about the penetration of SOE. However, if you could arrange it, we would very much like him to be asked by the French the particulars of any agents whom he knew to have been dispatched to the UK or British Empire during the war.'[36]

Philby sat on his hands until MI5 wrote again two months later, repeating the request to interview Christmann. It was another fortnight before Philby finally replied on 9 September, three months after the first MI5 request, writing one terse statement confirming that he had arranged for the French to be contacted by MI6's representative in Paris.[37]

In the meantime, Philby had managed to persuade the Americans to pass him a copy of Christmann's interrogation notes. On 11 October, Philby sent an abridged version of the American interrogation report to MI5.[38] When MI5 sent their first request to Philby about Christmann in June 1946, Lindemans was still alive.

Now Lindemans, who only a few weeks earlier had betrayed the Russians, was dead and Baber could not put the new Christmann evidence to him.

The question of whether Lindemans had been part of a Russian spy ring when he betrayed Market Garden also died with him.

Meanwhile in Holland, Christiaan Lindemans became a cause célèbre, his treachery and motivation bitterly argued over by politicians, historians and journalists.

Oreste Pinto and Kas de Graaf wrote books and articles on the affair. Pinto repeated his long-held assertion that Lindemans' treachery had directly led to the defeat at Arnhem.

And in an unexpected turn of events, de Graaf agreed, having a radical change of heart, and publishing material saying he now believed that his old resistance friend Christiaan Lindemans was undoubtedly responsible for the betrayal of Arnhem.[39]

Prince Bernhard's early Nazi links meant the Dutch royal family were caught up in the betrayal story. There were even stories that both men, who loved fast cars almost as much as they did chasing women, had driven down to Paris for a night out carousing Parisian fleshpots. Bernhard's insistence, against a welter of testimony, that he had not met Lindemans, as well as his refusal to surrender documents on the case, only added fuel to the conspiracy theories that Lindemans had learned about Market Garden from the Prince or one of his officers. When the American historian Cornelius Ryan came to write his seminal work, *A Bridge Too Far*, Bernhard persuaded him to drop any mention of a betrayal.[40]

In 1957, the former military intelligence officer E H Cookridge,[41] who after the war had embarked on a career as a historian, decided to take another look at the Lindemans' story. One of his first ports of call was his friend Guy Liddell, who must have told him enough to justify his further digging. He managed to track down two of the Lindemans brothers, Henk and Cornelius, and interviewed them in 1962. They had gone to The Hague hospital where Christiaan had been taken after his overdose on 26 July 1946.[42] Both now agreed to tell their story of what they saw as well as what they had been told about their brother's death, although Cookridge said that after nearly 20 years, they remained fearful of what might happen to them. The brothers said that Christiaan had in fact survived the drug overdose and had tried to leave his cell when he was attacked by a group of prisoners who bludgeoned him to death with bed boards.[43] When Henk and Cornelius arrived at the hospital they found that Lindemans' corpse was so severely battered that his eyes were no longer in their sockets. The brothers were adamant Christiaan would not have taken his own life on the eve of his trial as he was looking forward to putting his side of the story, including the work he had done for the Dutch, French and Belgian resistance. They were convinced beyond doubt his death was an act of murder. But without any corroborating evidence or access to any of the British files held by the Public Records Office (The National Archives), Cookridge dropped the book.

In 1969, the respected French author Anne Laurens did write a book about Lindemans' role in the Arnhem betrayal in which she suggested he may not have been working for the Germans at all but another unnamed third power. Laurens had spoken to French security officials and appeared to have interviewed one of Lindemans' daughters, to whom she dedicated the work.

Later, Dutch journalists started to cast doubt on whether Lindemans had died at all. There were suggestions that a Palestinian shopkeeper lay in Lindemans' grave in the Crooswijk cemetery, Rotterdam, and that the Dutchman had been secretly whisked off to South America.

There was enough uncertainty over Lindemans' death to cause the mayor of Rotterdam to order the body to be exhumed in 1984 and have it forensically tested.

Early on a June morning, Henk Lindemans and Christiaan Lindemans' two daughters stood at the side of the grave as a police work party retrieved the body still sandwiched between his mother and father's rotting, wooden coffin.[44]

Henk, who always believed his brother had only done what he had done to save Henk's life, did not need to wait for the DNA results on the corpse. He immediately recognised the outline of Christiaan's unmistakable hulking, misshapen physique.

The pathologist report which was published a few days later confirmed this, but with one further finding. Tests showed traces of arsenic, raising suspicions that Lindemans was poisoned by a third party. Unfortunately, the only witness to Lindemans' death was now also dead. Tine Onderdelinden, the nurse who had been accused of a suicide pact with Lindemans, had been killed in a mysterious car crash in South Africa in 1952. It later emerged that her father had worked for Dutch intelligence[45] on the Lindemans case.[46]

But even that was not the end of the story. Two years later, in 1986, a court case forced the Dutch security service, the BVD, to open its files on Lindemans.[47] What emerged was fascinating. There were testimonies from prisoners and investigators implicating Wim Sanders, the socialist politician with the dubious war record who had been named by Lindemans before he died.

A 32-year-old female prisoner held at Scheveningen at the same time as Lindemans said she had heard from fellow detainees that Sanders, who was working for the BNV[48] (a forerunner of the BVD), had the 'the murder of King Kong on his conscience'. The secret papers showed that Tine Onderdelinden had also given evidence about a feud between Sanders and Lindemans. Sanders was quick to deny the new allegations, claiming he had never met Lindemans and that the female prisoner named in the disclosed report had once wrongly accused him of having an affair with her.

Throughout all this, the British refused to release their own voluminous files on Lindemans, including Baber's report about Lindemans' evidence of post-war infiltration by the NKVD throughout Western Europe and the list of names of Russian agents that included Wim Sanders.

In the 1980s, the allegation of an Arnhem betrayal was examined more thoroughly as part of Frank Hinsley and C A G Simkins' work on British intelligence in the Second World War. The authors were given unrestricted access to files concerning MI5 and MI6 during the war. Appendix 14 of Vol IV was devoted to the Lindemans' case. Their unsatisfactory conclusion was that it was 'profitless to speculate how King Kong obtained the information which he delivered on September 15th' although they were at pains to stress it could not have come from Prince Bernhard because they said Lindemans first visited the Prince's quarters after Arnhem.[49]

Then in 1997 a two-page letter[50] purported to be written by Lindemans mysteriously surfaced and is now held at the Dutch national archives. The barely legible scribbled note was said to have been found in his Scheveningen cell after his death. In it, Lindemans accuses Prince Bernhard of 'treachery' and said he had passed on to Captain Baber and Kas de Graaf important intelligence about the Prince's role in the war in September 1944. He claims that at all times he had acted out of his love for Holland. But nowhere in the note did he say he intended to take his own life, and so the note only adds to the mystery and conspiracy surrounding his death.

In 2001, M R D Foot published his history of the SOE in the Low Countries. Foot had been an intelligence officer throughout the war and concluded that Lindemans had not known the full details of Market Garden, only 'gossip' about the abandoned Operation Comet, a forerunner of the plans for the Arnhem landings.[51]

But Foot's findings were overtaken by the transfer of secret materials from the security and intelligence service to the National Archives after 2001, which contained statements from at least four senior Abwehr officers who all said that Lindemans' intelligence directly related to Market Garden.

In 2004, Mia Meersman, the alleged German agent and Lindemans' lover, published her personal account of King Kong and Market Garden.[52]

She said she had overheard Christiaan Lindemans telling his brother Henk he had 'paid far too high a price' for Arnhem. Tellingly, she wrote: 'I am convinced that Lindemans betrayed the impending Operation Market Garden to the Germans.' But she made a further claim: 'I informed the English through my superiors

[Meersman claimed to have been secretly working for the British] months earlier. But the operation went ahead and failed, thousands of British and American paratroopers were killed uselessly.'[53]

Chapter 27

Bridge of Lies

After the war, the British government asked Colonel Roger Hesketh, one of the officers in charge of the D-Day deception team, to write an official classified account of Operation Fortitude. It was strictly for senior Whitehall consumption only and not released to the public until 2000.

In it, Hesketh considered the role played by Karl Heinz Kraemer during D-Day informing the Germans of supposed Allied plans. With access to the OKW's official intelligence records,[1] he discovered that in the month after D-Day more reports were sent by 'Josephine' than the combined output of Garbo and Brutus. He said these mostly mirrored Garbo and Brutus and helped the Germans to be taken in by Fortitude, adding plaintively, 'we had no idea Kraemer was playing with our toys.'[2]

Hesketh's assumption was that Kraemer was reading the Garbo and Brutus reports and then embellishing them in order to serve them up as his own. Yet this was an intelligence gathering risk of which Berlin was acutely aware and so did not routinely share intelligence from Garbo and Brutus with the other 'German' agents. It was precisely to stop this kind of cross-contamination that they kept all their agents operating out of silos.

By the time he left MI5, Anthony Blunt had done an excellent job downplaying the significance of Kraemer in the eyes of British intelligence. But in May 1946, more troubling questions emerged about the case.

The Americans had interviewed[3] a German intelligence officer who had served with Kraemer in Stockholm. His name was Major Friedrich Busch, the German assistant air attaché. He was convinced[4] that at least one of Kraemer's sources was a 'controlled agent' working for the British who also had ties to the Russians. Busch, a fervent and 'sincere' anti-Nazi, also said Kraemer had sold German military secrets to the Russians in return for intelligence concerning British and American deployments. He cited one instance of collusion with Moscow where Kraemer had tried to bury[5] a report about Soviet troop dispositions on the Eastern Front. When these allegations were first aired in Berlin towards the end of 1944,[6] Kraemer was recalled[7] to the capital and interrogated for four hours by the Gestapo. That was the offical story anyway.[8] But the truth was that Busch was not the only German intelligence officer who suspected Kraemer of playing a double game. The evidence against Kraemer had reached a critical mass. At least three other intelligence officers had raised concerns, culminating in a thorough audit of all the Josephine material sent to Berlin.[9] The investigation was led by Count von Posadrosky, who concluded that Kraemer's intelligence was a carefully blended mix of falsehoods, truths and half truths planted by the Allies as part of a sophisticated deception plan.

Such damaging conclusions about Germany's star agent at this stage in the war were not received well in Berlin. Heinrich Mueller, the head of the Gestapo, decided to shoot the messengers and instead of charging Kraemer with treachery removed von Posadrosky from his post and threatened Busch with prosecution before a Nazi court.

Busch told the Americans that Mueller knew Kraemer was working for the Allies and so 'must have had his own reasons' for protecting him.[10] After the war, the CIA concluded[11] that at the end of 1944, Mueller was already collaborating with the Soviets. His 'own reasons' for keeping Kraemer in Stockholm were likely aligned with the NKVD, who through Blunt would have been able to use Kraemer to feed the Germans intelligence about the Western Allies.

Busch also told the Americans that Onodera, the Japanese diplomat who passed on the background intelligence to Kraemer about the set-up for the Arnhem operation on 14 September, was working closely with the Russians. In fact, MI6 had also received intelligence Onodeda was using a contact man called Dimitrewski the British suspected of being a Russian agent.[12]

Dimitrewski was a name that had already cropped up in the Josephine investigation. Kraemer told[13] his interrogators at Camp 020 that Onodera had a Russian source based in London who was connected to the War Office and used a 'Russian typewriter'.

MI5 had failed to confirm his Russian identity and ended up downgrading his association with Kraemer, chararacterising Dimitrewski as of 'no interest'. The author of that finding was Anthony Blunt.[14]

When the Americans started asking questions about the Busch claims, they were robustly informed[15] by the British that Busch's evidence could not be relied upon because of an unspecified 'personal animus' between Busch and Kraemer. As a result, nothing further was done about Busch's allegations.

Yet Busch's testimony laid out a direct trail of evidence linking Kraemer to both British and Soviet intelligence – it just required one inquisitive and alert officer in British intelligence to join up the dots.

In the spring of 1946, the British officer[16] responsible for the Kraemer file was Kim Philby, the head of Russian counter-intelligence section at MI6, who now asked MI5 to send him any new material relating to the Josephine affair.

Kraemer was still being held by the British at the Combined Services Detailed Interrogation Centre, located at Bad Nenndorf (CSDIC WEA), a spa town near Hanover in Lower Saxony.

Philby said he had lost all 1,000 of the Kraemer teleprint messages sent to Berlin that had been clandestinely copied by SIS officer Peter Falk's agent, who had access to Kraemer's office. Philby asked MI5 to send him their copies so they could be shown to Kraemer and he could attribute a source to each of the messages.

Philby also requested the CSDIC interrogators put seven questions to Kraemer. Philby's first question was:[17] 'We would like to know for example which of the Fuellop reports came from Fuellop and which of the reports came from other Fuellop sources.'

If ever there was a question designed to elicit whether Kraemer knew the true source of the Arnhem intelligence this was it.

On 1 July 1946, the Spanish police informed the British authorities in Gibraltar they had arrested a Hungarian diplomat who had information which they believed MI6 would be very interested in.[18]

The diplomat in question was Josef Fuellop.

Arrangements were made for Fuellop to be flown to the UK, where he was held at Brixton prison. During his interrogation he categorically denied passing the Arnhem warning to Kraemer, explaining that he had never used a microdot file and that most of his intelligence reports were copied from magazines or made up. Those that were genuine came from Japanese diplomatic sources.[19]

Despite these admissions, no one at MI5 or MI6 thought it necessary at the time to reconsider the Kraemer file or question who might have been the real source of the Arnhem leak.

The Americans, however, had not given up on the Kraemer case and hoped to interview Fuellop, who they suspected might be able to throw light on intelligence leaks about the US landings in the Philippines.[20] Philby made sure this didn't happen. On 3 July 1946 he wrote to Joan Chenhalls at MI5: 'With reference to our telephone conversation this morning regarding Josef Fuellop... As you will know Feullop was Karl Heinz Kraemer's principal source in Spain and for that reason it is desirable that he should be interrogated [at] CSDIC/WEA, rather than be transferred to the American zone, as is the customary procedure for Iberian repatriates. It would be appreciated if you could make the necessary arrangements for his reception…would you kindly treat this matter as urgent.'[21]

MI5 contacted an intelligence officer attached to the British Army of the Rhine (BAOR) to make arrangements for Fuellop's transfer to a detention camp in Germany. That officer's name was the Soviet agent Leo Long, now one of the officers in charge of intelligence and security matters in Germany.[22]

In May the following year (1947), correspondence between MI5 and MI6 shows that an unnamed officer thought it was 'politically desirable' that Fuellop should be released and repatriated to Soviet Hungary, where his prospects as a former German spy held by the Allies would not have been good.[23] Whether he was liquidated by the NKVD or miraculously survived, Fuellop was now conveniently and permanently out of reach of the British security and intelligence services, should they wish to revisit the Arnhem betrayal.

The publicity which always surrounded the larger-than-life Christiaan Lindemans and the breathtaking scale of his treachery helped create the idea there was only one traitor responsible for betraying Market Garden. The legend of King Kong drowned out questions being raised about other possible betrayals. King Kong was simply too good a story. But the truth was the traitors who really mattered in post-war Europe, Anthony Blunt and Kim Philby, had avoided any scrutiny and had got clean away with their treachery. Anthony Blunt had become the Surveyor of the King's Pictures, but before he took up his post, King George VI had sent him on a very delicate and very secret mission to Germany in August 1945 to recover politically sensitive letters written by Edward VIII to well-known Nazis during the war. Blunt secretly made microdot copies of the letters and sent them to Moscow under cover of diplomatic mail.[24]

Chapter 28

Orders of the Kremlin

Stalin's malign influence in the democratic elections of new post-war governments across Eastern Europe was the defining condition of the Cold War in the late 1940s and early 1950s.

The seeds of communist tumult in France, Belgium and Holland were sown by the Red Orchestra and supported by the secret Pickaxe operations that relied so heavily on the resources of the RAF and SOE.

Rather late in the day, MI5 arrived at the worrying conclusion that the Russians may have used the Second World War as a cover to plant agents and set up cells in Britain and across Europe to help Russia install Russian-friendly governments at the end of the war. So it was hardly surprising that MI5 would eventually turn to the intelligence officer who had been instrumental in the training of the Pickaxe agents and who was now in charge of the SIS counter-Soviet section. It was, however, unfortunate for British interests that this officer was Kim Philby.

In November 1946, P J Small of MI5 wrote to Philby about a Russian agent called Elena Nakatina, who had been dropped in Europe by the RAF in February 1944, one of 25 Russian Pickaxe agents carried by the RAF on behalf of the NKVD. Small asked Philby: 'I wonder if it would be possible for you to let us have a description and some particulars of Elena Nakatina as, if she is still alive, it seems just conceivable that she might be used again by the Russians. It has occurred to us that there may be other Russian agents who were trained by SOE for work on the Continent about whom you may have full particulars. These people being thoroughly trained agents might, we feel, at any time be used again, perhaps even for work against this country. We should like therefore to have some record of them.'[1]

P J Small had no idea that by addressing his concerns to Philby he was asking the Russians to give up their own agents. On Nakatina, Philby simply said he had nothing to add.

A further request was sent to Philby for information about another Pickaxe agent, Anna Frolova, who had worked with Leopold Trepper. Philby passed MI5 the wrong photograph and then suggested she had perished in Auschwitz.

Enquiries with Philby about Kruyt, the resourceful NKVD officer who had linked up with the Dutch underground, also drew a blank.[2] Philby surmised Kruyt had been executed by the Germans.[3] Kruyt had in fact been operating as an active Soviet agent in Holland from D-Day and Arnhem through to the end of the war.

Philby later wrote to MI5 officer Roger Hollis deliberately playing down the role of the Pickaxe agents: 'The material is not in itself particularly interesting ... It also proves that the NKVD agents parachuted into France by SOE were given political rather than intelligence assignments – a conclusion which SOE had themselves arrived at.'[4]

In the same year (1946), Philby set in train one of the biggest wild goose chases in the history of MI5. In September 1946, Philby reported that[5] Leopold Trepper had been traced to an address in Harrogate, Yorkshire. According to a female Rote Kapelle agent interrogated by the Belgian Sûreté, Trepper was reported to be staying with Wilhelm Hofstadter, a priest and trainee furrier.[6]

The intelligence said that Trepper, the head of the Rote Kapelle, was 'in trouble' and was seeking refuge in England. Trepper was in fact 1,500 miles away, languishing in a Russian prison. He had fallen victim to Stalin's paranoia about agents who had spent too long in the West. Recalled to Moscow, he was summarily tried for treason and sentenced to a long period of imprisonment. He was eventually released in 1955.

Under Philby's directions, the search for Trepper ran across Yorkshire to London and back again. MI5 placed tails on Hofstadter and his extended family, tapped his phone and intercepted his mail. Sir Percy Sillitoe, the new head of MI5, was completely taken in by Philby and his 'Soviet intelligence'.

Sillitoe wrote to the Chief Constable of West Riding, Captain H Studdy, informing him he believed Hofstadter was 'harbouring a most important Soviet agent' and that the case must be treated with the 'most extreme discretion'.[7]

When after several weeks there was no sign of Trepper, Sillitoe was forced to write to Studdy conceding that it was 'unlikely' Trepper was in the country.[8]

The Cold War was now officially under way. Churchill gave his famous Iron Curtain speech in America in 1946, and by 1950, Klaus Fuchs, a German-born physicist who had been part of the British team at Los Alamos, had admitted to being a Soviet spy (it had been Jane Archer who had first raised doubts about him), and this led to a slew of further arrests and then Guy Burgess and Donald Maclean fled to Russia in the summer of 1951, although not before stopping off to meet their old friend and comrade in treachery, Anthony Blunt. Attention once again began to be turned to Russian operations in Britain during the war.[9] MI5 officer Evelyn McBarnet was asked to review the whole Soviet residenzia in London, not just the Russian links to Burgess and Maclean, who had been run by the NKVD during the war.

In many respects, McBarnet was the perfect officer for the job. In his book *Spycatcher*, Peter Wright describes[10] her as a 'strange woman with a large birthmark running down one side of her face'. She appeared to live her entire life at her desk with no perceptible social life while harbouring a sharp distaste for Freemasons, who she believed had a pernicious influence in the 'office'.

She had worked for MI5 longer than any of the male mole hunters brought in after the defection of Burgess and Maclean and had been certain for many years that MI5 and MI6 had been penetrated by the Russians. In her safe she kept a very secret book compiled by her predecessor Ann Last, who shared McBarnet's suspicions and theories. It contained a list of cases from the war that Last had collated from the MI5 Registry. Against each case was a specific allegation relating to the penetration of MI5 and MI6. Wright doesn't say whether Josephine was mentioned as one of Ann Last's suspicious cases.

But McBarnet, now seized by her colleague's prescience, began a full re-examination of all the evidence.

When it emerged that Burgess was the 'originator of the SOE training school idea', McBarnet's focus switched to Philby's role at SOE's 'Station 17', where the Russian agents were trained before being dropped in Europe.

The ever-artful Philby deflected attention on to two other MI5 officers, John Hacket and Tomas Harris, who he said were 'Burgess' closest associates'.[11] In August 1954, McBarnet was also passed information about Guy Liddell's links with Chichaev, the senior NKVD officer based in London during the war and who after returning to Moscow played a 'prominent role in planning the escape of Burgess and Maclean'.[12] Chichaev had recently replaced Pavel Sudoplatov as the head of Soviet Atomic Espionage.

Questions were asked about Chichaev's wartime contacts with MI5. In particular, McBarnet wanted to know what lay behind Liddell's plan to put Ustinov in close contact with Chichaev, an idea that had 'appalled' the MI5 director at the time.[13] McBarnet concluded: 'There is of course no doubt that Chichaev's agents were intended to operate as Soviet spies and those who survived probably joined up with established networks in occupied Europe.'[14]

She noted tellingly: 'nothing is known of the fate' of five of the agents including Kruyt, Danilov, Rodionov, Ouspenskaia and

Frolova. They had all survived the war and were busy following Kremlin orders in Europe supporting communist parties.

Philby was able to lend a hand deflecting attention away from a wartime MI5 officer who MI5 now believed a paid agent working for the Soviets. His name was Bill Hooper, the same officer who had been cleared of communist links in 1941 by Anthony Blunt. The new evidence[15] had emerged after Hooper had been recognised at Camp 020 by Hermann Giskes, who said he had used him as an agent before the start of the war in Holland. Giskes told MI5 he soon discovered that Hooper was also working for Henri Pieck, the communist Dutch spymaster. MI5 promptly kicked Hooper out of the service and placed him under surveillance, which soon revealed he was still in contact with Pieck. MI5 passed the correspondence on to Philby, who wrote[16] to MI5 declaring the letters to be of no interest as they concerned purely domestic matters. But the correspondence would turn out to be written in code and part of a chain of communication revealing a network of communists at work across Holland after the war. Nothing was said of Hooper's younger brother, Herbert 'Jack' Hooper, who had replaced Kas de Graaf as Prince Bernhard's senior aide in the wake of the King Kong scandal.

Yet again, Philby and Blunt, the two most influential Soviet agents of the war who were hiding in plain sight in Britain, escaped serious scrutiny. Instead, the spotlight fell on Blunt's boss, Guy Liddell, who had been widely expected to be a future Director General. He was now thought to have been suspiciously close to Burgess and Maclean, leading to unsubstantiated claims that Liddell was the so-called 'fifth man'. As a result, he was passed over for the top job before being allowed to quietly retire from the service in 1955. He died of a heart attack in 1966, two years after Anthony Blunt finally 'confessed'.

As with so much of Blunt's career, his confession is one of the more remarkable coups in a life not short of breathtaking achievements. Blunt had been the last 'friend' Burgess and Maclean had seen before fleeing to Russia in 1951. Likewise in 1963, when the net had finally closed round Philby, Blunt found himself the guest of the British ambassador in Beirut and so once again read his fellow spy's 'last rites'. Nevertheless, it was the beginning of the end for Blunt.

In January 1964, Tomas Harris, fellow member of 'the Group', the old friend and generous host to Blunt and Philby during the war who had been living in Majorca but had recently been identified as a potential Russian spy, died in a mysterious car crash in Spain. There was widespread suspicion that he had been murdered by the KGB. Shortly afterwards, Blunt 'confessed'.

It was the testimony of an American recruited by Blunt at Cambridge that led to his ultimate downfall. Blunt had already survived 11 interrogations by MI5.[17]

Only when Michael Straight told the CIA about his recruitment at Cambridge was MI5 able to extract a 'confession' – one that required the Attorney General to first grant Blunt immunity from prosecution.

According to the official case history[18] of Anthony Blunt prepared in 1978 by Cabinet Secretary John Hunt, the government knew of one other agent who had been 'dealt with' by the Russians after Blunt passed on intelligence about him. But the Hunt report[19] concedes: 'Efforts to extract additional information from him [Blunt] have been largely unsuccessful.'

It was a confession without penalty. He was allowed to keep his job as Surveyor of the Queen's Pictures, and the Queen herself was personally briefed about the matter and gave her consent. It can only be wondered what role the intelligence Blunt had gathered on her uncle Edward VIII (and one assumes other royal Nazi sympathisers) played in ensuring that he be allowed to continue to enjoy his liberty without recourse to the Treachery Act. Certainly, while the rumours continued to swirl about Blunt, he continued to live a very agreeable life. He had many friends in high places who regarded his betrayals as little more than misplaced idealism. He was able to take up well-remunerated teaching jobs and enjoy holidays around the world with his plentiful supply of rich friends.

Blunt's life was in stark contrast with his fellow Cambridge spies. In particular Philby, generally regarded as the 'greatest' of them, was living a life of alcoholic bitterness in Moscow. The Russians kept him jobless and at arm's length in a small Moscow apartment, where he was reduced to scouring weeks-old copies of *The Times* for cricket reports and begging friends to send him marmalade.

After Blunt's confession in 1964, Josephine would have faded away for good had it not been for the publication in 1971 of *The Game of the Foxes* by the improbably named Ladislas Farago, a Hungarian writer on military and intelligence matters who had been a Chief of Research and Planning in the US Navy's Special Warfare Branch. The book is an account, based on a huge trove of Second World War Abwehr files which he claimed to have discovered in US archives, of a range of Nazi intelligence activities against both the British and Americans during the war. It contained several chapters on Kraemer and Josephine.

Farago is a far from reliable source, yet he claimed to have interviewed Kraemer over several days in the late 1960s so his account bears some scrutiny.

As we have seen, Kraemer joined the Abwehr early in the war as a junior intelligence officer. He quickly established both a Hungarian and a Swedish connection and began to make a name for himself by supplying high-quality bombing targets for the Luftwaffe.

Farago quotes a letter from Karl Ritter, the senior Nazi diplomat who liaised between the OKW and the German Foreign Office,[20] to von Ribbentrop in support of Kraemer being attached to the Swedish embassy in early autumn 1942: 'Dr Kraemer works for the Luftwaffe. He has longstanding connections in Britain and is receiving continuous reports from inside England about factories engaged in war production. The authenticity and accuracy of his reports has been proven. At this time his information is regarded as the most valuable contribution to the target intelligence the Luftwaffe Staff needs in planning its campaign against British war industries.'

It is worth noting that Fritz Kolbe, who worked in Ritter's office, was the spy who first alerted OSS officer Allen Dulles in Switzerland to the existence of Karl Heinz Kraemer and Josephine. Equally, 'longstanding' implies that Kraemer – and the earliest incarnations of Josephine – may have been feeding the Luftwaffe targets during the Blitz. It's a bleak thought but it also raises the question of whether Pinto's suspicions about the precision bombing of Wormwood Scrubs in 1940 may have been correct.

This intelligence was being routed via Sweden and he clearly felt some fondness for the country. In 1941, he even married his German wife in Stockholm.[21]

Because of these Swedish connections he was officially posted as an air attaché in 1942. There he seems to have lived something of a charmed life. He had mysteriously acquired large amounts of money at his disposal and instead of adopting the discreet persona of an intelligence officer, he was a highly visible, not to say flamboyant, figure. Farago has him driving at high speeds around the Swedish capital in flashy sports cars, taking a succession of young women who worked in the embassies out to expensive restaurants and then, if he could, on to the three or four 'safe houses' the Abwehr maintained in the city. When he did this he made no attempt at discretion, but would park his car right outside.

Nevertheless, Farago calls him a 'genius' and a prototype James Bond because he seemed to break every single rule of the intelligence book and yet month after month he delivered an astonishing quantity of high-quality material to Walter Schellenberg in Berlin. It's a picture which seems calculated not to make sense. Especially when one considers that from late 1943 to the end of the war, Peter

Falk, MI6's man in Stockholm, had the key to Kraemer's personal safe and unfettered access to his household without Kraemer ever appearing to be aware.

Kraemer himself described his network as being 'my direct connections, often of a strictly personal character. I cooperated partly with friends in intelligence matters and not with agents, if the word "agent" means "cash and carry for intelligence". Naturally, I asked some of my friends to look out for agents and these I provided with money for the agents. That means that the list of my real agents must be a relatively poor one. What I know are intermediaries, which enabled me to get intelligence.'[22]

In other words, by his own admission Kraemer didn't run a single secret agent or V-man, instead relying on diplomats and known purveyors of intelligence. The thought that it may have been them who were manipulating him seems never to have occurred to him.

During their investigation of him, MI6 were able to confirm not only that he spent a 'great deal of money' but also that 'his financial transactions were very muddled'.[23] One of the last glimpses we have of Kraemer in Stockholm is just a week or two before the war ended, where he threw a party to celebrate the death of Franklin D. Roosevelt and where he was apparently discussing his plans for his summer holidays as if he hadn't a care in the world.

As early as December 1946, the commandant of the Combined Services Detention Interrogation Centre wrote:[24] 'It is not felt that Kraemer is endeavouring in any way to conceal information, at this late stage in his detention. No purpose would be served in doing so.'

So it is strange that an order was placed on his file in the MI5 Registry stating that under no circumstances must anything said by Kraemer be relied upon unless checked with another source. That order still sits there today on top of the voluminous Kraemer files held in the National Archives in Kew.[25]

Kraemer was officially deemed by MI6 and MI5 an 'inveterate liar – a most convincing liar – a totally unreliable source of information'. Because of this, when the American OSS asked to see his file, they were denied. The investigation was not merely closed. It was buried.

After his release, Kraemer returned to his home town of Gottingen, where he took a job as a travelling salesman for a sewing machine company. But instead of quietly melting away into West German society, he used his new job as cover to continue trading in military secrets. It was evident that Kraemer was being fed intelligence by the Soviets, although MI6, with Philby at the peak of his powers, was determined to prove that he had no real sources.

An MI6 report on his acquisition of intelligence from East Germany regarding aeronautical technology and a jet propulsion factory in Leningrad were dismissed as examples of 'fabricated intelligence reports [given] to Western intelligence services in Germany'.

The unnamed MI6 officer concluded:[26] 'He tends to specialise in fabrication dealing with aeronautical matters, such as AIR OB, armaments, development, experimentation and production. Subject has also put out reports dealing with scientific development in the USSR and with German scientists in the USSR.'

The impression was that Kraemer was up to his old tricks and could not be trusted.

In 1951, the Americans asked the British for help in resurrecting their own investigation into Kraemer. This time the CIA (which had taken on the role of the OSS) also requested[27] information about Kraemer's loyal secretary Nina Siemsen, who had been detained alongside her German spy boss in Camp 020.

The Americans had discovered that Siemsen had an English grandmother and had been in England before the war working for an American national.[28] They wanted to know about her 'political affiliations', although one memo makes clear they were 'dubious' about getting any meaningful cooperation from the British.

MI6 told the Foreign Office:[29] 'Please express to the American Consulate our regrets that the records of Siemsen's interrogation in

London in 1945 are no longer available. For your own information we do not consider, in the circumstance, any useful purpose can be served by setting in motion the rather lengthy procedure of obtaining her personal file from archives.'

As late as 1954, the Counter-Intelligence Corps, the American agency working against the Soviets by stopping them recruiting German scientists for their rocket programmes, was so concerned about the activities of Kraemer that they issued a 'blacklisting'[30] against his name.

But the last official word on Kraemer in the first years after the war must go to Kim Philby, who turned the intelligence community's consensus on its head when he wrote[31] to John Halford at MI5 describing Kraemer as 'the very successful German I.S. Officer with whom we knew Fuellop was in touch'.

After Arnhem, Kraemer had largely served his purpose and perhaps Philby simply couldn't resist the temptation of goading British intelligence about the truth of Kraemer's (and of course Philby's and Blunt's) success in the Second World War.

Chapter 29

Drawing Up the Bridge

While the Farago version of events is clearly to be taken with considerable doses of salt, it appears to have had one very significant effect.

The most intriguing and most detailed report concerning the Kraemer affair was written by Patricia McCallum, a former MI6 officer who had been commissioned by the British government to examine the Josephine files. Her report was only released in 2003.[1] And the released version is a redacted second draft. Nevertheless it represents the fullest picture we have of MI5's official view of the 'Kraemer (or Josephine) case'. While the report is undated it was clearly in some sense prompted by Farago. McCallum makes four references to *The Game of the Foxes* in the course of the report. No other book is referenced in this way and the 300-page report must therefore in some way be seen as a response to and possibly a rebuttal of Farago.

It is a very curious document. On the face of it, McCallum, who had worked for MI6 during Operation Fortitude,[2] served in the MI5 Registry and was later head of the Cabinet Office Historical Section, is an ideal choice and the report seems thorough and balanced on first reading.

It takes the reader on a tour of the investigations into Josephine – starting with the 1943 discovery of Josephine by the OSS and ending with the closing of the case in 1946 with Kraemer denounced as an 'inveterate liar'. She decries this judgement as unfair and found it 'peculiar' that no full investigation into the Arnhem betrayal had taken place at the time.

She said it was significant both that Josef Fuellop had denied sending the Arnhem message and that he was unfamiliar with microdot communication technology.

It was the timing of the leak that bothered the MI5 investigator the most. 'It seems staggering,' she wrote,[3] 'that information could have reached Stockholm, by a somewhat round-about route from the Iberian Peninsula, within three days.'

Yet the overwhelming impression gained by reading the report is that the identity of Josephine must forever remain a mystery, impossible to untangle.

This is at variance with the evidence in her own report that clearly shows by the end of Kraemer's interrogation at Camp 020 Paul Mason (MI6), Edward Stamp (MI5, who after the war became a Lord Justice of Appeal)[4] and Michael Ryde (MI5) and Robin Stephens (Camp 020) all believed the German spy must have had at least one source passing him secrets from London. The only officers involved in the case who believed he didn't were Anthony Blunt and possibly Herbert Hart.

Just as significantly, the Swedish authorities, who conducted their own investigation into Kraemer both during and after the war, were certain Kraemer had not received any of his intelligence from any member of the Swedish military or diplomatic corps in Stockholm and concluded he had only named individuals in order to shield his real informants who they said could have been based in the UK.[5]

Professor Harry Hinsley, the trusted Bletchley intelligence officer commissioned by the spy chiefs to write the history of British intelligence in the Second World War, relied on McCallum's report when he was the first to publish an official view of the Kraemer files in his 1990 Volume IV.

Hinsley noted the troubling divergence of opinion between MI5 and MI6 on Kraemer.

Blunt had tried to pin the blame on Cervell, the Swedish air attaché, and other Swedish and Japanese diplomats, but SIS always believed the 'Josephine' source was much closer to the British government.

McCallum wrote:[6] 'In spite of the fact that Kraemer himself maintained that these were cover-names for types of information ... Berlin appeared to regard them as real individuals. It is clear that Kraemer was as much a mystery to his own people as he was to the Allies. Although information about him was now coming from a number of captured Abwehr officials, who had known and even worked alongside him, little was emerging to help solve the central mystery.'

She concluded: 'Finally, it must be admitted that the Kraemer case is and will always remain something of a mystery.'

What McCallum and no one else appears to have done is to consider the possibility that Soviet agents played a role in the transfer of critical intelligence from the Western Allies to the Germans. Moreover, McCallum decided to 'deliberately exclude' from her report intelligence gathered by Heinrich Wenzlau, the Abwehr officer working alongside Kraemer in Stockholm who had developed Russian contacts, 'since this dealt with Russian material'.[7]

Karl Heinz Kraemer, the man who passed the Arnhem message to the Germans on the eve of the battle, seems never to have ever known who Josephine was or who had been responsible for the microdot intelligence that arrived in his diplomatic bag. This was still the case when he was held at Camp 020 and Blunt was leading the 'Josephine' investigation and directing the interrogation.

But if Kraemer did not know about Blunt, how, if Blunt was Josephine, did Blunt find Kraemer? After all, in order to pull off being Josephine he would have needed an Abwehr officer intelligent enough to be a plausible conduit for intelligence as high-quality as Josephine, but not so diligent as to start asking too many awkward questions.

This is where Blunt's intervention to personally take over the interrogation at the point at which Anton Grundboek enters the picture is potentially very telling. Grundboek was described by Blunt as a 'rather low-grade Hungarian intelligence officer' but he is characterised in the Fuellop files as 'very shrewd'. He was undoubtedly very rich and well connected, frequently travelling around Europe for business. He was also an experienced Abwehr agent who had known Kraemer long before they both turned up in Stockholm in 1943. He was also the person who linked Kraemer to the Fuellop/FULLOP network in Spain, with its ties to Kim Philby and the Iberian section of Section V. Blunt, with his control of the Swedish diplomatic traffic, and Philby, who ran the British intelligence operations in Lisbon and Madrid, had unique access to the channels of communication between London, the Iberian Peninsula and Stockholm.

Is Ivan Chichaev (also Chichayev, Tchicaev, Tchitchaev etc.), who had spent the first two years of the war in Stockolm building a spy network,[8] the missing link in the chain? Is he Blunt and Philby's 'Karla'? Certainly there is some sort of Hungarian–Swedish–English triangle at the heart of Josephine. There is also little doubt that in 1941 the man sent to head up Pickaxe will have been a trusted, serious player. He had a clear Swedish link and Chichaev, who was suspected of being 'the head of the Russian intelligence abroad'[9], would also go on to be suspected of playing a 'prominent part in planning the escape of Burgess and Maclean'. He even went on to follow in Pavel Sudoplatov's shoes as head of Russian Atomic Espionage in 1954, which also means he was shrewd enough to navigate the death of Stalin in 1953 and the execution of Lavrentiy Beria in December 1953.

The single strangest thing about what is on first reading a frank and shrewd investigation into the Josephine affair is what McCallum doesn't say. Anthony Blunt appears numerous times as Maj. Blunt without comment and without reference to the fact he was a soviet spy. McCallum was either a serving or possibly retired British intelligence officer. It is inconceivable that she would have been unaware of who Blunt was. Of course it might be said that if she was a serving officer of SIS, it was her duty not to pass on secrets, but the effect is to wholly distort the picture. For instance when, having exhausted Onodera as a potential fit for Josephine, the interrogators turn up the pressure and Kraemer starts talking about Grundboek – the man with ties to the Hungarian secret service that was viewed as entirely taken over by the NKVD: at once Maj. It is at this point that SIS started to receive reports from captured Abwehr officers and German diplomatic staff, claiming Kraemer was working 'unconsciously or consciously for the Russians.' Ryde of B1A who had been leading the interrogations is 'replaced' by Maj. Blunt the NKVD spy. The absence of any alarm bells is glaring.

Neither does McCallum make a single reference to the fact that Blunt had been the first to seriously investigate Josephine's identity in 1943 and 1944. It is another bizarre omission.

Throughout her report, Blunt is hiding – or being hidden – behind the simplistic fiction that because Josephine was supplying information to the Nazis she must have been on their side. Yet the two most important releases of information Josephine passed over to Kraemer and which form the centre of the report, at D-Day and at Arnhem, mislead the Germans over D-Day, thereby facilitating the success of the landings but gave them the right information at Arnhem, thereby contributing to the Allies' slow progress towards Berlin.

The D-Day deception is particularly instructive. After the war, Jodl was quite clear that it was the combination of the Garbo/Fortitude deception originating from Spain in combination with the Josephine material coming from Sweden which convinced the Germans to hold their armour in reserve for a crucial period, still expecting the main attack on the Pas-de-Calais. McCallum even says, in tones of jocular incredulity, that 'one thing is certain, had Josephine been a real agent she would have to have been a member of the deception staff!'[10]

It stretches credulity to believe that post 1971, after Farago's book was published, McCallum could innocently write that sentence without referring even in passing to the fact that the Major Blunt popping in and out of her narrative was not only a member of the deception staff but had since 1964 been a confessed double agent.

She even doubles down on the thought, noting elsewhere that 'it was also suggested that he was a British double agent which in view of the Fortitude material he (Kraemer) was reporting was not without its amusing side.' Later on she says with respect to Market Garden that 'it is one of the peculiarities of the case ... that no full investigation (by MI5) seems to have been made.' It is hard to avoid the thought that there is a deliberate intention to mislead.

There are other omissions. There is, for instance, a lengthy section dealing with the Spanish Fuellop/FULLOP network, which Grundboek was Kraemer's link to. Yet by D-Day and Arnhem, Grundboek was dead and had passed on the control of the conduit to Horvath in Berlin, yet McCallum makes no mention of Horvath.

Reading McCallum, one is left with the impression that with the best will in the world, the identity of Josephine is lost to the mists of time, a mystery it is no longer possible to disentangle. A conclusion which, intentionally or not, chimes exactly with the official view of Blunt. So it seems worthwhile to briefly speculate why the McCallum report came to be written.

It is undated, but as we have seen it had to have been written after *The Game of Foxes*, which was published in 1971, and it seems certain that it was written partly in response to that and partly in response to the drumbeat of rumours about Blunt which grew so strong in the course of the 1970s that Margaret Thatcher was forced to address them in the House of Commons in 1979 and publicly out Blunt as a traitor.

The report has all the makings of a pre-emptive rebuttal, should MI5 find themselves needing to answer questions about Josephine and Blunt. It is long enough and detailed enough to satisfy and baffle even well-informed inquiry and does what MI5 most wanted it to do, which was keep Josephine and Blunt as far as possible apart from each other.

Even now, the idea that Blunt was responsible for the deaths of tens of thousands of Allied soldiers and civilians is shocking. In the 1970s when the family and comrades of the people Josephine betrayed were very much alive, it would have been truly horrifying.

In the end, the McCallum report was not needed. The speculation around Blunt settled on the well-worn relationships with his fellow Cambridge spies and the post-war Cold War period popularised by John le Carré and so many others. Patricia McCallum's report was quietly entered into the official record and released without any attention in 2003.

The case for Blunt being Josephine is of necessity circumstantial. Smoking guns, if there are any, remain under lock and key in the MI5, SIS and Kremlin archives. Nevertheless, there is a long list of circumstantial clues which point to him. They are explored in greater detail in Appendix 1. But perhaps the strongest case for Blunt being Josephine lies in exactly the mystification McCallum leaves us with. Josephine could have any number of explanations she in effect says, throwing up her hands at the impenetrability of it all.

But in reality, if Josephine was NOT Blunt, then the options for whom she might have been are very limited. There are just three credible possibilities.

One is that Kraemer was, as Farago would have us believe, a 'genius' magicking up on the basis of a single three-month visit to England on the eve of the war an Abwehr agent in the heart of the British establishment. The trouble is that there is nothing to give us any idea how this was possible. Every other German intelligence asset in Britain was rolled up shortly after the war started and yet Kraemer, a young and wholly inexperienced officer, is supposed to have found a source of the quality and stature of Josephine.

It is worth comparing Kraemer with that other star officer of the Abwehr, Hermann Giskes. In him one can see all the diligence, tough-mindedness, courage, initiative and hard work that are so lacking in Kraemer. Giskes' successes with Englandspiel and with Lindemans make sense. There is a chain of cause and effect which adds up to a coherent whole. With Kraemer there is no chain: there is simply a spout which gushes forth intelligence with zero understanding of how that has come about.

There is no doubt that Giskes would not have accepted knowing so little about where the Josephine material was coming from, and that his instant belief would have been that if intelligence was just landing in his lap that would be because someone was putting it there and he would have not rested until he had found out who was playing him and how. There is no evidence that at any point Karl Heinz Kraemer investigated who or what Josephine was.

Giskes' doubts about Lindemans' motivations for spying for him so late in the war are also instructive. If Josephine really was a Nazi spy, then she would have needed to be unusually devoted to the cause, repeatedly risking her life until the very last days of the war in support of a losing cause. Equally, if there was such a high-ranking Nazi in the British military and intelligence establishment, it seems surprising that neither MI5, MI6, OSS or the NKVD ever seemed to catch the faintest whiff of who that was.

The second option is that Kraemer was a liar who was simply making it all up by reading newspapers and magazines and gossiping with embassy staff over lunch in Stockholm. The trouble with that is that far too much of the material was of too high a quality for this to be an option. Even Philby was careful to just characterise Kraemer as an 'very successful intelligence officer'. Too many of his colleagues were too clear that Josephine, while undoubtedly patchy, was at times frighteningly accurate.

Above all, if he really had been making it up, why not admit it? After all, that was the story the British would have been most happy to hear. There could be no blame attached to him navigating a difficult predicament as an officer of the Abwehr and trying with all his might to hold on to the cushy berth he had for himself and his young family in Stockholm. But the reality is that while some of the Josephine material was of poor quality, there are either explanations for that – such as the period after Blunt had fingered Cervell as Josephine, when it made sense for the quality of the material to drop. At crucial moments, the intelligence was of a startlingly high quality which it would have been impossible to invent.

The last option is that Kraemer was indeed a pawn of the Russians, but that Josephine was someone other than Blunt. This supposes the possibility that Josephine was one of the other Cambridge spies. They almost certainly contributed to the Josephine material but none of them had anything like the access that Blunt did, not just to material, but also to the means of getting it to Kraemer in Stockholm.

The alternative is that there was a sixth man – but again that begs the question, what were the Russians using Blunt for? As has been demonstrated, perhaps no spy in history has had the range of access to the crucial intelligence that Blunt had. What bigger project than Josephine might the Russians have held him back for? Arguably the atomic bomb, but there were already agents in place passing on that information and on a horses for courses basis, the linguist and art historian Blunt would be an odd choice for passing on theoretical physics which he was unable to fully comprehend. Certainly, from 1941 to 1945, the project of ensuring that Stalin won the peace at the end of the Second World War was at the very least of equal strategic importance to the atom bomb.

In other words, it is harder to think of an explanation for Josephine that does not involve her being Blunt than the other way around.

Chapter 30

After the Battle

Whether Blunt was Josephine or not, the question remains, how much did Josephine's betrayal of Market Garden affect the outcome of the battle? In the days after the Battle of Arnhem, Field Marshal Bernard Montgomery claimed that Operation Market Garden was 90 per cent[1] successful. Prince Bernhard's response was to dryly comment that the people of Holland could ill-afford another one of Monty's successes.

Ever since the last British paratroopers were evacuated[2] from the north bank of the Lower River Rhine in Holland, historians have been battling over the causes of the failure of the Arnhem landings.

The operation itself was inherently risky and bedevilled by mistakes and unforeseen setbacks from the start.

There were insufficient transport aircraft and gliders and so the landings had to take place over two days. Bad weather delayed reinforcement drops and the soldiers' radios didn't work.

Intelligence failures meant reports of the arrival of two Panzer divisions in the Arnhem area were ignored, partly as a result of the legacy of Englandspiel and assessments of the Dutch underground as being infiltrated. According to a military review of Arnhem after the war a warning about the presence of both SS divisions was prominent in the plans for Operation Comet but missing in Operation Market Garden.[3]

It is at the very least interesting that Blunt's agent, Leo Long, played a central role at SHAEF in assessing and briefing German military strength. It must be considered a serious possibility that he colluded with Blunt in minimising intelligence which might have seen Market Garden called off. Perhaps the most universally accepted reason for the failure of Market Garden lies in the fact that Montgomery and his commanders had an over-optimistic belief in the poor morale and combat status of the German army after D-Day. The Germans proved they were in fact far from beaten and were masters of improvisation, cobbling together disparate units of 'kampfgruppen' fighting groups. It is here that Josephine may have had the greatest impact. Or rather, as with D-Day, it was the combined impact of Lindemans' betrayal, the initial Josephine intelligence and then on the day itself the detailed order of battle. It was intelligence which enabled the German commanders to act with decisiveness and confidence which must surely have communicated itself to their troops.

Brigadier General Jim Gavin wasted men and time defending his flank from a possible counter-attack through the Groesbeek Heights by deploying troops that could have helped take part in the capture of the Nijmegen bridge. Lt General Brian Horrocks was accused of failing to press on to Arnhem after the river was finally crossed. The landing zones for the first British drop were too far from the vital bridge at Arnhem, British radios didn't work, Browning placed his headquarters too far back from the advance force and the resupply drops were plagued by bad weather.

But there is also a widespread consensus that despite all that did go wrong, Market Garden nevertheless came perilously close to succeeding. In the light of the more comprehensive picture of the degree to which the whole operation had been compromised, it does seem worth questioning whether the betrayals added up to the few percentage points that turned victory into defeat.

Betrayal has never been taken seriously as a possible reason for the failure. This is partly because the German commanders did not name a traitor or attribute their hard won victory to base treachery.

The German generals would have been unaware of the source of the intelligence reports they received before and during the battle. They couldn't have known whether the OKW or intelligence units of Walter Model's Army Group B (Heeresgruppe B) were sending them reports based on intelligence supplied by Karl Heinz Kraemer or Christiaan Lindemans or any other intelligence source. They were concerned solely on the end product and the importance the OKW attached to it. By the time anyone got round to establishing the Wehrmacht version of the battle, the three key German generals at Arnhem were either dead (Walter Model took his own life in April 1945) or facing war crime trials (Wilhelm Bittrich and Kurt Student both served prison sentences). And Alfred Jodl, who was interviewed by Hesketh in 1946, told the British general that Josephine was the Germans' best agent. Jodl, however, was executed for war crimes in October in 1946. Moreover, they were interrogated after their capture from a military perspective not, in any real depth, from an intelligence one. Military honour will have encouraged them to downplay the role treachery will have played in what was the last German victory of the war. Equally, it is unlikely to have seemed wise to them to suggest there was a highly placed traitor in their captors' ranks.

Most Dutch historians today have no doubt that Christiaan Lindemans betrayed Arnhem. The question in recent years has been what effect this betrayal had on the outcome of the battle.

As long ago as June 1981, Louis de Jong, the director of the Netherlands State Institute for War Documentation, concluded that the betrayal case was compelling. Harry Hinsley described Lindemans' actions on 15/16 September as the only potentially important success of the reformed Abwehr under Schellenberg during the last year of the war.

In 1997, the Dutch historian and intelligence expert Bob de Graaff found there was now enough evidence to prove a betrayal as well as a cover-up of the King Kong case that was partly instigated by Prince Bernhard and aided and abetted by the British government. However, determining exactly what impact the Lindemans' betrayal had on the battle has been more problematic.

At least four Abwehr intelligence officers – Giskes, Huntemann, Marcus and Christmann – all told their Allied military intelligence interrogators after the war that Lindemans' reports affected the outcome of the battle. Oreste Pinto, the head of Dutch counter-intelligence at SHAEF, continued to publish articles and books repeating his conviction that Lindemans' betrayal had cost the lives of thousands of British and American servicemen. Even Pinto's old adversary, Kas de Graaf, was latterly persuaded of Lindemans' guilt.

Perhaps the most critical voice of the period was the US Army's chief combat historian Sam Marshall, who had been at Arnhem. He concluded in 1950: 'The battle had been lost because of errors of omission and commission and the betrayal by Christiaan Lindemans, whose part in this great story has only just come to light.'[4]

More recently, in 2019, Wim Klinkert, professor of military history at the Netherlands Defence Academy and the University of Amsterdam, concluded:[5] 'Lindemans had brought Arnhem to the attention of the Germans' but it was only part of their intelligence picture which they had been building since the end of August.

Klinkert says: 'Lindemans' information might have had more effect on the German countermeasures against the ground attack, south of Eindhoven. Based on Lindemans' information, Student had sent reinforcements to that area, effectively delaying the ground attack on the 17th.'

Since the post-2001 release of voluminous files at the National Archives concerning Lindemans and Abwehr operations, it is possible to paint a much fuller picture of the King Kong treacheries and the motivation for these betrayals. The testimonies of many different witnesses, not least Lindemans' own admission about what he knew of the NKVD organisation, show that the

Dutch traitor had three masters – the Western Allies, the Germans and the Soviet Union.

Stalin had much to gain by slowing down the British and American advance into Germany in the wake of D-Day. The German military command had not, as the Russian leader hoped, switched vast divisions from East to West to contain the rapid breakout from Normandy. Indeed, the SS Panzer 9th and 10th divisions stationed in Arnhem were destined to be sent east to bolster the fight against the Soviet advance.

After the breakout of Normandy, the road to Berlin looked to have opened up for the Western Allies. By the end of August 1944, the Americans, British and Russians were all united in the belief that there would be a German collapse in the West leading to a political settlement that would isolate Stalin and keep the Red Army out of Berlin.

The top-secret plans for the Arnhem landings were not finalised until 10 September, yet within five days the Germans had received two clear and accurate warnings of the Allies' intentions – one from Lindemans and one from Karl Heinz Kraemer (the more general 'Onodera' warning reached Berlin on 14 or 15 September).

Stalin had everything to lose should Market Garden have been successful and the British and Americans reached Berlin before the Red Army as Churchill intended.

While Lindemans' early warning of an Anglo-American airborne assault is well known, the second intelligence breach has been largely ignored. This is because Kraemer's microdot report was delayed so that it arrived at the same time as the Anglo-British forces were arriving over Holland.

However, Walter Schellenberg, the head of German intelligence, was convinced it helped the Germans to understand the battlefield at a vital point in the battle.

The combined effect of the Lindemans and Kraemer (1st) warnings was to alert the Germans to the Allies' plan for an airborne operation in Holland. The degree of counter-paratroop training is evidence of that. The Germans would have realised from the on-the-ground reports that the Allied landings indicated a thrust towards Arnhem. But in the absence of air reconnaissance and the distraction of Allied deception reports of a sea landing the intelligence picture was confusing – Model thought the British paratroopers had come to capture him. Kraemer's second report was much more detailed and helped Model and Bittrich to understand the Allies' intention during the early phase of the battle and mount an effective counter-attack as well as bring in reinforcements to defend the known British and American objectives. It was this speed and certainty of action by the Germans (the deployment of SS 9 and SS 10 divisions) that Field Marshal Montgomery and the British generals believed defeated Market Garden.

Klinkert believes: 'The Germans were more successful in their use of human and signals intelligence and successfully deployed their forces to hand the Allies an ignominious defeat.'[6]

Bob de Graaff, the historian entrusted to write the official history of the Dutch secret services, concludes: 'Lindemans' betrayal of Arnhem and Kraemer's intelligence report made a difference that together may well have affected the outcome of the battle.'[7]

* * *

At the end of 1945, Blunt left MI5, physically and mentally exhausted. With the war over, his value to the Russians had significantly diminished. Their attention now shifted to Philby in MI6.

But Blunt's role in the betrayal of Market Garden was not his last mission as a Soviet agent.

In 1946 the Soviet spy held two meetings with his Russian handlers (16 September and 9 December) when he passed on information about the reorganisation of MI5. He also continued to supply intelligence from his sub-agent and communist protégé, Leo Long, about the intelligence division of the British Control Commission in Germany.[8] Blunt acted as a go-between for Burgess, Philby and the Russians, keeping them both in touch with the Centre.

He used his private office at the Courtauld Institute to photograph Foreign Office papers obtained by Burgess. Blunt was praised by Moscow for the quality of this photographic work. On 22 March 1948, Blunt reported to his handlers: 'with good contact with Liddell and Robertson (TA) I think I will be able to get information about MI5 that will be interesting enough for us.'[9] On the same day he produced a key for a Foreign Office safe and asked the Rezidentura to make a copy, a trick he had learned from Peter Falk, who had done the same with Kraemer's safe.

From then until his public exposure as a Russian spy in 1979, Blunt lived a blemish-free and grand life working for the Royal Family. He died four years later.

Yet there were plenty of missed opportunities to catch the Russian agent.

In 1951, Goronwy Rees, a military intelligence officer linked to the Cambridge spies, told Liddell that he suspected Blunt and Burgess had been active communists from 1937. Blunt denied it and the intelligence chief refused to believe Rees, dismissing it as a hangover from Blunt's misspent time and associations at Cambridge. Blunt was again investigated in 1957 and the Attorney General at the time was informed of the allegations, but once again nothing came of it. There were nine more inconclusive investigations into Blunt while he was working as Surveyor of the Queen's Pictures.

In 1964, Blunt was finally exposed, on the testimony of American Michael Straight, as one of the Cambridge spies and in return for immunity from prosecution agreed to provide intelligence about other Soviet agents.

Free from the threat of prosecution he changed his attitude and was clearly helpful to MI5, who were still using his intelligence in a live operation against the Soviets as late as 1975.[10] When he first agreed to cooperate with MI5 in the 1960s, it was the height of the

Cold War and the aftermath of the Cuban Missile Crisis. His value was very current and MI5 were solely interested in combating the existing threat to the West. MI5 was less interested in his historic treachery committed during the Second World War when he was working for Britain's Russian ally than they were in countering the new threat from the USSR and the devastating impact on Anglo-American relations of the other Cambridge spies.

Blunt of course had nothing to gain by volunteering acts of treachery from the last year of the war, including Arnhem, when he wasn't being pressed for it by his interrogators.[11]

MI5 officer, Peter Wright, one of Blunt's interrogators, describes in his book *Spycatcher* how Blunt was evasive and only made admissions grudgingly, when confronted with the undeniable.

Blunt, of whom Wright says 'he felt no guilt',[12] stubbornly clung to the claim that nobody had died because of his treachery until Wright was able to name names.[13]

The Cambridge spy knew he was also partly protected by the realpolitik of the day. MI5 had much to lose if Blunt's treachery became public or he followed Burgess, Maclean and Philby, all MI6 traitors, to Moscow. At this point, no high-profile traitors had been found to be working for MI5. According to Peter Wright, Roger Hollis, whom he wrongly accused in his book of being a Russian agent, told him to go easy on Blunt. And the Palace, with perhaps even more to fear from a spy scandal, instructed Wright not to mention any of Blunt's post-war covert operations on behalf of the King. MI5 and the Palace both feared a spy scandal that would topple the Tories and usher in a retributive Labour government.

Like so many other MI5 officers who came into contact with Blunt, Wright was partially beguiled by his quarry. 'Blunt,' Wright wrote,[14] 'was one of the most elegant, charming and cultivated men I have ever met. He could speak five languages and the range and depth of his knowledge was profoundly impressive.'

But just like his skilful non-investigation of Kraemer, Blunt backtracked, obfuscated and distracted until no one could be sure what the Cambridge spy knew or whom he knew it from.

Blunt's confession remains a secret document, although it is doubtful whether it contains many real secrets. Those lie under lock and key in the Lubyanka, Moscow.[15]

His treachery was finally made public in a statement to the House of Commons read by Margaret Thatcher in 1979 when she was also forced to deny media reports that Blunt had betrayed dozens of British and Dutch agents to the Germans during Englandspiel. The *Sunday Telegraph* had confused him with the British officer Charles Blizard under his alias 'Major Blunt', the name the SOE chief had mysteriously used during his time in the service.

It is a curious irony that when Blunt was finally revealed to be a Soviet spy in 1979 it was immediately and incorrectly linked to Englandspiel. The *Sunday Telegraph* devoted a front page to the story and Margaret Thatcher, when she gave her full statement to the House of Commons, singled it out, specifically to debunk it. It may be that the Blizard/Blunt confusion was simply a case of the *Telegraph* journalist getting the wrong end of the stick and it is a mere coincidence that it treads so closely on the real secret about Blunt. But it should also be pointed out that Kenneth Rose, whose story it was, would pop up 20 years later as the official biographer of Victor Rothschild (serialised by the *Sunday Telegraph*), who not only got Blunt his job in MI5 but was recorded as having him as a lodger as late as 1966. So there is more than a touch of accidentally on purpose about the Rose story, especially when one considers that Rothschild would go on to serve as Margaret Thatcher's adviser on security matters.

On 25 June 1993 the *Guardian* newspaper quietly reported that some of the sensitive Englandspiel files relating to MI6 and SOE had been destroyed the year before.[16] The signature on the destruction order was a senior Cabinet official working for John Major's government.

Since the *Telegraph* story no mention has been made of Blunt betraying British intelligence to the Germans in support of the military and political goals of Russia. Yet according to Professor Christopher Andrew, the former official historian of MI5, Blunt was prolific in terms of the volume of secret documents passed to his Soviet handlers, running to 1,771[17] and much remains unknown about what he got up to during the war.[18] MI5's official record of the amount of material that he handed to his Russian masters in the Second World War describes it as being 'phenomenal'.[19]

Yet we know next to nothing about the content of this intelligence.

What we can say is that if Blunt was Josephine – and at the very least there are reasonable grounds for suspecting he was – then Blunt can be argued to be the most devastatingly successful and destructive spy in history. Thousands of soldiers may have died as a result of Josephine's treachery. Many thousands more civilians died of starvation. And if one accepts that Josephine delayed the end of the war and allowed Stalin to win the race to Berlin, then millions more were condemned to lives of cruel oppression under the Soviet regime. Furthermore, without Soviet expansion into Eastern Europe, would there have been a domino theory? And without that, would there have been a Korean or Vietnam War? A Bay of Pigs?

The Traitor of Arnhem. Dutch intelligence officer Oreste Pinto helped to uncover Christiaan Lindeman's treachery and, after the war, told his story.
(Reach PLC. Image created courtesy of THE BRITISH LIBRARY BOARD.)

Poisonous death. How the British media reported the 'suicide' of Christiaan Lindemans in Juy 1946. (The National Archive, KV-2-237 p13.)

TOPSECRET AND PERSONAL.

Secret.

In reply, state NUMBER and DATE.

CX / V.F.20 dated 23.6.45.

Dear Anthony,

I note that a diplomatic transit visa has been granted to Captain Arnold KARCH, Swiss Military and Air Attache in Stockholm.

KARCH has been reported on various occasions as a source of General ONODERA's. It is also learnt from JMAs that [RUTH] Swiss Military Attache in Helsinki, was supplying information to the Japanese there.

There is presumably no action we can take, but I thought you might be interested in his background.

Yours sincerely,

(For Major P.G. Mason)

Major A.F. Blunt,
M.I.5.

THIS IS A COPY
ORIGINAL DOCUMENT RETAINED
IN DEPARTMENT UNDER SECTION
3 (4) OF THE PUBLIC RECORDS
ACT 1958. Oct '99

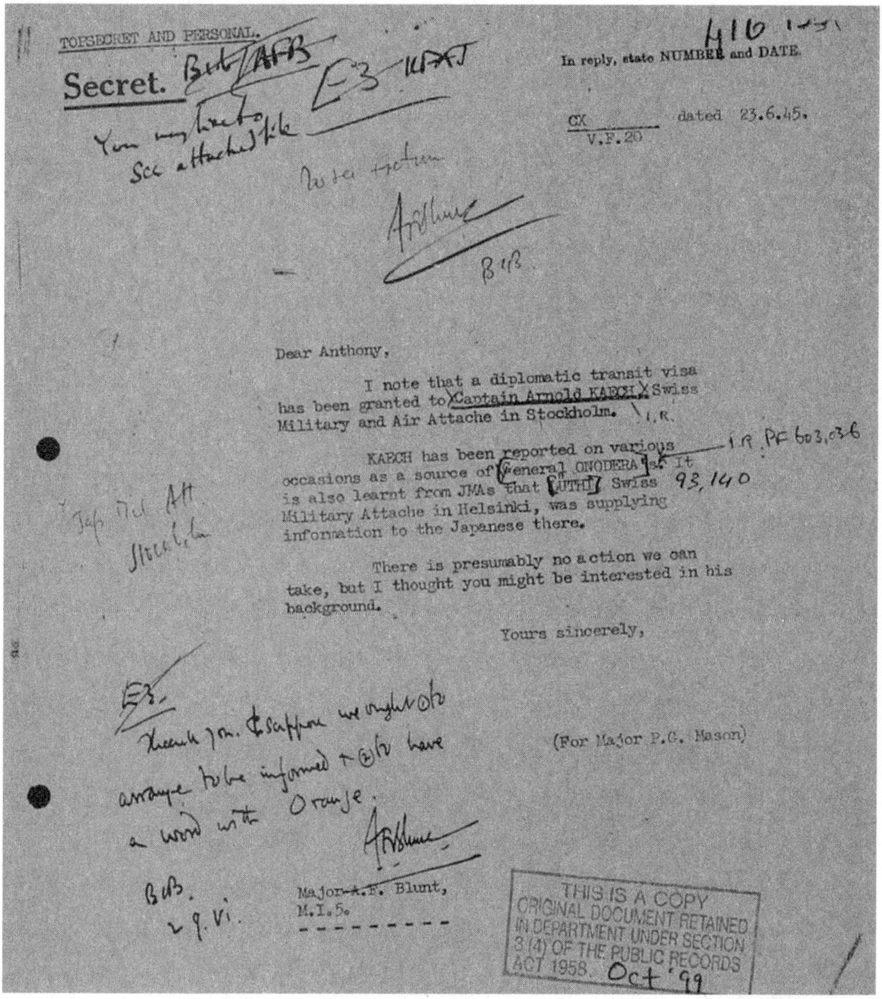

Blunt's scribbled note putting Agent Orange on the Kraemer case. Orange was Eric Kessler, a Soviet spy who Blunt helped recruit to MI5 and who could be relied upon to support Blunt's version of events. Dated 23 June 1945. (The National Archive, KV 2/150 (2), p.27.)

SECRET.

CAMP 020.

REPORT dated 19th October, 1945.

KRÄMER.

With reference to B.1.B's (Major Blunt's) memorandum of 27.8.45., the papers and teleprints concerning KRÄMER forwarded therewith are now returned, as the case is now closed.

M. Dundison
For Lt. Col. Stimson.

/EMB.

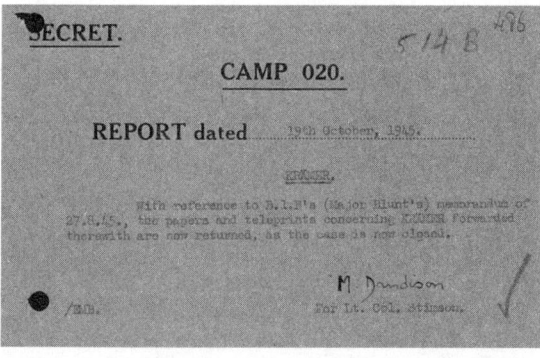

Blunt quietly closed down the investigation in October 1945 – his last act as an MI5 officer. Kraemer is sent back to Germany. (The National Archive, KV-2-153 (1) p.10.)

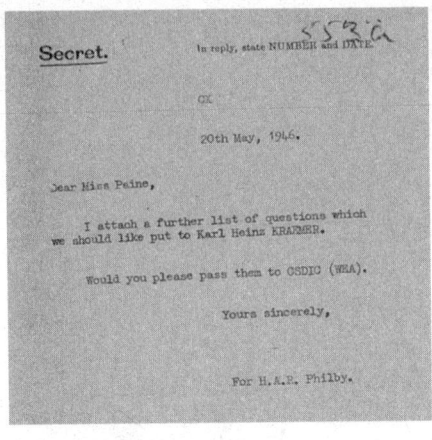

In May 1946 Blunt's Cambridge spy colleague Kim Philby is in charge of the investigation into Kraemer while he is detained by the British in Germany. (The National Archive, KV-2-154 (2) pp 24 25.)

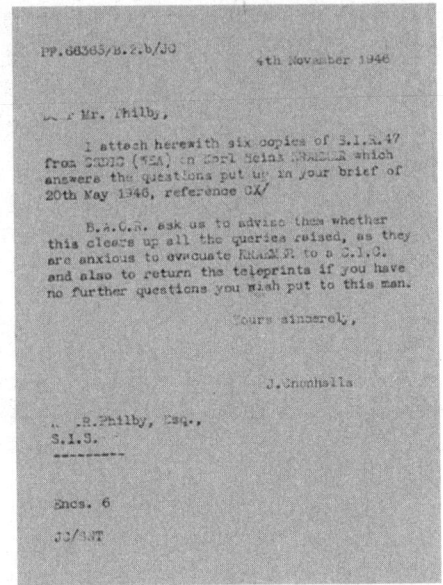

Philby closes the case.
(The National Archive, KV-2- 154 (1) p73.)

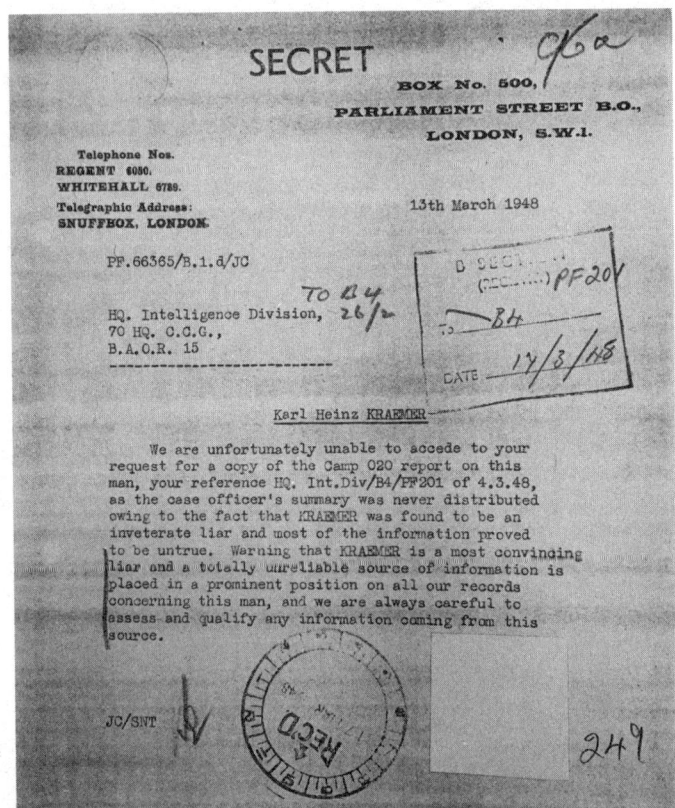

When the Americans pick up the trail of Kraemer two years later in 1948, they are denied access to the British papers on the grounds that Kraemer is deemed to be an 'inveterate liar.'

(The National Archive)

The American Office of Strategic Services (OSS), a forerunner of the CIA, find Josef Fuellop, (Kraemer's Arnhem source) living in Spain and arrange for him to be entrapped in Gilbraltar. Philby immediately takes over the case and ensures that Josef Fuellop is kept out of the hands of the Americans. (The National Arvhice, KV-2-242 (2) p.58.)

Josef Fuellop is handed over to Leo Long in Germany, a Soviet agent recruited to MI5 by Anthony Blunt. (The National Archive, KV 2/242(1) p.4.)

Philby clears the path for Fuellop to be sent back behind the Iron Curtain where he is never heard of again. (The National Archive, KV 2/242 (1) p.16.)

Epilogue

Exploding Chocolates

Shortly after midday on Monday 23 May 1938, two key figures in the fight for Ukrainian independence arranged to meet at a hotel restaurant in the centre of Rotterdam.

Yevhen Konovalets, a mathematician from Lviv now exiled in Holland, was the leader of the nationalist movement, the Ukrainian Military Organization. His close ally Pavel Sudoplatov was from Melitopol, eastern Ukraine. They warmly greeted each other before sitting down in the dining room of the Atlanta Hotel on Coolsingel, Rotterdam's cosmopolitan bustling high street.

Sudoplatov clutched a box of Belgian chocolates wrapped in paper decorated with the Ukrainian national colours. He remembered Konovalets had a sweet tooth and placed his gift in the centre of the table. They had much to discuss. War was in the air and Ukraine's resistance leaders sensed a moment of opportunity as the Nazis and Soviets faced off against each other.

But Sudoplatov told Konovalets that he would not have time to finish their plans for armed revolution that afternoon. His travel arrangements had changed at the last minute and he was due aboard a Ukrainian ship leaving Rotterdam within the hour.

Before parting, they embraced each other, promised to meet soon and vowed to continue the fight for Ukrainian independence. There was just time for Sudoplatov to apologise[1] for breaking up the party and express his wish that Konovalets enjoy the box of chocolates, which he had carefully placed upside down on the table where his friend was sitting.

At 14 minutes past midday, Harm de Jonge, a 41-year-old taxi driver, left his car and was strolling down Coolsingel towards the Atlanta Hotel.[2] As he crossed Aert van Nesstraat, his attention was drawn to a man with a pencil moustache and a grey fedora walking in great haste, carrying in his left hand a small parcel covered in yellowish brown paper.[3]

After leaving the Atlanta Hotel, Sudoplatov turned immediately right and found himself in a side street lined with shops: 'I entered one shop that sold menswear and purchased a hat and a light raincoat,' he later recalled.[4] 'As soon as I left the shop I heard a loud bang; it sounded like a blown tyre. People were running towards the restaurant.'

When de Jonge reached the Lumiere cinema he was halted in his tracks by the flash of a blue flame immediately followed by a deafening explosion: 'I saw the body of a man being blown to the right, towards the pavement, where it landed close to the litter bin at the kerb. Part of one of his legs fell in front of me. Blood from the leg covered my shoes. I picked the leg up carefully and put it down by the body.'

Sudoplatov headed for the railway station and boarded the first train to Paris.

After safely crossing the safety of the Belgian border, his thoughts turned to the events of the year before that had brought him to Rotterdam with his box of exploding chocolates.

It was November 1937, just after the annual celebrations of the October Revolution. Sudoplatov was driven to the Kremlin by Nikolai Ivanovich Yezhov, the head of the NKVD, the People's Commissariat for Internal Affairs. This was Stalin's secret police force that between 1937 and 1938 had murdered 680,000 political opponents, White Russians, suspected Western spies, loyal communists, farmers and people who happened to be in the wrong job at the wrong time. Sudoplatov was taken[5] to the doors of a spacious, spartan office with walls covered from floor to ceiling in a utilitarian brown wallpaper. Behind a large, wooden desk sat a man in a brown military tunic of the Soviet Army.

The young Ukrainian stood to attention: 'I was 30 years old and still not in control of my emotions. I was overwhelmed and could not believe that the leader of the country would meet with a rank and file case officer. When Stalin shook my hand I could not collect myself to report to him succinctly.'

Stalin smiled: 'Young man, don't be so excited. Report the essential facts. We have only 20 minutes.'[6]

Sudoplatov laid out his plan in detail, explaining that the bomb he intended to use to assassinate Konovalets had been designed by the director of the Soviet technical bureau of secret weapons. Its advantage over more sophisticated bombs was that it did not depend on a hidden switch. Instead, the explosive would be detonated 30 minutes after the box was moved from the vertical to the horizontal position.[7]

Stalin, who appreciated unfussy ingenuity in the art of assassination, was impressed. He told Sudoplatov: 'This is not just an act of revenge, although Konovalets is an agent of German fascism. Our goal is to behead the movement of Ukrainian fascism on the eve of the war and force these "gangsters" to annihilate each other in a struggle for power.'[8]

It was no accident that Pavel Sudoplatov had chosen Holland to carry out the assassination.

The Dutch were the only Western power to have refused to recognise the legitimacy of the Soviet state after the 1917 Revolution.

Holland was also far enough away from Moscow for Stalin to plausibly deny any involvement and too militarily and politically weak to cause any trouble, should anything go wrong.

The body of Yevhen Konovalets, a hero in the fight for an independent Ukraine, is buried in the Crooswijk cemetery,

Rotterdam, just a few metres from that of the 'traitor of Arnhem', Christiaan Lindemans.

* * *

History is not frozen in time. Events that took place in the Second World War continue to shape the geopolitics of our world today. The repercussions of the failure of Arnhem were profound. The Western Allies' failure to capture the German capital before the arrival of the Red Army has allowed the Russians to impose a map of Soviet rule in eastern Europe that has been used by Stalin's successors to lay claim to territories that were once free.

On 24 February 2022, Vladimir Putin invaded Ukraine after weeks of denying he had any plans to launch a military offensive. The next day his armies attacked the Ukrainian city of Melitopol. After heavy fighting and determined resistance from the civilian population the city fell to the invaders.

Among the Russian forces was the newly formed Pavel Sudoplatov Battalion, named after Stalin's favourite assassin and composed of pro-Russian Ukrainian and foreign fighters.[9]

One of Putin's first acts after capturing the city was to erect a monument in honour of Pavel Sudoplatov.

Appendix 1

If Anthony Blunt had never been involved in the hunt for Josephine and Hector, would we have ever considered that he could be the source behind them? Is it just the fact of his proximity that leads us to suspect him?

On the face of it, that seems like a reasonable doubt, but there are significant reasons why it is not true. The first must be that Blunt had motive, means and opportunity. While that is easily apparent to us now, it is important to recognise that in 1943/44 – and to a lesser degree in 1944/45 – he would have appeared *not* to have motive.

It would have seemed inconceivable that a man as cultivated as Blunt, a homosexual, a man with close Jewish friends, could possibly be aiding and abetting the Nazis. Few people were able to see that if one was a committed communist, there were significant reasons for helping the Nazis in the Western theatre.

The reluctance to acknowledge the intentions of Stalin was widespread and born out of a number of factors. There was the much-cited class element – members of the British upper classes giving each other a latitude which astonished the Russians and ironically meant they never fully trusted any of the Cambridge spies. Add to that a widespread cultural leftism, where being a 'bit of a communist' was of no more consequence than liking the poems of W H Auden. Then of course there was the appalling scale of Nazi evil. It was so big, and in 1940 the British were so on their knees that it really isn't that surprising that people could only concentrate on slaying the dragon that was trying to kill us right now. The thought that Stalin was every bit as evil as Hitler must have seemed too ghastly to contemplate.

It is only with the benefit of a longer lens that the intentions of Stalinism become clearer and that to be a bit of a communist is not to be a communist at all. Blunt was too much of an intellectual not to realise that. It is an unfortunate irony that Walter Krivitsky, the man who could have put a stop to all of them if he had been heeded in 1940, was quite explicit in his conversations with Jane Archer that the British were mad not to be rounding up and interning communists in exactly the same way we were with Nazis.

Much of what he said to her was about how the Russian secret services saw subversion and sabotage – for them less about blowing up stuff than a far subtler process of 'decomposition'. His words bear revisiting to this day.

Stalin demanded that the British open up a second front within eight days of Barbarossa and the end of the Molotov–Ribbentrop Pact and while it is hard not to do a double take at the hypocrisy of that, it is entirely consistent with the way he conducted the entire war. From the outset, Stalin was convinced that the British had somehow lured the Germans into becoming paranoid that the moment they launched an all-out attack on Britain, Russia would send troops pouring in at their backs. It seems entirely possible that was a hope the British had, just as it seems equally likely that the Russians did also hope that the Nazis would destroy the great imperialist enemy of Britain and at the same time either weaken themselves in so doing or strand a significant portion of their army on the British Isles and afford the Russians the perfect opportunity to sweep westward.

Certainly, Hitler may have admired the British and been reluctant to humiliate us, but the Battle of Britain may have been less of a factor in Hitler's diffidence about invasion than his reluctance to send his armies over the Channel.

APPENDIX 1

For the British, the war was about defeating Hitler and the Nazis. We stood to gain very little from it and indeed in 1940 the rational, self-interested thing to do would have been to make peace. For Stalin it was always the 'Great Patriotic War'; more than just about Hitler and the Nazis, it was quite explicitly about advancing national aims.

Blunt had means, motive and opportunity: via Triplex, Twist, his role briefing Churchill on the whole range of British intelligence activities. All of that gave him a key to every door, an authority which raised him above suspicion and gave him access to multiple routes for transmitting his information. It is impossible without access to files which will never be made public to say how many people had access to *both* the information required to mirror the Garbo material in the way Josephine did at D-Day *and* the detailed order of battle for Market Garden. It would be surprising if it was a number that reached double figures. The list of people who could have been Josephine is very short.

There is this strange mismatch in the narrative around Blunt. You have the towering intellect, the maths scholar who shifts first to French and then art history, mastering each equally. There is the great espouser of the Forsterish cult of friendship, who saw no conflict between his Marxism and love of the high life (and whose friends had a nasty habit of dying young). Above all there is the amazingly competent spy – promoted to high heavens by the British and held in unique esteem (of all the Cambridge spies) by the Russians and yet who apparently didn't really do anything very important. Yet he sent more than 1,700 secret documents to Moscow during the course of the war.

Even the barest facts, which are that while Burgess and Philby were drowning their sorrows in dingy Moscow flats, Anthony Blunt continued – after his confession even – to move in the highest circles, demonstrate that Blunt by any objective yardstick got away with it. That fact alone is enough to make one wonder if it was not he, much more than Philby, who was the master spy.

The 'nothing to see here' narrative spun by him as it was spun by the British establishment of the day never made sense. He always had to have done more. The question was what? Why would it make sense for there to be such a concerted attempt to downplay the impact of what he did?

One answer to that question is that it was because it was of such a scale that revealing it was unthinkable for all concerned. Imagine if in 1945 it had been revealed that a British spy had betrayed the 17,000[1] Allied servicemen killed, wounded or captured at Arnhem? Been responsible for the 20,000 Dutch citizens who had died in the famine that followed? Been revealed as sending the Luftwaffe bombing targets during the Blitz even? The howl of rage from all concerned would have been deep and damaging. Would that have spilled over into calls for war with Russia? Political upheaval? Both seem possible. At the very least it would have destroyed British credibility and ended the 'special relationship' before it had even begun. The consequences would have seemed unthinkable. It is still shocking to this day.

Even the Russians had no reason for their annexation of Eastern Europe to be presented as anything other than the heroism of the Great Patriotic War and the will of the proletariat to be freed from the yoke of Nazi imperialism. Laying the credit at the treacherous feet of an effete, British intellectual was not a narrative the Great Helmsman was about to encourage.

This perhaps explains another mystery, which is the way in which Kraemer and Josephine disappear from view at the end of the war. In 1945 it is quite clear that Jodl, the German Chief of Staff (regarded by most historians as the pre-eminent military mind in the OKW), and Walter Schellenberg, the chief of the secret service, both regarded Josephine as the Nazis' top source of intelligence in the Western theatre. It was material which was frequently handed direct to Hitler but which came via a junior German intelligence officer in Sweden who admitted to running no agents himself and appeared to have no idea where his stream of gold came from.

The identity of Josephine was, from a British point of view, the great intelligence mystery in 1945 and yet while just about every spy story of the Second World War has been the subject of numerous books and films, you will struggle to find any record of Josephine and Karl Heinz Kraemer either on the internet or even in the indexes of the big histories of the war. Why have they disappeared from view?

It is even odder because the Cambridge spies remain a global obsession. It is no longer possible to count all the books, films and other representations of this group and yet the focus is always on the latter part of their careers, not the part where they built their reputation. Again, why is that? Could it be that the reason why Josephine has disappeared from view are the same as the reason why it has been so hard to get a clear handle on what Blunt and Philby did in the war?

But then, if they are linked, is there anything which linked Blunt to Kraemer? After all, you can't just broadcast this kind of information to German intelligence willy-nilly. Not if it is to be believed and not if it isn't going to come back and bite you. If Blunt was Josephine, he needed a Kraemer to be his patsy, so how did he find him?

The answer to that is explored more fully in the text, but a significant part of the reason why Josephine disappears from view is that Blunt and Philby set about burying it. The American OSS were not allowed to even see the transcripts of the interrogation. Kraemer, they were told, was such an inveterate liar that there really was no point. Fuellop, the one person who knew enough to cause trouble, was sent back to disappear in Hungary. By as early as 1946, Josephine, like the Cheshire Cat, was vanishing from view: even Hesketh, tasked with writing a report on the D-Day and Arnhem deception, appears to have been wholly unaware that there were two Arnhem leaks and that it was the second which contained the devastating (from a security point of view) detail.

Quite quickly, Josephine became a mirage, a thing not worth investigating or writing about when there were so many more promising avenues to explore. After all, who in 1946 wanted a tale of betrayal and failure? What people wanted were stories which reflected the very real heroism of the countless millions who did risk their lives to fight Hitler.

And, of course, once the finger of suspicion began to be pointed at Maclean, Burgess, Philby, Blunt and Cairncross, the British security establishment, reeling from the humiliation of American contempt, would have been utterly aghast at the prospect of the heroic narrative of the Second World War being stripped from them too. And so it stayed. Even now, long after all the protagonists are long, long dead, it still feels only just time for us to ask the kind of hard questions about the depth and scale of Anthony Blunt's treachery during the Second World War.

The case for Blunt being Josephine

If there are any smoking guns identifying Blunt as Josephine they will be under lock and key in either the British or Russian secret service archives and are unlikely to ever see the light of day. Nevertheless the list of circumstantial evidence pointing to the identification of Blunt as Josephine is a long one and will no doubt be extended.

1943/44

1. Anthony Blunt was uniquely placed to be Josephine. By 1944 he had established himself in a key role in British intelligence, with the right to access every kind of secret material. He has motive, means and opportunity.
2. He was one of the first MI5 officers to become aware of Kraemer.

APPENDIX I

3. Blunt was central to the investigation of Josephine from the very first time the British became aware of her existence in 1943 and at every stage he steered the investigation away from British Intelligence and away from any Russian links.
4. After months of fruitless investigation he settles on and sells the Cervell/Oxenstierna story, which collapses with D-Day but that raises no red flags.
5. He had sub-agents (exclusively working for him) who had infiltrated the Swedish embassy in London (Agent Lemon and Jack Hewit). The only direct evidence against Frank Cervell came from Lemon.
6. Again, after Arnhem and the other Josephine intelligence, there are no red flags about the fact that after more than a year investigating Blunt and MI5 still have it so wrong. Of course it is unthinkable to his colleagues in 1944 that Blunt could be passing secrets on to Nazis.
7. The way the Arnhem message evaded all the usual radio and telephone surveillance of German communications undertaken by British Intelligence in the war. MI6 even had an agent working as a teleprint operator in the German embassy who collected Kraemer's secret messages. The Arnhem warning still somehow slipped the net.
8. In February 1944 Kraemer says he knew the British were trying to get him thrown out of Stockholm. Who warned him of this?
9. Why does Blunt not tell anyone about Peter Falk's meeting with him at the Reform Club in London?
10. Why does Blunt lose his cool with Falk when Falk raises a concern about Kraemer's possible links to Russia?
11. The way Blunt resists Menzies' idea of planting a 'rather hot' piece of intelligence on the Swedish diplomats to try to trap them.

1945/46

1. Who warns Kraemer to go to Flensburg? McCallum says MI6 were trying to get him arrested by the Swedes as this would keep him out of the hands of MI5.
2. In Camp 020 Blunt 'takes over the interrogation' by June from Major Michael Ryde, who had started to change his view and side with MI6 over the possibility of a London mole.
3. Both Hesketh and McCallum say that D-Day material (if not invented) could only have come from someone on the deception staff. Blunt was on the deception staff (Twist).
4. Similarly, the Arnhem material was only known by a very small number of very senior officers: Blunt was similarly in a position to know.
5. The number of people able to access *both* the D-Day deception and the Arnhem order of battle was minute.
6. Roger Hesketh was not made aware of the 2nd (detailed) Arnhem communication in his report. Had he been, he may well have started to ask questions about a possible London mole.
7. The fact that (according to McCallum) there was never an MI5/6 investigation into the betrayal of Arnhem.
8. Jodl and Schellenberg both testified that Josephine was regarded as the Germans' top intelligence source in the Second World War and yet by end 1946 the search for Josephine is over: she is decided to be an amalgam of Kraemer's inventions and open sources.
9. The way Kraemer is interrogated for weeks and only talks about Onodera. After the interrogations increases in intensity (a 'blitz') and secures a 'break' Kraemer admits to Grundboek. It is at this point that Blunt steps in to take over.
10. Blunt tries to hobble the Kraemer investigation by failing to address Major Paul Mason's question about a possible Russian link. On 20 July 1945, Major Mason, who had been given access to Schellenberg's first interrogation report before he was

APPENDIX I

brought to Camp 020 from Germany, wrote to Anthony Blunt, telling him: 'Schellenberg is of the opinion that Kraemer's intelligence comes from the Russians.'²

11. The fact that OSS were denied access to the Kraemer interrogations because by the end of 1945 MI5/MI6 concluded he was such an 'inveterate liar'. Despite the fact that OSS had first alerted the British to Josephine.
12. The fact that Philby takes charge of the Kraemer case after Blunt leaves MI5.
13. The fact that Leo Long (named by Blunt as a Soviet agent in his 1964 'confession') has a key role in Kraemer's and Josef Fuellop's ongoing custody after their return to Germany.
14. Blunt put Camp 020 interrogators off the scent of Russian agent Dimitrewski, who was alleged to be feeding Onodera with intelligence from Britain.
15. Blunt kills the investigation into the Moscow/Tedder link by telling MI6 they are 'flogging a dead horse'.
16. The way Philby sends Fuellop back to Soviet-controlled Hungary to disappear in 1946.
17. Blunt refused to re-interrogate Kraemer's secretary despite MI6's request and Mason's insistence that she was key to uncovering Josephine.
18. Blunt's determination to prove there was no British agent working as Josephine source. SIS, Ryde, Stamp and Stephens all believed there was.
19. An emotional Blunt had a meeting with his Russian handlers in London on 15 September, saying he was quitting MI5. The same day as Kraemer received the Arnhem microdot.
20. According to an NKVD report Blunt was paid a large sum of money and highly praised by his Russian handler in the days after Arnhem. KBG defector Oleg Gordievsky says that files from the NKVD Moscow archives show Blunt was personally praised by Moscow which was 'highly unusual'.

21. Blunt wrote on 2 November 1944 thanking the NKVD for his money and their praise for the important work he had recently carried out. Says he couldn't have achieved all he had without the help of Krotov.
22. The Arnhem warning was sent in microdot form. Fuellop told MI5 he had never used microdots. It is a specialist form of communication of which Blunt was a recognised expert by MI5/6.
23. The Russians referred to their spy inside MI5 as 'our girl' – Josephine?
24. Busch and Riedel (both German Intelligence), who were close to Kraemer in Sweden, were either convinced Kraemer had a British source or he was working for the British and/or the Russians as a controlled agent. Blunt does not ever answer the Russian connection.
25. MI5 officer Edward Stamp told Col Stephens he thought that the reason Kraemer was lying was because he had been 'unconsciously or consciously working for the Russians.'
26. The Americans (OSS) reported in 1945 that Kraemer had access to a 'great deal' of Russian intelligence.
27. Kraemer never knew who Josephine was.
28. In 1945 Blunt was allowed to 'leave' the service of NKVD unhindered because he had done such valuable work.
29. Blunt's very last act as an MI5 officer was to close down the Josephine investigation.

1947 to present
1. The way that Patricia McCallum's undated, but definitely post-1971, report on the 'Kraemer (Josephine)' affair makes repeated references to Major Blunt without ever referring to the fact that he is Anthony Blunt, the confessed Russian spy.
2. The way McCallum never mentions that the original investigation 1943/4 into Josephine was jointly led by Blunt – despite mentioning that investigation many times.

APPENDIX I

3. McCallum concluded that if Kraemer did have a source providing him with intelligence from London then the messages were probably being transmitted by 'diplomatic cable', a form of communication of which Blunt was something of an expert.
4. The way McCallum never mentions Horvath despite 10+ pages reviewing Fuellop's interrogation, which is quite explicit about Horvath.
5. The way the Fuellop interrogation characterises Grundboek as 'very shrewd' and close friends with both the former and current heads of Hungarian SIS, but McCallum quotes MI6, dismissing him as 'low grade'.
6. McCallum describes MI6 searching all of Europe for Josephine, but does not once ask if a spy handing over British military secrets may have been working in Britain.
7. McCallum undermines SIS insistence that there is a London mole, downplaying it as an 'article of faith' that is 'mythical, almost mystical'.
8. There is not a single reference by Blunt in the 2,500 pages of the Kraemer/Josephine files to Arnhem or D-Day.
9. The way in which Josephine and Kraemer have been all but forgotten: there is almost nothing out there. The Nazis' top agent excluded from major histories.
10. After the war the Swedish authorities investigate Kraemer and find he didn't have any military contacts in the Swedish government, armed forces or diplomat corps. They conclude that he may have had sources in London.
11. Burgess, Maclean and Philby all turn to Blunt in their last hours before defecting. Indicative that it was he who was their leader, or at the very least that it was his secret which had to be protected.

Appendix 2

THE ARNHEM WARNING 1

Christiaan Lindemans 'King Kong'

22 August 1944
Bletchley Park decrypted report[1] based on Lindemans' intelligence that featured in German intelligence signal:

'22.8. Subject: enemy intentions. Source: proven V.Mann CC [Lindemans' German code name] of Frontaufkl. Kdo 3017 – ... all activists who can be spared [are being dispatched] to the Maas line and are assembling at many fixed points due East of the Maas. West of the Maas remain only small sabotage groups to carry out regular sabotage against traffic. The enemy is planning the dropping of great numbers of parachute troops in the assembly areas of the insurgents (Maas line) ... V.Mann CC has urgent assignment to clear up: 1) Number of armed insurgents. 2) Main assembly centres on which the ABS [Belgium resistance] is counting. 3) Time at which dropping of airborne troops is expected.'

15 September 1944
Afternoon: Vught, General Kurt Student's HQ in Holland. Lindemans met[2] Kurt Student's intelligence chief (and according to

APPENDIX 2

one report[3] even Student himself) and passed on detailed accounts of British armour positions, including 300 Shermans preparing to move against Eindhoven in two days' time on 17 September. Lindemans must[4] have also outlined in more general terms what he had found out about the airborne element of Market Garden from his time with senior Allied officers including Lt Commander Philip Johns, Captain Peter Baker and Captain Kas de Graaf.

Student's intelligence chief reported[5] Lindemans' intelligence to Walter Model, head of Army Group B, at 10.50pm on 15 September.

An Ultra intercept[6] picked up German intelligence on 15 September sent to Fremde Heere West, Foreign Armies West (the military intelligence department of the OKH). It made it clear that the Germans believed the concentrated Allied airborne assault was now expected at Eindhoven through to Arnhem with the intention of cutting off German forces:

Ref: CX/MSS/T308/16,17,18,19,20
   IN SEVEN PARTS
   PART ONE
   ALLIES IN GERMAN REPORTS. ADDRESSED TO UNSPECIFIED ROMAN ITEM CHARLIE EVENING NINTH
   THIRTY BRITISH CORPS (TWO BRITISH ARMY) BETWEEN ANTWERP AND HASSELT.
   BRINGING UP OF FURTHER TROOPS. POSSIBLE ONE TO FOUR DIVISIONS WITH EIGHT TO NINE HUNDRED TANKS. INDICATE PROBABLE INTENTION IS THRUST MAINLY ON WILHELMINA CANAL ON BOTH SIDES EINDHOVEN INTO ARNHEM (FURTHER SPECIFICATION OF AREA INCOMPLETE BUT INCLUDES WEST OF NIJIMIGEN AND WESEL). TO CUT OFF AND SURROUND GERMAN FORCES.

Evening: Driebergen, German intelligence HQ in Holland. According to Richard Christmann: 'CC' further reported that he had succeeded in getting American and British officers to talk about a big aerial landing to take place on the 17/18 September. 'CC' gave us the positions of 400 heavy guns [there were actually 350]. From 16 September all the Dutch special troops [Dutch resistance] were to be mobilised. The aerial landings were to take place in Eindhoven, Nijmegen and Arnhem ... with the goal to drive a wedge into the German front, to reach Bremen.'[7]

German intelligence officers[8] at Driebergen say that Lindemans mentioned Arnhem as an intended objective.

Hermann Giskes, head of German military intelligence in Holland, said that Lindemans told Kiesewetter, 'English and American parachute divisions were standing by in England for a big airborne operation which is just about to be started ... there was no mention of Arnhem – King Kong had not mentioned it probably because he simply did not know in what area the Airborne attack was going to be made.'[9]

THE ARNHEM WARNING 2

Karl Heinz Kraemer 'Josephine'

14 September 1944
Kraemer received a report[10] from Onodera, head of Japanese intelligence in Stockholm, about an imminent airborne attack on Holland. It included the precise location in England of the British 1st, US 82nd and US 101st Airborne Divisions. He received this in his diplomatic bag, via the Japanese diplomatic staff attached to the Stockholm embassy. Onodera also verbally told Kraemer about the planned attack on Holland.

'About 2 or 3 days before the actual Arnheim operation, Onodera told me to have received from the Swedish general Staff,

APPENDIX 2

in exchange to other intelligence, the dislocation report that the 1st British, the 82nd and 101st USA Airborne-Division were now in England since about a month. Together with this he had got other dislocation reports concerning the Western Front. The whole dislocation report was handed over to me by Onodera. I remember that we wondered about the new dislocation of the Airborne Divisions, which were supposed to be in France. Onodera added verbally that: the Swedish General Staff expected a big Anglo-American Airborne operation in Holland as immediately imminent; it was further reported that the 1st British Airborne Division was in sealed camps. I knew what it meant to keep Airborne-units in "sealed camps" and reported this very important information to Berlin as quickly as possible und the cover designation "Quelle 10" (Source 10). This announced that the report was based on the official opinion of the Swedish General staff. This report of mine arrived in Berlin in due time.'

It has not been established whether this first, but less detailed, of Kraemer's two warnings about an imminent airborne landing in Holland was passed on to Field Marshal Walter Model, head of Army Group B, before 17 September, the start of Market Garden.

15 September 1944

Kraemer received a microdot report[11] containing detailed intelligence about the Arnhem landings.

'I had got the report from Fuellop in the form given above without further comment and without further reference to the original source. The report was sent to me by diplomatic mail, which arrived on a Friday night (from Madrid by Hungarian diplomatic bag towards Berlin and there received by Mr. Horvath at the Hungarian Legation, in Berlin. Here the message-letter was put into a new envelope and sent by German/Hungarian (diplomatic) mailbag towards the German Legation in Stockholm) [14 September]. I had a look on the (microdot) mail the same night and found that the mail consisted of 16 or 17 microphotos; in the night and the following morning, Saturday, I read through the reports and found on one of the microphotos the "Arnheim" information. Immediately I gave the information to the Air Attaché's teleprinter-office (FS) with the order to forward it to Berlin I-Luft as "KR-Blitz" (Kriegsentscheidend), the signification for the most urgent importance of the message. From there the message should have, immediately, been transferred on to the Milamt in charge of matters of I-Luft. The delay might have been caused in this quite long chain of directions. Conform to the original message and as usual in the case of Fuellop-intelligence, which dealt with strategical matters, I chose the cover designation "Zuverlässiger V-Mann" (Reliable agent). By several mishaps, interrupted of communication-lines (maybe first at: Das Auswärtiges Amt, and from there internally in Berlin to "das Milamt"), delay by coding and decoding etc, the telegram was received by Abwehr I-Luft only after the actual landing-operation had already begun.'

Walter Schellenberg, the head of German intelligence,[12] said Lindemans' intelligence was passed to field commanders on 17 September, which he said helped them understand the British and American attentions after the landings.

The MI5 report[13] of Schellenberg's interrogation from 1945 reads: 'Schellenberg states that the Luft Attaché passed the information to the Luftwaffenführungsstab [German air force command] from whence it was passed to the Wehrmachtführungsstab [Germany army command of the OKW led by Colonel General Alfred Jodl]. As to reliability, the information was received too late for assessment prior to the acts to which it related, though the serious intentions of the landing were appreciated. The information had originally been passed from Stockholm at about 18–24 hours prior to the landing. The information was received by Mil Amt C [the successor to the Abwehr under Schellenberg] some hours after the landing had occurred, and all that Milamt C could

APPENDIX 2

do was stress to the Staffs concerned the seriousness of the position. The information was also received several hours subsequent to the landing by the Luftwaffenführungsstab from the Luftwaffe Attaché.' On 17 September, the German High Command (OKH) sent this message[14] to field commanders: 'In connection with the air landings which have taken place, particular attention is deserved for an agent's report which has only just come in and predicted these air landings correctly. ... The agent above considers that reports, particularly emanating from diplomatic circles, about landing intentions against Norway and Denmark are deliberate camouflage.'

On 17 September, Wilhelm Bittrich, the commander of the 2nd SS Panzer Corps (9th and 10th SS Divisions), received two messages[15] about the airborne attack.

The first was around 1pm when the Allied air armada arrived over Eindhoven, Nijmegen and Arnhem. This told him that Allied paratroopers were being dropped.

The second message, from the Luftwaffe Communications Network, received soon afterwards that day contained vital intelligence about the positions and intentions of the Allied forces.

After the war Wilhelm Bittrich told Lt Colonel Theodor Boeree[16] of the Dutch army: 'In view of this information I issued the following orders by telephone:

To the 9th Panther division:

1. Division to reconnoitre in the direction of Arnhem and Nijmegen
2. The Division to go immediately into action, occupying the area and destroying the enemy forces which have landed to the west of Arnhem at Oosterbeek.

To the 10th SS Panzer Division:

1. Division to proceed immediately deny against, occupying the main bridges in strength and defending the bridgeheads.'

By 18 September, the Germans were able to say with confidence: 'the main objective of the airborne operation is the capture of the crossings along Eindhoven–Arnhem line in order to facilitate a quick thrust by the main forces of the Second English Army through Holland to form a bridgehead at Arnhem. This confirms the intention already suspected to cut off the German forces in Holland and at the same time to win a base from which to continue the operation east of the Rhine.'[17]

Acknowledgements

I owe a colossal debt of gratitude to five Dutch historians and academics who were so generous with their time and expertise. Bob de Graaff, Holland's foremost historian on Dutch intelligence and security, agreed to read parts of the manuscript and opened up his personal archive at his home. Frans Dekkers, one of the first writers to uncover the Lindemans' story and interview the family, helped me with my research into Eddy Verkaik's role in the Dutch resistance and his connection to the traitor. Wim Klinkerts, professor of military history at the Netherlands Defence Academy and the University of Amsterdam, shared his expertise on the intelligence battle fought during Operation Market Garden. Writer Willem Hogendoorn, whose father interrogated Lindemans in 1946, provided a unique insight into the history of King Kong. Jory Brentjens, curator of the Airborne Museum at Hartenstein, Arnhem, offered wisdom and critical challenge to the evidence I adduced to demonstrate the traitors' impact on the outcome of the Battle of Arnhem. In the UK, Jon Baker, curator of the Airborne Assault Museum, IWM, Duxford, was generous with his time and expertise. I'm also grateful to Mark Dunton (National Archives, Kew), Christopher Andrew, Mark Urban, Craig Mckay and Mark Pitt for their judicious direction. Craig's early work on Karl Heinz Kraemer and his interrogation of the Swedish documents, before the British archives were released, set the ball rolling on the Josephine intrigue. A special note of appreciation for Lyuba Vinogradova for all her research efforts on the Russian side of the story. Similarly, I wish to acknowledge the toiling of Sol Barasan, Triveni Srikaran and Philipp Steinhoff in the Dutch archives in The Hague and Amsterdam, McMaster archives in Canada and Bundesarchv in Freiberg, respectively. Veteran Fleet Street correspondent Michael Binyon, whose father was killed at Arnhem and who after the war interviewed General Heinz Harmel, offered invaluable insights. Thank you to Headline for backing the book and to my inspirational editor, Oliver Holden-Rea, enthusiastically supported by Rebecca Bader, Isabelle Wilson, Marta Juncosa and Raiyah Butt. Also, a tip of the hat to Alex Allden, who designed the cover. This book would not have been possible without the extraordinary narrative talents of my agent, Piers Blofeld. His thoughtful collaboration from beginning to end has allowed the story to be written on a much bigger canvas.

Netherlands
Bob de Graaf, Frans Dekkers, Wim Klinkert, Willem Hogendoorn, Jory Brentjens, Romy Nicholson, Sol Basaran, Hubert Berkhout, Marjon van der Veen and Katie Digan. NIOD Institute for War, Holocaust and Genocide Studies is a national and international centre of expertise for interdisciplinary research into the history of world wars, mass violence and genocides, including their long-term social consequences. Erwin van Loo, NIMH Netherlands Institute for Military History (Department for Defense), David Verkaik, Bill Verkaik, Sally (Verkaik) Le Marquand, Eddy and Matt (Verkaik) Le Marquand. Stan, Walter and Max Verkaik. Isaac, Louis, Travis, Emma, Fiona and Harry Verkaik.

UK
Craig Mckay, Jon Baker, Mark Urban, Christopher Andrew, Ben Hill (Airborne Assault Museum), Gemma Hollman (Liddell Hart Papers, King's College London), Chris Knowles, Jessica Collins and Nicole Allen (Churchill Archives Centre). Michael Binyon,

ACKNOWLEDGEMENTS

Mark Dunton, Mark Pitt, Richard Kerbaj, Jonathan Ames and Matthew King.

Germany
Philipp Steinhoff. (The Germans destroyed all their documents concerning intelligence matters held at the Stockholm embassy just before they pulled out of Sweden in 1945. See KV 2/148 (2), p.26. So Philipp's research in the Bundesarchiv was essential.

Russia
In 2021 Russia's Defence Minister issued orders that effectively blocked foreign access to Russian military archives from the period of the Second World War. I used two Russian researchers to help me with the Russian archives who I have chosen not to name due to the security situation in that country.

US
Suzanne Zoumbaris (Textual Reference Archives II Branch National Archives at College Park, MD), Dr. A M Weimer (Supervisory Archivist Special Access and FOIA Program National Archives and Records Administration).

Canada
Triveni Srikaran, Renu Barrett (McMaster University Archives).

Belgium
Montasser AlDe'emeh.

Bibliography

Aldrich, Richard J and Cormac, Rory, *The Black Door*, William Collins, 2016.
Andrew, C and Gordievsky, O, *K.G.B: The Inside Story*, Hodder & Stoughton, 1990.
Andrew, Christopher, *The Defence of the Realm: The Authorized History of MI5*, Penguin, 2009.
Arnold-Baker, Charles, *For He is an Englishman*, Jeremy Mills, 2007.
Baker, Peter, *My Testament*, John Calder, 1955.
Bauer, Cornelis, *De Slag By Arhem (The Battle of Arnhem)*, Fonthill Media, 1963.
Beevor, Antony, *Arnhem: The Battle for the Bridges*, Viking, 2008.
Beevor, Antony, *D-Day: The Battle for Normandy*, Viking, 2009.
Birstein, Vadim J, *Smersh: Stalin's Secret Weapon*, Biteback, 2013.
Boyle, A, *The Climate of Treason: Five Who Spied For Russia*, Hutchinson, 1979.
Bulloch, John, *Akin to Treason*, Arthur Barker, 1966.
Bullock, Alan, *Hitler and Stalin: Parallel Lives*, HarperCollins, 1991.
Caddick-Adams, Peter, *Snow & Steel: Battle of the Bulge, 1944–45*, Arrow Books, 2014.
Card, Tim, *Eton Renewed: A History from 1860 to the Present Day*, John Murray, 1994.
Carter, Miranda, *Anthony Blunt: His Lives*, Macmillan, 2001.
Cave Brown, A, *Bodyguard of Lies*, Fletcher & Son, 1976.
Cave Brown, Anthony, *Treason in the Blood: H. St John Philby, Kim Philby And The Spy Case of the Century*, Houghton Mifflin, 1994.
Churchill, W S, *The Second World War, Volume VI*, Cassell, 1949.
Cookridge, E H, *Set Europe Ablaze*, Arthur Baker, 1966.
Costello, John, *Mask of Treachery: Spies, Lies, Buggery & Betrayal. The first documented dossier on Anthony Blunt's Cambridge Spy Ring*. William Morrow, 1988.
Costello, John and Tsarev, Oleg, *Deadly Illusions: The KGB Orlov Dossier Reveals Stalin's Master Spy*, Century, 1993.
Day, Peter, *Trotsky's Favourite Spy: The Life of George Alexander Hill*, Biteback, 2017.

BIBLIOGRAPHY

Deeley, Graeme, *Worst Fears Confirmed: The History of Intelligence Corps Airborne Units and the Intelligence Gathering & Security Measures Employed for British Airborne Operations*, Barny Books, 2005.

de Gaulle, Noel, A J, *Desparate Carnival*, Wyman and Sons, 1955.

de Graaff, Bob, *Dood van een dubbelspion. De laatste dagen van Christiaan Lindemans*'s-Gravenhage, Sdu, 1987.

de Graaff, Bob, *Spion in de tuin. King Kong voor en na zijn dood*, Lindemans's -Gravenhage, Sdu, 1992.

de Graaff, Bob, 'King Kong and the Canadians: A Day in the Life of the Traitor of Arnhem', *Uncertain Horizons: Canadians and their World in 1945*, Greg Donaghy (ed.), published by the Canadian Committee for the History of the Second World War, 1996.

de Jong, Louis, 'Was Arnhem Betrayed?', *Encounter*, June 1981.

Dekkers, F, *King Kong Leven Dood En Opstanding Van Een Verrader*, HP-Balans, 1986.

de Meersman, Maria, 'Spy in the Third Reich: A Flemish Woman in the Resistance', Van Halewyck, Leuven. John Deccok De Standaard, 3 June 2004.

Dourlien, Pieter, *Inside North Pole*, William Kimber, 1953.

Farago, Ladislas, *The Game of Foxes*, Hodder & Stoughton, 1971.

Folly, M H, Roberts, G, Rzheshevsky, O A, *Churchill and Stalin: Comrades-in-Arms During the Second World War*, Pen and Sword Books, 2019.

Foot, M R D and Langley, J M, *MI9 Escape and Evasion, 1939–1945*, The Bodley Head Limited, 1979.

Foot, M R D, *Holland at War Against Hitler: Anglo-Dutch Relations 1940–45*, Routledge, 1990.

Foot, M R D, *SOE in the Low Countries*, St Ermin's, 2001.

Fry, Helen, *The London Cage: The Secret History of Britain's World War II Interrogation Centre*, Yale University, 2017.

Gerth, Matthew, 'British McCarthyism: The Anti-Communist Politics of Lord Vansittart and Sir Waldron Smithers', History: The Journal of the History Association,Vol. 107, Issue 378, December 2022, pp.927–948.

Gilbert, Martin, *The Second World War: A Complete History*, Weidenfeld & Nicolson, 1989.

Giskes, H J, *London Calling North Pole*, William Kimber, 1953.

Gorodetsky, Gabriel, *The Maisky Diaries: Red Ambassador to the Court of St James's, 1932–1943*, Yale University Press, 2015.

Haines, Joe, *Maxwell*, Macdonald, 1988.

Hesketh, R, *Fortitude: The D-Day Deception Campaign*, PXX St Ermin's Press, 2000.

Hinsely, F H and Simkins, C A G, *British Intelligence in the Second World War*, Vol. 4, HMSO Publications Centre, 1990.

Holt, Thaddeus, *The Deceivers*, Scribner, 2004.

Horrocks, Brian, *A Full Life*, Leo Cooper, 1974.

Jeffrey, Keith, *MI6: The History of the Secret Intelligence Service, 1909 1949*, Bloomsbury, 2010.
Johns, Philip, *Within Two Clocks: Missions with SIS and SOE*, William Kimber, 1979.
Kerbaj, Richard, *The Five Eyes: The Untold Story of the International Spy Network*, Blink, 2022.
Kershaw, Robert, *It Never Snows in September: The German View of Market-Garden and the Battle of Arnhem, September 1944*, Ian Allan Limited, 1994.
Klinkert, Wim, *The Intelligencer Journal of U.S. Intelligence Studies*, Vol. 25, No. 2, 2019.
Langley, J M, *Fight Another Day*, Collins, 1974.
Laurens, Anne, *Betrayal at Arnhem*, Award Books, 1969.
Lownie, Andrew, *Stalin's Englishman: The Lives of Guy Burgess*, Hodder & Stoughton, 2015.
McKay, C G, *Intelligence and National Security, The Krämer Case: A Study in Three Dimensions*, Taylor & Francis, 1989.
Margery, Karel, 'Operation Market Garden Then and Now', Vols 1 and 2, *After the Battle*, September 2002.
Macintyre, Ben, *Agent ZigZag: The True Wartime Story of Eddie Chapman*, Bloomsbury, 2007.
Macintyre, Ben, *A Spy Among Friends: Kim Philby and the Great Betrayal*, Bloomsbury, 2014.
Mitchell, John and Feast, Sean, *Churchill's Navigator*, Grub Street Publishing, 2010.
Modin, Yuri, *My Five Cambridge Friends*, Headline, 1994.
Middlebrook, Martin, *Arnhem 1944*, Penguin, 1994.
Montefiore, Simon Sebag, *Stalin: The Court of the Red Tsar*, Vintage, 2003.
Montgomery, B L, *The Memoirs of Field Marshal Montgomery*, Collins, 1958.
Neave, Airey, *Saturday at MI9*, Pen and Sword, 1969.
O'Sullivan, Donal, *Dealing with the Devil: Anglo-Soviet Intelligence Cooperation During the Second World War*, Peter Lang, 2010.
Payne Best, S, *The Venlo Incident*, Skyhorse, 2016.
Penrose, Barrie and Freeman, Simon, *Conspiracy of Silence: The Secret Life of Anthony Blunt*, Grafton Books, 1986.
Philby, Kim, *My Silent War*, MacGibbon & Kee, 1968.
Pimlott, B, *Hugh Dalton: A Life*, HarperCollins, 1995.
Pinto, Oreste, *Spycatcher*, T Werner Laurie Limited, 1952.
Pinto, Oreste, *The Spycatcher Omnibus*, Hodder & Stoughton, 1952.
Pinto, Oreste, *Friend or Foe?*, T Werner Laurie Limited, 1953.
Pinto, Oreste, *Spycatcher 3: Exciting True Stories of Wartime Spies and Counter-Spies*, New English Library, 1960.
Reynolds, David and Pechatnov, Vladimir, *The Kremlin Letters*, Yale University Press, 2018.

BIBLIOGRAPHY

Roberts, Andrew, *Leadership in War*, Viking, 2019.
Rose, Kenneth, *Who Loses, Who Wins: The Journals of Kenneth Rose, Vol II, 1979–2014* (Thorpe, D R (ed.), Weidenfeld & Nicolson, 2019.
Ryan, Cornelius, *A Bridge Too Far*, Simon & Schuster, 1974.
Schechter, Leona P, *Special Tasks: The Memoirs of an Unwanted Witness*, Little, Brown, 1994.
Simons, Martin, *German Air Attache: The Thrilling Story of the German Ace Pilot and Wartime Diplomat Peter Riedel*, Airlife, 1997.
Stafford, D, *Britain and the European Resistance, 1940–1945: A Survey of the Special Operations Executive*, Macmillan, 1980.
Stanton Evans, M and Romerstein, Herbert, *Stalin's Secret Agents. The Subversion of the Roosevelt Government*, Threshold, 2012.
Stephens, Robin, 'Digest of Ham, Camp 020', p.148, Public Records Office 2000.
Sudoplatov, Pavel and Sudoplatov, Anatoli, with Jerrold, L and
Tarrant, V E, *The Red Orchestra: The Soviet Spy Network Inside Nazi Europe*, Arms and Armour Press, 1995.
Thomas, Hugh, *SS 1: The Unlikely Death of Heinrich Himmler*, Fourth Estate, 2001.
Trepper, Leopold, *The Great Game: Memoirs of a Master Spy*, Michael Joseph Limited, 1997.
Trevor-Roper, Hugh (Harrison, Edward (ed.)), *The Secret World: Behind the Curtain of British Intelligence in World War II and the Cold War*, I.B. Taruris, 2014.
Tucker-Jones, Anthony, *The Devil's Bridge: The German Victory at Arnhem, 1944*, Osprey, 2020.
Urban, Mark, *Red Devils: The Trailblazers of the Parachute Regiment in World War Two: An Authorized History*, Viking, 2022.
Urquhart, Roy, *Arnhem*, Cassell, 1958.
Wentling, Michel & Klaas Castelein, *The Dutch Resistance, 1940–45*, Osprey, 2022.
West, N and Tsarev, O, *The Crown Jewels: The British Secrets at the Heart of the KGB Archives*, HarperCollins, 1998.
West, Nigel, *The Guy Liddell Diaries, Vol II: 1942–45*, Routledge, 2005.
West, Nigel and Tsarev, Oleg, *Triplex: Secrets from the Cambridge Spies*, Yale, 2009.
West, Nigel, *Churchill's Spy Files: MI5's Top-Secret Wartime Reports*, The History Press, 2018.
Whiting, Charles, *The Search for 'Gestapo' Mueller*, Leo Cooper, 2001.
Wood, James A, *Army of the West: The Weekly Reports of Germany Army Group B from Normandy to the West Wall*, Laurier Centre for Military, Strategic and Disarmament Studies, Stackpole Books, 2007.
Wright, Peter, *Spycatcher*, William Heinemann, Australia, 1987.

Notes

Prologue
1 Bauer, Cornelis., *De Slag By Arhem (The Battle of Arnhem)*, 1963 p.31.
2 Montgomery, B L, *The Memoirs of Field Marshal Montgomery*, p.331, Collins, 1958
3 WO 106/4410.
4 Kershaw, Robert., *It Never Snows in September. The German View of Market Garden and the Battle of Arnhem*, September 1944. p.39, 2015, Ian Allen. The 9th SS Panzer Division was located around Arnhem but its commanding officer had sent some patched up units to plug the gaps in Kurt Student's defensive lines near the Dutch-Belgian border.
5 https://www.ww2marketgarden.com/battleatbest101stairbornedivision.html
6 Beevor, A, *Arnhem*, p.115.
7 Marshall, S L A, US Deputy Theatre Historian, *The Sunday Star*, 4 June 1950.
8 Beevor, p.114.
9 The Pegasus Archive, Airborne Assaults Museum. File No 58 (2). Dutch resistance report of the build of German forces around Arnhem. Major Sepp Krafft's report to Heinrich Himmler, January 1945, about his role in the Battle of Arnhem. Gelders Archief. 2171 Boeree Collection.
10 4F3 2.10.17 Airborne Assault Archive, Diary of SS Panzer Grenadier Depot and Reserve Battalion 16 p-1-2.
11 4F3 2.10.17 Airborne Assault Archive, Diary of SS Panzer Grenadier Depot and Reserve Battalion 16 p-1-2.
12 Urban, Mark, *Red Devils: The Trailblazers of the Parachute Regiment in World War Two: An Authorized History*, Viking, 2022, pp.219–24.
13 Middlebrook, Martin, *Arnhem 1944*, London: Penguin, 1994, p.325. https://www.ww2marketgarden.com/marketgardenorderofbattle.html
14 CAB 106/1111.
15 CAB 106/1054, Brian Horrocks' notes made after Operation Market Garden.

Chapter 1
1 Giskes, H J, *London Calling North Pole*, 1953, p.7.
2 KV-2-967 (4), p.53.
3 KV-2-961 (1) p.53
4 HS6/750, 5 June 1945, Camp 020 progress report on the interrogation of Hermann Giskes.
5 Ibid.

NOTES

6 Giskes, Nordpol p.15.
7 Giskes, p.8.
8 Foot, M R D, *History of the SOE*, 2001, p.9.
9 Giskes, p.13.
10 KV-2-136, p.142.
11 Giskes, p.15.
12 Ibid.
13 KV-2-1170.
14 Giskes, p.28. Also, Verloop's file KV-2-139.
15 Giskes, p.24.
16 Giskes, p.31.
17 Ibid.
18 Giskes, p.33.
19 Ibid.
20 Among this mix of resistance fighters, cut-outs and couriers was a young man called George Behar who escaped to England, changed his name to George Blake and ended up spying for the KGB.
21 Cookridge, E H, Box 24 Fond 5, McMaster University Library. The V-man, according to Cookridge, was Jos F C Hoosemans, a 67-year-old leader of a gang of fascist informants. Cookridge said Lindemans bragged about his role in the attack.
22 Giskes, p.35.
23 Giskes, H. *London Calling Nordpol.* p.36
24 Giskes, p.36.
25 Cookridge, E H, Box 24 Fond 5, McMaster University Library.

Chapter 2

1 Interviews with Henk and Cornelius Lindemans, 1962, Cookridge, E H, Box 24 Fond 5, p.2, F.3 'King Kong', Draft manuscript of story of Christiaan ('King Kong') Lindemans. E H Cookridge fonds, 1905–1979, 15.35 m of textual records and graphic material. Series 1–7, McMaster University.
2 Interviews with Henk and Cornelius Lindemans, 1962, p.2, F.3 'King Kong', Draft manuscript of story of Christiaan ('King Kong') Lindemans. E H Cookridge fonds, 1905–1979, 15.35 m of textual records and graphic material. Series 1–7, McMaster University.
3 Interviews with Henk and Cornelius Lindemans, 1962, Cookridge, E H, p.2, F.3 'King Kong', Draft manuscript of story of Christiaan ('King Kong') Lindemans. E H Cookridge fonds, 1905–1979, 15.35 m of textual records and graphic material. Series 1–7, McMaster University.
4 KV-233, MI5 report, p.10.
5 MI5 report on interrogation of Christiaan Antonius Lindemans, p.7, KV-2-233, November 1944, Camp 020.
6 De Graaff, Bob, 'King Kong and the Canadians: A Day in the Life of the Traitor of Arnhem', *Uncertain Horizons*, p.53.
7 Laurens, Anne, *The Betrayal at Arnhem*, 1969, pp. 52, 58.
8 KV-2-235, p.58, MI5 report on Lindemans' interrogation at Camp 020.
9 KV-2-235, p.58, MI5 report on Lindemans' interrogation at Camp 020.
10 KV-2-231–238. MI5 files on C. Lindemans. Instituut Militaire Historie. Bureau Nationale Veiligheld (BNV) (Dutch security service) July 9.7.46

Scheveningen BNV 93 CB2354 - 10.000-11-45 vervolgblad proces verbaal dutch. Various statements taken from the interrogations of C. Lindemans at Camp 020, Breda and Scheveningen.
11 KV-4-14, Digest of Ham Vol 3. Stephens, R Camp 020, p.332 and KV-2-139.
12 HS6/750, Interrogation of Giskes and Huntemann at Camp 020.
13 KV-2-139 p.55, Verloop interrogation by MI5.
14 KV-2-139 p.55
15 Ibid.
16 KV-2-235, p.59, Interrogation of Christiaan Lindemans at Camp 020, November 1944.
17 KV-2-235, p.59, Interrogation of Christiaan Lindemans by MI5 at Camp 020, November 1944.
18 KV-2-235, p.59, Interrogation of Christiaan Lindemans by MI5 at Camp 020, November 1944.

Chapter 3
1 Foot, p.58.
2 Foot, p.109.
3 Foot, p.113, Lauwers/Giskes, pp.82, 177.
4 Foot, p.114.
5 Foot, p.115.
6 NIOD. Institute for War, Holocaust and Genocide Studies, Amsterdam. Document on Dutch resistance shows that the Russians had a controlling influence on CS-6 and other groups. Credit Bob de Graaff.

Chapter 4
1 KV-2-233, Lindemans' statement to MI5.
2 KV-2-235, p.60.
3 KV-2-231–238.
4 KV-2-235, p.59.
5 KV-2-235, p.62.
6 KV-2-235, p.60.
7 The Hepburn Nazis https://medium.com/@susangardiner1878/audrey-hepburns-greatest-charade-8b3fb03f4a34)
8 Laurens, Anne, *Betrayal at Arnhem*, p.65.
9 KV-2-232, p.13.
10 HS 9/284/3.
11 https://www.weggum.com/July_September_1944_part_1A_test.html
12 Wenting, Michel, Castelein, Klaas, *The Dutch Resistance 1940 to 1945: World War Two Resistance and Collaboration in the Netherlands*, Osprey, 2022.
13 *Biographical Dictionary of the Netherlands* 2 (The Hague 1985).
14 HS 9/284/3 SOE report on De Graaf and Celosse.
15 HS 9/284/3.
16 HS 9/284/3.
17 Ibid.
18 HS 6/728 Dutch resistance plans. Reports on King Kong and 'Rob', a Dutch resistance organiser based in Rotterdam.
19 Interrogation of Celosse, 4 March 1944, p.6, HS9/284/3.
20 Ibid.
21 KV-2-233, p.57.

NOTES

22 HS9/284/3, Interrogation of Celosse, 4 March 1944, p.6.
23 Laurens, Anne, *Betrayal at Arnhem*, Allan Wingate, 1971, p.114.
24 Ibid.
25 Ibid.
26 Ibid.
27 https://dambustersblog.com/category/fred-sutherland/
28 HS7-161 (1), SOE history of Dutch resistance.
29 IWM. Reel 4. Sydney Hobday https://www.iwm.org.uk/collections/item/object/80007101
30 https://www.oranjehotel.org/downloads/gedenkboek-oranjehotel-namenlijsten-van-_103.pdf
31 US FOIA: 5709392-806-34-Henrik. Compensation claim for helping US and RAF airmen. Claim made on 6 November 1945 gave food and shelter for two days. Personen die u de bekend zijn welke geallieerd personeel helpien: (person known to you who helped Allied personnel) FA van der Nagel Noordsingel 182 C A Lindemans Westzeedijk 21 Rotterdam C J A Lindemans Staatweg 136 Rotterdam.
32 Hobday IWM. Reel 4, Groeneveld, Arie Leendert NAID: 286657005 https://catalog.archives.gov/id/286657005?objectPage=6 Record Group 498: Records of Headquarters, European Theater of Operations, United States Army (World War II) Series: Case Files of Dutch Citizens Proposed for Awards for Assisting American Airmen.
33 IWM. Reel 4. Sydney Hobday https://www.iwm.org.uk/collections/item/object/80007101
34 Ibid.
35 Ibid.

Chapter 5
1 Door de Graaf, Obituary, *Daily Telegraph*, 2 March 2011.
2 KV-6-37-(1).
3 HS 9/1569/1 Wegner NA file.
4 Giskes, H, *London Calling North Pole*. p.135
5 HS7-159-1a Sent by Dobson – Seymour Bingham relieved of his command on 26 February 1944.
6 KV-235. Lindemans' statement to MI5, November 1944.
7 Laurens, Anne, p.104.
8 Laurens, Anne, p.32. Laurens says Lindemans reviewed the situation after the Allied advance 'had been checked' and he talked about Holland being a 'hollow, unyielding country'. p.157 Lindemans described the war as an 'atrocious comedy'.
9 HS 6/728.
10 KV-2-235, p.61.
11 Reel 4. IWM. Sydney Hobday https://www.iwm.org.uk/collections/item/object/80007101
12 https://www.oranjehotel.org/downloads/gedenkboek-oranjehotel-namenlijsten-van-_103.pdf
13 Laurens, p.118.
14 Laurens, p.120.
15 Laurens, p.120.

16 Laurens, p.121.
17 KV-2-235, p.61, MI5 report on Christiaan Lindemans.
18 KV-2-235, p.61.
19 Giskes, pp.130, 135.
20 KV-2-967 (2) Huntemann interrogation at Camp 020.
21 KV-2-139, MI5 file on Verloop, p.60.
22 *London Calling North Pole.* p.141-142
23 Giskes, p.142.
24 Giskes, p.143.
25 Ibid.
26 Giskes, p.144.
27 KV-2-233, p.8, MI5 report says Henk Lindemans was still being held after June.
28 KV-2-139, MI5 report on Verloop, p.60.
29 Bob de Graaff. Interview with the author, February 2023.
30 Foot, p.217.
31 NIOD-248-1059A and 248-A1059A. Files on Lindemans which explore the idea that he was involved in the SD arrests at the Montholon Hotel, Paris.
32 https://www-oorlogsbronnen-nl.translate.goog/tijdlijn/Viktor+Johannes+Mari+Swane/85/7223449?_x_tr_sl=nl&_x_tr_tl=en&_x_tr_hl=en&_x_tr_pto=sc&_x_tr_hist=true
33 Letuppe, Gilou testimony to Nuremberg. Trial of the Major War Criminals Before the International Military Tribunal, Nuremberg, 14 November 1945–1 October 1946, VOLUME XXXVII, Numbers 257-F to 180-L.
34 https://wwii-netherlands-escape-lines.com/airmen-helped/karst-smit-reports-by-and-about-him/interview-with-karst-smit-by-baarle-nassau-radio-1994/
35 Laurens, p.119.
36 Giskes, H, p.155
37 Letuppe, Gilou testimony to Nuremberg. Trial of the Major War Criminals Before the International Military Tribunal, Nuremberg, 14 November 1945–1 October 1946, VOLUME XXXVII, Numbers 257-F to 180-L.
38 Ibid.
39 Foot, p.218.
40 Foot, p.217. Cornelis Verloop first gave this figure when he was interrogated at Camp 020. Frans Dekkers says that it was much smaller.
41 Interview with Karst Smit, 6–7 July 2002. https://wwii-netherlands-escape-lines.com/airmen-helped/interview-with-karst-smit-july-6-7-2002/

Chapter 6
1 HS 6/750 1945 Interrogation of Giskes and Huntemann. Giskes, H J, *London Calling North Pole*, p.147.
2 Giskes, p.147.
3 Giskes later recalled in *London Calling*: 'These two men, however, could no longer do us any direct harm by what they could tell in England, and the influence and standing of Lindemans, which was my immediate concern, would be immensely increased if he was able to carry the business through to a successful conclusion.'
4 Foot, p.196.

NOTES

5 Foot, p.196.
6 Giskes, p.148.
7 HS9/284/3.
8 HS 9/1433/7
9 HS9/284/3.
10 Foot, p.216.
11 Foot, p.218.
12 Giskes, p.151.
13 Giskes, H J, *London Calling North Pole*, William Kimber (1 January 1953), p.151.
14 Giskes, p.151.
15 KV-2-235, p.64, Lindemans' interrogation at Camp 020.
16 KV-2-237, p.31, Giskes' interrogation and account of the Devisen Schutz Kommando.
17 KV-2-232, p.13, Kas de Graaf's account.
18 KV-2-235, p.64, Lindemans' interrogation at Camp 020.
19 Roelof Van Nagel and Karst Smit.
20 KV-2-232, p.15, What KK told De Graaf.
21 KV-2-235, p.65.
22 KV-2-232, p.15.
23 Foot, p.216.
24 Giskes, p.153.
25 Giskes, p.153.
26 KV-2-237, p.34.
27 Giskes, p.154.
28 KV-2-235, p.65, Interrogation of Lindemans.
29 KV-2-232, p.18, MI5 interrogation of Verloop, Camp 020.
30 KV-2-235, p.86.
31 KV-2-237, p.32, MI5 interrogation of Giskes, Camp 020.
32 KV-2-232, p.39.
33 Giskes, p.155
34 KV-2-235, p.67.
35 Laurens, pp.129, 133, 149.

Chapter 7
1 Giskes, p.146.
2 Giskes, p.146.
3 Archives du groupe de résistance armée Witte Brigade (Fidelio), 1941–1993 https://www.the-low-countries.com/article/why-the-belgian-resistance-deserves-more-attention
4 Giskes, p.147.
5 KV-2-232, p.38.
6 KV-2-235, p.65, Lindemans' interrogation.
7 KV-2-233, p.66, KV-2-967 (4), p.44, Huntemann.
8 Ibid.
9 KV-2-237, p.58.
10 Ibid.
11 KV-2-237, p.60.
12 Ibid.
13 Ibid.

14 KV-2-235 -237 Meersman later reported that Lindemans 'received all his orders direct from Inter.Serve as an individual agent. All other agents were under him.' But Meersman's German handlers failed to grasp the significance of what the drunken Lindemans was telling her.
15 KV-2-235, pp.68, 70.
16 Ibid.
17 KV-2-236, p.12.
18 KV-2-235, p.76.
19 KV-2-237, p.60.
20 KV-2-237, p.60.
21 KV-2-237, p.61, SD report on Meersman.
22 KV-2-235, Lindemans' statement to MI5.
23 Ibid.
24 KV-2-237 pp57,58

Chapter 8

1 KV-2-231, p.48, MI5 'CC' report of Bletchley Park intercept. KV-2-236, p.34, MI5 report on Lindemans.
2 Ibid.
3 KV-2-231, p.48, MI5 'CC' report of Bletchley Park intercept.
4 Giskes, p.165.
5 Ibid.
6 HS9/413/2. MI5 report on de Graaf November 1944 accessed under the Freedom of Information (closed extracts HS 9/413/10) Act, May 2023.
7 Bob de Graaff, 'King Kong and the Canadians', *Uncertain Horizons: Canadians and their World in 1945*, 1996, p.57.
8 Giskes, p.162.
9 KV-2-235, p.68.
10 Pogue, Forrest C. *The Supreme Command, (United States Army in World War II: The European Theater of Operations)* p.294
11 Giskes, pp.166–67.
12 KV-2-236, p.12, Urbain Renniers' statement, 30 November 1944.
13 KV-2-237, p.59, SD report on Lindemans.
14 De Graaff, Bob, *Uncertain Horizons*, p.55.
15 Neave, Airey, *Saturday at MI9*, p.278.
16 Johns, Philip, *Within Two Clocks. MIssions with SIS and SOE*, p.192. When he first arrived in Belgium, Johns requisitioned a large five-storey residential building nearby on the corner of the Avenue des Arts and Rue Beliard, where he directed resistance and special forces operations.
17 Johns, p.196.
18 Beevor, A, p.27.
19 WO 205/693 Operation Market Garden: reports and instructions September 1944 to February 1945.
20 Beevor, A, p.59.
21 Tucker-Jones, Anthony, *The Devil's Bridge: The German Victory at Arnhem, 1944*, Osprey, 2020, p.51.
22 De Graaff, Bob, *Uncertain Horizons*, p.58. A & WI, 31; DMH, Boeree Papers, Box 586B, Stainworth to Boeree, 26 March 1957.

NOTES

Chapter 9

1. After the war, Peter Baker founded a publishing company, was elected as a Conservative MP and spent seven years in Wormwood Scrubs for fraud.
2. KV-2-237 pp.34–36 MI5 interrogation of Huntemann.
3. KV-2-237 pp.34–36 MI5 interrogation of Huntemann.
4. KV-2-235, p.68, Baker, P, *My Testament.*, p.110.
5. KV-2-235, p.68.
6. Langley, J M, *Fight Another Day*, p.227.
7. Christmann, Richard, Interrogation by US Army, September 1946, document release date 21 May 2021, Sequence Number: Case Number: F-2019-02151. https://www.cia.gov/readingroom/docs/RICHARD%20CHRISTMAN%5B15921665%5D.pdf
8. De Jong, Louis, 'Was Arnhem Betrayed?' *Encounter*, p.13.
9. De Jong, Louis, 'Was Arnhem Betrayed?' *Encounter*, p.13.
10. KV-2-946 (1), p.21.
11. KV-2-946 (1), p.22. Interrogations of Richard Christmann by OSS and MI5.
12. Frans Dekkers' interview with the author, January 2024. Dekkers interviewed Christmann after the war. Dekkers, F, *King Kong Leven Dood En Opstanding Van Een Verrader*, pp.48, 49.
13. Margery, Karel, *Operation Market Garden Then and Now. Vol 1 and 2. After the Battle*, September 2002.
14. Ibid.
15. Frans Dekkers' interview with the author, January 2024. Dekkers interviewed Christmann after the war. Dekkers, F, *King Kong Leven Dood En Opstanding Van Een Verrader*, pp.48, 49.
16. KV-2-946 (1), p.21.
17. Klinkert, Wim, *The Intelligencer Journal of U.S. Intelligence Studies*, Volume 25, Number 2, 2019.
18. Hinsley, p.376.
19. Tucker-Jones, p.60.
20. Frans Dekkers' interview with the author, January 2024. Dekkers interviewed Richard Christmann in Germany after the war. Dekkers, F, *King Kong Leven Dood En Opstanding Van Een Verrader*, pp.48, 49. OSS interrogation of Christmann.
21. Ibid.
22. Frans Dekkers' interview with the author, January 2024. Dekkers interviewed Christmann after the war. Dekkers, F, *King Kong Leven Dood En Opstanding Van Een Verrader*, pp.48, 49. Hinsley, H, p.377, KV-2-946 (1), p.21.
23. De Jong, Louis, 'Was Arnhem Betrayed?' *Encounter*, June 1981, p.14.
24. De Jong, Louis, 'Was Arnhem Betrayed?' *Encounter*, June 1981, p.14.
25. Beevor, A, p.75.
26. Margery, Karel, *Operation Market Garden Then and Now. Vol 1 and 2. After the Battle*, September 2002.
27. De Graaff, B, *Uncertain Horizons: Canadians and their World in 1945*, 'King Kong and the Canadians', 1 January 1997.
28. Dekkers, F, Interview with the author, January 2024. Dekkers interviewed Eddy Verkaik and other members of the Eindhoven resistance cell in the 1980s. https://www.eindhoven4044.nl/10/Verkaik.html https://www.pegasusarchive.org/arnhem/RepDutch.htm https://marketgarden.com/2010/UK/studies/resistance.htm

29 Beevor, A, p.168.
30 Frans Dekkers' interview with the author, January 2024. Dekkers, F, *King Kong*, pp.52, 53.
31 De Jong, Louis, 'Was Arnhem Betrayed?' *Encounter*, June 1981, p.14.
32 De Graff, B, *Uncertain Horizons*, 'King Kong and the Canadians', p.62.
33 Nederlands Instituot voor Militaire Historie. Slag om Arnhem (Operatie Market Garden) 46. Marshall, Sam. Brigadier General Samuel Lyman Atwood Marshall, the US Army's chief combat historian during the Second World War. 'Story of the Spy Sheds Light on Arnhem Disaster', The *Sunday Star*, 4 June 1950. 'New Light Cast on Allies' Big Arnhem Defeat', *Chicago Tribune*, 4 June 1950. Bob de Graaff, *Uncertain Horizons*, p.61.
34 Hinsley, H, Simkins, C A G, *British Intelligence in the Second World War Vol 4*, p.377, Christmann, Richard. Interrogation by US Army. 24 September 1946, KV-2-946, p.22.
35 Kershaw, Robert, *It Never Snows in September*, p.34.
36 Kershaw, p.74.
37 Kershaw, p.35.
38 Hinsley, p.377, Christmann, Richard. Interrogation by US Army, 24 September 1946, KV-2-946, p.22.
39 Airborne Assault Archive 4F3 2.10.17 Diary of SS Panzer Grenadier Depot and Reserve Battalion 16, 17 September 1944. Klinkert, W, *The Intelligencer Journal of U.S. Intelligence Studies*, Volume 25, Number 2, Fall 2019: 'As early as 3–4 September, they had already put in place some precautionary measures: a SS-battalion under Sturmbannfürer8 Sepp Krafft was sent to Arnhem, with the assignment to prepare for an airborne attack in that region. Similar preparations were made in other areas as well. Krafft's unit was very effective on 17 September, when the attack actually began.'
40 Airborne Assault Archive 4F3 2.10.17 Diary of SS Panzer Grenadier Depot and Reserve Battalion 16, 17 September 1944.
41 Urquhart, R, *Arnhem* (Cassell & Co, 1958), p.54.
42 Montgomery, BL, p332
43 Hinsley, p.377, KV-2-946 (1), Christmann, Richard. Interrogation by US Army, 24 September 1946, p.22.
44 Frans Dekkers' interview with the author, February 2024.
45 Beevor, p.46.
46 Beevor, p.47.
47 Cookridge, E H and Boeree, T A, p.53, Fond 2 Box 24. 'King Kong'. Series 1–7, McMaster University Library, Canada.
48 Kersten, Felix, *The Kersten Memoirs, 1940–1945*, 19.12.44, Tilberg, the Black Forest (Hutchinson and Co, 1956), p.268 Doubt has been cast over the veracity of some of Kersten's stories as he was found to have fabricated documents to support exaggerated claims about his efforts to save Dutch Jews during the war.
49 General Bittrich's interview with T A Boeree 15 November 1953, p.4. Fond 2 Box 24. 'King Kong'. E H Cookridge fonds, 1905–1979, 15.35 m of textual records and graphic material. Series 1–7, McMaster University Library, Canada.
50 Bauer, Cornelis, Boeree, Theodor, *The Battle of Arnhem*, p.41.
51 Airborne Assault Museum. File 58. The Dutch Resistance Movement & the Arnhem Operations. p.1.

NOTES

52 Rauter's interview with T A Boeree, p.5. Fond 2 Box 24. 'King Kong'. E H Cookridge fonds, 1905–1979, Series 1–7, McMaster University Library, Canada.
53 Richard Christmann, in charge of Giskes' V-men, told the Americans Lindemans volunteered his services to the Abwehr in April 1943, KV-2-946 (1), p.22. US interrogation of Richard Christmann 24 September 1946 (APO513) https://www.cia.gov/readingroom/docs/RICHARD%20CHRISTMAN%5B15921665%5D.pdf

Chapter 10

1 KV-2-157 (4) McCallum, P, Appendix III 'The Arnhem Report', KV-2-153 (2), pp. 68–70, Statement by Karl Heinz Kraemer about Arnhem made on 24 September 1945 at Camp 020.
2 KV-2-157 (4) McCallum, P, Appendix III 'The Arnhem Report', KV-2-153 (3), p.16, Hinsley, Harry Prof Sir. *British Intelligence in the Second World War*, Vol IV, p.278.
3 Hinsley, H, p.278.
4 KV-2-152-1 Captain Scott Harrison's questionnaire for Schellenberg, 20 August 1945, sent to Lt Col Stimson, KV-2-152 (2), p.59.
5 Kershaw, R, p.133.
6 KV-2-157 (4) McCallum, P, Appendix III 'The Arnhem Report', KV-2-153 (2), pp.68–70, Statement by Karl Heinz Kraemer about Arnhem made on 24 September 1945 at Camp 020.
7 Hesketh, R, *Fortitude*, p.308.
8 Hesketh, R, *Fortitude*, p.309.
9 Appendix to Lagebericht West (OKH) No.1391, 17 September 1944, Hesketh, R, *Fortitude*, p.309.
10 KV-2/152-1, Captain Scott Harrison's questionnaire for Schellenberg, 20 August 1945, sent to Lt Col Stimson KV-2-152 (2) p.59, Hinsey p.279.
11 KV-2-152 (2), p.59.
12 McCallum, P, KV 2/157 (3) MI5 report on Kraemer, p.42.
13 McKay, C G, Intelligence and National Security, 1989: *The Krämer Case: A Study in Three Dimensions*, p.280.
14 General Bittrich's interview with T A Boeree, 15 November 1953, p.4.
15 Montgomery, B L, *The Memoirs of Field Marshal Montgomery*, p.297, Collins, 1958.

Chapter 11

1 Payne Best, S, *The Venlo Incident*, Skyhorse (24 May 2016).
2 https://www.sis.gov.uk/our-history.html
3 KV 4/185 Vol 1. Guy Liddell Diaries, December/February 1939/40.
4 https://www.iwm.org.uk/history/a-short-history-of-the-winter-war
5 Hinsley, F H, Simkins, C A G, p.19, *British Intelligence in the Second World War*, Vol 4, HMSO Publications Centre, 1990.
6 Costello, J., p.237 and p.279. Costello says another mysterious East European GRU agent 'Otto' was also involved in Blunt's recruitment. This was first established by Peter Wright during his interrogation of Blunt, *Spycatcher*, p.227.
7 British Library MS.88902/2, Blunt says he visited Russia with his brother Wilfred and a group of Cambridge communists including Michael Straight,

Charles Rycroft, John Madge, Brian Simon and Charles Fletcher-Cooke. He gives the date as 1935 but the majority of other sources give the date as 1933/34. https://www.nytimes.com/1988/05/12/obituaries/kim-philby-double-agent-dies.html

8   It is also possible that Burgess, the older of the two, recruited Blunt. Blunt says so in his self-serving memoir, but John Costello believes this was said to disguise the true extent of his influence in the group. He argues that Blunt was the 'first man' and early driving force behind the Cambridge spies: pp.230–235, p.279.
9   West, N, Tsarev, O, *The Crown Jewels*, Blunt's account of his life given to NKVD in 1943, p.130.
10 Blunt, A, Memoirs, British Library MS 88902, Andrew, Christopher, *The Defence of the Realm*, p.268.
11 Blunt, A, Memoirs, British Library MS 88902/2.
12 Blunt, A, Memoirs, British Library MS 88902/2.
13 Cave Brown, Anthony, *Treason in the Blood*, p.223.
14 Blunt, Memoirs, British Library, Costello, p.372.
15 MI5's own history of the Security Service during WW2. https://www.mi5.gov.uk/world-war-ii
16 Liddell attended the University of Angers in France.
17 Andrew, Christopher, *The Defence of the Realm*, p.232.
18 Carter, Miranda, *His Lives*, p.256.
19 Philby, K, *My Silent War*, p.35.
20 Andrew, Christopher, p.270. Burgess was recruited shortly afterwards and Blunt ran him as agent Vauxhall.
21 KV 4/185 Vol 2, Liddell Diaries, 25/26 September 1940.
22 Liddell Diaries, 25/26 September 1940.
23 Pinto, O, *Friend or Foe?*, p.150.
24 Pinto, O, *Friend or Foe?*, p.150.
25 KV 4/185, Vol 2, Guy Liddell Diaries, 20 August 1940.
26 Liddell, G. *Liddell Diaries*, Vol 2 KV/4/186
27 KV-2-802 – 805. Files on the debriefing of General Walter Krivitsky by MI5 in January 1941.
28 Bullock, Alan, *Hitler and Stalin: Parallel Lives*, Published by HarperCollins, 1991, p.674.
29 KV-4-228, Report into MI5's surveillance of the Comintern during the Second World War.
30 KV-2-802-805. The Krivitsky files.
31 KV-2-4347, MI5's files on William Hooper.
32 There were already question marks over Jack Hooper, but not apparently intelligence ones: 'After lunch,' wrote Guy Liddell, 'I discussed with Valentine Vivian [MI6] and Felix Cowgill [MI6] the question of [Hooper], who is working with Commandant François van't Sant, the head of the Dutch Combined Intelligence Bureau. It seems that there has been some inter-office intrigue with Claude Dansey [head of the secret Z organisation] employing an agent to watch him. He is apparently associating with Mrs Tregenna who is of foreign extraction. I do not think there is anything in it except sex but we are going to make further enquiries.', p.64. Hooper was appointed intermediary between MI6, the Dutch government in exile and François van't Sant

NOTES

CBE, head of the new Dutch intelligence service in London, the Centrale Inlichtingendienst (CID). Van't Sant had been adviser to Queen Wilhelmina and Hooper had known him for years.
33 KV2/4346 (1) p.1 Report on William (Bill) Hooper. Liddell, Guy. Diary entries 4, 18 March 1941.
34 KV2/4346 (1) Page 1 Report on William (Bill) Hooper.
35 KV2/4346 (1) Report on William (Bill) Hooper, p.1
36 KV-2-802-805 The Krivitsky files.
37 KV-2-805, Krivitsky interview with MI5.
38 KV-4-228. Four-page report on the operations of F2C in connection with Russian Intelligence during the Second World War. A central point made is that the fact that the USSR was an ally caused the Foreign Office to lay down rigid rules restricting MI5 action against Soviet Intelligence to the barest minimum. Vernon Kell, then head of MI5, had concluded shortly before the start of the war that Soviet activity in England was 'non-existent'.
39 Andrew, C, *The Defence of the Realm*, p.220.
40 KV-2-805.
41 Lownie, Andrew, *Stalin's Englishman*, p.111.

Chapter 12
1 Folly, M, Roberts, G, Rzheshevsky, O, *Churchill and Stalin: Comrades-in-Arms During the Second World War*, 2019, p.15.
2 Churchill, WS., Vol III p320; Hinsley, H., p.99
3 Folly, M, Roberts, G and Rzheshevsky, O, *Churchill and Stalin: Comrades-in-Arms During the Second World War*, Pen and Sword, 2019, p.12.
4 Sudoplatov, *Pavel Special Tasks*, p.118.
5 Smith, Chris, *The Last Cambridge Spy*, p.92.
6 Sudoplatov, p.118.
7 Trepper, L, *The Great Game*, pp.125–6.
8 Trepper, L, *The Great Game*, p.126.
9 Glantz, David, *Operation Barbarossa: Hitler's Invasion of Russia 1941*, The History Press, 2011.
10 Blunt, A, Memoirs.
11 Sudoplatov, P., *Special Tasks*, p.138

Chapter 13
1 Pimlott, B, *Hugh Dalton: A Life*, p.23.
2 KV-2-4101.
3 Card, Tim, *Eton Renewed: A History from 1860 to the Present Day* (London: John Murray, 1994), p.186.
4 http://www.lalkar.org/article/3894/hero-of-the-working-class-kim-philby
5 https://lend-lease.net/articles-en/raf-hurricanes-in-russia
6 KV-2-2827 (1), Survey of Joint Subversive Policy p.19.
7 KV-2-3227, p.19.
8 KV-2-3227, p.50.
9 aka Ivan Tchitchaiev.
10 KV-2-3226 (1), p.5.
11 Wright, P, *Spycatcher*, p.182.
12 KV-2-3226/7 The Chichaev files.
13 Guy Liddell Diaries, 2 November 1942.

14 KV-2-2827 (1), p.17.
15 Foot, pp.39–41.
16 KV-2-3227, p.7. Dick White claimed SOE didn't want MI5 to have contact with Chichaev.
17 KV-2-3226 (1).
18 KV-2-2827(1), pp.33, 37, 38, 51. KV-2-3226 (2), pp.6, 11, KV 2/4101.
19 KV-2-2827 (1), pp.44, 52, Card, p.186.
20 KV-2-2827 (1), p.44.
21 Donal O'Sullivan, *Dealing with the Devil*, p.72.
22 Foot, p.40.
23 KV-2-2827 (1), p.55.
24 Donal O'Sullivan, p.127.
25 Liddell Diaries, 14 August 1942.
26 KV-2-2827 (1), p.54.
27 O'Sullivan, p.134.
28 Charlotte Philby.
29 KV-2-3227, p.49.
30 KV-2-3226/7 The Chichaev files.
31 MI5 official history. https://www.mi5.gov.uk/world-war-ii-0 Andrew, C, *The Defence of the Realm*, p.231.
32 Blunt, A, Memoir, p.31.
33 West, N, Tsarev, O, *The Crown Jewels*, Blunt's account of his life given to NKVD in 1943, p.139.
34 West, N, Tsarev, O, *The Crown Jewels*, Blunt's account of his life given to NKVD in 1943, p.175.
35 West, N, Tsarev, O, *The Crown Jewels*, Blunt's account of his life given to NKVD in 1943, p.175.
36 West, N, Tsarev, O, *The Crown Jewels*, Blunt's account of his life given to NKVD in 1943, p.152.
37 KV-2-4526, p.151.
38 KV-2-4526, p.168.
39 Wright, P, *Spycatcher*, p.101.
40 Andrew, Christopher and Mitrokhin, Vasili, *The Mitrokhin Archive: The KGB in Europe and the West* (Allen Lane, 1999), p.110.
41 Hastings, Max, *Secret War: Spies, Codes and Guerrillas 1939–1945*, p.314.
42 KV-4-205.
43 KV-4-205 Menzies letter to Liddell appointing Blunt as intelligence go-between. 20.5.1942.
44 KV-2-2074 (1), MI5 report on Leopold Trepper, p.40.
45 KV-2-2074 (1).
46 KV-2-2074 (1).
47 KV-2-2827 (1) p.56, 1947 MI5 report.

Chapter 14
1 KV-2-157 (3) p.40e. McCallum report on identification of Karl Heinz Kraemer.
2 KV 4/192 Guy Liddell Diaries Vol 8, 27 August 1943.
3 Liddell, G, Diaries, 27 August 1943. KV-2-157-3, p.39d. Pat McCallum says the agent's nationality was Irish. A strange conclusion given how much we

NOTES

know about Fritz Kolbe's work in Switzerland and his involvement in the Josephine tip-off.
4 KV-2-144 (2), p.30a.
5 KV-2-144 (2).
6 Liddell, G, Diaries, 29 August 1943.
7 KV 2/144 (2) p.7, MI5 B3 memo on Josephine's Salerno intelligence sent to Herbert Hart.
8 Hinsley, p.200.
9 KV-2-144, KV-2-146-(2) p.2.
10 KV-2-144-1, p.45b (minute 55a), 'Josephine reported 5 October Vickers Armstrong's strike at Barrow considerably affected Lancaster production. Strike due to communist agitation. At Cabinet discussion of strike, [Stafford] Cripps accused Bevin [of] false policy and inefficiency. Sgd. Kraemer.'
11 KV-2-157 (3) McCallum. P, Josephine report.
12 KV 4/192 Guy Liddell Diaries.
13 Jennifer Hart was private secretary to the influential Home Office permanent under-secretary, Sir Alexander Maxwell, who had resisted MI5's attempts to round up fascist and communist aliens. After the war, the BBC accused her of being a sleeper Soviet agent.
14 KV 4/192 Vol 8. Liddell Diaries, 6 August 1943. The agent, based in one of the London embassies of a neutral government, was known to be in contact with the Abwehr and T A, Robertson, head of the Double Cross Operation, told Liddell she would make an excellent double agent for passing on misleading intelligence to the Germans. Blunt, who was already working with her on diplomatic counter-intelligence, wanted to run her himself and had clashed with another MI5 officer, Richman Stopford, who had laid claim to her as his agent. Liddell ruled in Stopford's favour.
15 KV-2-144-1, p.11, 12 January 1944, Hart's memo to Blunt, who had been brought into the case the previous year.
16 KV-2-145 (3), pp.3, 21, 40.
17 KV-2-145 (3), pp.3, 21, 40.
18 KV-2-145 The Kraemer file relating to MI5 investigations during 1944.
19 KV 2/1702. Files on Karl Theo Drueke [Drücke] (German), Werner Heinrich Waelti (Swiss), Vera Wedel (Erikson) (German).
20 KV-2-1705 (1).
21 Stephens, Robin, Digest of Ham, Camp 020, p.148, Public Records Office 2000 and KV-4-13–KV-4-15.
22 HO 405/41939 Author's FOI request: A redacted version of this record was made available for public viewing at The National Archives, Kew by 13 October 2023. We have had to carry out a public interest test. This was because some of the information you requested is covered by the Section 23(1) exemption, which by virtue of Section 64(2), becomes a qualified exemption where information falling within it is contained in a historical record in a public record office, such as The National Archives. Section 23 exempts from public disclosure, information that is directly or indirectly supplied by, or relates to, certain organisations dealing with security matters listed at Section 23(3).
23 Pinto, O, *Spycatcher*, p.132. *Time*, 29 September 1961.
24 Stephens, Digest of Ham, p.19.
25 Pinto, Oreste, *Spycatcher 3: Exciting True Stories of Wartime Spies and Counter-Spies*, pp.36–52, New English Library, 1960.

26 Ibid.
27 Ibid.
28 KV-2-1705 (1), p.6.
29 Farago, Ladislas, *The Game of Foxes*, p.182, Hodder & Stoughton, 1971. KV-2-448–451, The Snow Papers.
30 Farago, L, *The Game of Foxes*, pp.538–56.
31 Cave Brown, A, *Bodyguard of Lies*, p.471.

Chapter 15
1 KV-2-145 (3), p.48, Robert Seeds' memo, March 1944.
2 Ibid.
3 Ibid.
4 Ibid.
5 KV-2-145 (1), p.3.
6 Ibid.
7 KV-2-145 (1), p.6.
8 KV-2-156-7. McCallum, P, Report into 'Josephine'.
9 KV-2-145(2), p.32 and KV-2-145 (1), p.51.
10 *Triplex*, West, Nigel, and Tsarev, Oleg, p.1, Yale, 2009.
11 West, N, Tsarev, O, *The Crown Jewels*, Blunt's account of his life given to NKVD in 1943, pp.142–43.
12 Josephine was the first in a long list of code names used by Kraemer. For the sake of simplicity – and following MI5's own lead – we collapse them all into a single heading.
13 *Triplex*, West, Nigel and Tsarev, Oleg, p.6, Yale, 2009.
14 West, N, and Tsarev, O, *Triplex*, p.23.
15 West, N, Tsarev, O, *The Crown Jewels*, Blunt's account of his life given to NKVD in 1943, p.151.
16 West, N., Crown Jewells.
17 West, Nigel and Tsarev, Oleg, *Triplex*, p.11, Yale, 2009.
18 Ibid.
19 West, Nigel and Tsarev, Oleg, *Triplex*, pp.12 and 13, Yale, 2009.
20 West, Tsarev, *Triplex*, p.12.
21 Thomas, Hugh, *The Unlikely Death of Heinrich Himmler*, p.64.
22 Ibid.
23 Thomas, Hugh, *The Unlikely Death of Heinrich Himmler*, p.65.
24 Ibid. Falk later said he believed some of the secret material had been acquired by either Cairncross or Blunt, although he offered no explanation as to why the Russians would want to give it to the Germans at this juncture in the war.
25 Thomas, Hugh, Falk Memoir, p.64.
26 Thomas, Hugh, p.66.
27 KV 2/146-(2), p. 23.
28 KV-2-146 (2), MI5 memo to Menzies, 13 February 1945.
29 KV-2-144-1, p.17. SIS memo to Herbert Hart at MI5.
30 Blunt, Memoir, p.35.
31 West, N, Tsarev, O, *Triplex*, p.316.
32 West, N, Tsarev, O, *The Crown Jewels*, Blunt's account of his life given to NKVD in 1943, p.151.
33 West, N, Tsarev, O, *Triplex*, p.316

NOTES

34 West, N, Tsarev, O, *Triplex*, p.13.
35 West, N, Tsarev, O, *Triplex*, pp.277–78.
36 KV-2-145 (3), p.1, Courtenay Young MI5 memo to SIS.
37 KV-2-145 (1), p.41.
38 KV-2-145 (1), p.44.
39 West, Nigel and Tsarev, Oleg, *Triplex* (Yale, 2009), p.289.
40 Andrew, C, *The Defence of the Realm*, p.280, and West, N, *Triplex*.
41 *Triplex*, West, Nigel, and Tsarev, Oleg, pp.141, 173.
42 Ibid.
43 Ibid.
44 Ibid.
45 Hansard HC Deb, 9 November 1981, vol. 12 cc40-2W.
46 Costello, John, *Mask of Treachery* (William Morrow, 1988), p.431.
47 Cecil, Robert, Former MI6 officer. https://www.tandfonline.com/doi/abs/10.1080/02684529408432253?journalCode=fint20
48 Andrew, C, Mitrokhin, V, p.167.
49 Costello, J, p.432.
50 *The Crown Jewels*, p.329. Philby was taken in by the Fortitude plans and was reporting to Moscow about the real existence of invented US Army FUSAG in the run-up to D-Day.
51 Andrew, C, *The Defence of the Realm*, p.280.
52 The *Crown Jewels*, p.331. One of the agents warning Stalin of a D-Day disaster was Kim Philby.
53 Trevor-Roper interview 1985 with Barrie Penrose, Simon Freeman, *Conspiracy of Silence*, p.286.
54 Costello, J, p.432.
55 Costello, p.435.
56 Hinsley, p.278.
57 KV-4526, pp.148,149.
58 KV-2-156 McCallum, P. Report on Josephine.
59 KV-2-157 (4) and Hesketh, R, Report on Fortitude.
60 KV-2–145 (2), p.28.

Chapter 16
1 KV-2-157 (4).
2 Hinsley, p.278.
3 KV-2-157 (4), Patricia McCallum report on Hesketh's inquiry into Fortitude.
4 Andrew, C, *The Defence of the Realm*, p.309.
5 KV-2-157-4, p.38bk, The Kraemer Report Appendix 1. Colonel Hesketh's inquiry into Operation Fortitude.
6 Ibid.
7 Ibid.
8 KV-2-2068 (2), p.114.
9 KV-2-2074(1), p.69.
10 Ibid.
11 CIA Narrative History of the Rote Kapelle. https://archive.org/details/rotekapelleci00unit/page/124/mode/2up?view=theater
12 KV-2-2074(1), p.69.
13 London, KV-2-2827 (2) p17.

14 KV-2-1971, Karl-Heinz Pannwitz interrogation.
15 https://www.nytimes.com/2004/06/08/news/dday-60-years-later-for-russia-opening-of-a-second-front-in-europe-came.html
16 Reynolds, D, Pechatnov, V, *Stalin's Wartime Correspondence with Churchill and Roosevelt*, Yale University Press, 2018, pp.28,29.
17 Reynolds, D, Pechatnov, V, *Stalin's Wartime Correspondence with Churchill and Roosevelt*, Yale University Press, 2018, p.29.
18 CIA report, p.123 https://archive.org/details/rotekapelleci00unit/page/112/mode/2up?view=theater
19 Costello, p.436.
20 Costello, p.436.
21 Costello, p.436.
22 West, Nigel, *Churchill's Spy Files*, p.17.
23 West, Nigel, *Churchill's Spy Files*, p.151.

Chapter 17

1 Smuts Telegrams to Churchill, Churchill Society No: 20170115.
2 West, N, *Triplex*, p.142.
3 West, N, *Triplex*, p.106, Philby's report to the Kremlin.
4 *Triplex*, p.144.
5 *Triplex*, pp.143–4.
6 *Triplex*, p.145.
7 Macintyre, B, *A Spy Among Friends*, p.89.
8 KV 4/196 Vol 12 Liddell, G, Diaries, 1 January 1945.
9 Modin, Yuri, *My Five Cambridge Friends*, p.141.
10 Ellis, L, F, Warhurst, A E (2004) [1968]. Butler, J R M (ed.), *Victory in the West: The Defeat of Germany*.
11 Churchill, W S, *The Second World War*, vol VI, p.187; Folly, M, *Churchill and Stalin, Comrades-in-Arms*, p.197.
12 KV-4-195, p.69.
13 Baker, P, *My Testament*, p.107.
14 HS7-159-1a, SOE update 1944, p.15.
15 Baker, p.114.
16 West, N, Tsarev, O, *The Crown Jewels*, Blunt's account of his life given to NKVD in 1943, p.156.
17 *The Crown Jewels*, p.167.
18 *The Crown Jewels*, p.153.
19 *The Crown Jewels*, p.170.

Chapter 18

1 KV-2-156/7 Patricia McCallum Report: Appendix II Arnhem.
2 Ibid.
3 KV-2-156/7 McCallum, Josephine report.
4 Ohletz and Berg were upbraided by Schellenberg for negligence. Kraemer's statement to MI5. KV-2-156/7 McCallum Arnhem report appendix III.
5 KV-2-152 (2), p.59, Hinsey, p.278.
6 Hesketh, R, *Fortitude*, p.309.
7 Appendix to Lagebericht West No.1392, 18 September 1944, Hesketh, R, *Fortitude: The D-Day Deception Plan*, p.309.

NOTES

8 General Bittrich's interview with T A Boeree, 15 November 1953, p.4. Fond 2 Box 24. 'King Kong'. Background material: newspaper clippings, photographs, carbon copy of Boeree, T A Series 1–7, McMaster University Library, Canada.
9 Bauer, C, p.103 and p.55.
10 Airborne Assault Museum AL2069. Bittrich's interview with Boeree, 1954. p.5.
11 General Bittrich's interview with T A Boeree, 15 November 1953, p.4. Fond 2 Box 24. 'King Kong'. Background material: newspaper clippings, photographs, carbon copy of Boeree, T A. E H Cookridge fonds, 1905–1979, 15.35 m of textual records and graphic material. Series 1–7, McMaster University Library, Canada.
12 KV-2-152 (2), p.59, Schellenberg interrogation questionnaire. When Schellenberg was interrogated by MI5 about the Arnhem warning he said after he received it, he passed it to OKW and the Luftwaffe. In this scenario the message had reached the Germans in the nick of time and it had helped them in their deployment of forces to counter the Allies' operation.
13 Bittrich interview with Boeree, 1953.
14 Des II.SS Pz.A.K ubder die Kampf im Raum Arnheim vom 10.9-15.10.44 Jory Brentjens/ Airborne Museum Hartenstein, Arnhem, Holland.
15 Urquhart, R, *Arnhem*, p.53.
16 http://www.battle-of-arnhem.com/walter-harzer-the-german-commander-who-eventually-defeated-the-british/
17 Urquhart, R, *Arnhem*, pp.52, 53.
18 Ibid.
19 Anlageband Heeresgruppe B. Ic Meldungen 1–30 September 1944, 2330 hrs, 17 September 1944. Kershaw, R, *It Never Snows in September: The German View of Market Garden and the Battle of Arnhem 1944*, p.132.
20 http://www.battle-of-arnhem.com/myth-market-garden-failed-because-the-germans-were-in-possession-of-the-original-attack-plans/ For further discussion of the value of the Waco glider plans, see Robert Kershaw's *It Never Snows in September*.
21 Hesketh, R, *Fortitude: The D-Day Deception Campaign*, pp.307, 308.
22 KV-2-156/7 McCallum report. Hesketh investigation of Fortitude.
23 KV-2-147 (2) Extract from report 1490, March 1945, Axis intelligence activities in Sweden.
24 WO 208/5213 12.10/46 seven-page report on the Fuellop source.
25 KV-2-3266 MI5 assessment of Ivan Chichaev, 1941–1943.
26 KV-3-142.
27 KV-2-197 (3), p.31, 7 December 1943.
28 Andrew, C, Gordievsky, O, *KGB: The Inside Story*, p.244.
29 Philby, K, *My Silent War*, pp.92–94.
30 Philby's family was personally close to Bernard Montgomery, the best man at Philby's father's wedding. Access to the British general who had devised the Market Garden plan would not have been difficult.
31 KV-2-2271 (4), p.16.
32 KV-2-2271 (4), p.P58, MI5 report on Fuellop.
33 KV-2-2270 (2), p.P29, Philby letter replying to Stopford, showing Philby's charm by shutting down the idea of having the Japanese embassy in Lisbon

watched – 'even MI5 on their home ground would hesitate to embark on such an enterprise!'
34 KV-2-2271 (4), p.P58, MI5 report on Fuellop.
35 KV 2/157 (4), p.43bp. McCallum report. Appendix III – Arnhem.
36 Hinsley, p.279.
37 West, N, *The Crown Jewels*, copy of Blunt's handwritten text to Moscow. Back cover.

Chapter 19
1 CAB 120/864. The Tolstoy files.
2 https://www.nationalww2museum.org/war/articles/allied-responses-warsaw-uprising-1944
3 Churchill, W S, *The Second World War*, Vol VI, p.187. The 'child' was the United Nations.
4 Library of Congress. W. Averell Harriman papers
5 *Field Marshal Lord Alanbrooke Diaries*, Weidenfeld & Nicolson (2001).
6 Ibid.
7 CAB 120/864. The Tolstoy files.
8 Prem 3/434/2. Records of meetings at the Kremlin, 9–17 October 1944.
9 CAB 120/864. The Tolstoy files and Prem 3 434/2
10 Ibid.
11 Churchill, W S, Vol VI, p.198.
12 Ibid.
13 Prem 3 434/2.
14 Ibid.
15 Churchill, W S, p.199.
16 Sudoplatov, p.196.
17 Andrew, C, Mitrokhin, V, p.150.
18 Sudoplatov, p.184.

Chapter 20
1 KV-2 231.
2 HO 405/41939 Home Office report on Oreste Pinto. Accessed under the Freedom of Information Act.
3 Ibid.
4 Pinto Omnibus, p.192.
5 KV6-37-2, p.29, 10 March 1944, RPS interrogations of de Graaf. (Oratory Schools, Stewart's Grove SW3 was where MI5 conducted interrogations in Room 050.)
6 KV-2-239 De Graaf memo about Pinto.
7 Pinto Omnibus, pp.192–95.
8 Pinto, O, *The Spycatcher Omnibus*, p.383.
9 Pinto, O, *The Spycatcher Omnibus*, p.383.
10 Ibid.
11 Ibid.
12 Pinto, O, *The Spycatcher Omnibus*, p.387.
13 KV-2-234, p.88.
14 Langley, James M, *Fight Another Day* (Collins, 1974), p.227.
15 Ibid.

NOTES

16 Baker, p.113.
17 Pinto, *Spycatcher*, pp.118–9.

Chapter 21

1 De Jong, *Encounter*, p.14.
2 Dutch Ministry of the Interior. Hogendoorn document Christiaan Lindemans (2 delen) (The Hague, 1986) (MI), P G Hogendoorn report on interrogation of Lindemans, 2 August 1946. Author's interview with Willem Hogendoorn, son of P G Hogendoorn, January 2023.
3 De Jong, p.14.
4 KV-2-232, p.16, Dutch Commission p.4. This became known as the 'King Kong is all right' note.
5 KV-2-232, p.16.
6 De Graaff, *Uncertain Horizons*, p.64.
7 De Graaff, *Uncertain Horizons*, p.64.
8 KV-2-231, p.45. https://gerard1945.wordpress.com/tag/christiaan-lindemans/
9 De Graaff, *Uncertain Horizons*, p.65.
10 Pinto, O, *Spycatcher*, pp.122–24.

Chapter 22

1 Educated at Rugby School and then Cambridge, the 34-year-old British officer had been an international buyer before being recruited to the Intelligence Corps on an emergency commission two years earlier.
2 HS9/1299/5.
3 Pinto, O, *Spycatcher Omnibus*, p.399.
4 KV-2-231, Sainsbury's report, p.14.
5 Ibid.
6 Ibid.
7 KV-2-231, pp. 15/16, DSO MI5 report to London.
8 KV-2-231, p.22 and p.29.
9 KV-2-232, p.100 Stephens' report on Lindemans' arrival at Camp 020.
10 Stephens, Robin, Hoare, Oliver, Camp 020 Public Record Office/Secret History Files, p.18.
11 KV-2-231, pp.22, 29.
12 KV-2-233, Appendix III p.34, KV-2-232, p.100, Stephens' report on Lindemans' arrival to Camp 020.
13 KV-2-233, Appendix III p.34, KV-2-232, p.100, Stephens' report on Lindemans' arrival to Camp 020.
14 KV-4-15, History of Camp 020, entitled 'A Digest of Ham'. Case histories of suspected spies interrogated in Camp 020 in the Second World War and subsequent interrogations in the British-occupied zone of Germany.
15 KV-2-139, Cornelis Verloop interrogation by MI5 at Camp 020, p.62.
16 KV-2-232, p.17, Verloop evidence against Lindemans.
17 KV-2-232, p.100, Stephens' report on Lindemans' arrival to Camp 020.
18 https://www.smithsonianmag.com/history/the-monocled-world-war-ii-interrogator-652794/
19 KV-2-232, pp.17, 33.
20 KV-2-232, p.95, Stephens' report of first interrogation of Lindemans.

21 KV-4-13-15.
22 KV-2-233, p.39. Lindemans' first confession, 6 November 1944.
23 KV-2-232, p.3, Col Stephens' report on KK, 4 November 1944.
24 Baker, Peter, *My Testament*, pp.122–52.
25 KV-2-233, p.48.
26 KV-2-233, p.100, Stephens' report on Cornelis Verloop's statement.
27 KV-2-233, p.47, Lindemans' second confession.
28 KV-2-233, p.47, Lindemans' second confession.
29 Liddell Diaries, Vol II, p.239, 5 November 1944.
30 KV-2-234, p.53, Stephens' reports, 22 November 1944.
31 KV-2-233, p.7, Liddell report on Lindemans, 18 November 1944.
32 West, Nigel, *Churchill's Spy Files*, p.340.

Chapter 23
1 Cave Brown, Anthony, *Bodyguard of Lies*, p.810.
2 Churchill, W S, *The Second World War*, Vol VI, p.243.
3 Churchill, W S, *The Second World War*, Vol VI, p.70.
4 KV-2-151(1), p.46. Liddell, G, Diaries, 6-7 February 1945.
5 Kraemer gave all his sources code numbers.
6 KV-2-151(1), p.46.
7 Hinsley, H, p.277.
8 KV-2-147 (3). Liddell Diaries, 7 February 1945. KV 4/186 Liddell Diaries, Vol II, pp.150–1
9 KV-2-151 (1), p.54.
10 Liddell, G, Diaries, 6 February 1945.
11 KV-2-147 (3), p.77.
12 Deeley, Graeme. Diary entry of Brereton for 29 October 1944. *Worst Fears Confirmed: The History of Intelligence Corps Airborne Units and the Intelligence Gathering & Security Measures Employed for British Airborne Operations*, Barny Books, p.104.
13 KV-2-151 (2), p.18.
14 KV 2/157(3), p.45 McCallum, P, Report on Kraemer.
15 OSS report on Walter Schellenberg. 27 June–12 July 1945. R6 226 Entry 123 A Box 2 Espionage. Credit: Bob de Graaff.
16 Ibid.
17 KV-2-147(3), p.48.
18 KV-2-147(3), p.48.
19 Ibid.
20 KV-2-147(3), Major Ryde, Room 055, War Office, p.22.
21 KV-2-147 (3), pp.9, 17, 18.
22 KV-2-147(3), p.53, Blunt internal MI5 memo.
23 KV-2-147 (3), 25 March 1945, p.7.

Chapter 24
1 KV-2-964 (1), p.37.
2 KV-2-964 (2), p.41.
3 KV-2-964 (2), p.41.
4 KV-2-964 (1).
5 KV-2-964 (1), p.30.

NOTES

6 KV-2-964 (1), p.23.
7 KV-2-964 (1), p.21.
8 KV-2-964 (1), p.36.
9 KV-2-964 (1), p.38.
10 Stephens, R, Camp 020, p.328.
11 Instituut Militaire Historie. Bureau Nationale Veiligheid (BNV) July 9.7.46 Scheveningen BNV 93 CB2354 - 10.000-11-45 Vervolgblad proces verbaal. Lindemans' confessions and statements in Dutch.
12 KV-2-236, Supplementary Report in the cases of Lindemans/Verloop/Damen December 1944, p.51.
13 KV-2-236.
14 De Yong, Louis, *Encounter*, p.13.
15 KV-2-235, Lindemans' four confessions at Camp 020, KV-2-946 (1), p.21, Christmann's statement to US interrogators after his capture in France.
16 KV-2-233, p.36.
17 KV-2-232, p.22.
18 Stephens, R, Camp 020, p.70.
19 KV-4-195 Vol 11 Liddell Diaries, p.266.
20 Pinto, O, *Spycatcher*, p.132.
21 Pinto, O, *Spycatcher*, p.132.
22 Pinto, O, *Spychatcher* p.133
23 Ibid.
24 HS-6-728, SOE memo, 20 February 1945.
25 Pinto, O, *Spycatcher*, p.132.
26 KV-4-195 Vol 11 Liddell, 2 February 1945, p.280.
27 HS-6-728.
28 HS-6-728, SOE memo, 20 February 1945.
29 KV-4-195 Vol 11 Liddell, G, 17 February 1945, p.273.
30 HS-6-728, Report of Special Forces conference held at SFHQ on 20 February, p.5.
31 Ryan, Cornelius, The digital collection of the Cornelius Ryan Collection of World War II, Ohio University.
32 The failure of the 82nd to secure the Nijmegen bridge on Day 1 of the operation delayed the XXX Corp relief column 36 hours and is considered one of several key reasons for the failure of the entire operation.
33 Ibid.
34 HS-6-728, Report of Special Forces conference held at SFHQ on 20 February, p.5.

Chapter 25
1 KV-4-196 Vol 12 Liddell Diaries, 11 May 1945, Long and Blunt lunch with Liddell, p.291.
2 FCO 158/164 Leo Long was later, May 1946 to September 1946, Director of Operations at the HQ of the Control Commission at Herford. From 1946, one of five regional intelligence officers and chief political officer. Penrose, B, *Conspiracy of Silence*, p.299.
3 Stephens, R, Camp 020, p.354.
4 Stephens, R, p.354.
5 KV-2-157(3), Pat McCallum quoting from the Josephine files.

6 KV-2-157 (3), McCallum report.
7 KV-2-153 (2), Extract from C.S.D.I.C. (UK) interrogation of Obstlt Ohletz, OC (Leiter) Mil Amt C, RSHA.
8 Macintyre, Ben, *Agent Zig Zag*, (Bloomsbury, 2007), pp.292, 293.
9 KV-2-149, Stamp memo to Michael Ryde, June 1945.
10 KV-2-157.
11 Kv-2-150 (2), p.55. Stephens' report on Kraemer's interrogation.
12 KV-2-242
13 KV-2-147 (4).
14 KV-2-151 (2), pp.16 and 28.
15 KV-2-156 (3) McCallum report.
16 KV-2 -149. Stephens' memo to Blanshard Stamp, MI5.
17 KV-2-149 (1) p.33.
18 KV-2-149 (1) p.44
19 KV 2/150 (1), p.40, Blunt report to Stephens, 7 July 1945.
20 KV-2-150 (1), p.40, Blunt memo to Stephens at Camp 020.
21 KV-2-150 (1), 23 June 1945.
22 KV-2-151 (2), Blunt report to Stephens at Camp 020, 23 July 1945.
23 KV2-147-2, p.12.
24 KV-2-157, McCallum report on Josephine.
25 KV-2-157(3) McCallum's report on Kraemer, p.62.
26 KV 2/152-1, Captain Scott Harrison's questionnaire for Schellenberg, 20 August 1945, sent to Lt Col Stimson.
27 KV-2-157(4), McCallum report.
28 KV 2/152-1, Blunt Memo, 8 September 1945.
29 KV-2-144 (1), Monthly report on Axis Intelligence activities in Sweden, 8 February 1944. Jeorg Michael, Kraemer's brother-in-law, had arrived in the UK on 11 August 1943.
30 KV-2-152, Kraemer signed statement.
31 https://www.douglashistory.co.uk/history/carl_ludvig_douglas.html
32 KV 2/152-1, Mason memo to Blunt, 3 September 1945.
33 KV-2-152 (1), p.39.
34 Ibid.
35 KV-2-150 (2), p.21.
36 KV-2-150 Memo to Blanshard Stamp at WRC1, 22 June 1945.
37 KV-2-151 (2), p.17.
38 KV-2-151 (2), p.18, Camp 020 report, 23 July 1945, Captain Marseille and Sq Ld Beddard.
39 KV-2-151 (2), p.2, Bagyoni worked with Kraemer until March 1945 when he left Stockholm.
40 KV-2-147 (2).
41 KV-2-151 (2), p.50, Mason memo to Blunt.
42 KV-2-151 (2), p.42, 23.7.9 Blunt 020 report to Stephens.
43 KV-2-146 (2), Michael Ryde memo to the Foreign Office, 10 February 1945, about Kraemer's meeting with William Strang, the British diplomat who had been based in Moscow in the 1930s.
44 KV-2-146 (2), Michael Ryde memo to the Foreign Office, 10 February 1945.
45 Andrew, Christopher, *The Defence of the Realm*, p.268.
46 KV 2/152 (1).

NOTES

47 KV-2-151 (2), p.42 23.7.9 Blunt 020 report to Stephens.
48 KV-2-151 (2), p.3, Kraemer's office accounts 1943–1945 kept by his secretary Siemsen and copied by SIS.
49 KV 2/153-2, p.15. Kraemer's Arnhem statement.
50 KV-151 (12), p.12.
51 KV-2-150 (1), pp.19–20, Blunt's response to SIS about Kraemer's sources dated 15 July 1945.
52 KV 2/157-3, p.44
53 KV-2-155(1), p.21.
54 KV-2-150 (1), pp.19–20, Blunt's response to SIS about Kraemer's sources dated 15 July 1945.
55 KV-2-153 (1) p.10
56 KV-2-154 (2), p.72.
57 KV-2-154 (2), p.100, MI5 report, 27 October 1945.
58 CIA report Theodor Paeffgen. Gestapo Mueller believed Kraemer was working for the British and had him interrogated after Arnhem. https://www.cia.gov/readingroom/docs/PAEFFGEN%2C%20THEODOR_0024.pdf KV-2-151 (2), p.46. PW: Offz Von zur Gathen 1945 OKL LW Fuhrungstsab Clerk who received the intelligence: 'Josephine provided the most important information on Great Britain including plans, troop movements, identifications etc. PW heard this source described as a neutral diplomat in Great Britain with excellent connections in high British military circles. Josephine, however, was suspected of working for British intelligence as well. Questions, the answers to which were known, were therefore put to this source but PW does not know what results were obtained.'
59 Penrose, Barrie and Freeman, Simon, *Conspiracy of Silence*, p.287. Simon Freeman's interview with Tar Robertson in 1986.
60 Andrew, C and Gordievsky, O, *KGB: The Inside Story*, p.244.
61 Rose, Kenneth, *Who Loses, Who Wins: The Journals Of Kenneth Rose*, Vol II 1979–2014 by Kenneth Rose and edited by D R Thorpe, Weidenfeld & Nicolson, 2019.
62 Flora Solomon was one. John Costello says there were others.
63 Churchill, W S, *The Second World War*, Vol VI
64 Churchill, W S, *The Second World War*, Vol VI
65 Churchill, W S, *The Second World War*, Vol VI, p.437.

Chapter 26

1 Haines, Joe, *Maxwell*. pp.119, 120. After Maxwell interrogated Giskes he wrote to London concluding that the SOE must have sent agents to Holland knowing they would fall into enemy hands as part of a deception plan for D-Day.
2 KV-2-967 (2), pp.15–17 Huntemann statement to MI5.
3 KV-2-237, p.33, KV-2-967, p.11 Huntemann statement.
4 US FOIA Document Release Date 21 May 2021, Sequence Number: Case Number: F-2019-02151. https://www.cia.gov/readingroom/docs/RICHARD%20CHRISTMAN%5B15921665%5D.pdf
5 USFOIA Christmann, R. Interview by US Army, September 1946. https://www.cia.gov/readingroom/docs/RICHARD%20CHRISTMAN%5B15921665%5D.pdf

6 Pinto, O, *Spychatcher*, p.133.
7 Ibid.
8 Ibid.
9 NIOD Institute for War, Holocaust and Genocide Studies. H4 Interrogations and statements of Lindemans, documents relating to the cause of death of Lindemans, the death certificate from the register of civil status in The Hague, 8 August 1946. Frederick Sutherland letter written on 8 July 1946: 'On 16th October 1943 Christiaan Lindemans at great risk to his own life, accompanied Sidney Hobday and myself from Scheveningen to Rotterdam where he kept us safely for several days. During this time he took us to the docks in Rotterdam so that we could gather information on German shipping to take back to England. Then he arranged for our transportation by rail from Rotterdam to Paris and accompanied us to the later point. During this trip we were searched by the Gestapo and Lindemans remained with us to answer questions as we were acting deaf and dumb. I believe that the efforts of CL were wholly responsible for our escape and safe return to England. And I make this affidavit so that the Dutch authorities become aware of the patriotic activities of CL during 1943 when he saved myself and my comrade from the German Occupation Forces.'
10 Pinto, O, *Spychatcher*, p.134.
11 Ibid, p.135.
12 AIR 81/8094. After the war Douglas Gordon Baber wrote several novels drawing on his experiences of captivity and his time at The Hague.
13 KV-2-237, p.14.
14 Ibid.
15 Ibid.
16 KV-2-237, p.14.
17 Pinto, O, *Spycatcher*, p.137.
18 KV-2-237, *Daily Express* report of Lindemans' death.
19 Pinto, O, *Spycatcher*, p.137.
20 KV-2-237, p.26.
21 KV-2-237, p.14.
22 Frans Dekkers' interview with the author, January 2024.
23 Nederlands Instituut voor Militaire Historie. Slag om Arnhem (Operatie Market Garden) 68. 15.1.1976 C.V.D interview with Lt Van Dijk.
24 KV-2-237, pp. 23–26.
25 KV-2-237, p.26, Lindemans' letter included in Sq Leader Baber's statement to MI5 after visit to Scheveningen Prison in 1946.
26 Nederlands Instituut voor Militaire Historie. Slag om Arnhem (Operatie Market Garden) 68. 15.1.1976 C.V.D interview with Lt Van Dijk.
27 KV-2-237, p.26, Sq Leader Baber's statement to MI5 after visit to Scheveningen Prison in 1946.
28 Ibid.
29 Ibid.
30 KV-2-237, p.26, Sq Leader Baber's statement to MI5 after visit to Scheveningen Prison in 1946.
31 Ibid.
32 KV-2-237, p.26, Sq Leader Baber's statement to MI5 after visit to Scheveningen Prison in 1946.

NOTES

33 NIOD Institute for War, Holocaust and Genocide Studies: a18 Report on statements about Lindemans, made after the war by Ellie Zwaan. She had been one of Lindemans' relations in Belgium illegally. Not signed, 7 August 1945.
34 Box 24 Fond 2 E H Cookridge fonds, 1905–1979, 15.35 m of textual records and graphic material. Series 1–7, McMaster University, Canada.
35 KV-2-946, p.81.
36 KV-2-946, pp.77–80. Correspondence between Philby and MI5.
37 Ibid.
38 Ibid.
39 Box 24 Fond 2 E H Cookridge fonds, 1905–1979, 15.35 m of textual records and graphic material. Series 1–7, McMaster University, Canada.
40 Bob de Graaff interview with the author, February 2024.
41 Box 24 Fond ¾, E H Cookridge fonds, 1905–1979, 15.35 m of textual records and graphic material. Series 1–7, McMaster University, Canada.
42 Lindemans' death certificate. Box 24 Fond 2 E H Cookridge fonds, 1905–1979, 15.35 m of textual records and graphic material. Series 1–7, McMaster University, Canada.
43 Lindemans' brothers' interview with Cookridge. Box 24 Fond 2 E H Cookridge fonds, 1905–1979, 15.35 m of textual records and graphic material. Series 1–7, McMaster University, Canada. This story is partly backed up Frans Dekkers, who later interviewed Henk Lindemans in the 1980s. Dekkers' interview with the author, February 2024.
44 NIOD Institute for War, Holocaust and Genocide Studies: g1 The report regarding the various investigations into the remains of J H Lindemans and C A Lindemans found at the opening of the family grave at the Crooswijk General Cemetery in Rotterdam. The research was carried out on behalf of the Ministry of Justice by the Judicial Laboratory in Rijswijk, 13 August 1986. https://www.upi.com/Archives/1986/06/17/A-Dutch-pathologist-positively-identified-a-skeleton-exhumed-today/8581519364800/
45 Frans Dekkers says that he found evidence that Onderdelinden didn't die in South Africa and was living in Holland after 1952.
46 Willem Hogendoorn (Tomas Ross) interview with the author, February 2023.
47 Bob de Graaff interview with the author, January 2024.
48 The Bureau Nationale Veiligheid (BNV) was a Dutch security agency that was founded in 1945 and succeeded in 1946 by the Centrale Veiligheidsdienst, which in turn was transformed into the Binnenlandse Veiligheidsdienst (BVD) in 1949.
49 Hinsley, pp.373–78.
50 https://www.nationaalarchief.nl/onderzoeken/archief/2.21.326 308 Brief account of the facts regarding the poisoning of King Kong (alias Lindemans) and Zr. T Onderdelinden by H Schokking, with accompanying farewell letter from King Kong. 1946 and two pieces.
51 Foot, p.399.
52 de Meersman, Maria, *Spy in the Third Reich: A Flemish Woman in the Resistance*, Van Halewyck, Leuven. John Deccok De Standaard, 3 June 2004.
53 Ibid.

Chapter 27

1. KV 2/157-4, page 39. McCallum report into Kraemer's role in Fortitude. In the vital days after the landing there were 25 Josephine messages contrasted with 10 from Garbo and nine each from Ostro (another German agent) and Brutus. Hesketh, R, *Fortitude: The D-Day Deception Campaign*, pp.207, 210, 356 PXX St Ermin's Press, 2000. According to Hesketh the Germans investigated Josephine and her puppet master in the aftermath of D-Day and concluded he was a 'controlled agent'.
2. KV 2/157 (4) p.39 McCallum report into Kraemer's role in Fortitude with reference to Roger Hesketh.
3. https://www.cia.gov/readingroom/docs/CIA-RDP78-03362A002500070002-3.pdf
4. KV-2-259 (2), p.2, KV-2-154 (2) SIS section V memo, 14 May 1946.
5. McKay, Craig, p.271.
6. KV-2-259 (2), p.2.
7. KV-2-259 (2), p.2.
8. McKay, C, p.274.
9. Ibid.
10. McKay, C, p.274.
11. https://www.cia.gov/readingroom/docs/SCHELLENBERG%2C%20WALTER%20%20VOL.%202_0026.pdf
12. KV-2-2128, MI5 files relating to the French diplomat Garnier, who was based in Stockholm.
13. KV-2-151 (2), p.10, Interrogation of Kraemer. Onodera was being fed by a Polish spy working for the British, but Michal Rybikowski left for England and then Italy well before Arnhem. No evidence he worked for the Russians. Possibly agent Sunrise: https://apjjf.org/2022/8/Edstrom.html
14. KV-2-149.
15. KV-2-259 (2), p.46.
16. KV-2-259 (1), p.25. Philby letter to MI5 about Kraemer, 20 May 1946.
17. KV-2-154 (2), p.14. Philby's correspondence with MI5 regarding Kraemer, 1946.
18. KV-2-242 (1), p.44.
19. KV-2-242 (1), p.36.
20. KV-2-242 (2).
21. KV-2-242 (2), p58.
22. KV-2-242 (1), p.7. Joan Chenhall's letter, 5 July 1947.
23. KV-2-242 (1), p.8.
24. Modin's interview with Roland Perry, Channel 4 documentary, *Royals Declassified: The Queen and the Russian Spy*, April 2021.

Chapter 28

1. KV-2-2827 (2), p.6
2. KV-2-2827 (2), p.21.
3. KV-2-991, p.30, letter to MI5 from Philby, November 1946.
4. KV-2-2827 (2), p.34.
5. KV-2-2074 (2), Philby correspondence with MI5, pp.7, 12, 74.
6. KV-2-2074 (2), pp.7, 74.
7. KV-2-2074 (2), p.47, Sillitoe letter to Capt Studdy.

NOTES

8. KV-2-2074 (2), p.9.
9. KV-2-3226 (2), p.5.
10. Wright, P, *Spycatcher*, p.187.
11. KV-2-2827 (1), p.17. Memo sent to Evelyn McBarnet.
12. KV-2-3226 (2), p.11.
13. KV-2-2827 (1), p.17.
14. KV-2-3226 (1), p.6.
15. KV-2-4347, Giskes' interrogation in relation to Hooper.
16. KV-2-4347, Philby letter to Marriot, 7 October 1946.
17. https://api.parliament.uk/historic-hansard/commons/1979/nov/21/mr-anthony-blunt
18. PREM 16/2230.
19. PREM 16/2230.
20. Farago, L, p.547.
21. KV-2-148-2, p.26.
22. Farago, L., *The Game of Foxes*.
23. KV-2-153.
24. WO 208/5213.
25. WO 208/5213. 'IMPORTANT All information from Kraemer must be taken as highly unreliable unless confirmed from other sources', 16 November 1948.
26. Ibid.
27. WO 208/5213.
28. Ibid.
29. Ibid.
30. Ibid.
31. KV-2-242, p.9, Philby's letter to John Halford, 2 January 1946 or more likely 1947.

Chapter 29

1. KV-2-157 (4). The report on this case written by Pat McCallum was produced during the preparation of Volume IV of the *Official History of British Intelligence in World War II*. The report is undated and the exact date of writing is not now known. Its transfer into the National Archives was not completed until after the rest of the pieces KV-2-144–157 and it was not in fact available to researchers until August 2003.
2. Howard, Michael Captain Professor, *A Life in War and Peace*, p.151, Bloomsbury Academic, 2006.
3. KV-2-157 (4).
4. https://www.specialforcesroh.com/index.php?media/edward-stamp.31718/
5. McKay, pp.286–89.
6. P McCallum said that it was Major Blunt who had taken over the investigation in MI5 from Major Ryde, who had quoted MSS (Most Secret Sources) to show that Berlin still thought that Josephine was a real agent based in London.
7. KV 2/157 (3), p.65.
8. KV 2/3226.
9. Ibid.
10. KV-2-157-4.

Chapter 30

1. WO 106/4410 21st Army Group Operation Market Garden. Montgomery's reference to the operation being 90 per cent successful comes from this official military analysis.
2. Operation Berlin.
3. CAB 44 254 Liberation Campaign North West Europe.
4. Nederlands Institut voor Militaire Historie. Slag om Arnhem (Operatie Market Garden) 46. Marshall, Sam, Brigadier General Samuel Lyman Atwood Marshall, the US Army's chief combat historian during the Second World War. Story of the Spy Sheds Light on Arnhem Disaster. The *Sunday Star*, 4 June 1950. New Light Cast on Allies' Big Arnhem Defeat. *Chicago Tribune*, 4 June 1950. De Grauff, Bob, *Uncertain Horizons*, p.61.
5. Wim Klinkert interview with the author, January 2023 and Klinkert, W, *The Intelligencer Journal of U.S. Intelligence Studies*, Volume 25, Number 2, 2019.
6. Ibid.
7. Bob de Graaff interview with the author, February 2024.
8. West, N, Tsarev, O, *The Crown Jewels*, pp.175, 176.
9. Ibid.
10. PREM 16/2230. John Hunt report on Blunt case, 1978.
11. PREM 16/2230. John Silkin memo to Callaghan.
12. Wright P, *Spycatcher*, p.225.
13. Wright, P, *Spycatcher*, Wright demonstrated how Blunt had betrayed Aleksandr Nelidov, p.220, Nigel West and Oleg Tsarev, *Triplex*, p.250.
14. Wright. P, *Spycatcher*, p.224.
15. The NKVD files are held at operations buildings of the Foreign Intelligence Service of the Russian Federation at Yasenevo, Moscow.
16. Norton Taylor, Richard, *Guardian*, 25.6.1993, p.6. One explanation for Englandspiel, often voiced by Dutch historians, is to blame the Russians for the infiltration of SOE to crush the social democrat resistance groups who would be competing against the communist groups for power after the war. Kim Philby and Guy Burgess were key figures in the training of SOE and agents sent to Holland in the early part of the war.
17. Andrew, Christopher, *The Defence of the Realm*, p.272.
18. Interview by email with the author, January 2024.
19. https://www.mi5.gov.uk/world-war-ii-0

Epilogue

1. Sudoplatov, Pavel and Sudoplatov, Anatoli. With Jerrold, L and Schechter, Leona P, *Special Tasks*, Little, Brown, 1994, p.27.
2. Rotterdam Police, Department ID, report concerning the murder of Konovalets written by police inspectors P W Schoemaker and J P Bontenbal, Rotterdam, 20 June 1938, folder 7, p.14, quoted in Marc Jansen Ben de Jong. Intelligence and National Security vol 9 number for October 1994, pp.676–94 published by Frank Cass, London.
3. Ibid.
4. Sudoplatov, P, *Special Tasks*, p.22.
5. Ibid.
6. Ibid.

NOTES

7 Ibid.
8 Sudoplatov, P, *Special Tasks*, p.23.
9 Tass News Agency, 13 January 2023: https://tass.com/politics/1561973

Appendix 1
1 Commonwealth War Graves Commission figure for estimated Allied casualties and POWs.
2 KV-2-151 (2) Mason memo to Blunt, p.50.

Appendix 2
1 KV-2-231 P46. MI5 'CC' report of Bletchley Park intercept. Liddell Diaries, Vol II, p.239, 5 November 1944.
2 De Jong, Louis, 'Was Arnhem Betrayed?' *Encounter*, p.13. KV-2-235 Lindemans' four confessions at Camp 020, p.68.
3 Lauren, Anne, *Betrayal at Arnhem*, p.8.
4 KV-2-946 (1) p.21 Christmann's statement to US interrogators after his capture in France.
5 De Jong, Louis, 'Was Arnhem Betrayed?' *Encounter*, p.13.
6 Margry, Karel, *Operation Market Garden Then and Now. Vol 1 and 2. After the Battle.*
7 KV-2-946 (1), p.21 Christmann's statement to US interrogators after his capture in France.
8 De Jong, Louis, *Encounter*, p.13, KV-2-237, p.33, KV-2-967 (2), pp.16–17 Huntemann statement.
9 Giskes, H, *London Calling North Pole*, pp.170, 171.
10 KV 2/153-2, p.16.
11 KV 2/153-2, p.16, Hinsley, Harry Prof Sir, *British Intelligence in the Second World War*, Vol IV, p.278.
12 KV 2/152 (1) Captain Scott Harrison's questionnaire for Schellenberg, 20 August 1945, sent to Lt Col Stimson.
13 Ibid.
14 Appendix to Lagebericht West (OKH) No.1391, 17 September 1944, Hesketh, R, *Fortitude*, p.309.
15 Colonel Theodor Boeree's interview with Wilhelm Bittrich, King's College archive. Cornelis Bauer, Boeree, T Arnhem p.103.
16 General Bittrich's interview with T A Boeree, 15 November 1953, p.9 Fond 2 Box 24. 'King Kong'. Background material: newspaper clippings, photographs, carbon copy of Boeree, T A, "Two Short Stories (with comment)" regarding the Battle of Arnhem. Owner: Brig W F K Thompson. E H Cookridge fonds. 1905–1979. 15.35 m of textual records and graphic material. Series 1–7. McMaster University Library,. Canada.
17 Appendix to Lagebericht West (OKH) No 1392, 18 September 1944, Hesketh, R, p.309.

Index

Abbeville Prison 30
Abwehr:
  abolished 48, 69
  'American offensive plan' 235
  The Game of the Foxes 296, 301, 306
  HQ 11, 33, 41, 51, 59, 220, 221
  I Luft 147, 260, 344
  IIIF section 11, 15, 17, 18, 41, 62, 75
  Liege report 73
  successor 255, 344
Agent Josephine 106, 107–10, 141–8, 149–58, 162–4, 165–6, 170–1, 178, 184, 189
  case for Blunt being 307, 334–9
  Churchill briefed on 152–5
  Internet 'blackout' 333
  McCallum investigation 301–9
  McCallum investigation/report 249–67
  microdot intelligence 179–80, 185–6, 260, 288, 289, 302, 303, 314, 337, 337–8, 343–4
Albrecht, Margaret 71–2, 218, 276
Albrecht, Margaret (Akke Volges) 276
Allied High Command 58
Andrew, Christopher 319
Anglo-Soviet agreement (1941) 131
Antwerp, liberation of 75–8
appeasement 115, 209
Archer, Jane 105, 121, 123, 141, 175–6, 259, 292
  described 197
Archive of Foreign Intelligence, Moscow xii
Armia Krajowa (Polish Home Army) 200
Army Group B (Heeresgruppe B) (Germany) 72, 94, 181, 312, 341, 343
Army Group G (Heeresgruppe G) (Germany) 166
Arnhem warnings 106, 107–10, 180, 182, 254–60, 269, 288, 335, 338, 340–6
Astor, Lord 163

Atlanta Hotel 325, 326
Atlantic Wall 30, 177
atomic bomb 205, 206, 244, 309
Auden, W H 329
Aufklärungs Abteilung 9 (SS) 183

Baatsen, Arnoldus 28
Baber, Douglas G 271
Bagyoni, Agent 258
Baker, Peter 78, 80–1, 82–5, 88, 94, 177, 198, 215, 217, 225–30, 269, 341, 347, 348
Band of Brothers 3
Barclay, Colville 175
Battalion Krafft 4
Battle for The Hague 21–2
Battle of Britain 330
Battle of Normandy, *see* Normandy Landings
Battle of the Bulge 233–9, 264
Bay of Pigs 319
BBC 65, 114, 118, 177
Beaufort, Agnès de 52–3
Belgian Sûreté 291
Belgium 31, 45, 54, 72, 92
  MI5 Defence Security Office 224
  resistance 44, 66–9, 73, 78, 80, 212, 213, 230, 281
Belorussia 168
Beria, Lavrentiy 129, 304
Berlin, Isaiah 123–4
Bernhard, Prince of the Netherlands 10, 80, 156, 198, 209
  Castle Wittouk HQ 215–16, 218, 224, 247
  Hotel Metropole HQ 78
Best, Sigismund Payne 275
Bevin, Ernest 142
Bingham & Co., Successors Ltd 42
Bittrich, Wilhelm ('Willi') 109–10, 181–4, 312, 315, 345
Blenheim Palace 118, 143
Bletchley Park 73, 125–6, 138, 142, 158, 160, 162, 187, 229, 234–6, 302, 340
Blizard, Charles Cecil 28, 42, 318
'Blue Jacket' ('BJ') decrypts 185

Blunt, Anthony 105, 114–20, 122, 124, 137, 151
  B1B 240
  Blizard/'Major Blunt' confusion 318
  Churchill briefings 170
  'confession' 294–6
  D-Day 168, 169–70
  described 197
  microdots expertise 186
  mitigation attempt 124
  Russian handler, *see* Gorsky, Anatoly
  as Surveyor of the Queen's/King's Pictures 278, 295, 316
  Thatcher House of Commons statement 306–7, 318
  Twist committee appointment 156
  XXX (Triplex) 151, 156, 185, 331
Blunt, Christopher 161, 163
Boeree, Theodor A 181–2, 345
Boetzelaer, Baron van (Jan Beaufort) 32, 53
Bohr, Niels 207
Bomber Command (Britain) 25, 158
Brereton, Lewis H 164, 237
British 1st Airborne Division (Britain) 1
British Army of the Rhine (BAOR) 289
British Control Commission 249, 315
British Empire 206, 279
British Expeditionary Force (BEF) 116
British Library 129
British Union of Fascists 114
Brixton Prison 288
Brooke, Alan 202
Brown, Anthony Cave 234
Brucker, Dr 63
Brussels, liberation of 71, 75–8, 215
Buchenwald 53
Bulgaria 172, 174, 176, 201, 205
Bulgarian Communist Party 174
Bundesarchiv (German National Archive) xi–xii, 349
Bureau Bijzondere Opdrachten (BBO) 209

384

INDEX

Burgess, Guy 106, 114–15, 118
  erratic behaviour 123–4
  flees to Russia 292
  SIS syllabus 131, 133
Busch, Friedrich 286–7, 338
BVD (Binnenlandse Veiligheidsdienst) 271, 282

Cabinet Office Historical Section 301
Cairncross, John 114–15, 126, 207
Cambridge Five 105, 114–15, 333–4 (*see also spies by name*)
Cambridge University 114–15, 141, 160, 207, 295, 316
Camp 020 145, 225, 242, 245, 250–9, 262, 287, 294, 299, 302–3, 336, 337
Canaris, Wilhelm 12, 15–16, 48, 54, 69
Castle (Château) Wittouck 212, 215, 218, 222, 223
Cave-Browne-Cave, Henry 238
Celosse, Jan 61
Celosse, Nicolaas 32, 34, 37, 39, 41, 58–62
Central Archives of the Ministry of Defence, Russian Federation xii
Centrum Sabotage 6 32
Cervell, Frank 106, 152–3, 155–7, 166
Château de Battel 63
Chenhalls, Joan 288
Cherbourg 30
Chesterfield Gardens 118
Chichaev, Ivan 106, 132–6, 140, 167, 185, 258, 293, 304
Christiansen, General 84, 90, 93
Christmann, Arnaud 243
Christmann, Richard 15, 83–5, 89, 90, 93, 95, 229, 243, 268–9, 278–9, 313, 342
Churchill, Winston ix, 92, 95, 113, 125
  Ascalon ('LV-633') 199–200, 202
  birth 118
  communist insurgency, Greece 235
  Iron Curtain speech 292
  Operation Tolstoy 199–207
CIA (Central Intelligence Agency), *see also* OSS 141, 237, 276, 295, 297, 299

Clichy, Madame 35
Cnoops, Tony 58, 61
Code Room (FO) 121
Cold War 140, 141, 267, 290, 292, 307, 317
Colditz 78
Cole, Paul ('Harry') 24
Combined Services Detailed Interrogation Centre (CSDIC), *see* CSDIC/WEA
Communist Party of Great Britain 114–15, 120, 135, 140, 143
concentration camps 43, 53, 252, 275
Cookridge, E H 280–1
Cooper, Duff 161
Corin, E J 272
Council of Resistance (Raad van Verzet, RVV) 32, 44–5, 58, 66
Counter-Intelligence Corps (US) 300
Courtauld Institute 115, 316
Cowgill, Felix 105, 138, 141–2, 174
Crete 83
Cripps, Stafford 131, 142
Crooswijk Cemetery 281, 327–8
CS-6 11, 32–5, 37, 58, 62, 66, 75, 198, 276
CSDIC/WEA 145, 262, 287–8, 298 (*see also* Camp 020)
Cuban Missile Crisis 317, 319
Cussen, Edward 247
Czerniawski, Roman ('Brutus') 163–4, 165, 166, 184, 285

D-Day 43, 57, 62, 65, 72, 156–64 (*see also* Normandy Landings)
  deception planning, *see* also Operation Fortitude 157–8, 165–6, 168, 180–1, 286
  Kraemer's reports 238
Dalton, Hugh 130
Dambusters (617 Squadron) 37, 39, 45, 270
Damen, Tony 242, 278
Danilov, Ivan 134, 293
Day-X (D-Day) 62, 65
De Gaulle, Charles 160
De Waarheid 135
De Weiss (Dutch guide) 82
Dekkers Frans 94, 347, 348
Delden, Margaretha 214
Denmark 109, 180, 249–50, 345
Department S (USSR) 207
Deutsche Lufthansa 155

Devise Anschutz Kommando (Foreign Exchange Protection Commando), 60
Dimitrewski (Russian agent) 287, 337
Doetinchem 109, 181–2
Donnet, Mr and Mrs 144
Dool, Nijs van den 38, 45–6
Dordrecht, RAF bombing of 59
Douglas, Carl 256
Dourlein, Pieter 41, 56
Driebergen 59–60, 83–5, 220–1, 229, 234, 243, 268, 278, 278–9, 342
Drücke, Karl Theodor 144
Duchess of Richmond 121
Dulles, Allen 141, 297
Dumbo, Agent, *see* Hewit, Jack
Dunkirk 22, 24, 118
Dutch Counter-Intelligence Mission 209
Dutch National Archives, the Hague xi–xii, 283
Dzhugashvili, Yakov 275

Eastern Front 168, 234, 286
Easy Company 506 Parachute Infantry Regiment 3
Eden, Anthony 202
Edward VIII 278, 289, 295
8th Army (Britain) 152
82nd Airborne Division (US) 4, 89, 107, 109, 178, 180, 228, 248, 342, 343
Eindhoven mission xi, 1–3, 75, 80, 82, 82–9, 94, 107–8, 177, 226–9, 243–4, 269, 313, 341–6
Eisenhower, Dwight D 77, 79, 80, 94, 145, 236, 245, 257, 264–6
El Alamein 80, 152
Elizabeth II 105, 295
Elliott, Nicholas 122
Englandspiel 9, 10, 25–9, 33, 41–50, 60–2, 80, 307, 310, 318–19
Erikson (Starizky), Vera 144, 146

Falk, Peter 150, 153–5, 185, 288, 297–8, 316, 335
The Fall of Berlin 265
Farago, Ladislas 296–7, 301, 306, 307
FAT 365 83
Fatherland Front 176
fifth columnists 117, 138
59th Division (Germany) 3
Fighter Command (Britain) 158
Finland, USSR invades 113,

385

126
1st Airborne Division
  (Britain) 1, 5–6, 91, 107,
  110, 178, 184, 265, 342,
  343
1st Allied Airborne Army
  (FAAA) 94, 237
1st Parachute Army
  (Germany) 108
1st Parachute Brigade
  (Britain) 85
1st Parachute Company
  (Germany) 82–3, 215
First World War 12, 112–14,
  117, 144, 145, 168
Fitin, Pavel 129, 178
Five-Day War 21
Fliegerdienststelle (Flight
  Advisory Service) 182
Foley, Frank 240
Foot, M R D 283
Foreign and Commonwealth
  Office (Britain) 114, 121,
  122–3, 153, 158, 240, 247,
  259, 299, 299–300, 316
Foreign Excellent Raincoat
  Company 139
Foreign Legion 11, 23, 198
Foreign Office (Germany)
  107, 167, 180, 249, 296
Foreign Office (Sweden) 155
4th Parachute Brigade
  (Britain) 5
Fraser, Bill 199
Freemasons 292
French National Committee
  160
French North Africa 173
French Red Cross 23
French Resistance 23–4, 74,
  139
Fresnes Prison 54, 71, 72,
  74, 269
Frolova, Anna 134, 291, 294
Frost, John 5, 91, 183
Fu-BStelle-ORPO 27
Fuchs, Klaus 292
Fuellop, Josef 180, 185–6,
  198, 252–3, 257–61,
  288–9, 300, 302, 304–6,
  333, 337–9, 343–4
FULLOP network 252, 306
Funkspiel (fake radio
  messages) 41, 166
Furstner, Admiral 16
FUSAG (First United States
  Army Group) 163

Garbo, Agent 165–6, 184,
  285, 305, 331
Gavin, Jim 248
GC&CS 126, 185
Geer, Dirk Jan de 209
General Strike 114

George VI 226, 278, 289
German Foreign Office 107,
  167, 180, 249, 296
German High Command
  (OKH) 85, 108, 110, 153,
  162, 163, 165, 254, 262,
  345
German National Archive
  (Bundesarchiv) xii, 349
Gestapo 12, 34, 36, 37, 39,
  44, 45, 52, 66, 70–1, 95,
  112, 157, 205, 213, 215,
  218, 226, 240–1, 286
GFP (Geheime Feldpolizei)
  (Secret Field Police) 62
Gibraltar 37, 39, 288
Giessen, Aart van der 41–2,
  56, 57, 67
Giskes, Hermann 9, 11–16,
  26–8
  diary entries 48, 53–4,
    65, 76–7
  'Dr German' code name
    83
  Hotel Metropole HQ 48,
    62, 78
  liberation of Brussels 75
Goorden, Cornelis 221–2,
  231
Gorsky, Anatoly 123, 159,
  169
Goudriaan, Max 47
Government Code and
  Cypher School (GC&CS),
  see GC&CS
Graaf, Bob de 86, 312, 315,
  347
Graaf, Kas de 10, 32, 34–9,
  41, 75, 80, 83, 198, 209,
  216, 218, 228, 231, 277,
  280, 283, 294, 312, 313,
  315, 341, 347, 348
Gräbner, Viktor 183
Great Patriotic War 331, 332
Great War, *see* First World
  War
Greece 172, 174, 201, 204,
  235
GRU 132, 139
Grundboek, Antal (Anton)
  252–4, 257, 303, 303–6,
  336, 339
Gurevich, Anatoly 139,
  166–7
Guyot, Raymond 134

H Company 3
Haaren Prison 41, 56, 57, 60,
  61, 67
Hacket, John 293
The Hague:
  Giskes posted to 13
  May 1940 air assaults 83
Halford, John 300

Halifax, Lord 121
Harker, Oswald 121, 123
Harriman, Averell 201–2
Harris, Tomas 118, 163,
  293, 295
'Harry' (resistance worker)
  31
Hart, Herbert 106, 143–4,
  150, 155
Harzer, Walter 183
Hasso, Peterson 235–6, 261
Hector, Agent 142, 143, 146,
  152, 157, 256, 329
Heemstra, Baron van 32, 43,
  229, 275
Heeresgruppe B (Germany),
  see Army Group B
Heeresgruppe G (Germany),
  see Army Group G
Helle, Paul 90, 93
Hendrickx, Jimmy 63, 68,
  71, 72, 229
Hepburn, Audrey 32, 43
Hesketh, Roger 163, 165–6,
  285, 312, 333, 336
Hess, Rudolf 127
Hewit, Jack 137–8, 163, 335
Hill, George 133
Himmler, Heinrich 12, 69,
  94–5, 154
Hinsley, Frank 282
Hinsley, Harry 187, 312
Hitler, Adolf:
  assassination plot 69,
    111–12
  Englandspiel 28
  Halifax meeting 121
  Normandy Landings 67
  V1/V2 rocket programme
    57
Hitler Youth 205
Hobday, Sydney 37–9, 45,
  270
Hofstadter, Wilhelm 291–2
Holland, *see* Netherlands
Holland Militia 85, 93
Hollis, Roger 291, 317
homosexuality 115, 137,
  226, 329
Hooper, Bill 117, 120, 122,
  228, 294
Hooper, Herbert 294
Hoosemans, Jos 17–18
Hoover, Herbert 117, 122
Horrocks, Brian 1–3, 5–6,
  77, 80, 86–7, 184–5, 248,
  311
Horvath, Janos 252–3, 254,
  257–8, 260, 306, 339, 343
Household Cavalry 76
Howard, Leslie 152
Hungary 150, 201, 205, 235,
  252–3, 289, 333, 337
Hunt, John 295

INDEX

Huntemann, Gerhard 83, 95, 268, 278, 313

Iberian Peninsula 186, 187, 302, 304
ID cards 30, 51
IIIF section HQ, *see* Abwehr
Indian Police 105, 141
Intelligence Corps (Britain) 115
Intelligence School 78, 198
internment 132, 149
Inter.Serve 69
Irish Guards 1
Iron Curtain speech 267, 292
Ismay, Hastings 202
IS9 79, 96, 215

Jackson, Captain (Prosper de Zitter) 70
Jahnke, Kurt 240
Jodl, Alfred 110, 165–6, 184, 254, 266, 305, 312, 332, 336
'Johnny' (secretary) 30, 63
Johns, Philip 75, 78, 80, 83, 341
Joint Intelligence Committee (Britain) 127, 156
Jong, Louis de 312
Jonge, Harm de 326
Josephine, Agent, *see* Agent Josephine

Kampfgruppe Walther 2, 87
Kastein, Dr Gerrit 32–4
Kent, Colonel (Winston Churchill) 199
Kersten, Felix 94
Kessler, Eric 138, 254
KGB 115, 263, 295
Kiesewetter, Ernst 62, 83–5, 88, 94–5, 217, 220–1, 243, 269, 342
King, John Herbert 121–2, 175
King Kong, *see* Lindemans, Christiaan
Kleyenstüber, Obstlt. 256
Klinkert, Dr Wim 313, 347, 348
Knight, Les 38
Knochen, Helmut 52, 54
Kolbe, Fritz 141, 297
Kommandantur (Paris SD HQ) 53, 54
Konovalets, Yehven 325–6, 327
Korean War 319
Koutrik, Folkert van 117, 120
KP (Funkabwehr) (Radio Defense Corps) 87–8
Kraemer, Karl Heinz 106, 141, 142, 143–4, 146–51,
153–8, 163, 165–6, 168, 170, 179–88, 306–7
Arnhem statement 259–61, 340–6
arrest 249–67
'blacklisting' 300
Camp 020 interrogation 298, 302–5, 336–7
confessions 240–8
Farago interview 296–7
Internet 'blackout' 333
'inveterate liar' 298–9, 301, 333, 337
microdot intelligence 179–80, 185–6, 260, 288, 303, 314, 337, 343–4
SHAEF 'veracity checks' 239
Western Front reports 236–7
Krafft, Sturmbannführer (Major) Sepp 4, 90–1, 95, 183
Kreshin, Boris, *see* Krotov, Boris
Krivitsky, Walter 105, 121–4, 129, 131, 175, 197, 330
Krotov, Boris (Boris Krötenschield) 106, 170, 178, 188, 338
Kruyt, Nicodemus 134
Kruyt, Wilhelm 134, 291, 293
Kup, Willy 9, 14, 26, 42, 48, 52, 59, 63, 66, 226

Lacoche, Monsieur 30
Landing Zone-Z (LZ-Z) 4
Langley, James 82, 215
Last, Ann 293
Latchmere House, *see* Camp 020
Laurens, Anne 46, 281
Lauwers, Huub 25–8, 61–2
Lebedev, Viktor 132
Leclerc, Philippe 74
Leibstandarte Adolf Hitler 21
Lemon, Agent 152, 335
Letuppe, Gilberte (Gilou) 9, 23, 31, 44, 46, 47, 52–4, 68, 71, 74–5, 198, 213, 222, 271, 274
Leuchars, RAF 185
Liddell, Guy 106, 132–3
Blunt PA to 118–19, 122, 137
diary entries 118–19, 123, 133, 141, 143, 155, 236, 245
Lindemans, Christiaan ('King Kong') 9, 18
Arnhem betrayal xi, 54, 70, 95–6, 96, 213, 222,
223–39, 245–6, 278, 312, 328
Belgian ('Brandt') alias of 71
capture and imprisonment 223–32
CC code letter 52, 63, 65, 73–4, 83–5, 268, 340, 342
Colonel Kiesewetter ID 217, 220–1
confession 240–8
education 19
Eindhoven 217–22
legend born 30–40
motorbike accident 20
Operation Comet 73, 181
other aliases 35, 82
Pinto's antagonism 211–13
playboy lifestyle 19–24
police informant 20–1
prison term 30
Lindemans, Christina 19, 46
Lindemans, Cornelius 19, 280
Lindemans, Henk 9, 20, 31, 45, 45–6, 49–50, 51–2, 75, 96, 198, 269, 280–2, 284, 1941
Lindemans, Jan 19, 31
Lindemans, Joseph 19
Lindo Garage 19–20
Lippert, Hans 90, 93
Liskow, Alfred 128
Lithuania 113
London rezidentura 116, 132, 135, 159–61, 167, 178, 186, 316
Long, Leonard 106, 160, 171, 197, 249, 262, 289
Louette, Marcel 65
Low Countries 67, 75, 283
Luftwaffe 2, 21, 23, 24, 44, 93–4, 109, 118–19, 144, 181–2, 208, 254–5, 296–7, 332, 344–5
Luftwaffe Third Fighter Division (Germany) 94
Luret, Henrietta 36
Luxembourg 75
Lvov–Sandomierz Offensive 168

Maas Line 73, 108, 340
McBarnet, Evelyn 292–3
McCallum, Patricia 154, 162, 166, 250, 262, 301–7, 336, 338–9
Maclean, Donald 114–15, 292
Major, John 319
Malines (Mechelen) 63, 70
Maly, Theodore 115

387

Marcus, Carl 240–1, 313
Marshall, Samuel 89, 313
Mason, Paul 256, 258, 259, 261–3, 302, 336–7
Maxwell, Robert 268
Maxwell, Somerset 152
Maxwell, Susan (Agent Lemon) 152, 156, 335
Meer, 'Wim' van der 31, 71
Meersman, Mia 9, 63–4, 67, 70–1, 214, 225, 229, 276, 283–4
Menzies, Sir Stewart 138–9, 141, 155, 160, 174, 239
Metropole Hotel 48, 62, 78, 82, 93, 177, 269
Michael, King of Romania 176
Middle Wallop, RAF 164
MI5 47, 70, 105, 108–9
  B Division 117, 118
  Blunt joins 116–17
  Blunt resigns 278, 285
  D Division 117
  Defence Security Office, Belgium 224
  Dutch Country Section (E1a) 122
  'the group' 118, 163, 174, 295
  'Kraemer (or Josephine) case' official view 301–9
  official history 319
  Registry 117, 119, 120, 143, 146, 154, 257, 293, 298
  Triplex (XXX) 151, 156, 185, 331
  WRC1 257
Mil Amt C 255, 344
MI9 247
Ministry of Information 120
MI6 105, 109, 122
  Burgess joins 130–1
  E-Division 122
  Englandspiel files destroyed 318–19
  Philby joins 116, 130–1
  Section D 130–1
  Section V 136, 138, 147, 161, 187, 240, 304
  SIS syllabus 131
  Venlo incident 111–12, 116, 127
Model, Walter 94–5, 180, 182, 312, 343
Modin, Yuri 176
Molotov–Ribbentrop Pact 113, 116, 330
Molotov, Vyacheslav 158, 203
Momotaro Enomoto 259
Montgomery, Bernard 6, 72, 76, 78, 79, 92, 110, 152,
171, 172, 177, 234, 246, 265, 310
Montholon Hotel 45, 52, 53
Mueller, Heinrich 286
Muller, Charles 82

Nakatina, Elena 290–1
National Hotel 203
National Socialist Movement of the Netherlands (NSB) 33
Naval Attachés 152
Neave, Airey 78
Ness, Lucien de 82
Netherlands:
  deportation 276
  National Archives, the Hague xi–xii, 283
  resistance movement 17, 211, 230, 244–5, 248
  Security Service (BVD) 271, 282
  Ypenburg RAF recruitment 271
Netherlands Communist Party (CPN) 16–17
Netherlands State Institute for War Documentation 312
9th Air Force (US) 163–4
9th SS Panzer Division (Hohenstaufen) (Germany) 4, 21, 85, 94, 109, 181, 183, 314, 345
NKVD:
  Cambridge Five 114, 118, 121, 128, 159–61, 292, 305
  official London presence, *see* London rezidentura
  post-war infiltration 282
  SIS 'call to arms' against 160
  TONY report 156
  'travel agents' 133–7
Norfolk House 161
Normandy Landings 4, 66–72, 78–81, 85, 90, 92–3, 110, 164–9, 172, 314 (*see also* D-Day)
Northolt, RAF 200, 224–5
Norway 109, 179, 180, 345
No. 21 Field Security Unit (Britain) 115

Octagon Conference 237
October Revolution 326
Office of Strategic Services (OSS), *see* OSS
Official Secrets Act (1911) (Britain) 121
OKH, *see* German High Command
OKW (Oberkommando der Wehrmacht) 85, 108, 180,
238, 254–5, 285, 296, 312, 332, 344 (*see also* Wfst)
Onderdelinden, Tine 272, 277, 282
Onderduikers, defined 30–1
101st Airborne Division (US) 2, 107, 178, 180, 342, 343
Onodera Makoto 251, 253–4, 256, 260, 287, 305, 314, 336, 337, 342–3
Oosterbeek 90–1, 95, 183, 184, 345
Operation Bagration 168, 172
Operation Barbarossa 125, 126 9, 131, 136, 158, 330
Operation Catarrh 25–6
Operation Comet 73, 181, 230, 283, 310
Operation Eclipse 2 265
Operation Fortitude 157, 162, 164, 165–6, 285, 301, 305, 306
Operation Garlic 37
Operation Grenade 236
Operation Lena 144, 147, 208
Operation Market Garden, *see also* Eindhoven mission; *also* Nijmegen xi, 2, 6, 79–97, 107–10, 162, 172, 177, 179–98
Operation Naples II 237
Operation Nordpol 26
Operation Overlord 157, 161–2, 168
Operation Sealion 144
Operation Tolstoy 199–207
Operation Torch 173
Operation Unthinkable 267
Operation Veritable 236
Oranjehotel, *see* Scheveningen Prison
Ordedienst (OD) 17, 26, 34
OSS (Office of Strategic Services) 142, 237–8, 256, 297, 299, 301, 308, 333, 337
Outin, Vladimir 328
Owen, Mary Josephine, *see* Josephine, Agent

Palace Hotel Brussels 215
Palestine 139, 281
Panzergrenadier Battalion 16 (Battalion Krafft) 4
Pas-de-Calais invasion 67, 162, 165, 165–6, 305
Pat O'Leary Line 24
Patton, George S 265
Pavel Sudoplatov Battalion (Russian Federation) 328
People's Commissariat for Internal Affairs, *see* NKVD

INDEX

Petrie, Sir David 143, 161, 170
Philby, Kim 105, 114–16, 118, 122, 122–7, 130–40, 147, 158, 158–61, 174–6, 186, 197, 234, 279, 287–96, 299–300, 304, 308, 315–17, 331–4, 337, 339
  described 197
  exile 296
  Iberian Peninsula 186–7
  Section IX 174–5
  SIS syllabus 131, 133
Philippines 237, 288
Philips, Emory 186
Phony War 116
Pickaxe mission 106, 131, 132–6, 140–1, 290–1, 304
Pieck, Henri ('Hans') 122, 294
Pinto, Oreste 145, 197, 208–16, 217–19, 227, 243, 245, 268–9, 277, 280, 313
  autobiography: *Spycatcher* 219
  Lindemans's arrest 223–4
Poland 92, 267
  Britain declares war on Germany over 200–1
  Germany invades 113, 116
Posadrosky, Count von 286
Potemkin 131
Prinz Eugen 27
Public Records Office (PRO), *see* National Archives, Kew
Putlitz, Wolfgang zu 138

Quebec 153, 237

Raad van Verzet (Council of Resistance) (RVV) 32, 44–5, 58, 66
Radio Security Service 135
Rauter, Hans 94–5
Red Army 1, 113, 128, 158, 168–9, 172, 175–6, 206, 233, 264–7, 314, 328
Red Cross 23, 149, 271
Red Orchestra, *see* Rote Kapelle
Reform Club 119, 153, 239, 248, 335
Reniers, Urbain 65–6, 69–70, 74, 76, 77–8
Revai, Andrew 138
Reydon, Hermanus 33
Rhine River 1, 73, 75, 78, 79, 85, 91
Ribbentrop, Joachim von 113, 116, 167, 296, 330
Ridderhof, Matthijs ('George') 10, 15, 26–8, 33, 45, 47, 96
Riedel, Peter 237–8, 338
Rietschoten, Jan van 41–2, 56, 67

Rissouw (Sizauw), Bart 135
Ritter, Karl 296–7
Robertson, TA 151, 316
Robigot, George 134
Romania 172, 174, 176, 201, 204
Rome, Maurice de 217–18
Rommel, Erwin 149
Roosevelt, Franklin D. ('FDR') ix, 140, 154, 158, 201–2, 205, 298
Ross, Major 82
Rote Kapelle (Red Orchestra) 29, 116, 125–9, 135, 136, 139, 140, 166, 178, 241, 266, 290, 291
Rothschild, Victor 116, 118, 318
Rotterdam 19–24, 31–2, 38, 44–6
Royal Air Force (RAF) 2, 26, 28, 38, 40, 59
Royal Canadian Air Force (RCAF) 70
Royal Nord Hotel 63, 67–8, 70, 72
Russian Federation Central Archives xii
Russian Front 33, 48, 90
Ryan, Cornelius 248
Ryde, Michael 192, 250, 251–3, 259, 302, 305, 336, 337

Sainsbury, Alfred Vernon 223–4
St Gilles Prison 224
St James's Park 112, 119, 161
Sanders, Huub 58, 61–2
Sanders, Wim 275–6, 276, 282
SAS (Special Air Service) 78
Schaefer, Han 155
Scharroo, P W 21
Schellenberg, Walter 12, 26, 28, 69, 106, 107–12, 127, 147, 154, 157, 179–80, 182, 226, 240, 254–5, 258, 260, 269, 297, 312, 314, 332, 336–7, 344
Scheveningen Prison 38, 45, 75, 269–73, 275, 282, 282–3, 283
Schmidt, General 21
Schneider, Franz 140
Schneider, Germaine 140
Schouten, Jan 135
Schreieder, Joseph 10, 15–16, 26, 33, 38, 41, 48, 60–2, 95
Schwenke, Dietrich 184
Scotland Yard 225
SD (Sicherheitsdienst) 15–18, 23–7, 32–5, 45, 45–6, 53, 57, 60–2, 65, 67
Second Army 182, 239, 346
2nd (II) SS Panzer Corps (Germany) 110, 181, 182, 345
2nd (II) SS Panzer Group (Germany) 109, 181
2nd Parachute Battalion (Britain) 91
Secret Intelligence Service (SIS), *see* MI6
Seeds, Robert 149
17th Airborne Division (US) 265
Seyben, Harry 58, 60–1
Seyffardt, Hendrik 33
Seyss-Inquart, Arthur 22
SFHQ conference 248
SHAEF 161–3, 169, 171, 209, 215, 219, 222, 235–9, 245, 266, 310–11, 313
'shoe shop' ID-card factories 30
Sicherheitsdienst (SD), *see* SD
Siegfried Line 2, 79, 240
Siemsen, Nina 256–7, 299–300
Sillitoe, Sir Percy 292
Simkins, C A G 282
SiPo (Sicherheitspolizei) 49–53, 62
'SIS plans for Anti-Soviet Operations' 159–60
SIS (Secret Intelligence Service), *see* MI6
SIS (Special Intelligence Service) 56, 112
6th Airborne Division (Britain) 238–9
Sizauw (Rissouw), Bart 135
Small, P J 290–1
Smirnov, N G: *Diary of a Spy* 139
Smuts, Jan 126, 172, 235
SOE (Special Operation Executive) 25, 28–9, 42, 56–7, 130
Soviet High Command 128
Spaak, Charles 167
Spain 31, 49
Spanish Civil War 22, 32, 123, 175
Special Operation Executive (SOE), *see* SOE
SS-Junker Schools 90
SS Panzer Grenadier Depot and Reserve Battalion 16 (Germany) 90
Stalin, Joseph ix, 95, 113, 121, 125
  D-Day 157–8, 161–2, 168–9
  death of 304
  expansionist plans 201–5

malign post-war influence 290–2
Starizky, Vera 146
Steenwijk 28
Stephens, Robin ('Tin Eye') 144–5, 197, 225–30, 242–4, 250–4, 259–60, 302, 337, 338
Stevens, Richard 112, 275
Stewart, Bob 135
Straight, Michael 295, 316
Studdy, Capt. H 292
Student, Kurt 3, 21, 83–4, 86, 108, 242, 243, 269, 278, 312, 313, 340–1
Sudoplatov, Pavel 126–7, 129, 132, 134, 169, 207, 249, 267, 293, 304, 325–8
Supreme Headquarters Allied Expeditionary Force (SHAEF), *see* SHAEF
Susloparov, Ivan 127, 139, 266
Sutherland, Fred 37–9, 45, 270
Swane, Victor 32, 52–3
Sweden 155
Swedish Air 152, 155
Swedish Foreign Office 155

Taconis, Thijs 25–7
Tchicaev (Tchitchaev), Ivan, *see* Chichaev, Ivan
Tedder, Arthur 262, 337
Tempsford, RAF 25, 134, 135
10th SS Panzer Division (Frundsberg) (Germany) 4, 85, 109, 181, 184, 314, 345
Tettau, Hans von 91
Thatcher, Margaret 306, 318
XXX (30) Corps (Britain) 1, 3, 5, 77–8, 86, 89, 234, 248, 269
Todt 30, 39, 53, 63, 68, 134
Tower of London 246
Treachery Act (1940) 278
Treaty of Moscow 113
Treaty of Versailles 13
Trepper, Leopold 134, 139–40, 166–7, 169, 291–2
Triplex (XXX) 151, 156, 185, 331
Tudor-Hart, Edith 135
Turkey 172
21st Army Group (Anglo-Canadian) 2, 72, 75–6, 84, 94, 171, 227, 230, 233, 238, 242, 265
Twist committee 156, 157, 331, 336
245th Division (Germany) 3
Ubbink, Johan 41, 56
UK National Archives, Kew xi, 154, 203, 281, 283, 298, 313, 347
Ukraine 11, 72, 114, 128, 168, 325–8
Ukrainian Military Organization 325
Ultra ciphers 73, 84, 86, 125–7, 138, 142, 160, 162, 234, 341
Urquhart, Robert ('Roy') 91, 184
US 101st Airborne Division 2, 3
US National Archives, College Park xi–xii, 349
US Navy Special Warfare Branch 296
USAAF (United States Army Air Forces) 44
USSR:
  Act of Military Surrender of Germany 266–7
  Atomic Espionage 106, 293, 304
  counter-intelligence 'stagnation' 173
  Department S 207
  expansionism 201–5, 319
  Germany invades 128
  non-aggression treaty 113
  Philby's exile in 296
  Section IX 174–5
Ustinov, Klop 133, 293
Ustinov, Peter 133
Utrecht 22, 33–4

Van Dijk, Lt 273–4
Venlo incident 111–12, 116, 127, 235, 236, 275
Verkaik, Eddy xi, 86, 87–8, 347, 348
Verleun, Jan 33, 34
Verloop, Cornelis 10, 23–4, 48, 52, 198, 219–22, 226–8, 230, 242, 273, 278
Vermeulen family 23
Viellot, Theresa 38
Vietnam War 319
Vistula–Oder Offensive 234
Vivian, Valentine 116, 121, 138, 141, 172–5
V-Men 12–18, 23, 44, 46, 60, 95
Volges, Akke, *see* Albrecht, Margaret 218
Volunteer Legion Netherlands 33
V1/V2 rocket programme 57, 243–4
Voorwinden, Eduard 275
Vos, Maurice de 222, 231
Voute, Anna ('Puck') 135
Vredenburgh, Freule von 32, 47–8, 54

Vrijwilligerslegioen Nederland 33
V2 project 243–4, 300
Vught 83, 184, 243, 340

Waal River 75, 89, 90, 108, 184, 228
Waals, Bio van der 33
Wach Battalion 3 90
Waelti, Werner 144, 145–6
Wallenberg, Henry 252, 258
Walther, Oberst Erich 2
Wandsworth Prison 146
War Office 132, 138, 149, 153, 238, 262, 287
Ward, Irene 150–1
Wegner, Antonius 41–2
Wehrmacht 2, 5, 11, 51, 108, 111–12, 134, 162, 177, 180, 254, 312, 344
Wehrmachtführungsstab, *see* Wfst
Wenzlau, Heinrich 303
Werff, Ellie van der 60
Wery, Betty (Betje) 60
West, Nigel 170
Western Front 12, 158, 160, 236, 343
Wfst (Wehrmachtführungsstab) 108, 180, 254, 255, 344 (*see also* OKW)
White, Dick 151–2
Wijk, Knut 152
Wilhelmina, Queen 17, 22, 26, 34, 209, 216
Williams, Edgar ('Bill') 79
Williams, Jenifer Fischer 143
Winters, Maj. Dick 3
Witte Brigade 65–6, 69, 86
Wormwood Scrubs 117–19, 120, 208, 297
Wright, Peter: *Spycatcher* 292, 317
Wurr, Walter 14, 48, 51–3

XXX (30) Corps (Britain) 1, 3, 5, 77–8, 86, 89, 234, 248, 269
XXX (Triplex) 151, 156, 185, 331

Yalta Conference ix
Yezhov, Nikolai Ivanovich 326
Yugoslavia 172, 174, 201, 204–5, 257

Zhukov, Marshal 92
Zitter, Prosper de 70
Zwaan, Ellie 63, 64, 214–15, 229, 277